38.50
2-6

Greek Tragedy and Political Theory

GREEK TRAGEDY
AND
POLITICAL THEORY

Edited by
J. PETER EUBEN

UNIVERSITY OF CALIFORNIA PRESS
BERKELEY   LOS ANGELES   LONDON

University of California Press
Berkeley and Los Angeles, California

University of California Press, Ltd.
London, England

© 1986 by The Regents of the University of California

Library of Congress Cataloging-in-Publication Data
Main entry under title:

Greek tragedy and political theory.

Contents: Introduction—Greek tragedy and society /
Charles Segal—Polis and monarch in early Attic
tragedy / Anthony Podlecki—[etc.]
  1. Greek drama (Tragedy)—History and criticism—
Addresses, essays, lectures. 2. Politics in literature—
Addresses, essays, lectures. 3. Literature and society—
Greece—Addresses, essays, lectures. I. Euben, J. Peter.
PA3136.G58 1986   882'.01'09   85-24623
ISBN 0-520-05572-1 (alk. paper)
ISBN 0-520-05584-5 (pbk. : alk. paper)

Printed in the United States of America
1 2 3 4 5 6 7 8 9

For my parents,
Arthur and Jean Euben

Contents

Preface

Political philosophy is tragic thought. . . . Without a dramatic sense of fate and mutability no rational intelligence would turn to this . . . subject.
—Judith Shklar on the occasion of the death of Hannah Arendt

1

Three related developments are responsible for my interest in editing a volume on the subject of Greek tragedy and political theory. The first is the crisis of American culture. I have no intention of rehearsing what is by now well known, and better said by others, except to note the obvious: as people, and as a people, we seem more confused than usual about what is worth cultivating, caring for, and nourishing. The second development is a parallel crisis in political theory. From one point of view the proliferation of journals and panels at professional conferences is a sign of political theory's vitality, as the preoccupation with method is indicative of its philosophical or scientific maturity. But from another point of view this proliferation simply replicates the division of labor and esoteric expertise that characterizes both the university and society in general; and the preoccupation with method has isolated theorists from politics. What makes all this ironic is that the great paradigmatic theorists aspired to integrate human activities, relationships, and beliefs into a theoretical whole so as to repair, reform, or transform a political whole.

A third development is a recent shift in the interpretation of classical texts and culture. Somewhere Goethe writes of classical Greece as a magic mirror in which, when living men and women gaze seeking the image of a culture long dead, they see not unreturning ghosts but the half-veiled face of their own destiny. What we now see in that mirror is Nietzsche.

For whatever reasons—the trauma of the newly past Holocaust and the threat of a new, nuclear one, the disappointment of revolutionary hopes (including those of the 1960s), the relentless brutality of "small" wars, the increasing centralization of the state and bureaucratization of society, the erosion of permanent ties of place and person, the corruption of our institutions and the blatant failures of our foreign policy—we read tragedy differently than previous generations. For those no longer enamored of technological utopias, less sure that history means progress and that more is better, and more aware of the finitude of our power and powers, the image of classical Greece is less one of serenity, proportion, and rationality than of turbulence, dissonance, and an ambivalent morality that plagues action and passion. As Charles Segal argues in his essay in this volume, it is the darkness tragedy contains and discloses that increasingly fascinates contemporary critics and readers. They find in it both the hidden patterns of contemporary life that the conscious mind is largely unwilling or unable to face, and the resources to explore "beneath the surface of [their] own highly rationalized, desacralized, excessively technologized culture." As this language suggests, the new interpretation of tragedy invigorates and gives depth to the pessimism of such modern social theorists as Max Weber (as evident in the concluding page of the *Protestant Ethic*), Jacques Ellul, the Frankfurt School, and Michel Foucault.[1] Bernard Knox gives an example of this shift in sensibility. Reviewing the Fagles translation of the *Oresteia*, he notes that an earlier generation read the trilogy as the triumph of civilization over the darkly mysterious forces of a sinister primitivism. For that generation the promise of wisdom born of suffering, the triumph of an ultimately benevolent Zeus, the joint human and divine consecration of a just Athens, in which all conflicting forces and principles were accorded due place and honor, seemed to mirror their achievements. But we are no longer so sure of ourselves, and so we read and watch Greek tragedy differently. Knox recalls a performance of *The Eumenides* in which the audience was roused to a high pitch of emotions, not by the plea of extenuating circumstances, or Orestes' acquittal of murder, but by the Furies' warning, "There is a time when terror helps," which Athene echoes: "Never / banish terror from the gates" (699).[2] It is no wonder that

1. This excludes Jürgen Habermas for whom the retrieval and preservation of the Enlightenment promise remains a fundamental hope and aim.
2. *New York Review of Books*, Feb. 5, 1976, p. 11.

Brian Vickers concludes his chapter on the trilogy by observing, "Reading the *Oresteia* makes one afraid for one's life."[3]

For all its pessimism, or perhaps because of it, this crisis in the conception of the classical can help clarify what is at stake in the other two crises. At least that is the overall assumption of my Introduction to this volume, and the direct argument of its concluding section. Here I do no more than list why I think this to be the case.

The juxtaposition of Greek tragedy and contemporary politics can enrich the way we talk about our public lives and stay the triteness that afflicts almost all cultural criticism. The juxtaposition can also provide a sensibility to express feelings and fears in public that are now expressed awkwardly and hesitantly. In this and other ways the reading of Greek tragedies can qualitatively expand the "political agenda," bringing before the public issues, such as mortality, madness, piety, and passion, that are usually consigned to specialists or private life. In addition, the content of tragedy and the place of the tragedians in public life may offer an example to confound the comfortable academic division of labor and the compartmentalization of life reflected and reified by that division. Doing so, it could reopen the question of how life and thought may be justly bounded, lived, and related.

The juxtaposition of Greek tragedy and contemporary political theory may be equally salutary. For one thing it may provide an example of how the most general ruminations on the human condition can take place within the traditions of a particular people, more specifically as part of a tradition of democratic citizenship. As such, tragedy may indicate how and why theorists need to engage the experience of their compatriots; why it is dangerous for the academy to privilege its speech; and what is lost when theories devolve into recondite abstraction.

As the very idea of juxtaposing Greek tragedy and political theory implies, I regard the former as analogous to, if not itself a kind of, theoretical activity. But it is a kind of activity that contains a distinct "politics of theory." By a politics of theory I mean something more than the political assumptions or implications of a particular theory. That more is the political message contained in the theory's structure and idiom, the degree to which its sensibility is esoteric and its language abstract or technical; its view of action (including itself as a theoretical act), and the way it reaches out to, turns away

---

3. Brian Vickers, *Towards Greek Tragedy* (London: Longmans, 1973), p. 425.

from, or selects prospective audiences. Joel Schwartz gives a sense of what I mean when he says in chapter 7 that Sophocles "wrote tragedy because there was no other genre that could both teach *and 'imitate'* in Aristotle's sense, the tragic form of life of the classical *polis*" (emphasis added). Studying Greek tragedy can alert us to the ways contemporary political theories and thought teach and imitate a modern culture Segal characterizes in chapter 2 as "rationalized, desacralized and excessively technologized." It might even be the basis for a critique of that imitation and so a foundation for reconstituting the politics of contemporary theory.

If I am right about all this, Greek tragedy might do for us what Socrates did for his fellow Athenians: help us determine who we are and what we are doing to ourselves and others, while making it clear that such questions are never fully answered or finally resolved.

2

What makes this volume possible (as distinct from my interest in editing it) is a recent confluence of concerns among classicists (usually educated in comparative literature programs) sympathetic to new trends in "literary" theory[4] and political theorists interested in classics, literature in general, or contemporary social theory, particularly hermeneutics.

Contemporary literary theorists (or cultural critics) whether structuralist or post-structuralist, Marxist or hermeneuticist,[5] have focused their attention on what might be called the "politics of interpretation."[6] They have urged or forced us to become critical of the language and categories through which we articulate the world,

---

4. I put *literary* in quotation marks because contributors to this new theory include philosophers, sociologists (Erving Goffman), and analysts (Jacques Lacan). For the mapping of this intellectual terrain, see Terence Hawkes, *Structuralism and Semiotics* (Berkeley and Los Angeles: University of California Press, 1977); Jonathan Culler, *On Deconstruction: Theory and Criticism after Structuralism* (Ithaca, N.Y.: Cornell University Press, 1982); Frank Lentricchia, *After the New Criticism* (Chicago: University of Chicago Press, 1980); Terry Eagleton, *Literary Theory: An Introduction* (Minneapolis: University of Minnesota Press, 1983); and Frederick Jameson, *The Prison-House of Language* (Princeton, N.J.: Princeton University Press, 1972).

5. The criteria distinguishing one "school" from another are so imprecise that most theorists are more than their self-chosen labels would suggest.

6. That is the title of a recent book edited by W. J. T. Mitchell (Chicago: University of Chicago Press, 1983); see especially the essays in part 3. Though there are overlaps, the politics of theory and the politics of interpretation are not identical.

to make background foreground, to "problematize" the most sacred demarcations of our culture. More specifically these theorists are concerned with themes such as reflexivity and perspectivism, poetics and meta-communication, tropes and critical meta-languages, semiotics and authorial presumptions, "texts" and the sociology of audience, marginality and otherness, strategies of argument and the decoding of discourses. Inspired by Nietzsche, Hegel, Marx, Freud, Saussure, Barthes, Jakobson, and Heidegger, they have loosened the hold of traditional academic disciplines and, in some cases, have been suspicious of disciplines generally. The redescriptions they offer of institutions, practices, and discourses not only undermine the sanctity of academic divisions; they suggest that these divisions as well as the compartmentalization of life and mind they legitimate are conventional, if not arbitrary and oppressive.

Though none of the essays in this volume deal directly with these developments in literary theory (with the obvious exception of Segal's), the book would not be possible without them, and several of the essays (by Zeitlin, Slatkin, Salkever, and Euben) show their influence.

At the same time that literary theorists became interested in politics,[7] political theorists were becoming more explicitly engaged by problems of interpretation. The sources of this interest are ancient (which is why I say "more explicitly") and manifold.

Political theorists have traditionally been preoccupied with many of the issues that now preoccupy literary critics. Writers such as Plato and Hobbes sought to elucidate and deconstruct (though also reconstruct) the implicit categories that unconsciously informed the individual and collective lives and discourses of their compatriots. Moreover, in the *Apology*, arguably the first work to define political philosophy, Plato offers an interpretation of Socrates' interpretation of an answer by the Delphic Apollo, who himself neither speaks nor conceals but gives "signs." As that dialogue makes clear, where and how Socrates practiced philosophy confounded almost all the conventional demarcations of his culture. Finally,

---

7. There is a tendency among such critics to see politics everywhere and to define it as power and domination, while insisting that political societies and political theories are "texts" to be studied according to the most advanced strategies of interpretation. It seems to me the definitions of politics and power and their equation are historically and analytically suspect and that the new literary imperialism (to put it uncharitably) threatens to make literary theorists the new arbiters of inquiry and culture just as the foundational pretensions of philosophy have been exposed.

Foucault's concern with, and view of, power/knowledge is anticipated by Plato in the *Republic*, which is itself about the interpretation of politics and the politics of interpretation, and a work of deconstruction that also deconstructs deconstructionism.[8]

There are other, more immediate sources for the interest of political theorists in problems of interpretation, literary theory, and
Greek tragedy. One is the influence of Hannah Arendt and Leo
Strauss. These students of Heidegger have (together with Eric
Voegelin) defined classical political theory as it is presently taught
in American universities. For somewhat different theoretical reasons and very different political ones, each found in classical authors or the *polis* a vantage point from which to criticize modern
social science, historiography, conceptions of reason, moral philosophy, and liberal politics. Though Strauss did not write on tragedy,
his emphasis on the dramatic aspects of Platonic dialogues encouraged his students to do so.[9] And while Arendt only referred to
Greek tragedies in passing, her overall emphasis on the prephilo-
sophical articulation of politics and her substantive concerns (with
action and speech, public and private life, heroism and immortality)
stimulated others to do so, even when they rejected her polarities.[10]

None of the following essays discuss Arendt and Strauss (except
in footnotes), but their influence is reflected in the essays by Saxonhouse, the Lanes, Salkever, Davis, and Euben.[11]

There is, finally, the feminist critique of "male-stream" thought
and politics. In an effort to disestablish the authority of those classical texts thought to legitimate the denigration of women, "private"
life, nurture, and the body, feminists have subjected the tragedians,

8. Plato's discussion of writing and language in the *Phaedrus* and of rhetoric and
dialogue in the *Gorgias* are important starting points for deconstructionist criticism.
9. Thus the "Straussian" *Interpretation* is the journal that most consistently pub-
lishes essays on Greek tragedy by political theorists.
10. The importance of classical texts for contemporary theory has come from another direction as well. Hans-Georg Gadamer (another student of Heidegger) and
Habermas have both taken much from Aristotle's discussion of *praxis, phronēsis* and
sophia (in the *Ethics*) and Plato's emphasis on dialogue (crucial to Gadamer's hermeneutics and Habermas's ultimate ambivalence about ideal speech situations).
They have been influential more in legitimizing classical study among those who
regarded social theory as beginning with Marx, rather than in directly stimulating
concern with tragedy (though Gadamer's own philosophical poetics has had a direct
impact, as I argue in the Introduction).
11. Podlecki's approach is closer to the distinguished tradition of historical
scholarship on Athenian democracy. See particularly his *The Political Background of
Aeschylean Tragedy* (Ann Arbor, Mich.: University of Michigan Press, 1966); and *The
Life of Themistocles* (Montreal: McGill-Queen's University Press, 1975).

Plato, and Aristotle to sustained critique. The ensuing debate has centered on Aeschylus's Clytemnestra and the *Oresteia*'s role in establishing Western misogyny, on the degree to which Sophocles' Antigone is a paradigm for contemporary arguments supporting "the family" and household against the state, and on the defensibility of Medea's words and actions in Euripides' play. It has also focused on the extent to which Plato is a source of women's political disenfranchisement and derogatory stereotypes even as he coopts feminist voices through "feminine" images (midwife, weaver, philosopher-queens) or whether his own critique of heroic hyper-masculinism provides a voice from which feminists might draw sustenance and ideas. Finally, it has forced political theorists to read Aristotle's *Politics* in the context of his biology and metaphysics, and to reassess his distinction between the public sphere where rational, free, and equal male citizens act collectively and the private sphere, where husbands rule wives (even if it is as a statesman to citizens) in a realm of necessity, production, and reproduction.

Feminist influence is obvious in the Lanes' essay, is present (with more French [12] than American feminist roots) in Zeitlin's chapter, and to a lesser degree appears in the essay by Saxonhouse (who is perhaps the foremost American political theorist writing on "the feminine" in Plato).

3

Whether the juxtaposition of Greek tragedy and political theory can do all I claim for it depends not only on my Introduction but on the essays it introduces. They represent a diversity of fields, interpretative principles, political stances, substantive concerns, and conceptions of (or degrees of indifference to) political theory. Though such diversity threatens to exacerbate the diffuseness that characterizes edited collections, I have not tried to impose my views on the contributors. (Indeed, I do not always agree with either their analyses or approaches). But I have asked that they deal with what I regard as an important political issue, and/or embody a significant approach to the study of tragedy.

I have not introduced each essay individually, though my Intro-

12. For an introduction to French feminism, see *New French Feminism*, ed. Elanna Marks and Isabelle DeCourtivron (New York: Schocken Books, 1981), esp. chs. 1–3.

duction refers to specific essays, as this Preface has to those of Segal and Schwartz. While I do not doubt that individual introductions can increase thematic unity, summarize arguments and controversies in ways that guide readers through sometimes murky intellectual terrain, and highlight particular substantive disagreements (such as the different conceptions of *philia* held by Salkever and the Lanes), my reluctance to provide such introductions is threefold: I am uneasy about so directly inserting yet another level of interpretation between author and reader; I have a sense that such introductions too often reduce complex sensibilities and insights in ways that seem initially helpful but are ultimately misleading; and I think the authors introduce their own essays well enough. Where they offer no elaborate introduction, as with Davis's essay, that refusal is purposeful and demands respect.

Rather I have written an Introduction intended to justify the volume as a whole and to provide a context in which the authors become participants in a conversation about shared concerns, much as Aristotle insists that for people to be citizens, sheer differences must become diverse points of view about a common life. Given the title and purpose of the book, this sort of introduction and context seemed most useful.

Of course it deemphasizes other kinds of otherwise relevant contexts. For instance, I say little about the origins of drama and how much those origins tell us about classical tragedy, though these issues remain topics of controversy. Nor do I say much about the fact that, or ways in which, epic (and lyric) influenced tragedy. I do not doubt that Homer's banquet was a veritable feast, but the history of Greek literature is best left to those (such as E. Fränkel, Werner Jaeger, Albin Lesky, Richmond Lattimore, Sir Maurice Bowra, Charles Rowan Beye, and John Finley, to mention a sample of writers whose works are available in English) who can tell it better than I can. Finally, and more seriously, the Introduction offers little in the way of historical detail (though several of the essays do). Again, I have no doubt that knowledge of the political, economic, and social developments in classical Athens (say the reform of the Areopagus, the centralization of the "state," Periclean power, and imperialism) can enhance our understanding of tragedy's concerns and place as a political institution (as Podlecki's essay and previous works make clear). Nor do I doubt that the substance and fortunes of tragedy were intimately connected with the vitality and corruption of the city. Clearly the decline of tragedy is linked to the political, spiritual, and physical exhaustion brought on by the protracted war with Sparta. Or so I will argue in my essay on the *Orestes.*

.　　　.　　　.

I would like to thank the Faculty Research Committee of the University of California, Santa Cruz, for generously supporting this project; Charlotte Cassidy and Judy Burton, whose expert typing helped it happen; and Chris Rocco for his help with the index. I would also like to thank Propyläen Verlag, Berlin, for permission to print Charles Segal's English translation of his essay, the German version of which appeared in Charles Segal, *Griechische Tragödie und Gesellschaft*, Propyläen Geschichte der Literatur, vol. 1 (1981).

.　　　.　　　.

My intellectual and political debts are many and I look forward to acknowledging them elsewhere. Here I want to record just one, though it is the most important one. This book is dedicated to my parents. By example and precept they taught me that drama, politics, and serious thinking are not the prerogative of specialists or professionals, but are, as George Steiner once said, best loved and best known by those who live most intensely.

Chapter One

Introduction

J. Peter Euben

Greek Tragedy and Political Theory is a provocative if not provoking title. For one thing it conjoins what seem disparate, even opposed, sensibilities, forms of discourse, and purposes. No less an authority than Plato insists on a longstanding disagreement or quarrel (*diaphora*) between philosophy or theory and tragic poetry, a quarrel that can only be resolved when the latter submits to the political, moral, and ontological tutelage of the former. No less an institution than the contemporary university legitimates their separation, consigning political theory to political science departments, and Greek tragedy to departments of classics or comparative literature. For another thing, the title invites comparison between a historically bounded achievement that ended with Euripides and a 2,500-year-old tradition of political reflection that (arguably) continues in our own day.[1] Of course Greek tragedians and a few contemporary playwrights stimulate political thought; and some political theorists (such as Plato, Machiavelli, Hobbes, Marx, Arendt) contain dramatic elements. But this "fact" hardly bridges the chasm between tragedy and theory.[2]

The title is not only provocative—it is ambiguous as well. How are Greek tragedy and political theory related? What kind of theory and to which theorists or dramatists does the title allude? Even if one could establish specific and significant continuities of theme,

---

1. There is an ongoing debate over the nature of that tradition. For John Gunnell (in his *Political Theory: Tradition and Interpretation* [Cambridge, Mass.: Winthrop Publishers, 1979], ch. III), it is a "myth." The charge seems less based on historical realism or sophistication than on a confusion about what political theory was, is, and can be.

2. There are common etymological roots to theory and theater. See the discussion in Karen Hermassi, *Polity and Theater in Historical Perspective* (Berkeley and Los Angeles: University of California Press, 1977), pp. 18–22.

form, and aim between Greek tragedy and classical political theory, what importance would or could that have for later, especially contemporary, political theory? Why turn to Greek tragedy when there are so many other political and theoretical resources closer at hand and closer to home?

This Introduction aims at offering enough of an answer to these questions to reduce (but not eliminate) the title's provocativeness and so justify this volume of essays. The answer makes three general claims, which are elaborated in four sections.

The first claim is that Greek tragedy was more than a casual antecedent in shaping the substantive concerns of classical political theory, the form that theory took, and the theorist's view of his own activity in relation to his fellow citizens.[3] Thus I do not regard the dramatic elements in Thucydides' *History*[4] or in the Platonic dialogues as vestigial remnants to be discarded as incidental, if not alien, to theory's main task and mode. Nor is discussing the "theoretical" aspects of Greek tragedy a promiscuous misuse of a word.

My second claim is that insofar as Greek tragedy shaped classical political theory, and we take the normative meaning of "classical" seriously, Greek tragedy also shaped the tradition of political theory as a whole.

A "classic" is an exemplar, at once distant and contemporaneous, an achievement that rebukes our insufficiency and invites our emulation. Unlike what is mundane, the classical "is something retrieved from the vicissitudes of changing times and tastes";[5] something that has so pared away the minor and incidental that the "organic structure of life stands whole."[6] The classic is self-sufficient and lit-

3. As the new historians of political theory have warned, establishing such influence is a precarious undertaking even when, as with Hobbes and Locke, we have considerable biographical and historical knowledge.

4. On the tragic structure and content of the *History*, see F. M. Cornford, *Thucydides Mythistoricus* (London: Routledge and Kegan Paul, 1965).

5. Hans-Georg Gadamer, *Truth and Method* (New York: Continuum Books, 1975), p. 156. This does not mean that a classic is above or outside of history: it is not a suprahistorical category but a mode of "being historical." Thus a classic's power to empower does not presuppose the suspension of critical historical analysis, but is enhanced by it; its legitimacy gains through such criticism. "The classical is what resists historical criticism because its historical dominion, the binding power of its validity that is preserved and handed down, precedes all historical reflection and continues through it. What we call classical does not require a separate act of overcoming historical distance. In its constant communication it does overcome it." The classical is timeless, "but this timelessness is a mode of historical being," a present contemporaneous with every age (pp. 255–57).

6. John H. Finley, *Four Stages of Greek Thought*, (Stanford, Calif.: Stanford University Press, 1966), p. 46.

erally auto-nomos,[7] yet possesses an expressive and generative power that is always greater than, and beyond, that of any specific statement that may be contained within it, or made about it. What is classic may change its aspect but not its core; is multivocal but not cacophonous or vague; speaks directly but anew to each age and people.

As an exemplar a classical work helps constitute and define a field, problem, or question. To know what the problem is, or the appropriate questions are, means having read the classic texts that formulated them.[8] If one's topic is justice or the nature of political theory, Plato's *Republic* is part of the definition of the subject. That does not mean Plato had the final word (or even first) on either matter; it does mean that one accepts or rejects specific theses on, or conceptions of, political theory and justice on the basis of reasons that owe much to Plato. The same is true for the meaning of tragedy and the reading of Greek tragedy.

The power of a classic is reinvigorated by the new facts of life each generation experiences as a condition of its interpretation and appreciation of the classic. These facts establish new resonances and disclose new lights within the classic, even as the classic reveals and elucidates the conditions of the interpreters.

But there are limits to how confidently one can establish continuities between Greek tragedy and classical theory, and limits to how far one can persuasively press the normative meaning of "classical." Clearly contemporary political theorists depart from ancient norms without any sense of embarrassment or loss. They do not write dramatic dialogues about heroic deeds. Nor are they much concerned with eros and friendship, mutability and piety, or tyranny and corruption. Political theory is an academic subject and so propounding visions of civic virtue is at best a peripheral concern.

These limits lead me to my third claim, having to do with the centrality of analogical thinking in, to, and for political theory. Margaret Leslie's essay "In Defence of Anachronism" elaborates both the meaning and relevance of the claim for my overall argument.[9]

---

7. Here is Marx in the *Grundrisse*: "The difficulty lies not in understanding that Greek art and epic are bound up with certain forms of development but that in certain respects they count as a norm and unattainable ideal" (trans. Martin Nicolaus [New York: Random House, Vintage Books, 1973], p. 111).

8. John H. Schaar, *Legitimacy in the Modern State* (New Brunswick, N.J.: Transaction Books, 1980), p. 13.

9. In *Political Studies* 18, no. 4 (1970): 433–47.

Leslie rejects the historical asceticism of those new historians of political theory who would rule out all but the scholarly uses of the past. In contrast, she suggests how and why the thought of our ancestors becomes relevant to our own thinking, that misinterpretations of past ideas may have valuable functions of their own, and that, in some cases, commitment to particular interests in the present may be a necessary condition for an adequate interpretation of the past.[10] Her primary example is Antonio Gramsci's reading of Machiavelli's *Prince*.

She argues that Gramsci's meditation on the *Prince* was a necessary condition of his originality. Yet it is a mistake to assume that his formulation of a position in the present and recognition of a parallel to the past were separate activities rather than a single dialectical process. Gramsci did not work out a political position and then apply it to understanding Machiavelli; nor did he study Machiavelli and then extract lessons relevant to his own situation and time. The insight that suggested a particular interpretation of Machiavelli was the same insight that gave rise to an original political position.[11] Thus his reading of the *Prince* presented Gramsci with an idea from which he drew the analogy of a "New Prince"— the Communist Party—and showed him the style in which to write about it. Once he conceived a parallel between his own situation and that of Machiavelli, he had both a historical interpretation and political inspiration "within a general political outlook which [was] his own."[12]

If Gramsci had observed the rigid separation between academic territories whereby historians understand the past while contemporary political theorists explore politics in the present, he never would have thought or written as he did. And his relationship to a past theorist is not unique—one can think of Hans-Georg Gadamer (or Alasdair MacIntyre or Jürgen Habermas) and Aristotle; Emile Durkheim and Rousseau; Hannah Arendt and the Greeks; Jacques Derrida and Nietzsche; Max Weber and Machiavelli. The methodological strictures commended by historical asceticism cut us off from understanding, let alone doing, political theory. Such insistence on the radical otherness of the past precludes the perception

10. Ibid., p. 436.
11. Ibid., p. 438. There is another level here, which Leslie omits: what Gramsci was doing to and with Machiavelli, Machiavelli did with Livy. In other words, Gramsci also learned how to "use" Machiavelli from reading Machiavelli.
12. Ibid., p. 439.

of similarity in otherness that is the lifeblood of analogical thinking; and analogical thinking is the commonest way in which we extend the "limits of our thought and break out of the straightjacket of commonplace assumptions."[13] Moreover, the zeal to recover the original meaning of a text from under the debris of centuries of "misinterpretation" may not only be futile (for hermeneutical reasons to be explored later), the very attempt is counterproductive. For if the incrustations of tradition have greatly enriched the original work and increased its resources of meaning, then the historian who recaptures the writer's "original intention" finds something considerably less interesting than the tradition he or she rejects.

All this may seem perfectly compatible with a division of labor between historians intent on recovering the exact context in which the classic texts of political theory were written so as to better understand them, and political actors concerned with monumental history. We need only be sure of what we are doing and avoid confusing truth and action. But this not only divides what political theorists had united, and so elides the distinctiveness of political theory and the paradox of being at once theoretical and political; it ignores the fact that having certain sorts of political preoccupations in the present may enhance our understanding of things in the past. As Leslie argues, it may be an advantage not to approach the past or past texts with an "open mind," but to become interested in a particular work or historical problem because it has links with one's own train of thought. Thus personal commitments and interests become a necessary condition for the successful pursuit of "historical truth."

This is particularly true with political theory. It is easy to see how political thinkers like Gramsci who are engaged in grappling with political experience and trying to get a conceptual grip on it have particular need of the store of ideas and images the past can provide and particularly strong motives for wrenching the ideas they use away from their "original meaning." What is less visible but equally crucial is how a close concern with politics in the present may also make possible a particular sympathy with the attitudes and intentions of political thinkers in the past. It could be that a person who is himself or herself involved in political activity is better able to understand the ways of thinking of past political writ-

13. Ibid., p. 442.

ers than an academic whose unconscious literary paradigm is the monograph or scholarly article.[14]

If Leslie is right, then the purpose of juxtaposing Greek tragedy and political theory is not to bring a laundry list of contemporary questions to the study of tragedy, nor to "apply" the "lessons" of the tragedy to contemporary politics and political theory. If we expect Greek tragedy or classical political theory (or even the tradition of political theory as a whole) to supply ready-made answers to preformulated questions, we are bound to be disappointed.[15] In our disappointment that Plato, for instance, cannot answer questions about nuclear disarmament or race relations, we are likely to conclude that nothing can be learned from the past, or to reject the historical study that led to that conclusion. The result is either completely to distance Greek tragedy and classical political theory or too easily to assimilate and adapt them to immediate prejudice.

There is another interesting implication in Leslie's argument. Theorists (and citizens) who care deeply about politics may, because of that fact, have privileged access to dimensions of Greek tragedy and political theory ignored by their more scholarly but unpolitical colleagues. Conversely, those canons of academic respectability intended to insure dispassionate objectivity may obscure as much as they disclose.

These then are my three claims: that Greek tragedy directly shaped classical political theory; that taking "classical" in its normative aspect means that political theory influenced by tragedy was exemplary for the tradition of political theory as a whole; that taking the idea of a "classic" seriously suggests the importance of analogical thinking for political theory. My assumption is that Greek tragedy (and classical political theory read in its terms) can stand to contemporary theory as Machiavelli stood to Gramsci.

My argument defending these claims and this conclusion has four parts. I begin with the once generally held view that tragedy and philosophy or theory [16] are diametrically opposed enterprises. Since this view is given legitimacy by, if it does not derive from, Plato's criticisms of poetry in the *Republic*, part 1 assays that critique.

14. Ibid., pp. 446–47.
15. As Robert Dahl is in his preface to *Modern Political Analysis* (Englewood Cliffs, N.J.: Prentice-Hall, 1964), p. viii.
16. In another context it might be important to distinguish between political philosophy and political theory. I am not much concerned to do that here, other than to say that philosophy is one way of theorizing, and that, if pressed, I would argue that political theory mediates and unifies philosophy and tragedy.

Since the posited opposition between Greek tragedy and philosophy or theory depends on a particular view of philosophy (as well as on the authority of Plato), part 2 turns to three contemporary thinkers (Richard Rorty, Alisdair MacIntyre, and Hans-Georg Gadamer) whose understanding and practice of philosophy is congenial to the poetic sensibility manifest in Greek tragedy. Whereas parts 1 and 2 question the definition of *philosophy* that sustains the opposition between political philosophy and Greek tragedy, part 3 questions the conception of *tragedy* that sustains it.

While parts 1 through 3 are critical, part 4 is constructive. Here my text is Sheldon Wolin's "Political Theory as a Vocation." Because the essay suggests and displays affinities between theory and tragedy, it serves as a preface to my outline of what a dialogue between Greek tragedy and contemporary political theory might accomplish.

1

In the *Republic*, Plato insists on a long-standing enmity between poetry (including tragedy) and philosophy. His critique of the former in the name of the latter is sustained, multifaceted, and powerful. Yet we are uncertain of how to assess that critique, and thus Plato's authority for the opposition between tragedy and political theory I am criticizing. Why is such a poetic, even tragic, work so unrelenting in its condemnation of poetry and tragedy? Are we to apply the *Republic*'s critique to itself? Is Socrates warning us about the enterprise as a whole (or is Plato warning us about Socrates), or does the *Republic* represent the kind of philosophical poetry and tragedy needed to replace a poetic and dramatic tradition that has lost its hold, point, and audience? How does this uncertainty and the discussion of tragedy generally relate to the status and aim of the dialogue as a whole, and to the three waves that threaten to inundate the search for justice? Is the paradox of philosophical poetry the fourth wave that, though unmentioned, encompasses all the other paradoxes in this richly paradoxical work? Or is this paradox resolvable and the quarrel capable of being healed, at least sometimes and in some places?

The first thing to say is that poetry and tragedy had *become* politically, morally, and ontologically corrupt and corrupting by Plato's time. As the reliance of Cephalus and Polemarchus on it demonstrates, poetry was no longer a world, but a series of excerpted maxims, removed entirely from an informing moral intention that might direct or limit their applicability. So far had the poetic tradition degenerated that instead of providing a binding political ethos, it had become a weapon to be manipulated by sophistic educators. When Thrasymachus and his view (that no one is just voluntarily) rule the city (or dialogue), the "pedagogical effect of poetry converts to its opposite." [17] However much poetry may have once provided appropriate moral exemplars, and however central it may have been in the political education of sons by fathers, it had become irrelevant and pernicious. Sons have already left their fathers: Polemarchus is down in the Piraeus worshipping a new god while his father is at home sacrificing to ancestral gods.

Though poetry may have recently become corrupting, that does not exonerate the poets. Insofar as Socrates' argument in the *Gorgias* that Pericles deserved the chastisement of the Athenians since he made them worse is more than ironic, the poets are responsible for their own corruption. [18] Or, to put it somewhat differently: the second thing to say is that poetry is corrupt in itself. But why is that?

One reason, suggested by Salkever in his essay on the *Poetics*, is that the *dēmos* taken as a whole, which is as tragedy must take it, is radically ineducable. Not only are attempts to provide a common public education in virtue futile, they can only reinforce the dream of tyranny that power is the aim of life. That is because this is the only ideal capable of integrating and giving form to an otherwise disorderly *dēmos*. [19]

A second reason is that poetry and tragedy do, and necessarily must, hold up contradictory ideals and immoral exemplars. While book 2 of the *Republic* objects to the moral inadequacy of particular imitations, book 10 insists on the ontological inadequacy of imita-

17. Hans-Georg Gadamer, "Plato and the Poets," in *Dialogue and Dialectic*, trans. with an introduction by P. Christopher Smith (New Haven: Yale University Press, 1980), p. 50.

18. Ironic, since Socrates' accusation against Pericles is the same as the accusation leveled at him. Their mutual involvement with Alcibiades suggests a further affinity.

19. It follows that one difference between tragedy and theory is their respective audiences. For Socrates and Plato education in virtue, if possible at all, can only take place singularly, not collectively. But it is important not to push this too far: democratic Athens was the birthplace of Socratic political theory as well as of tragedy; it is possible that tragedy did at one time educate a *dēmos* less factionalized and corrupt than the one confronting Socrates in his old age and Plato in his youth; the tragedians themselves admonished the *dēmos;* and his regarding the citizenry as collectively ineducable does not mean that Socrates regarded individual democrats that way.

tion itself. Poets, like painters, are three steps removed from reality, and so whatever they depict and offer confounds the soul and corrupts the city. Only if poetry can justify itself on philosophical grounds can it be permitted a place within the ideal city.

But the *Republic* repeatedly turns back on itself, calling attention to its own partiality and to disjunctions within posited analogies in ways that raise questions about its surface meaning and stated objectives. Thus we are left uncertain about whether the *Republic* is indeed an ideal city; whether "realizing" it means instantiation in the world or merely recognizing its ideality; and whether that world is the city or the soul. (Nor is it clear that it is *not* an ideal state intended to be realized in a city that might come to exist if the proper circumstances arose.)

Similarly the dialogue leaves us uncertain about what political philosophy is, can be, or should be. For there is a discrepancy, if not contradiction, between philosophy as practiced by Socrates *in* the dialogue (the conversation with the interlocutors), and the philosophical life that is the dialogue's conclusion (the philosopher-king). What makes this relevant to Plato's critique of poetry is that the poet and philosophers are rival political educators. That they are implies that drama is an inferior form of philosophy and philosophy a superior form of poetry. Thus it is possible that political philosophy is not only better than tragedy because it is philosophy, but because it is better tragedy. In these terms the *Republic* is an ideal tragedy as much as an ideal state. But if that ideality is questionable and the nature of political philosophy uncertain, then the *Republic's* critique of tragedy is too problematic a foundation for radically opposing philosophy and tragedy. Indeed, a case can be made for the *Republic* as philosophical tragedy.

For Plato political philosophy is necessary because of tragedy's failure to educate its citizen audience. That failure is a sign and further cause of the political factionalism that has made Athens into many cities rather than one. Thus philosophy has to turn away from existing cities to find another audience, or rather, the same audience now conceived not as a whole, but as individual souls whose moral self-ordering is a prerequisite for political reconstitution. Insofar as the city in thought and philosophy in general aims to bring something to light rather than to provide an actual design for an improved order in real life, the ideal state is a paradigm in heaven for one who wants to order himself; though as he recognizes himself in the paradigm, he also recognizes in himself the basis on which the reality of the city is built.[20] But insofar as the city in thought and philosophy does aim to provide a pattern for public life, the philosophical poetry of the *Republic* seeks to create an audience capable of appreciating it as the one true tragedy.

The *Republic* then attempts to waken the powers that form the state and audience as did tragedy. But since these powers are contradictory *and* complementary, energizing as well as destructive, its philosophical poetry must tune a dissonance. If human beings are to avoid being either slavish herd animals or tyrannical, rapacious wolves, the strife that plagues and benefits them must be calmed, but not eliminated.[21] That is why a true *paideia* is so difficult. It must sustain a dynamic tension between parts of the soul and city, establishing or reestablishing a unified ethos without obliterating difference and distinction.

This interpretation of the *Republic,* and so Plato's critique of poetry, has several interesting implications. For one thing, it suggests that the apparently ironic discussion of philosophical watchdogs is in fact a consideration of the human condition itself; that the "class of guardians is, properly speaking, the class of all human beings."[22] For another thing, the *Republic's* poetry makes it possible to unite theory or philosophy and practice or politics. For insofar as it cultivates our philosophical natures, which it also reconciles with those violent passions evidenced in the drive for power and self-preservation, it makes it possible for human beings to be human beings among human beings; that is, to be citizens. Finally, to think this way about the *Republic's* critique of poetry, its own poetry, and the *paideia* it commends, begins to specify the continuities between tragedy and theory. To interpret the *Republic* in terms of dualities that plague and enhance human life elaborates the human strangeness manifest in *Antigone* and described in the play's great choral ode. To regard these dualities as confounding our fondest hopes of mastery, so that we remain riddles, riddlers, and riddle solvers, recalls Oedipus. And, most of all, to suppose that justice is a temporary resolution of conflicting forces that are necessary for the whole they constantly threaten to disrupt reminds us of the *Oresteia*.

---

20. I draw on, but also disagree with, Gadamer's argument in "Plato and the Poets" (cited in note 17 above). I think he too readily dismisses (as almost all philosophical interpreters do) the possibility that the *Republic* is an actual design; a dream as well as a nightmare; the best and the worst of all regimes.

21. Gadamer, "Plato and the Poets," pp. 56–57.

22. Ibid., pp. 54–56.

The ending of the *Oresteia* is a joyful reconciliation that restores the balance of nature. The final scene of previously malevolent, life-destroying forces now gracious and generative is truly awesome. Finally the world has been set right and humankind has found healing and relief. But this ending is less an ending than a moment of respite in a never-ending attempt to reachieve an integration of passions and forces that continually threaten to splay the unity they help create and sustain. It is this literal open-endedness that brings suffering, now not to the protagonists, but to the audience. It is they who know that the prodigious feat celebrated at *The Eumenides'* close is a fragile achievement. Aeschylus's juxtaposition of an idealized Athens with the city his audience knew firsthand emphasizes the precarious nature of what has been gained and the proximity of loss. By reminding men and women of their mortality at the moment they are most tempted to forget it, the *Oresteia* teaches, by precept and example, that suffering brings wisdom, and wisdom suffering.[23]

Something similar happens in the *Republic*. Here again there is a promise of final resolution. Mortals can possess knowledge of goodness and know what a just policy is, even if the chance for realizing it is remote. But the ideal, as incarnated in argument and in dialogue, turns out to be problematically desirable and realizable. The "solution" to political and intellectual corruption is plural and incompatible, and so we are left, not with a happy ending or a rationalist politics, but with an achievement that calls its own greatness into question. It is no accident that no sooner has the ideal state been constructed than it is "deconstructed."

Plato's *Republic* is a tragedy of mind and intellect. Few works ask so much of their interlocutors and interpreters. Few give such substance to visions of ideality and longings for perfection, only to suggest the danger of precisely what they commend. With intensity and majesty Plato invites us to understand human experience in a comprehensive context of Being and time. Taking the Socratic injunction to know thyself with the utmost seriousness and piety, he guides us on the treacherous ascent to a promontory from which we can understand our own particularity with full universality. Looking down on the world complete, we can, godlike, be theorists of our own society and spectators of our own actions. Here is the chance to be playwright, actor, and judge. With such

23. I have elaborated on this at length in my "Justice and the *Oresteia*," *American Political Science Review* 76, no. 1 (March 1982): 22–33.

knowledge the mind can transmute social relationships, transform
public life, and recast human destiny. Because the dialogue's drive
for fullness of Being and comprehension is so exhaustive and ex-
hausting, its ultimate "failure" brings untold sorrow.

Failure is too strong a word and begs the question. The final assessment is more complex, the lasting impression more ambivalent. As Oedipus rises in defeat to a stature unattainable in triumph, the *Republic's* failure gives it incomparable dignity. Like
those heroes who confronted death with a courage that inspired
the storied awe of later generations, the *Republic* confronts the possibility that its claims and hopes for philosophy may be exaggerated,
and even pernicious. It is not only that the *Republic's* magnificence is
a testament to reason that belies the insufficiencies it depicts, but
that in displaying its own limitations and those of intelligence in
general, it reasserts the intention, capacity, and necessity of mind
to shape experience. Moreover, as we have seen, the sorrow of defeat is a spur to wisdom. And that wisdom, which consists in our
recognition of mortality and partiality, reminds us of our need for
one another and so for politics.

It is not only the possible failure of philosophy that brings suffering. The prospect of a perpetual quarrel between philosophers and
statesmen, of an irreconcilable opposition between what needs to
be a mutually enhancing partnership between philosophy and
statesmanship, of men of thought and men of action in uncompro-
mising antagonism or unpromising indifference to one another, is
an incalculable loss. The loss is perhaps greater for the city (since it
is possible to have a good person without a good city but not the
other way around), though philosophers cannot fulfill themselves
as philosophers outside the city. The *sense* of loss is no doubt greater
for the philosopher, since he or she, but not the city, knows the
stakes of their antagonism.

The prospect of philosophers being killed or exiled, or choosing
the latter as a preemptive defense, signifies an estrangement far
greater than that between tragedians and their fellow citizens. But
there is an ironic continuity between theory and tragedy even here.
To the extent that this literal or figurative exile imitates the strangeness of the Sophoclean hero,[24] political philosophy is an heir not

---

24. See Bernard Knox, *The Heroic Temper: Studies in Sophoclean Tragedy* (Berkeley
and Los Angeles: University of California Press, 1964), chs. 1 and 2.

only of tragedy's attempt to moralize the heroic ethic, but of that ethic itself.

In these and other ways the *Republic* is a tragedy and Plato an heir to the tragedian's civic task and vision of the world. But in the nature of the case inheritance requires a reconstitution of what tragedy can be. In Plato that reconstitution is achieved by absorbing tragedy into a vision of political philosophy. Having lost its place in a corrupt city/audience and so its purpose in the world, tragedy can only survive by being incorporated into political theory that absorbs its sensibility even as it criticizes what tragedy was and/or had become.

2

The claim that tragedy and theory (or philosophy) are radically opposed activities and sensibilities not only rests on an interpretation of Plato's critique of poetry, but on a view of philosophy as by definition antitraditional, ahistorical, conceptually self-conscious, intellectually privileged, and foundational. Whether deriving from empiricism or transcendent phenomenology, Cartesianism or Kantianism, such assumptions have come under increasing critical scrutiny. Thus recent works by Rorty, MacIntyre, and Gadamer,[25] though often different in agenda and aims, all castigate what they regard as the pretensions, sterility, remoteness, and triviality of most contemporary philosophy in terms that reopen the issue of philosophy's relation to poetry and tragedy.[26]

All three object to philosophers claiming privileged access to truth on the basis of an unproblematic grasp of external reality that presents itself as data for minds freed of bias by methodological purification. Here is Rorty:

Philosophy as a discipline thus sees itself as the attempt to underwrite or debunk claims to knowledge made by science, morality, art, [including po-

---

25. Richard Rorty, *Philosophy and the Mirror of Nature* (Princeton, N.J.: Princeton University Press, 1979); Alisdair MacIntyre, *After Virtue* (Notre Dame, Ind.: University of Notre Dame Press, 1981); and Hans-Georg Gadamer, *Truth and Method*, and *Philosophical Hermeneutics*, trans. and ed. David E. Linge (Berkeley and Los Angeles: University of California Press, 1977).

26. There is a certain paradox in philosophers claiming special expertise to show that philosophical expertise is an unwarranted claim for special recognition.

etry and drama], or religion. It purports to do this on the basis of its special understanding of the nature of knowledge and of mind. Philosophy
can be foundational in respect to the rest of culture because culture is the
assemblage of claims to knowledge, and philosophy adjudicates such
claims.[27]

But for Rorty there are no privileged foundational statements that
furnish us with self-evidently true first principles in terms of which
we can justify our beliefs and opinions. There are no grounds for
accepting the existence of an uninterpreted, unconceptualized reality "out there" to which the ideas in the mind have to correspond.[28]
He admires those philosophers, such as Wittgenstein, Dewey, and
Heidegger, who broke free of the Kantian conception of philosophy as foundational and spent their time (as does Rorty) warning
us against those very temptations to which they had themselves
succumbed. Thus their later work is "therapeutic rather than constructive, edifying rather than systematic, designed to make the
reader question his own motives for philosophizing rather than to
supply him with a new philosophical program."[29]

All three authors insist on the fact that men and women are historical beings, partners in traditions that shape their lives and
minds even as they shape the traditions that shape them. This fact
is an obstacle or embarrassment to philosophy only if we accept the
Enlightenment's prejudice against prejudice, rather than recognizing that it is precisely those traditions and prejudices that make
philosophy possible in the first place. These traditions are not antithetical to reason; they teach us how to be reasonable. Which does
not mean they are always conservative. Sustaining them may require revolutionary reconstitution, lest they lapse into incoherence
and disrepair.[30]

For these authors there is no Archimedean point from which
right principles of action and thought can be inferred and no neu-

27. Rorty, *Philosophy and the Mirror of Nature*, p. 3.
28. See MacIntyre's review of Rorty in the *London Review of Books*, June 5–18,
1980, pp. 15–16.
29. Rorty, *Philosophy and the Mirror of Nature*, p. 5.
30. This was certainly Machiavelli's view, as it is MacIntyre's; whether it is Rorty's
depends on how one understands the positive conclusions of his book: whether, as
it seems, philosophy is over and *Philosophy and the Mirror of Nature* is its obituary
notice, or whether, as he says elsewhere, "As a practical matter, Socratic virtues cannot be defended save by Platonic means, that without some metaphysical comfort
no one will be able not to sin against Socrates" ("Pragmatism, Relativism and Irra-
tionalism," *Proceedings of the American Philosophical Association* 53 [1980], p. 737).

tral matrix or algorithm for assessing all forms of inquiry, types of knowledge, or modes of rationality.[31] We cannot stand outside ourselves and see our world and actions as objects. Nor can we use language as if it were a preexistent tool for designating a world already familiar to us by other means. To know a language is to be familiar with the world itself and how it confronts us. Language constitutes and bounds our world; it uses us as fully as we use it.

In these terms the ahistoricism, apoliticalness, and positivistic prejudices that characterize "analytic" philosophy[32] and its social scientific admirers are naive, self-serving, and dangerous. They are naive and self-serving because such philosophy assumes that it has no prejudices; that what it does *is* rational thinking. By regarding any questions about its own status and nature as a "philosophical" question in its sense of philosophy, it refuses to risk its own presuppositions in a genuinely dialogic encounter with other modes of thinking. Precisely because it is so critical, analytic philosophy is uncritical about its own commitment to criticism, and its inability to live up to that commitment as formulated.

Analytic philosophy is dangerous to philosophy because of its tendency to demystify the world and so deprive us of that wonder that drove men to philosophize in the first place. It is dangerous to the larger culture because it is uncritical of, if it does not contribute to, modern society's tendency to transform practical wisdom into technical knowledge, turn education (in the sense of *Bildung* or *paideia*) into vocational training, identify political practice with technical manipulation, and confound *praxis* (collective deliberation and action undertaken by a collectivity of relative equals) with *poiēsis* (the implementation of a plan by experts to manage other human beings assumed to lack independent wills, intentions, and voices).

---

31. In some respects, MacIntyre and Rorty are at cross-purposes. MacIntyre seeks to resuscitate an Aristotelian tradition of virtue purged of its reactionary politics and outmoded biology. His aim is to do what Rorty criticizes; find a "rationally defensible standpoint from which to judge and to act and in terms of which to evaluate various rival and heterogeneous moral schemes which compete for our allegiance" (p. viii). For MacIntyre deconstruction is as much part of the problem as construction, whereas Rorty worries about the latter rather than the former. But the discrepancies lessen when we read the passage quoted in the previous footnote, and when, given the plurality of virtues he uncovers, MacIntyre is forced to confront Rorty's dilemma.

32. I put *analytic* in quotes because the critique applies as much to Husserl as to the early Wittgenstein. There is, of course, a question about who is and who is not part of the analytic tradition.

If philosophy has a role to play, it is to enrich our moral vocabulary and so our moral lives; to re-enchant the world by respecting contradiction and paradox; to undermine the triumph of especially those experts and that expertise that reduce political and social life to problem solving and efficient management; and to recapture the sense of mortality and mutability that inspired Greek tragedy and Socratic political philosophy.

For philosophy to play that role it must become less stubbornly analytic and more like drama and poetry. Each author insists on the philosophical respectability of poetry, the need for poetic philosophy, and even provides an example of such a unity in their works. This is true of Rorty, whose ideal of edifying philosophy is a self-conscious identification with classical education and poetry against the systematic philosophy and scientific education,[33] and whose own work exhibits striking inversions akin to those of Greek tragedy.[34] It is also true of Gadamer. His concern with "the tragic" in modern society, his purposeful extension of the language of theater and play, and emphasis on the aesthetic alienation of consciousness has led one critic to characterize his hermeneutics as a "prolegomenon to a philosophical poetics."[35] But most of all it is true of MacIntyre. *After Virtue* is less a prolegomenon to a philosophical poetics than an example of it.

MacIntyre intentionally exploits the conceptual affinities and common vocabulary of politics, morality, and drama to bring urgency and dimension to contemporary discourse and action, including his own discourse in *After Virtue*. The book's voice and mood owe as much to Sophocles as to Aristotle. MacIntyre apparently discovers in Greek tragedy (as Gramsci did in Machiavelli) some whispered revelation of our present moral and political calamity, an animating sensibility for his own necessarily different enterprise, and the profoundest statement of the human condition.

As I read him he, like (his) Sophocles, thinks there is an objective

33. The matter is more complicated, since edifying philosophy is parasitic on systematic philosophy, which means if the former truly does its job the latter cannot exist and both kinds of philosophy disappear. In his distinction he follows Gadamer. See "Philosophy and the Mirror of Nature," chs. vii and viii, esp. pp. 365–72.

34. See Richard Bernstein's review of Rorty, "Philosophy in the Conversation of Mankind," *Review of Metaphysics* 33, no. 4 (June 1980): 758–59.

35. David Couzens Hoy, *The Critical Circle* (Berkeley and Los Angeles: University of California Press, 1982), p. viii. Gadamer has argued that the quarrel between philosophy and poetry that supposedly stems from Plato is, in fact, an enlightenment reconstruction of Plato. For Gadamer Plato's criticism of poetry is, paradoxically, the result of imitating the tragedians' moralizing of the heroic ethic.

moral order. But since, as mortals, our perceptions of it are necessarily partial, we can never bring rival understandings of it into complete harmony with each other.[36] Virtue, or the virtues, make incompatible claims on us, and we cannot default on any one of them. As in Greek tragedy (and in the *Republic*), choosing one does not exempt us from the authority of the claim we choose against.[37] So even if the world is intelligible in principle and coherent "in fact," we, as partial beings, are constantly confronted with new truths that remind us that our most confident criteria of rationality may be questionable in the future as they have been in the past. As Sophocles and Socrates understood, "we can never be sure that we possess the truth or are fully rational."[38] Always there loom unsuspected dissonance, startling reversals and inversions, violated expectations: witness Aeschylus's *Agamemnon*, Sophocles' *Oedipus Tyrannos*, and most plays by Euripides.

MacIntyre regards dramatic narrative as the crucial form for understanding collective as well as individual action.[39] Here he is on Sophocles: "It is the individual in his or her role, representing his or her community, who is . . . the dramatic character. Hence, in some important sense the community too is a dramatic character which enacts the narrative of *its* history."[40] He elaborates the point in an essay entitled "Epistemological Crises, Dramatic Narrative and the Philosophy of Science." Confronted by such crises we construct "new narratives which enable the agent to understand both how he or she could have held their original views and how he or she could have been so drastically misled by them. Thus the narrative in terms of which he or she first understood and ordered experience is itself made into the subject of a larger, more inclusive narrative."[41] What is interesting about these quotes is how applicable they are to Greek tragedy, Plato's *Republic*, and *After Virtue*.

MacIntyre's own book is a narrative that shows how, and that our individual and collective fate now hangs in the balance.[42] Like trag-

36. It may be that the moral order is objectively plural or even contradictory, though at some point we might get uneasy about calling it an "order."

37. *After Virtue*, pp. 129–36.

38. MacIntyre, "Epistemological Crises, Dramatic Narrative and the Philosophy of Science," *Monist* 60 (1977): 455.

39. Ibid., p. 464.

40. *After Virtue*, p. 135. Notice how similar this is to Vernant's description of Athenian tragedy discussed below in section 3.

41. "Epistemological Crises," p. 455 and passim.

42. Whether his diagnosis is right is another matter. See the sharply critical review by John Wallach in *Telos*, no. 53 (Fall 1983): 233–40.

edy, it seeks to push its audience to a more inclusive understanding
of their predicament. And like the tragedians, MacIntyre warns his
citizen audience of their moral transgressions, the necessity of political reform, and their finitude.

I do not mean to exaggerate; MacIntyre himself reminds us of the
specific historical achievement of tragedy and the gap between
ancient Athens and contemporary America. Because in classical
Athens "politics and philosophy were shaped by dramatic form,
the preoccupations of drama were philosophical and political, and
philosophy had to make its claims in the arena of the political and
dramatic," the Athenians had what we lack; a public, generally
shared communal mode for representing political conflict and for
submitting politics to philosophical questioning.[43] Yet the contrast
not only serves to distance Athenian tragedy from us but invites us
to judge our deficiencies from that distance. Though we obviously
cannot reestablish Greek tragedy, the form, content, and even
status, of that tragedy ought to inform any serious reconstitution
of our moral and political lives. As I said, MacIntyre's reading of
tragedy plays a role similar to Gramsci's reading of Machiavelli and
indicates again the importance of analogical thinking.

Like Rorty and MacIntyre, Gadamer regards most modern philosophy as trivial, inflated, and technocratic. Though he is less
desperate than MacIntyre about our moral crisis, and Greek tragedy thus informs his vision of modernity less, Gadamer's work is
nevertheless a preface and invitation to philosophical poetry. And
though he does not wholly share MacIntyre's aim of reviving the
Aristotelian tradition of virtue, he too looks to the *Ethics* for an argument, sensibility, and langue by which to reject technical conceptions of theory, of practice, and of the relationships between
them. But it is not this aspect of Gadamer's argument that interests
me. Here I am more concerned to show how his hermeneutics
offers a philosophical elaboration and justification of Leslie's political defense of anachronism.

Fundamental to the argument that philosophy (or theory) and
tragedy are diametrically opposed is the assertion that those who
conflate them ignore the historical context in which tragedy arose
and was performed. As a result they overintellectualize its content,
overemphasize the sophistication of its citizen audience, and under-

43. *After Virtue*, pp. 129–30.

estimate the degree to which tragedy conformed to popular tastes. There are two assumptions here: ordinary citizens could not have possibly understood, let alone rewarded, plays that failed to pay obeisance to their prejudices; and the reconstruction of context is not itself an interpretative activity. Since I deal with the first assumption in the next section, I turn to the methodological assumption in this one.

No doubt understanding a "historical context" enhances the understanding of a text. The question is, how are we to understand history, context, and understanding? For instance, how can we delimit a context without having to defend a context for our definition of context, and so on? In what sense is the context a text and the text a context? Is the interpretation of one less "subjective" than the interpretation of the other? And, finally, how does our context shape the interpretation of what a context is and the particular context within which the text is to be explicated? [44]

For Gadamer the definition of a context is no less an interpretative activity than the interpretation of a text. In neither case is there one final or privileged interpretation, any more than an action, person, culture, or tradition is ever finally complete or fully bounded. Understanding is the continuous elaboration of what is implicit in, but not dictated by, a particular text or form of life. That does not mean that all readings are equal, or that we lack standards for adjudicating contradictory readings, at least up to a point. [45] The fact that there is no unproblematic historical context from which to derive an unproblematic reading of a text, or that interpreters always bring to their interpretation a certain horizon of expectations in consequence of their own historical situation, is only a sign of intellectual failure *if* we embrace an objectivist epistemology and ontology. That interpreters never wholly bridge the distance between their present and past or their culture and another culture is not pathological, but a recognition of human plurality. Interpretation is a fusion of horizons in which, like participants in a Socratic dialogue, we seek to understand a text, action, or culture and ourselves as understanders, actors, and cultural beings.

44. Though the point is abstractly put, the stakes are clear. One need only think of revisionist history, or the impact of Marx, Foucault, and Braudel, to see how political the definition of context really is.

45. The sense in which we do is discussed by Hoy, *Critical Circle*, passim, and Richard J. Bernstein, *Beyond Objectivism and Relativism: Science, Hermeneutics and Praxis* (Philadelphia: University of Pennsylvania Press, 1983).

To even talk about "a" context is misleading. A text is not bounded in a single moment but by a series of historical moments and readings. There is always a tradition of interpretation that constitutes text and context at once. To discard that tradition as an intrusive cultural prejudice standing in the way of truth and freedom is self-deluding and self-defeating.

It is self-deluding because, as we have seen, every culture has assumptions that lie beyond the explicit consciousness of even its most persistently critical minds. Even the most radical dissolution of traditional forms and practices obscures remaining solidarities of sentiment. It is precisely such solidarities that constitute resources for rejuvenating languished or distorted elements in traditions of discourse and action.[46]

It is self-defeating because, insofar as the goal of impersonal investigation is achievable, it leaves us with an impoverished sense of self and a truncated capacity to know the questions worth asking and the answers worth hearing. It is self-defeating, too, because it would transform understanding from a hermeneutical approach whose aim is a practical and informative understanding of a text, action, or culture as it relates to the self-understanding of a particular community into a purely cognitive enterprise concerned with abstract individuals.[47] Finally, discarding traditions is self-defeating because it stifles precisely that dialogue with alien yet familiar texts and times that force us to test our fondest prejudices, including our prejudice against traditions.[48]

If Gadamer is right then there are good philosophical reasons for accepting Leslie's defense of anachronism and rejecting simple

---

46. For instance, attending to such resources could help resuscitate Aristotelian notions of *phronēsis* and *praxis* against the dominant culture of technique. Because traditions—such as liberalism or republicanism—are composites and multivocal, the resuscitation of a tradition may entail a change in emphasis that constitutes a revolution. Think how different liberalism would be if we took consent with the utmost seriousness; or how different our understanding of American politics might be if we drew out the suppressed, but unextinguished, republican sentiments in the *Federalist Papers*.

47. Gadamer, *Reason in the Age of Science*, trans. Frederick G. Lawrence (Cambridge, Mass.: MIT Press, 1981), pp. 126–30.

48. The cult of dialogue can easily go too far. As has been said by others (and increasingly recognized by Gadamer himself), Gadamer's hermeneutics are too philosophical and intellectualist. The practices of even the most academic philosophers are shaped by distinctive national traditions (including distinctive traditions of intellectual practice and academic behavior, many of which were adumbrated by Tocqueville), by the political, linguistic, and academic structures of power and powerlessness, and by the social and economic conflicts of the moment.

assertions of historical context. If Gadamer, MacIntyre, and Rorty are right then philosophy is akin to tragedy and the purported philosophical deficiencies of tragedy—its poetry, attention to a particular audience, and location within a specific tradition, the telling of stories—are not embarrassments but strengths. Indeed, some of them are necessary conditions for all thought, including philosophy.

3

Building partly on what they take to be Plato's understanding of democratic politics and philosophy, certain modern critics have insisted on the thoroughly untheoretical character of tragedy. For example, Denys Page's introduction to *Agamemnon* claims that while Aeschylus is a great poet and powerful dramatist, he lacks "the faculty of acute and profound thought." Because the dramatist uncritically accepts conventional opinions and adheres to traditional religious beliefs that "cannot be justified by any reasoning acceptable to man," the *Oresteia* contains a "simple and practical morality" that amply demonstrates the distance between tragedy and philosophy.[49] In a complementary argument another critic explains that modern readers of Greek tragedy underestimate this distance because, being remote from the political context of tragedy's invention and performance, they anachronistically overemphasize drama's abstract and intellectual qualities. Doing so, they ignore how severely constrained the tragedians were by the political predilections and intellectual deficiencies of a popular audience. Given such an uneducated citizenry, we cannot expect the tragedians to challenge, let alone contravene, the sentiments or prejudices of the ordinary Athenian. But that is exactly what we expect from philosophers. So, while dramatists are part of the "living world of the theater" concerned with practical matters commonly conceived, philosophers are "concerned with ideal situations" and truth regardless of common understanding. To insist on continuities or parallels between philosophy or political theory and Greek tragedy is to create a flimsy, if not wholly artificial, bridge over the "wide gulf [that] separates theory and practice."[50] Similar things are said

49. *Agamemnon*, ed. J. D. Denniston and D. Page (Oxford: Clarendon Press, 1957), p. xv.
50. Peter Walcott, *Greek Drama in Its Theatrical and Social Context* (Cardiff: University of Wales Press, 1976), p. 3.

about Sophocles (despite H. D. F. Kitto's *Sophocles: Dramatist and Philosopher*) and, with less certainty and consensus, about Euripides.

There is something to these views. Aeschylus's religious views do seem primitive,[51] intellectuals do overintellectualize, democrats do romanticize Athenian democracy,[52] and philosophers were relatively independent of popular recognition and acclaim. Moreover, tragedy, as opposed to philosophy, was entertaining as well as edifying, concentrating as much on affect as on effect, on exciting as on calming the passions.[53] Even the most dramatic of Plato's dialogues contains a level of conceptual self-consciousness, concern for logical reasoning, direct discourse, analytic rigor, explicit critique, and purposeful prescription absent in even the most intellectualist plays of Euripides.[54]

Something but not everything. For the contrasts they present and presuppose are overstated and so misleading. In the preceding section I criticized the idea of philosophy that underlies the supposedly "wide gulf" between theory and tragedy; in this section I want to criticize the idea of tragedy that underlies it.

Whatever its origins, fifth-century tragedy was a part of a religious festival and a political institution analogous to the *heliaia*, *boulē*, or *ekklēsia*. It was performed in public, for the public, largely by the public, and judged by the citizens it helped educate to the task of judgment. Tragedy's importance in sustaining the quality of public life is indicated by the fact that it was a liturgy equal to the maintenance of a trireme, as if to suggest that the cultural survival of the Athenians depended on the courage of its people in con-

51. Of course, Page assumes he knows what those views are. Here is E. R. Dodds: "Aeschylus did not have to revive the world of the daemons: it was the world into which he was born. And his purpose is not to lead his fellow-countrymen back into that world, but, on the contrary, to lead them through it and out of it" (*The Greeks and the Irrational* [Boston: Beacon Press, 1957], p. 40).

52. With our justified repugnance against slavery and the second-class status of women, the pendulum has swung the other way.

53. How much ancient philosophers were independent of popular attitudes and how indifferent they were to entertainment is open to question. Certainly the sophists and rhetoricians depended on pleasing their clients and that often included verbal pyrotechnics. It remains to be seen how independent contemporary philosophers are of our dominant academic and political ideologies. In any event they are almost certainly less entertaining than Protagoras.

54. See the discussion of tragedy and theory in the chapter on "Political Theory" by R. I. Winton and Peter Garnsey in *The Legacy of Greece*, ed. M. I. Finley (Oxford: Clarendon Press, 1981), esp. p. 38. I do not mean to beg the question: it is unclear whether, how, and in what sense, the *Republic* is prescriptive. Also, since I do not think Socrates is Plato's "mouthpiece," I am not sure the *Republic* is quite as direct in its discourse as most of its philosophical interpreters assume.

fronting the risks of tragedy in the same way as its physical survival depended on its sailors' courageously meeting the risks of battle. In the days preceding the performances, children of those who died for the city were presented, honors to outstanding citizens were proclaimed, ambassadors were publicly received and prisoners released from jail, as the city reconsecrated, remembered and re-dedicated itself to sustaining its traditions of collective life.[55]

Tragedy was also a democratic institution. Not only did it de-velop with other Athenian democratic institutions and practices,[56] but it was, in William Arrowsmith's words, a "democratic *paideia* complete in itself."[57] Thus citizens brought political wisdom in-formed by tragedy to the deliberations of the assembly, and the ex-perience of being democratic citizens in the assembly, council, and courts to the theater. That is one reason why, as Werner Jaeger wrote, the "Athenians regarded tragedians as their spiritual leaders with a responsibility far greater than the constitutional authority of successive political leaders."[58] It is at least suggestive that *didaskein* means both to teach, learn, or explain and to put on plays. This teaching helped collectivize (and moralize) the heroic ethic, creat-ing citizens whose drive for excellence took the form of surpassing others in contributing to common greatness. At least that is Pericles' boast in the Funeral Oration, where he proclaims democratic Athens a heroic city, great alike in speech and deed.[59] Finally, tragedy was a democratic institution because it helped to maintain a cultural equality that was part of, and a precondition for, *isonomia*, that equality under, by, and through the laws in which men became lawful because lawmakers and responsible because actors.[60] In sum, tragedy was a form of public discourse that inculcated civic virtue and enhanced the citizen audience's capacity to act with foresight and judge with insight.

55. Charles Rowan Beye, *Ancient Greek Literature and Society* (Garden City, N.Y.: Doubleday, Anchor Books, 1976), ch. 7, esp. pp. 247–48.

56. See the discussion in Gerald Else, *The Origin and Early Form of Greek Tragedy* (New York: W. W. Norton, 1965), ch. 2.

57. Arrowsmith, "A Greek Theater of Ideas," *Arion* 2 (Autumn 1963):33.

58. *Paideia: The Ideals of Greek Culture* (New York: Oxford University Press, 1945), p. 247.

59. See Cedric H. Whitman's argument that Athens is the repository of the heroic tradition in his *Homer and the Heroic Tradition* (New York: W. W. Norton, 1958), ch. 3.

60. I have argued this in "Political Equality and the Greek *Polis*," in *Liberalism and the Modern Polity,* ed. Michael J. Gargas McGrath (New York and Basel: Marcel Dekker, 1978), pp. 207–28. In his essay below Podlecki talks about tragedy as a col-lective sharing of responsibility.

The question is whether this discourse was uncritical; whether because the wisdom tragedy contained "lay open to the senses and thoughts of daily consciousness,"[61] it simply followed that consciousness; whether because tragedy was a literary genre uniquely rooted in reality, it merely reflected that reality;[62] whether being a democratic political institution precluded its being a theoretical one.

My answer is that tragedy was critical (though also conservative) and self-critical; that it provided an opportunity for the city as a whole to reflect on the cultural accommodations and political choices it had made and not made; and that, given its form, content, exploration of language, and context of performance, tragedy was an institution whose theoretical dimensions were made possible by a democratic culture it helped define, sustain, and question. Here is Jean-Pierre Vernant:

> By establishing, under the authority of the *archōn eponymos* in the same civic arena and following the same institutional norms as the assemblies or the popular tribunals, a performance open to all citizens, directed, played and judged by qualified representatives of the various tribes, the city makes itself into a theater; in a way it becomes an object of representation and plays itself before the public.[63]

Watching itself on stage in the distancing garb of Argive or Theban heroes enabled the citizen audience to initiate a dialogue about what it was doing to itself and to others; a dialogue whose concerns and form anticipated Socratic dialogue and so classical political theory as a whole.

Tragedy's structure contained a series of tensions between mythical origins and historical present, poetry and "prose," and heroic individuals and the collectivity. On the one side there were ancient legends of a mythical but still living past; on the other, the city's

---

61. Finley, *Greek Thought*, p. 32.
62. "Drama is the most social of literary forms. It exists fully only by virtue of its public performance. . . . This means that one cannot separate the condition of drama from that of the audience or from that of the social and political community" (George Steiner, *The Death of Tragedy* [New York: Oxford University Press, 1980], p. 113).
63. Jean-Pierre Vernant, "Tensions and Ambiguities in Greek Tragedy," in *Interpretations*, ed. Charles S. Singleton (Baltimore: Johns Hopkins University Press, 1969), p. 108. Froma Zeitlin's essay below elaborates and qualifies Vernant's statement: "If we say that theater in general functions as an 'other scene' where the city puts itself and its values into question by projecting itself upon the stage to confront the present with the past through its ancient myths, then Thebes . . . is the 'other scene' of the 'other scene' that is the theater itself," (pp. 116–17). As she notes, this lends another dimension to Oedipus's paradigmatic status.

present political and legal achievements purchased at the expense of that past. The tension is manifest in the juxtaposition of a mythical hero-protagonist played by a professional actor with an anonymous nonprofessional (but trained) chorus of citizens who express fears and hopes shared by the citizen spectators. The contrast is deepened and complicated by another set of tensions, which reinforce but also cut across these. While the hero and heroic past are made immediate through the contemporary language, the citizen chorus is distanced by its lyric songs.

The content of tragedy seconds and elaborates the tensions embodied in its structure. Especially for Sophocles, human life and action are enigmas whose dualities can never be fixed or finally resolved. The paradigmatic case is Oedipus in *Oedipus Tyrannos*. Here is a man of extraordinary intelligence, decisive, perceptive, and profoundly concerned for the well-being of others. Yet his talents turn against him. He takes counsel with himself, weighs the pros and cons, judges the appropriateness of ends and means. But with all of that he cannot help but hazard himself in an inscrutable matrix of supernatural forces, whose surface congeniality is a treacherous mask for ruin.[64] Only in the end do actions reveal their true significance. Only in the end do agents discover their true identity. And by then it is usually too late, at least for the actors on stage.

Of course, not all of us are Oedipuses. But all of us are human. And so the enigmatic quality of his life is ours as well. The roots of our being riddles to ourselves and others lie in the duality that plagues and empowers us. In *Antigone*'s great choral ode the chorus sings of man as *deinos*—wondrous, awesome, marvelous, powerful *and* terrible, fearful, destructive, and violent.[65] We are simultaneously capable of prodigious power but often powerless to govern ourselves; able to control the forces of nature but not our own nature; inventors of civilization—that is, of language, thought, and the sentiments that make human concourse possible—and destroyers of what we have made, including tragedy and ourselves. Immediately upon the ode's conclusion a guard enters with Antigone. The chorus, seeing her and the meaning of her being there, cries out: "My mind is split at this awful sight." The direct reference

64. Vernant, "Tensions and Ambiguities," p. 118.
65. On the significance of the ode in the play and Hellenic culture generally, see Charles Paul Segal, "Sophocles' Praise of Man and the Conflicts of the Antigone," *Arion* 3, no. 2 (Summer 1964):46–66. See, too, Heidegger's discussion in *An Introduction to Metaphysics* (New Haven: Yale University Press, 1959), pp. 146–65.

is to the girl before them; the indirect one is to the "ontological" dualities of being human.

No other creatures are actors and acted upon, victimizers and victims, free yet constrained by necessity, simultaneously puppeteers and puppets, subjects and objects of their own destiny and character. Because this is our place and condition, drama unfolds both on the level of everyday existence in an opaque human temporality that is composed of successive and limited present moments; and on the level beyond earthly life in a divine temporality that embraces at every moment the totality of events, sometimes to hide them, sometimes to reveal them, always to insure that nothing and no one escapes or is forgotten.[66] Without that reality human suffering would have no larger meaning and so human life would be unbearable. That is why the chorus in *Oedipus Tyrannos* would rather the oracles were true and their beloved king be guilty of Teiresias' charges, than that he be innocent and the oracles wrong. His unspeakable pollution is made bearable only because of its connection with the gods. If the oracles are false then Oedipus's whole life is nonsense, since he has lived it in faithfulness to them. If his horrible deeds are nothing but inexplicable coincidence and erratic circumstance, then, literally, all is lost.

These dualities and the structural tensions they second are deepened and elaborated in drama's recognition of, and teachings about, the equivocal character of language. Examining how the tragedians make a clear point about the ambiguity of language also indicates how much the content of tragedy depended on the context of performance.

Repeatedly drama presents men and women who misunderstand one another. Whether out of fear (the nightwatchman in *Agamemnon*), or out of purposeful duplicity (Clytemnestra), or because of the inadvertent but necessary mishearing, misspeaking, or misanswering that infects all speech, the words on stage function less to establish communication than to establish barriers to it. In such circumstances language functions not to disclose but to enclose; not to make known but to keep obscure. Rather than reminding us of a common fate and predicament, speech encourages a disdainful imperviousness to the intentions and characters of others, thereby constricting and impoverishing thought rather than enlarging and enriching it.

66. Vernant, "Tensions and Ambiguities," p. 118.

But by making the ambiguous and equivocal nature of language clear in the play, tragedy helps obviate the problem outside it. "From the author to the spectator" language recovers the "full function of communication which it had lost on stage." But what is communicated "is precisely that there exist, in the words exchanged by men, zones of opacity and incommunicability."[67]

Aeschylus and Sophocles display both the capacity and opacity of human thought, the power of mind and action to shape the world and the imperviousness of the world to the light of the mind and the shaping hand of action. Alive to the contradictoriness of experience and ironies of action and mind, their tragedies explore dissolution and dissonance within the firmly defined structure of theater, play, and ritual. But when that structure itself dissolves, as in the late plays of Euripides, the world simply becomes opaque. Then language cannot recover because the breakdown of speech on stage mirrors the linguistic combat and verbal isolation of the factionalized audience. By bringing the contemporary world more fully onto the stage and projecting what is on stage out into the audience, dramas such as *Orestes, Heracles,* and *The Bacchae* suggest that both tragedy and politics have become radically problematic enterprises.

To put the matter this way suggests that tragedy could be radical, critical, and self-critical because it was conservative. As a communal act and part of a religious festival, tragedy reaffirmed the city's political traditions, rituals, and gods. But this did not lead the tragedians to accept uncritically the context that made performance of their plays possible. On the contrary, tragedy explored passions and actions no public life could countenance, and problematized the city's most fundamental cultural accommodations, whether these were sexual, generational, institutional, or intellectual. This paradox parallels the situation of the tragic hero who is both a liberator/creator of and threat/destroyer to his community. A similar ambivalence applies to the tragedians and political theorists.

What makes this conservatism particularly interesting (and the paradox all the more acute) are the ways in which, as a form of public speech about public speech, tragedy was self-reflective.

To the degree that tragedy dramatized the problematic aspects of

67. Ibid., p. 117. See also Charles Paul Segal, "The Music of the Sphinx: The Problem of Language in *Oedipus Tyrannus,*" in *Contemporary Literary Hermeneutics and the Interpretation of Classical Texts,* ed. Stephanus Kresic (Ottawa: University of Ottawa Press, 1981).

the *polis* of which it was an integral part, it explored its own preconditions, status, and prospects. Insofar as the dualities it contained
in its form and depicted in its stories was a kind of self-examination
that promoted collective self-examination, tragedy anticipated the
theoretical vocation as it is described by Socrates in the *Apology*.

More specifically: tragedy was a form of action concerned with
the ironies of action and part of a religious festival concerned with
piety and impiety. Dramatizing the problem of leadership, the tragedian was, as Jaeger suggests, himself a political leader. Interested in the interplay of passion and reason, tragedy not only
sought a balance that enhanced both, but provided an example of
such balance in its very form. Probing the shaping force of institutions and traditions, tragedy was itself a political institution and
part of a tradition. Educating the judgment of the political community, it thereby nurtured an audience capable of appreciating what
it was and did.[68] Critical of heroism, it was itself a heroic effort to
represent human life within the bounded context of theater, stage,
and play.

In this the playwrights were in danger of imitating the presumptions of their heroic characters. By its nature tragedy comes close to
imitating Oedipus's imprudent confidence[69] that the world is fully
intelligible to human understanding. In these terms the enigmatic
quality of *Oedipus Tyrannos* becomes an act of piety (though piety is
no guarantee of the gods' favor).

As all this implies, drama both embodied and defined the cultural tensions it portrayed. To the degree that tragedy embodied
these tensions, it was fully part of the city and looked outward toward the audience as did the actor on stage. In this sense, and like
him, it was precluded by limits of time and space from knowing the
full context of its own undertaking. But to the degree that tragedy
defined, rather than embodied, these tensions, to the extent that
(like some Sophoclean hero) it explored the outermost realm of
otherwise barely intimated, usually unspoken, cultural accommodations, it looked down on the actors in the political arena as the

68. Or, as with Euripides, tragedy indicated how the corrupted judgment of a
corrupted city deprived it of its place and point.

69. In Slatkin's words Oedipus's "problem is not one of moral deficiency but of
imperfect comprehension, of flawed insight into the circumstances of his existence.
Without acknowledging this limitation as the link between human nature and human suffering, society cannot begin to deal justly with the individual and his experience of life" (p. 215 below). I think this is also Socrates' view in the *Apology*, and
Plato's in the *Republic*.

audience did at the actors on stage. In this respect the dramatist could claim a privileged understanding of collective life, though to the extent that his plays educated his audience to share his insight, it was a privilege shared with his community. Without separating their activity or thought from that of their fellow citizens, the tragedians achieved what was at one and the same time a unique distance from, and integration with, the sustaining visions of their *polis*. In this, as in other ways, they once more anticipated the intellectual endeavor and the ultimate dilemma of their theoretical successors.

By now it is clear that tragedy was as close as one could come to a theoretical institution. In its form, content, and context of performance, tragedy provided, by example and by precept, a critical consideration of public life. Unlike other political institutions, but like many political theorists, tragedy did not provide specific remedies or recommendations. Freed from the urgency of decision and the exigencies of the moment, tragedy drew its citizen audience to reflect on the latent pattern of their lives as that was disclosed in the play and lived outside it. Here was an opportunity to think about what they were doing in systemic and structural terms without losing touch with the traditions of their city and the concrete dilemmas it faced.

Putting the matter this way suggests that tragedy was able to unite thought and action not because it applied the former to the latter, but because drama was itself a theoretical act. The theater was an occasion, place, and way for theoretical considerations to become relevant to practical affairs without violating the irony, rhythms, or contingency of action. This was possible because the citizen audience were simultaneously spectators and actors. As spectators of the action in the play, they could see a whole denied those who enact their part and are by definition bound to the particular. But as political actors themselves, they took part in a whole they could only partially comprehend.

Tragedy cannot be characterized as accommodating to popular prejudices, or primitively religious, or unphilosophical. As we have seen the tragedians were popular *and* left none of the city's ideals, aspirations, achievements, or resolutions outside the problematizing of paradox and contradiction. They validated the city's institutions *and* called them into question; reaffirmed its structure of order *and* pushed the mind beyond that order to face the chaos those structures had exorcised.

Here again there are striking parallels and continuities between tragedy and political theory as the latter is discussed and exemplified in the *Apology* and *Crito*.[70] In those dialogues, Socrates implies that membership in the democratic community of Athens is a prerequisite for political philosophy. He, and his way of doing philosophy, have a dual parentage: the mortal city of Athens and the god Apollo. Since the city is a parent to the man and vocation, Socrates owes it a double respect (provided that respect does not entail disrespect for his divine parent).

But his need to remain in Athens in order to be philosophical is not only a matter of respect. His kind of philosophy can only be done in Athens, among, if not with, his fellow Athenians. Other kinds of philosophy can be done anywhere, but not Socratic philosophy. The sophists may have no home and so may avoid taking responsibility for what they say, but he does and so cannot. More than that, what Socrates does, including what he criticizes, he owes (partly) to the city he is criticizing. And that city, particularly its tradition of critical reflection, has been partly constituted by tragedy. From this point of view, Socrates' simultaneous critique and defense of his native city is not new; it elaborates and makes explicit a tension present in tragedy.

In certain respects the *Republic* can also be seen as an elaboration of this tension, especially given a "structuralist" interpretation of tragedy as I have rendered it and as it is surveyed in Segal's essay in this volume. When Segal argues that tragedy is committed to a political, linguistic, psychological, and cosmic order it also shows as precarious, that it invigorates our appreciation for form by displaying the chaos and formlessness that lurks beneath the surface and at the borders, he could well be analyzing the *Republic*. As the memory of *Agamemnon*'s corruption and chaos suffuses the joyful reconciliation of *The Eumenides*, so the image of Thrasymachean tyranny remains as context and threat throughout the *Republic*. Similarly, as the *Oresteia*'s concluding vision of a fully just Athens stands in contrast and as rebuke to the factionalism of Aeschylus's city, so, too, do the well-ordered individual and city stand to the cave and Plato's Athens. Moreover, the *Republic*, like tragedy,[71] is concerned to re-

70. I have argued this at length in "Philosophy and Politics in Plato's *Crito*," *Political Theory* 6, no. 1 (May 1968): 149–172.

71. It is important not to exaggerate the similarities: tragedy was a political institution, political theory was not. Socrates and Plato are skeptical that tragedy can be the cathartic *paideia* essential to a democracy. There is, moreover, a distinction

pair, reestablish, and sustain linguistic constancy and so the possibility of political and moral discourse. When words change their meaning in the ways Thucydides so masterfully portrays at Corcyra and throughout his *History*, they become weapons, violence by other means. In such contexts men and women can neither deliberate, reason, nor communicate.

When, borrowing from Victor Turner, Segal calls attention to the liminal status of the hero as outcast, suppliant, and liberator, as one who threatens the old order and creates a space in which "the old pieces can be reshuffled in new combinations" and "new alternatives . . . can be imagined," he is describing Socrates and Plato as well as Oedipus and Sophocles.

Finally, Socrates and Plato join the tragedians in detaching heroic virtues from a predominantly warrior ethic and reassigning them to citizenship, goodness, or philosophy. This heroic attempt to moralize the heroic ethic is evidenced by Aeschylus's Agamemnon, who goes too far (in both senses); in Sophocles' warnings against intellectual pride; in Euripides' conflation of the cowardly Trojan slave and the "heroic" Orestes; in Socrates' misquotation of Homer in the *Apology* and rejection of Crito's traditional definition of heroism at the beginning of the *Crito*; and in Plato's rejection of Polemarchus's equally traditional definition of justice as helping friends and harming enemies.

4

If my argument has been persuasive, opposing tragedy and theory underestimates the continuities between Greek tragedy and classical political theory and presupposes a "positivist" interpretative principle that obscures the normative force of "classical" and the importance of analogical thinking to political theory.

But much of this argument has been critical and negative, as much a prolegomenon to the juxtaposition of Greek tragedy and

---

"between the tragedian's mode of engagement with political themes and the more rigorously analytic approach that developed around the middle of the fifth century. The emergence of the latter marks the beginning of Greek political theory as such" (R. I. Winton and Peter Garnsey, "Political Theory," p. 38). But in the *Apology* Socrates argues that he, not his accusers, is a true Athenian; that he, rather than they, represents and embodies what is most noble in a free people. The tragedians too, were critical of the *dēmos* and explored the possibilities and prospects of their success as political educators; it is important not to identify theory with analysis for reasons discussed in parts 1 and 2.

contemporary theory as the doing of it. In this last section I want to remedy the deficiencies. To reiterate: the point of juxtaposing tragedy and theory is to enrich the latter while disclosing neglected aspects of the former.

I begin the section with an analysis of Sheldon Wolin's by now "classic" essay, "Political Theory as a Vocation."[72] I start with Wolin because his critique of Cartesianism adds a political dimension to similar criticisms offered by MacIntyre, Rorty, and Gadamer; because his own combination of radical critique and conservatism parallels that of the tragedians; because his conception of epic theory derives from tragedy and classical political theory, and, most importantly, because his portrait of political theory helps specify the theoretical aspects of tragedy and how incorporating tragedy in the study of political theory can sustain and enhance the vision and vocation of theory he admires.

Wolin begins his essay with a critique of what he calls "methodism," the attempt to substitute a prescribed set of mental steps for inherited knowledge and tradition. Methodists believe that only a mind purged of such knowledge and so rid of any distorting preoccupations and preconceptions can discern natural regularities. Not only is their method untainted by personal bias, it is the shortest, most efficient means of gaining self-mastery, the mastery of nature, and path to truth. Given their conception of truth as economical, replicable, and easily packaged, knowledge is properly presented in propositions that are rigorously formulated, logically consistent, empirically verifiable, and independent of historical or political context. Dualities, incoherence, dissonance, or ties to the complex historical sensibility of a people all interfere with the compactness and manipulability that are the essential attributes and signs of genuine knowledge.

Paradoxically, methodism's questioning of tradition does not lead to a genuinely skeptical temper, but to a single-minded preoccupation with order. With both Descartes and contemporary political science, methodism's systematic doubt leads to a desperate though irrational affirmation of whatever political and social arrangements happen to exist. For a mind turned in on itself and stripped of its acquired habits, beliefs, and values, yet pledged to support exist-

---

72. Reprinted in *Machiavelli and the Nature of Political Thought*, ed. Martin Fleisher (New York: Atheneum, 1972), pp. 23–75.

ing political regimes and moral schemes that it nevertheless regards as provisional, is likely to avoid "fundamental commitment and critique."[73]

Political theory, on the other hand, is critical because of its commitments, regards education as a form of apprenticeship rather than the learning of rules, and is concerned with political wisdom rather than political science.[74] Political wisdom inheres in historical knowledge of institutions, legal analysis, and past political theories. Because it does, political theory's mode of activity is less the search than reflection, and, while mindful of logic, it is even more so "of the incoherence and contradictoriness of experience." For the same reason it is distrustful of rigor, believing that political life does "not yield its significance to terse hypotheses but is elusive and hence meaningful statements about it often have to be allusive and imitative."[75] Where methodism discards historical and political context, political theory regards context as supremely important, "for actions and events occur in no other setting. Knowledge of this type tends, therefore, to be suggestive and illuminative rather than explicit and determinative."[76]

We can see now why education is a form of cultural initiation or political apprenticeship rather than instruction, socialization, or training. The knowledge it offers accrues over time, and never by means of a specified program in which particular subjects are chosen in order to produce specific results. Rules, intellectual shortcuts, and detailed procedures advocated and adopted by methodists are self-defeating. Not only do they foster a technicism, instrumentalism, and impatience that obscure political complexities, they impoverish the mind and so the world the mind sees, starving rather than nourishing the theoretical imagination from which even the idea of method arose. As opposed to this, the political theorist aims to "preserve our understanding of past theories, sharpen our sense of the subtle, complex interplay between political experience

73. Ibid., p. 38.
74. Wolin is rightly reluctant to give up "political science" to political scientists, since Aristotle's notion of political science (or practical wisdom and moral virtue) is similar to Wolin's understanding of political wisdom.
75. Wolin, "Political Theory," p. 45. *The Pentagon Papers* offers a good example of what happens when the world *is* seen to yield its significance to terse hypotheses. On this, see Hannah Arendt's discussion of problem solving among defense planners in her "Lying in Politics," in *Crisis of the Republic* (New York: Harcourt Brace Jovanovich, 1972) ch. 1, esp. pp. 19–20.
76. Wolin, "Political Theory," p. 45.

and thought, and preserve our memory of the agonizing efforts of intellect to restate the possibility and threats posed by political dilemmas of the past."[77]

This is both a conservative and radical task, and one because of the other. It is conservative in its concern to preserve the past, respect for knowledge that accrues over time, attentiveness to the complexities of collective life, and patient care for relationships, sensibilities, and cultural resources discarded by the methodist in his embrace of rules, shortcuts, manipulable knowledge, and mastery. It is radical in the double sense of going to the root of things, and in rejecting the methodist's implicit reliance on an ideological framework that simply reflects the politics of the community he is ostensively studying objectively.

Unlike systems theories, communications theories, and structural-functional theories, which are unpolitical in their desire to explain certain nonpolitical phenomena and untheoretical in their refusal to engage in critical analysis of the quality, direction, or fate of public life, political theories expose what is systemically corrupt and systematically mistaken. Not only do they expose basic principles that produce mistaken arrangements and wrong actions, they offer visions of an alternative, uncorrupted whole whose principles can form the foundation for juster beliefs and actions.[78]

If Wolin is right, then the choice of a method, or between a method and a theory, or among theories, is not an innocuous choice among intellectual constructs or conceptual schemes, but a choice among rival ways of constituting the world, living a life, teaching and learning, and knowing. To choose a theory is like choosing a self.[79] It initiates a new way of thinking, evaluating, intuiting, and feeling, and demands a substantial sacrifice in the existing forms of these same human processes.[80]

What is so striking about Wolin's essay are the parallels between his discussion of political theory and my earlier analysis of Greek

77. Ibid., p. 62.
78. Ibid., pp. 26–27, 71.
79. "For there is a far greater risk in buying knowledge than in buying food and drink. The one you purchase of the wholesale or retail dealer, and carry them away in another vessel, and before you receive them into the body as food or drink, you may deposit them at home and call in an expert. . . . But you cannot buy knowledge and carry it away in another vessel; when you have paid for it you must receive it into the soul and go on your way, either greatly harmed or greatly benefited" (Plato *Protagoras* 314a–b, Ostwald's revision of the Jowett translation).
80. Wolin, "Political Theory," pp. 56–57.

tragedy. The qualities Wolin deems essential to theorizing—playfulness, the juxtaposition of contraries, astonishment at the variety and subtle interactions of things, attention to the contradictions and incoherence of experience—are also central to drama.[81] Moreover, it was precisely the achievement of Greek tragedy that it captured the imitative and allusive quality of public life that methodism cannot see or tolerate. In addition, Wolin's claim that political theories try to locate the divisions in the world and embody them in a theoretical form that, though a whole itself, does the least violence to the existence of separate provinces is equally the aim (or achievement) of tragedy. Furthermore, tragedy's emphasis on turbulence, tensions, and dissonance is matched by the theorist's refusal to regard knowledge and truth as present only in rigorous, precise, and quantifiable statements. The tragedian's portrait of the riddling dualities and ultimate strangeness that mark the human condition is matched by the theorist. Both reject the problem-solving mentality that helped Oedipus toward his ruin, as it may hasten us to ours. And when Wolin affirms that nothing is more necessary for theorizing than that facts be respected as multivocal and that "multifaceted facts are more likely to yield to the observer whose mental capacities enable him to appropriate a known fact in an uncongenial way,"[82] we are reminded that one of the essential aspects of Greek tragedy was that action took place on both a human and a divine plane, so that every incident or fact presented itself in a double aspect, as the choice of the actor and as a fate both implicit in his character and ordained by the gods. This duality is not only present in Sophoclean tragedy; it reappears in the secular paradoxes and purposeful ambiguities of the *Republic*.

When Wolin writes of the theoretical vocation as preserving the past, sharpening the interplay between political experience and thought, and preserving the memory of the agonizing efforts to es-

---

81. I think there is a tension between epic theory and theories that are reflective, respectful of incoherence, allusive, playful, etc. However much he may rely on metaphor (for strategic or other reasons), and however aware he may be of the subtle interconnections between things, an epic theorist like Hobbes is impatient with both and castigates ambiguity, allusiveness, and the multifacetedness of facts. Indeed, as Wolin's own writings on Hobbes make clear, *Leviathan* espouses technique, rules, and method, and this may be a necessary concomitant of epic theorizing. The tension is present in the *Republic*'s two modes of philosophizing. (Hobbes admired the *Republic*, but thought it failed in a similar enterprise because it asked too much of sovereigns and knew too little geometry.) Thus the dialogue contains an immanent critique of its own heroic impulses and a critique of that critique.

82. Wolin, "Political Theory," p. 53.

tablish political order, he might well be analyzing the *Oresteia*. And it is the *Oresteia* that presents us with an idealized image of Athens, just as theorists offer a vision of justice against which the systemic corruption of their times can be measured and judged.

Finally, Wolin's political theorist is a political educator. He or she, like the tragedian, is concerned with the quality, direction, and fate of collective life. Each is, in somewhat different ways, intent on nourishing what Wolin calls the theoretical imagination—that is, furnishing rather than purging the mind, so that it can take account of and appropriately embody (in form and content) the ironies, ambiguities, and tensions that attend mortality.

Precisely because Wolin's vision of political theory echoes and parallels my understanding of Greek tragedy, his essay is an appropriate preface for directly proposing how Greek tragedy can enrich contemporary political theory (even as such theory reveals obscured dimensions of tragedy). The point of such juxtaposition is not to make Greek tragedy overly congenial or completely alien, either of which would deprive it of its power to shock and disorient.

The first thing the juxtaposition of political theory and Greek tragedy might accomplish is to provide resources of sensibility, language, and perception for invigorating, extending, and deepening the diagnosis of those crises that define our age. For instance, a democratic nation of former foreigners and exiles is particularly plagued by problems of collective identity and selfhood, of inclusion and exclusion, of the proper balance between plurality and unity. So, too, were the tragedians of democratic Athens. As the essays by Slatkin, Zeitlin, and Saxonhouse in this volume make clear, tragedy and old comedy were preoccupied with membership and community, with being among friends and enemies, fellow citizens and strangers, comrades and exiles. In part that preoccupation stemmed from the double boast of the Athenians that they were autochthonous and a city that welcomed outsiders, outcasts, and suppliants. But it also derived from their recognition that what is new and outside must often find place and respect inside if what is traditional and old is to be renewed. As Slatkin suggests, that is part of the benefit Oedipus bestows on Athens; as Zeitlin suggests, that is what Thebes was unable to do. Thebes was incapable of extending itself (in both senses), incapable of elaborating its foundations. Instead, it turned back and in upon itself, replicating in ever-narrower compass a pattern of destruction until, like Oedipus, it was everything to itself and so nothing at all.

As this Introduction and the essays in this volume suggest, Greek tragedy was about boundaries of space, time, and place, about being inside and outside. It was also about how such boundaries, divisions, and oppositions are born, maintained, and justified. Prominently included were divisions of sex and gender. Such concern with sexual politics is a second instance of where the juxtaposition between Greek tragedy and political theory could deepen conversation and debate. Tragedy called into question the dominance of *polis* over household, the enforced silence of women, the traditional masculine drive for glory and power, and the division of public and private in terms of rigid gender distinctions. To appreciate what the Lanes call Antigone's demonic eros, which "empowers her to break through the conventional gender-based limitations and to champion the civic principle of lineage pride and *philia*," is to alert us to the political voices of women now and enlarge our understanding of women as "political actresses." (That the phrase sounds politically inappropriate in a way that "political actors" does not is interesting in itself.)

A third example of an issue where the juxtaposition of tragedy and theory might be illuminating centers on the Greek distinction between nature (what is necessary and given, or essential, completed and proper) and convention (what has come into the world by human effort, what differs according to circumstance and time). Questions of knowledge and authority, the moral status of laws and constitutions, the purpose and place of politics in human life, and the relationship of men and women to nature were debated in those terms. Insofar as contemporary environmentalism aims to remind us that, as natural beings, our exploitation of nature is also the exploitation of one another and so of ourselves in ways we cannot know or predict, Greek tragedy can add dimension to the reminder. (The choral ode on man in *Antigone*, the fate of Oedipus, Aeschylus's *Prometheus Bound*, and Euripides' *The Bacchae* come to mind.) To the extent that such mastery of nature remains clothed in the rhetorical tunic of heroism and is justified by abstract arguments of purportedly universal significance and validity, Greek tragedy offers two cautions. The first is that any heroic impulse unrestrained by patient care for place and life will destroy both.

That is, I think, the basis for tragedy's warnings against *pleonexia* (a greediness for more than one's share, or an abrogation of what is rightly other and other's), tyranny, and imperialism. The second is that any justification so abstract that it fails to disclose the specific consequences to and for particular lives is an ignorance that insures catastrophe. Thus Oedipus's answer, "man," ignores the riddle's specific applicability to himself and so fails to discern the defeat inside his victory. Or, in more contemporary terms, problem solvers who fail to recognize that problem solving is part of the problem are prone to a tyranny of mind and blindness that accompanies those who cannot hear, see, or honor the world's complexity.

One could go on enumerating other examples—the foundations of legitimacy and accountability, the relationship between democracy and empire, oligarchy and violence, the idea of thoughtful loyalty and critical patriotism, the importance of *isēgoria* (equal right to speak and be heard as a participant in common deliberation), the appropriate reciprocity between passion and reason, how to think about justice and corruption—but the general point is made.

Ancient tragedy can also provide a language and sensibility for saying more clearly what is difficult to say in a contemporary idiom. For example, in an effort to make the unprecedented nature of the Holocaust intelligible without compromising its radical newness, Hannah Arendt recalls the sensibility and dilemma at the heart of Aeschylus's *Oresteia*. Quoting Yosal Rogat, she suggests that there are crimes of such horror and scope that "the very earth cries out for vengeance"; that there are evils so malevolent that they violate "a natural harmony which only retribution can restore"; that there are some wrongs so destructive of a world community that the collectivity "owes a duty to the moral order to punish the criminal."[83]

Not only can a reading of Greek tragedy offer an incisive alternative to currently fashionable formulas about contemporary issues and provide a sensibility to recall long forgotten but now needed sentiments, it can also offer a conception of public life that implicitly denies the compartmentalization of academic disciplines and communal activities we largely take for granted. What we consign to peripheral disciplines (such as theology), or separate depart-

83. *Eichmann in Jerusalem* (New York: Viking Press, 1963), p. 277. For the significance of the transformation of crimes such as parricide from being violations of the cosmic order constituted by parallel hierarchies of being, goods, meaning, and truth into crimes against individuals or particular groups, see Michel Foucault's *Discipline and Punish* (New York: Random House, Vintage Books, 1979).

ments (literature, philosophy, economics), or private life, Greek tragedy regarded as a whole, and so part of public life. Its themes were thus fate and mutability; mortality and finitude; pollution (*miasma*), eros and madness; pride and heroism; the relations of gods and men; suffering and wisdom. To reinsert such themes into political theory would not only add power and poignancy to our understanding of the ironies of action and give insight into the double vision that afflicts and ennobles the human condition, it would also remind us that part of the raison d'être of tragedy, the *polis*, and classical political theory was to help us confront the "emotional terrors of vulnerability, separation and total helplessness."[84] Refocusing contemporary political theory away from its increasing preoccupation with method would expand theory's audience and concerns, and its capacity to learn from fellow and sister citizens.

Reading Greek tragedy would not only assist in the articulation of what is already being said and make divisions in and out of the academy problematic, it would also provide a way of seeing and assessing the politics of contemporary theory. As the Preface indicated, by the politics of contemporary theory I do not mean the political assumptions or implications of a particular theory. I have in mind a theory's structure of intentions, linguistic texture, and implicit claims to authority, as well as the examples it uses, the experiences it invokes, the conception of evidence and argument it relies on, and the audience it anticipates. Some questions will clarify the issue.

What are we to make of a theory of emancipation or liberation whose technical jargon and esoteric arguments leave those whose liberation is projected indifferent, intimidated, or further alienated? Is there something contradictory about a theory of democracy that only a few experts can understand? What would democratic theorizing, as distinct from a theory of democracy, look like? Who could participate and where would it take place? Is there a way of doing democratic political theory such that the very act of theorizing educates citizens for democratic practices? More generally, are most social science and analytic philosophy so reflective of the political community they analyze that they are unlikely or unable to raise fundamentally critical questions? More pointedly still: are

84. The words are those of John H. Schaar in *Legitimacy in the Modern State*, p. 248.

there homologies between the technological society (exaggeratedly, but provocatively, depicted by Jacques Ellul), the bureaucratic state (as analyzed by Max Weber), and analytical philosophy, such that no matter how explicitly critical the latter may be, it necessarily reinforces the others?[85]

Greek tragedy alerts us to these questions because its politics of theory is so different from our own. Tragedy and Socratic dialogue were politically theoretical in form and texture as well as in subject matter and substance. The poetry of drama points outside itself to a depth beneath and beyond the confines of its structure, just as Socratic dialogue is a dialogue about dialogue even as it explores the meaning of justice, piety, friendship, or knowledge. Both let us know that ignorance is the foundation of knowledge; mortality, the foundation of ignorance; and that all wisdom, including their own, is incomplete. There are no endings, only respites and accommodations; no final triumph of reason, only a wisdom dependent on suffering passions that threaten as well as invigorate; no final decisions but a dialogue between play and audience, Socrates and interlocutor. The contingency of action, the need continually to reaffirm justice and rewin freedom, and the sheer fact of human becoming and passing away, is embedded in the very structure of drama and dialogue.

Such a political theory invites interlocution and encourages participation in a way prepackaged knowledge does not, whatever the content of that knowledge may be.[86] Rather than reifying cultural accommodations, tragedy and Socratic philosophy make them

85. Foucault makes a similar argument in his discussion of the politics and political economy of truth and in his warning against totalizing theories, which he sees as inevitably integrated into, and constitutive of, the supervisory institutions and practices that characterize modernity. Thus he endorses the liberation of subjugated discourses, the dispersal and localization of theories, and revolutionary practices that avoid reproducing those forms of control that exist in the structure against which such practices rebel. (On these matters see *Power/Knowledge: Selected Interviews and Other Writings 1972–7*, ed. Colin Gordon [New York: Pantheon Books, 1980], chs. 5 and 63, and Foucault's "Afterward" in Herbert Dreyfus and Paul Rabinow, *Michel Foucault: Beyond Structuralism and Hermeneutics* (Chicago: University of Chicago Press, 1982).

86. Who can participate, where such participation takes place, and with what political import, is another matter. As I mentioned in note 48 above, there is a danger of romanticizing and idealizing dialogue as if the political, economic, and social preconditions were somehow incidental. In this regard it is hardly surprising or wrong that many students regard Socrates as a slyer Thrasymachus, and see dialogue as a covert form of domination.

problematic even as they warn us of problematizing.[87] Rather than succumbing to the mind's propensity for closure and reductionism in the name of consistency and coherence, tragedy and Socratic dialogue make the danger and necessity of such closure and simplification public. Rather than presenting and re-presenting thinking as analogous to *poiēsis*, the imposition of an idea on inert and inanimate materials, both regard theory as a form of *praxis*. In all this they anticipate Aristotle's warning: "It is the mark of a well-educated or well-bred man [*pepaideumenou*] to expect that amount of exactness in each subject matter as is appropriate to its nature."[88] Finally, Greek tragedy can make our theoretical and political accommodations as problematic as it did those of its contemporaries.

Most political theorists have forgotten, or no longer find disturbing, the fact that at its origins, political theory was as paradoxical a phrase and vocation as political astronomy. While politics took place in a contingent world subject to human decisions and purposes, theory involved contemplation of permanent truths about nature, the cosmos, and Being.[89] Thus two questions were present in the mere connection of theory and politics: are there truths about politics analogous to those about nature? and, are all truths, even those about nature, somehow political? Since "politics" and "theory" interrogated the legitimacy of the other's presence in "political theory," political theory was uniquely self-critical about its possibility, status, and point.

It is no accident that who Socrates was and what he was doing confused even his closest friends. Nor is it accidental that his explanation and example of political philosophy in the *Apology* leaves us uncertain about what political theory is, who could and should

---

87. Thus "deconstruction" is as much part of the problem as of the solution, as much in danger of becoming mechanical and rigid as the linguistic codes it seeks to expose and demystify. There is an important political point in deconstructing the encoded linguistic, methodological, and mythical structures that sustain the microdomination of power. But if capitalism is a system that demands continual dislocations and discontinuities in the interest of maintaining a hegemonic ideology, then the task is sustaining and constructing as much as deconstructing, protecting and expanding those attachments to persons, places, and tasks that modernity destroys in order to "progress" as well as to unmask structures of domination.

88. 1094b25.

89. As Bernstein points out in his conclusion to *Beyond Objectivism and Relativism*, Aristotle's separation of *phronēsis* and *sophia* does not resolve the paradox, but restates or even intensifies it. See also Werner Jaeger's *Aristotle: Fundamentals of the History of His Development* (Oxford: Oxford University Press, 1948), appendix 2, for a fine statement of the problem.

practice it, where "it" should be practiced, and how "it" should be judged. Political theorists no longer question their place in an academy, or express unease about their own professionalism or specialized languages. This is a troubling development. It is troubling not only because of the politics implied by such accommodations, but because it cuts contemporary theorists off from the political impulses of their greatest forebears. And this is an incalculable loss in our attempts to make sense of the political and intellectual crises of our times.

Chapter Two

Greek Tragedy and Society: A Structuralist Perspective

Charles Segal

1

Over the past two or three decades the study of Greek tragedy has shown an increasing concern with conceptual patterns, with structures of thought, action, language. A greater circumspection about the nature of character in ancient drama has lessened the tendency to view the plays in terms of psychological realism. Earlier in the century the "Cambridge School" of Jane Harrison, Gilbert Murray, and Francis Cornford stimulated interest in the social and ritual structures reflected in the plays and pointed students in the direction of underlying patterns rather than surface literalism. At about the same time the work of Freud and Jung laid the foundation for the recovery of underlying patterns of a different nature. From the thirties on, especially in Germany, scholars devoted special attention to tragedy's formal and dramatic structure: dialogue and monologue, the patterning of the odes, the messenger's speech, patterns of intrigue and deception.

In America the "New Criticism" of the fifties focused on patterns latent in the poetic language of the plays. Studies like R. F. Goheen's of *Antigone* and Bernard Knox's of *Oedipus Tyrannos* tried to discern the relation between the poetic texture and the intellectual armature of the work.[1] Repeated images, clustered about certain characters or the attitudes embodied by those characters, could help articulate the main concerns of the play and relate them to patterns of language and action. Anthropologically or psychologically ori-

---

1. Robert F. Goheen, *The Imagery of Sophocles' Antigone* (Princeton, N.J.: Princeton University Press, 1951); Bernard M. W. Knox, *Oedipus at Thebes* (New Haven: Yale University Press, 1957).

ented scholars like E. R. Dodds, A. W. H. Adkins, J.-P. Vernant, Alvin Gouldner, and Philip Slater have also viewed Greek tragedy as the battleground for conflicting value systems and latent tensions within society.[2] Vernant especially, concerned with the question of how the social order deals with the antinomies it contains, has stressed the role of tragedy as the field of the problematical, the area where the familiar institutions are called into question and the moral vocabulary, no longer adequate, becomes ambiguous or self-contradictory.

Society, on this approach, appears not as a crystalline, coherent entity inherited by each of its members, but rather as an ongoing process of constructing, abandoning, and readjusting systems of analogies and interlocking relations. Interaction and continuous development of individual institutions in their relations to one another, rather than the unity of the centralized entity, emerge as the dominant subject for scrutiny. This view of the ancient Greek city stresses "the study of relations of complementarity or conflict between the behavioural norms associated with different contexts of interaction."[3]

The structuralist's position has some analogies with that of the sociologist. "Reality" has its existence in its relation to the mental, social, linguistic constructions of the thinking subject. Like a literary work, the social system is viewed, as Roland Barthes would say, in the present rather than the perfective tense. Social man is not a being secure in a given nexus of familial, ritual, political ties with which his life is held together, but rather a being continually engaged in the creating of that nexus. "Ultimately, one might say that the object of structuralism is not man endowed with meanings, but man fabricating meanings, as if it could not be the *content* of meanings which exhausted the semantic goals of humanity, but only the act by which these meanings, historical and contingent variables, are produced. *Homo significans:* such would be the new man of structural inquiry."[4]

2. E. R. Dodds, *The Greeks and the Irrational* (Berkeley and Los Angeles: University of California Press, 1951); A. W. H. Adkins, *Merit and Responsibility* (Oxford: Oxford University Press, 1960); Jean-Pierre Vernant and Pierre Vidal-Naquet, *Mythe et tragédie* (Paris: F. Maspero, 1969); Alvin Gouldner, *Enter Plato* (New York: Basic Books, 1965).

3. Arnaldo Momigliano and Sally C. Humphreys, "The Social Structure of the Ancient City," *Annali della scuola normale superiore di Pisa,* Classe di lettere e filosofia, 3rd ser. 4 (1974):366.

4. Roland Barthes, "The Structuralist Activity," in *The Structuralists from Marx to Lévi-Strauss,* ed. R. and F. DeGeorge (Garden City, N.Y.: Doubleday, Anchor Books, 1972), p. 153.

The structuralist emphasis, therefore, falls not so much upon the dominant, ideal values at the surface of the culture, but rather on the subsurface tensions within the system, the dynamic pulls the culture has to allow, resist, and contain in order to exist. The "achievement" of classical Athens, then, appears less as the crystallization of a marmoreal harmony than as an open equilibrium between competing values and unresolvable polarities.

On such a view tragedy will reflect the anxieties rather than the confident verities of its audience. Rather than "those Greek qualities of goodness and beauty" that Browning's Balaustion found in "that strangest, saddest, sweetest song"[5] of Euripides, recent critics find themselves more attuned to the dissonances, contradictions, and harsh archaic residues the tragic poet's reworking of myth heaves back to the surface.

The rationality of the form of Greek tragedy only sets off the irrationality it reveals just below the surface of myth, cult, and other social forms. Literary critics influenced by both the Freudians and the Frazerians have increasingly probed for these latent, often darker, meanings because they seem to hold more of the hidden patterns and unquestioned assumptions of the society or more of the knowledge that the conscious mind is unwilling or unable to face. In this way the darker side of Greek civilization, as expressed in its creation of tragedy, has enabled modern man, too, to confront the darker side of his own existence and explore beneath the surface of his own highly rationalized, desacralized, excessively technologized culture. From Nietzsche on, Greek tragedy has been felt to hold the key to that darker vision of existence, the irrational and the violent in man and the world. Its rediscovery and popularity since World War II have filled a need for that vision in modern life, a need for an alternative to the Judeo-Christian view of a world order based on divine benignity and love.

2

Because it approaches myth as a system of tensions and oppositions, the methodology of Claude Lévi-Strauss is especially suited to explore the conflictual aspect of tragedy. For Lévi-Strauss, mythic thought operates in terms of bipolar oppositions. The function of myth is to mediate fundamental contradictions in human exis-

---

5. Robert Browning, *Balaustion's Adventure*.

tence, man's relation to man in society, and man's relation to nature in the external world.[6] Recognizing the extent to which our perception and representation of experience are structured by coded patterns of language, gesture, ritual, and so on, structuralism provides a frame in which we can more precisely and thoroughly formulate the interrelation between the political, linguistic, religious, psychological, and other levels of dramatic action.

In a structuralist analysis the details of kinship, dress, architecture, eating, ritual, and so forth are not merely isolated data or *Realien*, but elements of a structured message, a "code." Each code expresses in its own terms—the "language" of ritual, kinship, diet, and so on—a microcosm of the social order. In the analysis of a myth or of a literary work it is not the surface details in themselves that are important, but the relational patterns, the configurations, of these details in the various codes, the "analogy of functions" rather than the "analogy of substances."[7]

Whereas the "New Criticism" tends to isolate the work in a cultural vacuum and to limit itself to verbal structures of internal coherence, structuralism seeks to relate the value structures of the society to the aesthetic structures of the literary work. Its concern, however, is not so much the internal logic and coherence of the codes per se as the cognitive patterns of the culture they imply and the correspondence between the semantic structures of the literary work and the social structures of the culture as a whole.

When we turn from structures of society to structures of literary texts, however, we encounter a fundamental difficulty. The literary work imposes a secondary structure of language and meanings upon the given structures of the society. Unavoidably it utilizes the codes that constitute the mental patterns of the society; and it could be analyzed, at one level, solely in terms of those accepted, normative codes. But at the same time it deliberately manipulates, distorts, or otherwise transforms those patterns in the special self-conscious structures—linguistic, psychological, societal—superimposed by its own internal aesthetic coherence. To put

6. See, for example, Claude Lévi-Strauss, "The Structural Study of Myth," in *Structural Anthropology*, trans. C. Jacobson and B. G. Schoepf (Garden City, N.Y.: Doubleday, Anchor Books, 1967), pp. 202–28; also his "Four Winnebago Myths," in DeGeorge, *Structuralists*, pp. 195–208.

7. Barthes, "Structuralist Activity," p. 150. On codes in classical texts see my *Tragedy and Civilization: An Interpretation of Sophocles*, Martin Classical Lectures, vol. 26 (Cambridge, Mass.: Harvard University Press, 1981), pp. 14–20.

it differently, the work of literature overlays the "codified contiguity" of *signifiant* and *signifié* with a new internal coding wherein the relationships between sound and sense, between overt and latent meaning, between the literal and figurative significance of words change from the familiar (i.e., the precoded) to something unexpected, novel, striking.[8]

Tragedy's relation to the expression of the social order encoded in the myths is particularly complex. As part of a public festival, a ritual in honor of the god Dionysus, tragedy validates the social order. Its demonstration of the dangers of excess, impiety, overconfidence within a coherent system of symbols representative of the divine, political, and social order—the gods who often appear on stage, the palace of the king, the altars and shrines, the oracles, the house—creates a microcosm of the totality of that order. At the same time the violence of its action, its radical questioning of justice, both human and divine, its searching explorations of the failure or the betrayal of public and private morality take us outside of that order. In the magical circle of the orchestra the normal coherence that distinguishes and balances good and evil, love and hate, friends and enemies, kin and strangers, reality and illusion breaks down. The world order is stretched to its limits; its intelligibility is suspended.

Thus while affirming the interrelatedness of all parts of the human and divine order through its densely woven web of symbolic imagery, tragedy also has the special peculiarity of calling the normative codes themselves into question. Both in language and in its enacted narrative it effects a violent derangement of the codes, a deliberate de-structuring of the familiar patterns of order. In tragedy, as to some degree in all literature, the "message" of the specific text not only brings something that was not in the code itself, but can actually threaten to destroy the code.

The parallelism between the strained diction, violent metaphors, perverted rituals, and inverted sexual roles in the *Oresteia* shows the violence done to the linguistic, ritual, and familial codes. *Oedipus Tyrannos* develops an elaborate correspondence between the confusion of language in the riddles of the Sphinx and in the oracles of the gods (the two polar forms of utterance have a discon-

8. Another, more formalistic way of describing the process is Roman Jakobson's much-quoted dictum, "The poetic function projects the principle of equivalence from the axis of selection into the axis of combination" ("Linguistics and Poetics," in DeGeorge, *Structuralists,* p. 95).

certing unity), the social inversions of king and scapegoat,[9] the ritual inversions of pollution and purification, and the domestic confusion of father and husband, father and brother, wife and mother.
Here, as in the *Oresteia*, the linguistic, political, ritual, and familial
codes are all involved simultaneously in the unstable situation from
which the tragic suffering arises. Confused intermingling, inversions, troubling identifications replace reassuring demarcation or
differentiation. The original structures are suspended, forcing the
mind to reach beyond those structures in the painful search for
other principles of order or in the even more painful admission that
there are no principles of order. Here men must face the chaos their
mental structures—social, linguistic, political, sexual, spatial—deliberately shut out.

3

A Greek tragedy is a very special kind of mythical narration. We
cannot approach it exactly as Lévi-Strauss approaches a given
myth, reconstructing an underlying pattern by comparing the corresponding terms ("mythemes") in a large number of variants.[10]
The literary critic is concerned not with the core structure of the
myth as it is revealed and realized in its variants, but rather with
the particular "variant" constituted by the literary work. The structuralist analysis of the coding processes of language can trace the
relation between aesthetic patterns and patterns of order in the society as a whole.

To take a specific example, to which we shall return in more detail later, Sophocles' *The Trachiniae* utilizes a system of analogies
based on an underlying opposition of god and beast, civilization
and savagery.[11] The play opens with Deianeira anxious about the
long absence of Heracles, her husband. She laments the cares of
her life and Heracles' frequent absences. She tells of how the monstrous river-god Achelous and Heracles fought to win her hand, a
battle described in a later choral ode (497–530). A messenger an-

9. For king and scapegoat, see Vernant, *Mythe et tragédie*, pp. 101–31, especially
pp. 114–24; further references in my *Tragedy and Civilization*, p. 453 n. 3.

10. For example, Claude Lévi-Strauss, *The Raw and the Cooked: Introduction to a
Science of Mythology*, vol. 1, trans. J. and D. Weightman (New York: Octagon Books,
1970); see also the references cited in note 6 above.

11. See my *Tragedy and Civilization*, ch. 4; also my essay, "Mariage et sacrifice
dans *Les Trachiniennes* de Sophocle," *L' Antiquité classique* 44 (1975):30–53.

nounces Heracles' return. Deianeira sees the young and beautiful Iole in the entourage and soon learns that she is destined for Heracles' bed. At first calm and forgiving, she later returns to the stage resolved to try a love charm given her in another violent wooing, the Centaur Nessus's attempted rape long ago. Fatally wounded by Heracles' arrow, poisoned with the Hydra's venom, Nessus instructed Deianeira to save the blood clotted around his wound as a love charm. All these years she has kept it stored in the inner chambers of the house. Now she anoints a robe with it and sends it to Heracles for his sacrificial celebration at Cape Cenaeum across the water from Trachis. Her son Hyllus arrives soon after with the news of the robe's effect: Heracles, in the midst of slaughtering bulls at the sacrificial fires, was suddenly seized by terrible agony. He is now coming to Trachis to exact vengeance from Deianeira. Realizing what she has done, she exits in silence; her suicide in the bed-chamber is soon described. Ferocious in his pain, Heracles arrives, ready to kill Deianeira with his own hands. When he learns the details of the poison and hears the name of Nessus he realizes that he is doomed, in accordance with an old oracle from Zeus. He forces the reluctant Hyllus to marry Iole and makes him promise to take him to Mt. Oeta, where he is to be burned on a funeral pyre. In a last speech he checks his cries of pain with heroic endurance and exits with son and followers for Oeta. Hyllus (or the chorus) closes the play with a lament about the remoteness and indifference of the gods.

From this rather complicated action emerges the symmetrical relation between Nessus, the beast-man, and Heracles, the man who stands in a special proximity to the gods. Structurally the success of Nessus's revenge and the deaths of Heracles and Deianeira can be described in the form of a series of failed mediations between the poles of bestiality and divinity. Heracles acts out the anomalous role of a beast-god insofar as he, the son of Zeus, repeats the violence of the Centaur. Sacrifice in the ritual code, marriage in the sexual code, the safe interior of the house in the spatial and familial codes are all isomorphic expressions of this basic failure of mediation, the destruction of the mean where civilization is possible. The normal communication between man and god is destroyed. This disruption also collapses the hierarchical relationship of beast, man, and god, the equilibrium of the violent sexual instincts that links man with the beast, and the coherent social and cosmic order that links man with the gods. The triumph of the "beast," Nessus, through his poisoned blood, a specious love charm that reaches back to the destructive monstrosity of the Hydra, the resultant perversion of the sacrificial rite into the killing of the god-man by the man-beast, and the destruction of the house and marriage are not only elements in a causal sequence but also simultaneous manifestations of an underlying structure—or rather the disintegration of structure. Achelous and Hydra, for example, are agents within a causal series culminating in Heracles' death; but they are also ever-present forces in the action, existing simultaneously with and parallel to Nessus and the bestial aspect of Heracles himself.

Sacrifice, which plays a central role in this and other tragedies, functions as the mediating vehicle within the system of relations and communications that link gods and men. Sacrifice validates the world order by affirming the hierarchical relation of god-man-beast. The immortal gods receive the airy smoke that mounts up from the hard, durable bones on the altars. Mortal men sustain themselves with the roasted meat of the perishable flesh and vital organs. The human celebrant who offers the victim to the gods is as far above the beast as he is below the god who receives the offering. The ritual stylization of killing in sacrifice and the roasting of the flesh to be consumed by the celebrants after the sacrifice separate the structured world of "culture" from the savagery of wild "nature." By establishing a system of conjunctions and disjunctions, sacrifice makes manifest the implicit logic of the world order. It separates gods from men and men from beasts, but also opens a way of access from men to gods.[12] In tragedy that system of logical relations is overthrown or confused, sometimes to be recreated on a new basis. The centrality of sacrifice as a symbolic expression of that system explains, in part, why sacrifice and its distortions or perversions play such an important role in tragedy: one thinks of the stories of Thyestes, Iphigeneia at Taurus and at Aulis, Medea, Ajax—all recurrent subjects of tragedy and all characterized by perverted sacrifice.

Kingship, like sacrifice, is not merely a one-dimensional social category (political in the case of kingship, religious in the case of

12. For this view of sacrifice, see Marcel Detienne, *Les Jardins d' Adonis: La Mythologie des aromates en Grèce* (Paris: Gallimard, 1972), pp. 71–113; also his *Dionysos mis à mort* (Paris: Gallimard, 1977), pp. 164–207. See also Henri Hubert and Marcel Mauss, *Sacrifice: Its Nature and Function,* trans. W. D. Halls (Chicago: University of Chicago Press, 1964).

sacrifice). In tragedy, as in early Greek myth and literature generally, the king occupies the point of symbolic intersection between
the human and the divine, the natural and supernatural worlds.[13]
His sufferings represent the efforts of the society to maintain those
relations with the cosmic order on which its physical and spiritual
life depends. Thus in the *Oresteia* Aeschylus takes great pains to
establish the spatial coordinates of this kingship in a large framework. The suffering and death of the king stand at a point of crossing between elemental opposites: sea and fire (*Ag.* 281–83, 650–
51, 958), winter and summer (966–72), upper and lower limits (cf.
hyper-, *hypo-*, "above," "below," in *Ag.* 786), divine honor and bestial degradation. It is not just the suffering of Agamemnon as an individual that moves us, but the cosmic, religious, and social vi-
brations in the drastic reversal and fearful collapse of polarities
defining the ordered structure of the society and the natural and
supernatural order. Hence Agamemnon's walking on the carpet is
not merely an act of individual pride that provokes the "envy" of
gods and men (cf. *Ag.* 921–25, 947), but a terrifying confusion of
boundaries in the figure who is charged with the sacred task of mediating between human and divine, making visible in his own person the numinous order of the gods.

The Greek tragic hero, then, is not a "character" quite in the
sense of the hero of a modern fiction or drama, an individual with a
three-dimensional idiosyncratic personality. He is, rather, both an
individual caught in a moral conflict and a symbolic element in a
complex socio-religious structure. He both carries the linear flow
of the action and is a constellation of patterns present simultaneously in all parts of the action. Alongside the individualized personalities of Aeschylus's Agamemnon, Sophocles' Oedipus, or Euripides' Pentheus stands the role of sacral kingship wherein each of
these figures concentrates in himself the crisis in the relation between the human, natural, and supernatural worlds that forms the
starting point for the tragic action.

In *Oedipus Tyrannos*, for example, the plague, manifestation of a
disturbance in the relation between man and god, both reveals and
engages the hero at the point of maximum exposure to the unknown. It forces him to take responsibility for the troubled cosmic
order and propels him into the reversals of power and helpless-

13. On the sacral function of kingship with reference to Greek tragedy, see my
Tragedy and Civilization, ch. 3.

ness, knowledge and ignorance, divine and bestial in the ensuing dramatic action. The king supplicated with nearly divine honor in the prologue (*OT* 31–54) proves to be the beastlike pollution wandering "in the savage woodland, the bull of the rocks" (*OT* 477ff.). The spatial coordinates of this reversal in the ritual and biological codes are clearly demarcated in the "tyrant's" fall from rooftop to ground in the third stasimon (863–79). A horizontal axis from palace to wild, city to mountain, man to beast, intersects a vertical axis from highest to lowest, king to scapegoat. At the point of intersection stands Oedipus, the figure whose identity consists precisely in this intersection of contradictions, this co-presence of polarities.

To describe these structural and spatial coordinates of Oedipus's tragic situation is to supplement, not deny, our affective reactions of pity and fear to the undeserved agonies of a great-souled man as they unfold sequentially before us. A structuralist approach to Oedipus's tragedy reinforces its connections with the patterns of sacral kingship that link him with Aeschylus's Agamemnon, with Euripides' Heracles and Pentheus, or even with Shakespeare's Lear and Hamlet. Within the limits of the play itself, it helps us appreciate the cosmic implications of Oedipus's ruin and hence the underlying *seriousness—spoudaiotēs* in Aristotle's terminology—of our involvement in that ruin. It is not just an ordinary individual who undergoes this suffering, but a paradigmatic figure whose fate must deeply concern us because it involves the fundamental issue of the order or chaos of our world and the capacity of our social and intellectual constructs to contain that chaos.

Like psychological analysis, a structuralist reading seeks to uncover the latent, subsurface meanings, implicit rather than explicit structures. Thus a structuralist view of sacrifice focuses on the nexus of logical relations described above. From a psychological point of view, however, sacrifice expresses the violence beneath the surface of the social order and the need for the expulsion of that violence. In the work of René Girard, who has approached tragedy from this point of view, the tragic action sacralizes violence by the choice of an arbitrary victim, a *pharmakos* or scapegoat, whose death or suffering removes violence from the realm of men and gives it back to the gods.[14] In the sacrificial action of tragedy, the hero doubles with his bestial opposite—Heracles with Nessus in

14. René Girard, *La Violence et le sacré* (Paris: B. Grasset, 1972), translated as *The Violence and the Sacred* by P. Gregory (Baltimore: Johns Hopkins University Press, 1977).

The Trachiniae, Pentheus with Dionysus in *The Bacchae*—only to draw apart from him in the sacrificial death that reestablishes distinctions and gradations and thereby prevents a further collapse into chaos.

The cultural meaning of certain symbols does not, of course, preclude psychological significance. To the cultural historian, for example, the opening of *Oedipus at Colonus* certainly reflects the Greeks' religious concern with pollution and purification and with the rites of supplication. To the Freudian critic Oedipus's blind entrance to an inviolate grove of hallowed female goddesses is not only the ritual frame for the ensuing drama, but also the significant reenactment of a prior pattern in Oedipus's life: it recapitulates at a new level the hero's transgressive entrance into a dark forbidden place of the mother, connected with her mysterious power of creating life. Entrance to the grove is a movement from the "bad mother" who cast him out into the wild to the nurturant mother who receives and shelters him.[15] Cruel expulsion from the womb, from Jocasta's body to Cithaeron (symbolical of the bad mother), is answered by acceptance back into the womblike earth of the generous mother that is the pious city of Athens.

In moving from *Oedipus Tyrannos* to *Oedipus at Colonus*, Sophocles' symbolism shifts from an infantile world of primary acceptance or rejection to a public realm of civic action. Through the symbolism of the Eumenides and their grove the civic frame of Athens in *Oedipus at Colonus* seems able, finally, to reconcile the "two faces" of woman, the generosity and the destructiveness of the mother as perceived by the totally dependent infant to whom her alternation of presence and absence means denial or fulfillment.

From a structuralist perspective the grove is also the point of conjunction between the city and the wild, the place of shelter and the exposed world of the polluted outcast. It is also the focus for a vertical spatial axis between upper and lower worlds, gods and men. It unites the two polarities of Oedipus's status *below* the human as the despised, impure, exiled parricide and incestuous criminal and his status *above* the human as a hero mysteriously called by divine voices that come from both above and below.

15. See Barbara F. Lefcowitz, "The Inviolate Grove: Metamorphosis of a Symbol in Oedipus at Colonus," *Literature and Psychology* 17 (1967):78–87, and Helen H. Bacon, "Women's Two Faces: Sophocles' View of the Tragedy of Oedipus and His Family," in *Science and Psychoanalysis*, American Psychoanalytic Association Decennial Memorial Volume (New York: 1966), pp. 10–27.

Mother, mother earth, womb, and city are all parts of a single symbolic complex. Instead of a nubile youth's deed of violence in winning the body of his biological mother in incestuous marriage, the aged hero of *Oedipus at Colonus*, purified by years of suffering, blind, and enfeebled, can win, metaphorically, the "body" of a symbolic mother, the earth of Athens that receives him, as a surrogate for the maternal earth of Thebes, at the transitional point of the Furies' grove. The good order of Athens replaces the dark curses of Thebes. The surrogates of the evil mother, the Furies who pursue crimes of violated kin ties and aggressively take the mother's part in Aeschylus's *Oresteia*, are now transformed into Eumenides, the Kindly Ones. Although the mystery of numinous power still attaches to them, they are also associated with the city as a whole, the political and civic space of Athens as a well-governed *polis*. Hence the famous ode that praises Colonus's grove as a place poised between the powers of life and death (688–719, especially 671–80) ends with images of Athens as a political and military entity and with the power and solidarity of the city that are under the control of the male ruler and the male warriors (cf. 699–703, 711, 714–19). The creative energies of the goddesses' grove, connected with the chthonic realm of Hades and the female realm of the Eleusinian divinities (674–78, 683–85), pass to the Olympian goddess Athene, daughter of Zeus and divinity of Athens.

At the same time Oedipus's acceptance by Athens in this play marks a shift from the polluted and exiled king's unmediated swing between godhead and bestiality so dangerous in *Oedipus Tyrannos* to the king's restoration to a civic frame: he himself becomes the mediator between chthonic and Olympian powers and stands in a privileged relation to the goddesses who embody both the destructive and creative forces of nature. His marginal status thus parallels that of the Furies/Eumenides themselves. Like them he is an ambiguous figure whose place is at the fringes of the city, the liminal space at the borders of the land. Like them he dispenses both curses and blessings. Received back into the city, he has a place of honor as a "hero"; but he is still in a sense outside, for his tomb is unknown to all but Theseus, and his end is hidden in mystery and associated with places of mysterious transition between worlds, the "brazen-footed road" and its "bronze steps" into the earth (*OC* 57, 1590f.).[16]

16. For this liminal aspect of Oedipus, see my *Tragedy and Civilization*, pp. 363–65, 371–76.

4

Lévi-Strauss's view of myth as exploring and validating the opposition between nature and culture, the "raw" and the "cooked," is substantiated by a great deal of Greek tragedy.[17] Here the tension between *nomos* and *physis*, "culture" and "nature," often takes the form of a tension between the spheres of confident human authority and divine autonomy: on the one hand the *polis* and its Olympian-sponsored, male-oriented institutions, the area where man imposes structure and the ordering conventions of *nomos* upon the potentially threatening impulses of *physis;* on the other hand the power of the gods in its elusive, unknown aspects, the chthonic divinities and the areas of human life under their supervision, the stain of impurity, the threatening realm of women, the biological processes of birth and death, the demands of "nurture" (*trophē*) and blood ties, and the curses produced or transmitted in the area of such blood ties.

The origins and development of civilization, the emergence of law (*nomos*) and justice (*dikē*), the mastery over the savagery both in nature and in man himself are important themes in all the surviving tragedians, as well as in contemporary thinkers such as Herodotus, Protagoras, Hippias, Hippocrates, Democritus, and others. Aeschylus's Prometheus trilogy (of which only *Prometheus Bound* survives) deals with the origins of civilized technology. In his *Oresteia* the juridical resolution of homicide in the city evolves out of primitive blood-vengeance in the family. Sophocles won his first victory with a play about a culture-hero, the *Triptolemus* (468 B.C.). His lost *Palamedes, Nauplius*, and probably *Daedalus* seem to have been based on similar subjects. The first stasimon of *Antigone* (332–75) is one of the great texts of the fifth century on man's conquest of nature and brings this broad evolutionary perspective to the play's conflicts between political authority and the ties of blood, between the rationalism and Olympian religion supposedly governing the state and the emotional bonds among kin and the chthonic deities whose sphere is burial and respect for the dead. Sophocles' *Philoctetes*, whose hero has been described as an ancient Robinson Crusoe, draws heavily on Sophistic theories about the origins of culture to

17. See the references cited in notes 6 and 10 above. For classical applications, see my *Tragedy and Civilization*, ch. 2, with the literature there cited. For recent discussion, with useful bibliography, see K. R. Waters, "Another Showdown at the Cleft Way: An Inquiry into Classicists' Criticism of Lévi-Strauss's Myth Analysis," *Classical World* 77 (1983–84):337–51.

explore the paradox that the miserable outcast on a desert island may embody a more valid and humane vision of civilized order than the goal-oriented, unscrupulous, manipulative leaders of the Greek army at Troy.

Whereas Aeschylus sets these issues into a religious framework implicating the entire cosmic order, Sophocles tends to embody them in deeply involving personalities. Sophocles' richness of characterization sometimes calls attention away from the questions of social order and justice, but they are always strongly present nevertheless. In his *Electra*, for example, the heroine's personal suffering and endurance seem to be in the foreground. Yet they derive much of their impact and importance from the fact that she is the sole champion of justice in the corrupt land of Mycenae. The king has long ago been murdered by the selfish and licentious Queen Clytemnestra, and his death symbolizes the state of corruption in both the political and moral order. Rituals too are violated; family ties are turned from love to hate; the natural order is inverted. Orestes, coming from outside, bent on the practical fulfillment of the "deed" (*ergon*) of revenge in a male world of efficient action and a logically defined background of space and time, contrasts with Electra, confined to the house, involved in an inner, female realm of static "words" (*logoi*), uttering Niobe-like lamentations in a petrified timelessness (145–52). Electra's tragedy of sheer spirit, force of will, and feeling turned to hatred and killing, though relieved in part by the joyful reunion with her brother in the moving recognition scene of the play, remains defined by a larger supra-personal field of reversals, where life has become death, where the king's palace is a locus of corruption rather than order, and where justice, recoverable only at the cost of matricide, becomes confused and problematical.

The scale and violence of the Peloponnesian War, with its atrocities of Corcyra, Melos, and Mytilene, made men more keenly aware of how precarious the ordered forms of civilized life are. Euripides depicted the process of breakdown and disintegration in tragedies like *Medea, Hecuba, The Trojan Women, The Phoenissae,* and *The Bacchae. Medea,* produced the year the Peloponnesian War began (431 B.C.), shows the power of the unleashed violence of love turned to hatred, passion to ferocity. In this heroine the traditional passivity of woman changes to a murderous revenge that destroys a mother's love for her children and leaves the male antagonist impotent and shattered. In *Hippolytus* and *The Bacchae*, too, the potential destructiveness of emotional life also centers on women as the symbol and the focal point for the irrationality the *polis* must suppress. In *The Bacchae* that destructive power of the irrational annihilates the city itself. Dionysus, god of wine, religious ecstasy, madness, and illusion, retaliates against the Theban king, Pentheus, who has rejected his worship, by maddening the women of the city and driving them to the mountain, with the king's mother, Agave, at their head. The hierarchical separation of god, man, and beast breaks down as the god appears in the form of bull, snake, or lion and is present to his worshippers in the holy *thiasos*, the ecstatic band of Maenads. Pentheus, the substitute victim of the god, becomes a fearful human sacrifice, torn apart as a beast-victim in a sacrifice where the mother is the "priestess of the murder" (1114). The tearing apart of the king in the Dionysiac *sparagmos*, or ritual "rending apart," is a symbolic rending of the city itself, no longer able to integrate emotionality and religious ecstasy into the order of civic institutions and law. That order collapses with the centrifugal movement that ends the play, the exile of the queen mother, Agave, after she has killed her son and the bestial metamorphosis of the old king, Cadmus, the culture-hero who founded Thebes.[18]

Throughout Greek tragedy systems of linked polarity—mortal and divine, male and female, man and beast, city and wild—operate within the dense fabric of the language and the plot to include not just the emotional, interior world of the individual character or spectator but the whole of society in its multiple relationships to the natural and supernatural order.

5

The hero of Greek tragedy stands at the point where the boundaries of opposing identities meet, where "identity" in fact becomes the paradoxical conjunction of two opposites. To return to the example of Aeschylus's Agamemnon, the king, trying in vain to avoid the doom to which his own nature, his past actions, and the violent passions of his wife pull him inexorably, asks, "Revere me as a man, not as a god" (λέγω κατ' ἄνδρα, μὴ θεόν, σέβειν ἐμέ, *Ag.* 925). But then, by walking upon the carpet he overreaches to god-

---

18. See my *Dionysiac Poetics and Euripides' Bacchae* (Princeton, N.J.: Princeton University Press, 1982), pp. 206–14, 314–27.

like status, only to plummet suddenly in a dramatic reversal from
god to beast, sacrificed like a bull in an unholy and perverted rite.

Heracles in *The Trachiniae* follows a similar pattern. Son of Zeus
and conqueror of monsters, he fuses with the bestial victims he
sacrifices, "burned" and "devoured" by the Hydra's poison. His
pyre on Mt. Oeta is the place of both his triumph and his defeat. It
hints at his immortalization as a god, but also marks his subjection
to the still-unconquered bestiality in himself, symbolized by the
monsters of his past, the Hydra and Nessus, who have, in a sense,
vanquished him.

The perverted ritual, a recurrent feature of Greek tragedy, itself
indicates the destruction of the mediations between god and beast
the forms of civilized life assert. Whereas civilization separates
man from the "beastlike life" (*thēriōdēs bios*) on the one hand and
places him in a subordinate, but propitious, relation to the gods on
the other, the tragic hero is polarized at the opposite extremes: he is
either involved in bestial actions (incest, matricide, and patricide
all fall within this category too) or aspires to some form of godlike
power or autonomy.

Euripides' Hippolytus, placing himself outside the civilized
forms of sexual union and marriage, devoted to Artemis, virgin
goddess of the hunt, lacks a secure place in the *polis*. As both virgin
and hunter, he is in a sense uncivilized. He meets his death in the
wild realm, in a threatening borderland between land and sea. Yet
his force of will and integrity, the other side of his heroic status,
entitle him at the end to a kind of quasi-divine honor as the figure
to whom girls at marriage dedicate their offering of hair.

The bestowal of this honor upon a youth whose life has centered
upon total abstention from sex and marriage is an ironic inversion
that corrects, too late, the emotional imbalances in Hippolytus's
life. This restoration, however, takes place in a framework beyond
the hero's individual life, which is left shattered. It occurs for others,
not for himself, and at a point when his own repressed sexuality
has brought him death and sterility, the reverse of the marriage and
procreation implied in the rites that are to commemorate his sufferings (1423–30). In these rites his goddess offers the dying youth
"greatest honors" in the songs of girls dedicating locks of their hair
as they leave virginity for marriage, leave the realm of Artemis for
that of Aphrodite, her and Hippolytus's enemy. These ritual hon-

ors, therefore, reflect the tragic hero's place at the crossing of opposites, mortality and divinity, death and love, shame and honor. The songs at these rites, furthermore, will immortalize Phaedra's love for Hippolytus (1429–30). The hero whose aspirations are toward godlike purity receives his parcel of immortality, his everlasting fame, in its most repugnant possible form, the eros of a passionate woman, a form exactly opposite to the ideals of his life. The ritual act here, as generally in tragedy, perpetuates rather than dispels the contradictions in the hero's relations to both the divine and the social order.

In another way, too, *Hippolytus* shows how tragedy transforms the structures of myth and ritual from an affirmation of order to a questioning of order. As the rites commemorating Hippolytus's death imply, this hero is probably a vestige of the young consort of the Great Mother, a goddess of sex, fertility, marriage. As a fertility daimon subordinate to her power, he dies annually, to be reincarnated each year in the fresh vegetative life of the new crops, and then to die again, and so on. Euripides' tragedy, however, individualizes this figure into a unique personality who resists the biological drives toward sex and procreation. Instead he devotes himself to a transcendental ideal, symbolized by his pure goddess, the virginal Artemis. His effort is the tragic attempt of man to assert spiritual freedom amid the demands, instincts, and necessities of the animal half of his nature. Such an aspiration beyond the physical basis of the mortal condition has a price, a choice with tragic implications, insofar as it brings with it a rejection of certain ineluctable elements of existence, in this case the side of life symbolized by Aphrodite.

By placing himself outside these demands, Hippolytus also places himself outside the familiar norms of civilized life and stands therefore in a marginal relation to the city. Along with marriage, he also rejects political responsibilities (1013–20). His father's mode of life, both as husband and as ruler, is not the model that he would choose for himself. He would exist in a prolonged adolescence, between childhood and adulthood, between the city and the wild, between the divine (in his virginal purity) and the savage (in his hunting in the wild). On a structuralist reading it is tragically appropriate that this figure whose place has been on the margin of the city should be involved in the rites of passage that civilize the "un-

tamed" or "unyoked" maiden (1425) and mark her change from the
implicit "wildness" of her virgin state to the "civilized" status of
her place within the house (1423–27).[19]

Unlike ritual, tragedy stresses not the orderly process of transition from one stage of life to another, but the in-betweenness, the
marginality, the ambiguity in the juxtaposition of the two sides, virgin and marriage, beast and man, forest and city. Thus Hippolytus's "greatest honors" from the goddess to whom he has devoted
his life, and for whom, in a sense, he dies, both honor and dis-
honor him at the same time. He is defeated and abandoned in his
aspirations toward this divinity even as he receives the "greatest
honors" from her. The peculiar nature of this rite within the complex field of tensions that Euripides frames for it fixes the hero's ambiguity forever: he is both within the human world as the recognized exemplar of some of its noblest virtues and simultaneously
outside it as a threat, an anomaly, a source of disturbance and conflict. He slips beyond the mediations necessary to civilization both
from above, in his special relationship with Artemis, and from below, in his role as the savage hunter. His tragic situation lies in the
destructive coincidence of the extreme poles. He slides from one
polarity to the other without a middle ground.

In the cultic background of *The Trachiniae* the pyre on Mt. Oeta
was important in a ritual rewarding Heracles for his life of labors
that freed the earth of monsters and made it safe for civilized life. A
shrine on Oeta with burnt offerings from early archaic times attests
to this cult of the apotheosized hero. In Sophocles' play, however,
the pyre is part of the ambiguity between god and beast surrounding Heracles. By making the pyre so prominent in the promises
Heracles exacts from his son Hyllus at the end, Sophocles surely
raises the issue of the hero's apotheosis.[20] Yet there is no clear, un-
ambiguous reference to Heracles' future immortality on Olympus,
only dark and uncertain hints. In cult the pyre and the rituals
around it affirm the mediation between god and man; in tragedy
that focal point in the ritual becomes the center of the most prob-

19. On this aspect of *Hippolytus*, see my "Pentheus and Hippolytus on the Couch
and on the Grid: Psychoanalytic and Structuralist Readings of Greek Tragedy," *Classical World* 72 (1978–79): 129–48, especially pp. 134–39.

20. On the problem of Heracles' apotheosis, see my *Tragedy and Civilization*,
pp. 98–102, with the further references cited in nn. 119–20 on p. 431; also my essay,
"Sophocles' *Trachiniae:* Myth, Poetry, and Heroic Values," *Yale Classical Studies* 25
(1977): 138–41, with the references in nn. 94 and 95 on p. 139.

lematical part of the hero's existence, the mystery of his suspension between the highest and lowest extremes.

In Euripides' *Electra* Aegisthus's death, though just, is a kind of human sacrifice. In the grim justice of this play that quasi-sacrificial act has a spatial analogue in its location outside the *polis*, performed in honor of the Nymphs, divinities of forest and mountain who are also, ironically for this play, divinities connected with marriage. Marriage and sacrifice are here combined, as they are throughout this play, whose series of perverted rites weaves together familial, sexual, spatial, biological, and political codes in its violated cosmic and social order. Likewise in *Heracles Mad* the hero who ostensibly defends the civilized order comes to embody its destruction. After saving his family from the cruel tyrant Lycus, Heracles is afflicted with a homicidal madness in which he performs a perverted ritual: he "sacrifices" his children to the accompaniment of an insane inner dancing and song. Coming from the Underworld to purify himself from that dark realm, he reestablishes order, but then plunges into the even darker Hell of his own violence, from ritual purification to the most horrible pollutions.

The order affirmed by ritual is both literal and symbolic. The ritual represented as part of the tragic action is therefore a symbol within a symbol. It is both a literal recreation of the cosmic order in the regular succession of stylized acts performed just as they were *in illo tempore*, to use Eliade's terminology—the magical time of creation reenacted by myth, when order emerges from chaos[21]— and at the same time a symbolic expression of the order the rite reasserts through the symbolic or metaphorical meaning these acts have acquired by constant repetition over centuries.

For these reasons the perverted ritual of tragedy can serve as the most intense and inclusive focus of the disrupted cosmic order. The rituals mirrored in the plays enact the disruptions of that order in one particular code among other codes, but, at the same time, because ritual is itself the fullest symbolic expression of the harmonies between man and god and between man and nature, it includes all the other codes. Ritual's special symbolic and expressive function in the society, in other words, gives it a privileged status within the secondary, superimposed structure of the literary work. Here it is both a code among codes and the code whose function it

21. Mircea Eliade, *Cosmos and History: The Myth of the Eternal Return*, trans. W. Trask (Princeton, N.J.: Princeton University Press, 1954).

is to express the harmonious interlocking of all the codes in the order of the whole.

In the literary work, whose medium is words, language has a similar privileged function. The powerful effect of the Cassandra scene of *Agamemnon* rests in part on the close interlocking of both the ritual and linguistic codes. There is a parallel breakdown of the two most expressive, synoptic foci of the civilized and aesthetic order, each code functioning in the work as a metaphor virtually interchangeable with the other code and each functioning as a code that sums up all the other codes.

To return to Sophocles, the entity constituted by "Oedipus" in *Oedipus Tyrannos* similarly renders problematical the familiar configurations by which civilized man keeps chaos at bay. There is a reciprocal relation and interaction between Oedipus as an individual character and the function of Oedipus the King as focal point for the cosmic order. Oedipus polarizes the universe into unmediated extremes: overdetermination by the gods and utter chaos; gods who are providential and intelligent and gods who "leap" upon their victims like beasts of prey (*OT* 469, 1311, and cf. 263); the riddles of the bestial Sphinx and the oracles of Olympian Apollo. Simultaneously this ambiguous world order polarizes the unstable configuration of personal traits that make up the character we call "Oedipus." It leaves him in a precarious oscillation between the two opposite fields of his identity: quasi-divine power and bestial rage, strength and weakness, self-affirmation and utter helplessness, confident knowledge and abysmal ignorance of the most fundamental thing about himself, proud rationality and uncontrolled passion. As his world splits apart into its two increasingly disparate halves, so Oedipus too splits apart into the antithetical halves of a self that can no longer hold together on the old terms. He can no longer exist (or rather coexist) as both murderer and ruler, both destroyer and savior, but has to confront the identity-in-polarity of himself as *both* king and scapegoat. Whatever new unity and strength of self Oedipus possesses at the end rests on a new set of balances between authority and weakness, autonomy and subjection to forces beyond himself.

A structuralist approach illuminates the not-dissimilar features of the kingship of Pentheus in *The Bacchae*. Even in this highly psychologizing play we find that a tragic character is not merely a bundle of emotional tendencies or a psychological type, but also

constitutes a field where the basic codes of the civilized order intersect and their mediated polarities pull apart. It is, of course, typical
of Euripides that the psychological interpretation of the myth is
pushed into the foreground: the individual personality of Pentheus, with its pathology and its clearly delineated neuroses, as a
number of recent critics have shown, is more active and pressing in
the dynamics of the action than is that of Aeschylus's Agamemnon
or even Sophocles' Oedipus. Yet behind the dramatic action on the
stage stands the armature of several overlapping mythical structures.[22] The myth of origins in the history of Thebes (autochthonous
birth) contrasts with the myth of the god's miraculous birth from
the thigh/womb of Zeus. The Dionysiac myth of resistance to the
foreign god's arrival, as in the tales of the daughters of Minyas and
the daughters of Proetus, not only releases the female emotionally
repressed by the *polis* but also takes us back to Thebes's origins and
cancels out the civilizing work of the culture-hero Cadmus. At the
end his "sowing" of the filicidal Agave as the "best of daughters"
(1234) who destroys the last of the male line of Theban kings is
a counterpoise to his "sowing" of the earth-born men in the foundation myth of Thebes. Behind the death of Pentheus stands the
myth of Olympian gods battling Giants or other chaotic adversaries
sprung from the earth (see 538–44). The god's "chthonic" foe, however, proves to be not a fearsome monster of the subterranean
depths, but only an immature and unstable youth.

Pentheus's character and suffering entwine together the sexual,
biological, spatial, and generational codes. His conflict with Dionysus, his antagonist, but also his double, releases his total lack of
balance between these extremes. From the imbalance between male
authority and female emotionality, the collapse of polarities ramifies
to man and beast, hunter and hunted, child and adult, and so on.
As a result of this destruction of mediation, the advocate of maleness par excellence swings to the opposite extreme and becomes
one of those violently emotional, undisciplined Maenads whom he
so bitterly opposes. Dressed as a woman, he loses both his sexual
and his personal identity. As a pseudo-Maenad, he himself becomes a bearer of the emotional excitement and ecstasy he resists;
and he also releases, negatively, his own repressed sexual desire in
the form of a regressive voyeurism. In the ritual code, the king

22. See my *Dionysiac Poetics*, chs. 2–5, especially pp. 128–57, 180–85.

becomes the sacrificial victim; in the biological code the human hunter becomes the hunted quarry; in the generational code the "young man" (*neanias*, 274, 974; cf. 214) fails to make the crucial passage to adult warrior status and instead moves backward to infantile helplessness in the "hands" or "arms" of his mother (cf. 975, 1206).

Pentheus's psychic coherence is here homologous with his political coherence, for his regression to an infantile state also accompanies his failure in a king's most fundamental duty, to protect his city from invaders outside those gates or walls on which he so strongly insists (e.g. 653, 780–81). Inner and outer space are confused as the women of the city move out to the mountains from which the new god comes and as hoplite warriors, bulwark of the city, are routed by the anomaly of female warriors, bacchants who use not weapons fashioned by human technology but the thyrsus, which is barely separated from organic nature.

This inversion of nature and culture has its counterpart in the cosmic order. Dionysus, born from the "male womb" of Zeus (526–27; cf. 90–91) and carried from the mortal body of his mother, Semele, to Olympus, stands at the opposite extreme from Pentheus, who traces his ancestry to the "earth-born" Echion, one of the "savage" brood of the serpent, emblem of chaos and chthonic violence, killed by Cadmus, his maternal grandfather, as a necessary preliminary to founding the city. Sprung from the teeth of the serpent, these Spartoi or Sown Men, are violent, dangerous, hostile to the gods. Euripides repeatedly connects the "savagery" of Pentheus with the "savagery" of his chthonic, serpent-born ancestry (537–44, 995–96 = 1015–16).

The sexual code develops a polarity between the birth of Dionysus from Zeus's "male womb" and the chthonic affinities of Pentheus, between Olympian order, immortality, and divinity on the one hand and subterranean caverns, chaos, death, and bestiality on the other. Both extremes bypass the heterosexual union from which mortals are born, Dionysus from above (the male womb of Zeus), Pentheus from below (autochthonous birth, in his ancestry, and the "Sown Men").

The civilized institution of the city represents the mediate point where human civilization is possible. Psychologically it is analogous to the healthy, integrated personality of the hero-king. Here Agave, the mortal daughter of the Eastern culture-hero, Cadmus,

slayer of the serpent and founder of Thebes, can be united with the
earth-born offspring of the serpent, Echion, in Greece, to create the
heterosexual union of the family where a succession of kings seems
to be assured. That balance proves unstable, however, and the arrival of Dionysus repolarizes these elements—East and West, barbarian and Greek, disorder and order, bestial and human, youth
and adulthood, and so forth. Pentheus's denial by repression (or
neurotic displacement) of heterosexual union on the psychological
plane (which also includes his failure to achieve full adult male
status) is homologous, on the cultural plane, to the destruction of
the mediations by which civilized life is maintained: family, sacrificial ritual, agriculture (as opposed to hunting and the negative "sowing" of the serpent's teeth), the delimiting of inner and
outer space. On the plane of the cosmic order, these imbalances appear in the difference-in-identity between Dionysus and Pentheus,
Olympian "male womb" and chthonic ancestry, the eternal adolescence of the god and the unstable, fixated adolescence of the "young
man" who will regress to his negative "rebirth" at his mother's
hands. The rift between the two sets of polarities is then generalized
to the civic and cosmic order as a whole in the closing scene. Now
the culture-hero himself is transformed into a city-destroying serpent; and the pious and elderly ex-king bitterly questions a divine
order that permits so drastic and so little-deserved a punishment.

In the poetry of the plays metaphor facilitates the interconnec-
tion of the codes and the convertibility of one code into another. In
The Bacchae the wild Maenads who will destroy the king-victim
Pentheus on the mountain are "foals which have left their yokes"
(1056). The king who is "in the power of" this ambiguous god and
allows himself to be dressed as a bacchant speaks of "being dedicated" to him (*anakeisthai;* 934). Yet the god is also both the beast in
bull, serpent, and lion form (1016–17) and the hunter whose "noose"
will hurl the prey beneath the "herd" of Maenads that will destroy
him (1020–23). As in *Oedipus Tyrannos* this metaphorical interlocking is compounded by the ironies of double vision, madness, and
ecstatic transport, so that there are actually two levels of interlocking codes, one through metaphor and another through the ironic
interchange of appearance and reality. Through the peculiar nature
and powers of Dionysus as god of madness and illusion the trope
becomes the reality. That blurring on the level of language then cor-
responds to an analogous blurring on the level of perception (mad-

ness and sanity, illusion and truth) and ritual (celebrant and deity, sacrificer and sacrificed are confused). Pentheus, figuratively "savage" (*agrios*), and the offspring of a lioness (cf. 542, 988–90), is seen as an actual lion by the maddened Agave (1174, 1215, 1278, etc.) and himself sees the god in the form of the beast (e.g., 617–21, 922; cf. 1159).

Like *Oedipus Tyrannos*, *The Bacchae* is in a sense a paradigm of tragedy itself, simultaneously telescoping polarity and identity. The tragic king then functions as the figure who must occupy both extremes at the same time. Kingship occupies the isolated point of exposure to elemental forces and their abrupt reversal, the point where order crosses over into disorder, where apparent chaos harbors a hitherto unseen coherence.

6

Just as the king, standing at the summit of happiness and power, can suddenly move from highest to lowest through some chance event and/or the "envy of the gods" (Herodotus 1.207),[23] so the tragic hero, through accident or inner nature or some combination thereof, finds his strength turned to weakness, his prosperity to misery, until by his suffering and integrity of spirit he creates new definitions of these values.

Sophocles particularly depicts tragic figures who are more exposed than other men to the extremes of the human condition as they appear in the world and their own natures. "Such natures," as Creon says in *Oedipus Tyrannos*, "are justly most difficult for themselves to bear" (674–75). These figures, more intense in their reactions to these extremes, become paradigms of the precarious status of honor, power, and happiness. They have affinities with the savage world outside the limits of the city, but also possess qualities felt to be indispensable to their societies. Ajax, Antigone, Oedipus, and Philoctetes are or become outlaws; and yet they are also champions of values essential to civilized life: personal integrity, devotion to kin ties, energy and intelligence. The course of the tragic action takes these heroes through a sharp reversal of status and thereby requires a redefinition of basic values. In *Ajax* the trusty warrior becomes a hated criminal. In *Oedipus Tyrannos* the king

23. For a sociological and ritual interpretation of Oedipus's reversal from highest to lowest in *OT*, see Vernant, *Mythe et tragédie*, pp. 122–29.

who has saved the city becomes the source of its pollution. In the reverse direction, the helpless outcast becomes the true hero, the source of an inner strength invisible to others (*Philoctetes, Oedipus at Colonus*). In the boundary situations created by tragedy and occupied by the tragic hero, truth and illusion undergo paradoxical shifts. Apparent fragility may be the source of another form of power, and vice versa.

Anthropologists such as Victor Turner have called attention to the importance of these "liminal" situations and to the "liminal" status of the outcast and the suppliant.[24] These threaten and confuse the old order, but also create a kind of free space in which the old pieces can be reshuffled in new combinations, where new alternatives to the old conditions can be imagined. We have already noted how Aeschylus brings together the opposites of sea and fire, upper and lower, man and sacrificial victim for the suffering of Agamemnon. The first ode of *The Trachiniae* brings together death and life, birth and destruction in a cosmic frame for Heracles' imminent doom in a universe characterized by a disturbing violence and sexual quality in its basic processes:

> ὃν αἰόλα νὺξ ἐναριζομένα
> τίκτει κατευνάζει τε, φλογιζόμενον
> Ἅλιον Ἅλιον αἰτῶ . . .

You whom shimmering night, as she is slain, brings to birth and then lays to bed as you blaze in flames, Helios, Helios, I call upon you . . .

(*Trach.* 94–96)

The alternation of day and night here reflects not a stable, regular natural order, as in *Ajax* 672–73, but the violent death of the "mother," the female Night, who, as she "is slain" (the verb ἐναρί-ζειν describes violent death in Homer and the killing of Agamemnon in Aeschylus), "gives birth" to the "blazing" light of the new sun at dawn. Without going into the elaborate inversions of light and darkness, birth and death, which run beneath the action of the play, it is clear that the heavenly bodies' involvement, through metaphor, in the pain of the human life-cycle, provides a cosmic analogue to the sufferings of the protagonists and links the human

24. For liminality, see Victor Turner, *The Forest of Symbols* (Ithaca, N.Y.: Cornell University Press, 1967), pp. 93–111, drawing on the analysis of rites of passage by Arnold Van Gennep; see also Turner's *Dramas, Fields, and Metaphors* (Ithaca, N.Y.: Cornell University Press, 1974), passim.

action to the great rhythms of the universe.[25] Deianeira, like Night
here, is a *mater dolorosa* whose births are all pain (cf. 28–31, 41–42).
Like Night, too, she will be violently "slain" (indeed, ἐναριζομένα
could be read as a reflexive middle, "slaying herself," as Deianeira
does); and she is closely linked with night and night's rhythms in
her statement of her unhappy life shortly before (28–29): "For night
leads in pain and night in succession drives it away." Heracles, the
far-wandering hero whose journeys, like those of the sun, span
continents (100–101), ends his mortal life ablaze in his fiery death
on the pyre, where he has been "put to rest" (note the repeated
εὐνάσαι εὕνασον in 1005–6, 1041) through the agency of a female figure connected with birth and with darkness (cf. 573, 579,
685–92).

Scholars such as Bernard Knox and Cedric Whitman have sen-
sitively interpreted this isolated, asocial aspect of the tragic hero.[26]
A structuralist approach supplements their reading by emphasizing not the hero's affective responses to his world and that world's
rejection or acceptance of him, but rather the social and moral
structures themselves as they define the hero and are expanded,
redefined, or confused by him.

To dwell again on the Heracles of *The Trachiniae*, the issue for a
structuralist reading is not the worth or worthlessness of Heracles
vis-à-vis Deianeira or the assessment of her generosity over against
his brutality, important as these judgments are for a full evaluation
of the play, but rather the polarization of values as each figure
reaches outside the civilized world to a destructive bestial violence
of his or her past. The play then appears not just as the domestic
tragedy of a doomed house, nor as the personal tragedy of a man
and woman whose lives have carried them in opposite directions,
but as the tragedy of civilized values disintegrating under the impact of those powerful forces that always threaten civilization from
without and within.

The structural paradox of the tragic hero set forth by such an approach runs parallel to the paradox of the performance of which he

25. For this ode, see Thomas F. Hoey, "Sun Symbolism in the Parodos of the *Trachiniae*," *Arethusa* 5 (1972):133–54, and my "Sophocles' *Trachiniae*: Myth, Poetry,
and Heroic Values" (cited in note 20 above), p. 107.

26. Cedric H. Whitman, *Sophocles: A Study in Heroic Humanism* (Cambridge,
Mass.: Harvard University Press, 1951); Bernard M. W. Knox, *The Heroic Temper*
(Berkeley and Los Angeles: University of California Press, 1966).

is the center. The social context of that performance presupposes a safe, limited world, hedged about by the order of rituals and stable community and communication; but the action of that performance explores what transgresses that order. As a communal act, a part of the Dionysiac or Lenaean festival, tragedy affirms the solidity of the social forms and celebrates the gods of the *polis*. But the *content* of these tragedies stands in tension with their ritual and social context. That content holds the most terrible pollutions, the most feared crimes, the most puzzling and disturbing cruelties of the gods, the killing of parents by children and of children by parents (*Agamemnon, Heracles Mad, Medea*), incest (*Oedipus Tyrannos*), the death or prolonged suffering of the innocent (*Hippolytus, Philoctetes*), the triumph of the wicked and unscrupulous (*Hecuba, The Trojan Women*).

7

The ritual and social situation of the drama thus sets up a powerful tension between the fictional and the actual rite and between character and audience that is essential to Greek tragedy and possibly to all tragedy. A festival at the very heart of the city shows the social and ritual order of the city inverted and turned against itself in conflict and division. Yet it is part of the deeper social effect of tragedy that the citizens who behold this negation of their civic and religious order experience therein what that order signifies, what its limitations may be, what stands below or above it in the realm of the incomprehensible, the mysterious, the irrational.

This heightened sense of the preciousness and precariousness of that order, this intensified "cosmological consciousness," as it has been called, is at least as probable a social effect of tragedy as Aristotle's "cleansing" of violent emotions. Plato, well appreciating the subversive implications of Greek tragedy, was in this respect the more sensitive critic. As Brian Vickers has put it recently, "Reading the *Oresteia* makes one afraid for one's life."[27]

As we suggested above, the metaphorical and symbolic language of the plays function, in part, to interweave the multiple codes of this order. A passage such as *Agamemnon* 1384–98 provides a good illustration of the process:

27. Brian Vickers, *Towards Greek Tragedy* (London: Longmans, 1973), p. 425.

παίω δέ νιν δίς, κἂν δυοῖν οἰμωγμάτοιν
μεθῆκεν αὐτοῦ κῶλα, καὶ πεπτωκότι   1385
τρίτην ἐπενδίδωμι, τοῦ κατὰ χθονὸς
Διὸς νεκρῶν σωτῆρος εὐκταίαν χάριν.
οὕτω τὸν αὑτοῦ θυμὸν ὁρμαίνει πεσὼν
κἀκφυσιῶν ὀξεῖαν αἵματος σφαγὴν
βάλλει μ' ἐρεμνῆι ψακάδι φοινίας δρόσου,   1390
χαίρουσαν οὐδὲν ἧσσον ἢ διοσδότωι
γάνει σπορητὸς κάλυκος ἐν λοχεύμασιν.
ὡς ὧδ' ἐχόντων, πρέσβος Ἀργείων τόδε,
χαίροιτ' ἄν, εἰ χαίροιτ', ἐγὼ δ' ἐπεύχομαι·
εἰ δ' ἦν πρεπόντως ὥστ' ἐπισπένδειν νεκρῶι,   1395
τάδ' ἂν δικαίως ἦ, ὑπερδίκως μὲν οὖν·
τοσῶνδε κρατῆρ' ἐν δόμοις κακῶν ὅδε
πλήσας ἀραίων αὐτὸς ἐκπίνει μολών.

. . . I strike him twice; and with two cries there on the spot he let his limbs
go slack; and then, when he is down, I add a third stroke, a welcome
prayer-offering to the Zeus beneath the earth, the saviour of the dead. So
he belches out his own life as he lies there, and blowing forth the sharp
slaughter of his blood, he strikes me with a darksome shower of gory dew;
and I rejoiced no less than the crop rejoices in the rich blessing of the rain
of Zeus when the sheath is in labour with the ear.

So stands the case, noble elders of Argos here: be glad, if ye will be glad;
for me, I glory in it. And were it possible to pour libations over the dead
body in a manner that would suit the circumstances, this (my doing)
would be just, yea, more than just: so many are the curseful evils where-
with this man in his house has filled a bowl, a bowl which he now drains
himself on his return.

(E. Fraenkel's translation, slightly modified.)

This passage interconnects the ritual, familial, biological, and sexual codes. The very density of the closely packed metaphors creates
a special language in which the various codes of the civilized order
can come together to express a synoptic vision of the totality of that
order—political, religious, and domestic, natural and supernatural—at a moment of crisis when that order is pushed to its extreme
limits and questioned in its most fundamental values.[28] The *Oresteia*

28. For other aspects of the interlocking of codes in the *Oresteia*, see my *Tragedy
and Civilization*, pp. 55–58. For the interpretation of the violated rituals, the studies
of Froma I. Zeitlin remain fundamental: "The Motif of the Corrupted Sacrifice in
Aeschylus' *Oresteia*," *Transactions of the American Philological Association* 96 (1965):
463–508, with the "Postscript," ibid., 97 (1966):645–53. See also Vickers, *Towards
Greek Tragedy*, pp. 347–437, especially pp. 356–59 and 381–82; Vidal-Naquet, "Chasse
et sacrifice dans l' 'Orestie' d' Eschyle," in *Mythe et tragédie*, pp. 135–58; Walter Burkert, "Greek Tragedy and Sacrificial Ritual," *Greek, Roman and Byzantine Studies* 7
(1966):87–121, especially pp. 119–20.

is probably the richest development of this technique, and it may be that this deliberate interlocking of the various codes through repeated, expanded, and interwoven sequences of metaphor is the creation of Aeschylus, stamped upon Attic tragedy by his genius as one of its basic techniques.

This interlocking function of metaphor is also important in Sophoclean tragedy. The wound of *Philoctetes*, for example, is the focal symbol of an ambiguous divine order, a corrupt social order, and an inward sickness and "savagery" (*agriotēs*) that parallels the outward, physical sickness and the "savage" beastlike state of Philoctetes' life. Clytemnestra's dream of Agamemnon's "scepter by the hearth" "blooming" and "shadowing over" the land of the Mycenaeans (Soph. *Electra* 417–23) interconnects the familial, civic, biological, and cosmic order. Deianeira's comparison of Heracles to a farmer who plows an outlying field that he visits only at the time of sowing and the time of harvest (*Trach.* 31–33) brackets the familial order of the house with the biological order implicit in agriculture. As the play continues, an increasingly ironical discrepancy cracks open between fertility and destruction. Sophocles here draws on the interweaving of marriage and agriculture as the two basic civilizing acts. In the Athenian marriage ceremony the father bestows the bride on her husband "for the *sowing* of legitimate children" (ἐπὶ παίδων γνησίων ἀρότωι). What is probably a rather inert metaphor or vaguely felt parallelism in the social structure becomes operative as part of a system of signs, metaphors, and values within the secondary structure of the literary work. By this process the literary work exercises what Roman Jakobson and others term the "metalingual" function of language: language calls attention to its own coding of experience.[29] Moving from the linguistic structure to the social structure as a whole, the self-conscious interweaving of codes by metaphor also calls attention to the unconscious coding processes that go on as part of society's unification of the various human activities and roles, the interdependence of its various parts, and the interaction of the various codes in homologous areas.

The tragic force of *The Trachiniae* lies in the way in which the multiple codes of the civilized order are twisted together for their complete destruction. Both the models of the civilized life, the domestic wife who faithfully keeps house and hearth and the beast-

---

29. Jakobson, "Linguistics and Poetics," in DeGeorge, *Structuralists*, pp. 92f.

taming hero, come to embody what their basic social roles have most resisted.[30] The faithful wife destroys house and husband with the poison of the Hydra and the blood of the lustful beast-man; the hero famous for his civilizing triumphs reenacts the part of his bestial double, Nessus, sacking a city and annihilating a house (cf. 257, 351–65) for the sake of lust, raging with subhuman cries, and carried away by a blind thirst for bloody revenge (1066ff., 1133). The maiden Iole, taken within the house as if in legitimate marriage, is "yoked" (536); but this metaphor, which usually indicates the domestication of the "unyoked" virgin, who is felt to be part of the "wild" until she is "tamed" or civilized by marriage, points rather to the ominous beast-world of the mythical background. In the ode immediately preceding, Deianeira is the "heifer" fought over by two "bulls," Heracles and the river-god Achelous. Everything about this pseudo-marriage with Iole is awry. Coming as a kind of second wife into an already established ménage, as Deianeira bitterly complains (543–51), this "bride" destroys rather than unites the two houses in question. Rather than producing legitimate children in a fruitful marriage, she can only "give birth to a great Fury for this house" (893–95).

The homology between the familial and agricultural codes suggested by Deianeira in the prologue has its negative aspect too, for agricultural images describe the deadly effects of the love-charm, which Deianeira discovers too late (701–4). The inverted fertility of agriculture parallels the inverted significance of the love-gift. What was intended to unite the house dissolves it; what was meant to bring love brings the most deadly hate; what should have asserted the unifying bonds of civilized institutions manifests the vengeful power of a monstrous nightmare-world of Centaurs and Hydras.

While interlocking the various codes of civilization through its metaphoric language, Greek tragedy also makes language itself a sufferer, as it were, in the inversions or disintegrations that threaten all civilized norms. The tragic situation distorts normal speech into difficult paradoxes, oxymora like Ajax's "darkness by light, dimness most brilliant" (*Ajax* 393–95), Antigone's "holy impiety" (*Ant.* 74, 924, 943), and Oedipus's "wedless wedlock" (*OT* 1214; cf. 1256). Like ritual, language is both a code among codes and also the special mode of intercommunication among the different codes. Its

---

30. For this view of *The Trachiniae*, see my "Mariage et sacrifice" and my *Tragedy and Civilization*, ch. 4, especially pp. 62–79.

disintegration into ambiguity, paradox, or the celebrated Sophoclean irony signifies both a loss of coherence in the world and a loss
of the ability to grasp and communicate that coherence. The verbal
ironies of *Oedipus Tyrannos* reflect both the ultimate failure of Oedipus to solve the true "riddle" of the play—the riddle of the meaning
of life in a universe governed by chance or by distant and mysterious gods—and the very incoherence of a universe that *logos*,
reason-as-language, cannot make intelligible. The "bridling" of
Iphigeneia's mouth in the human sacrifice at the beginning of the
Oresteia (*Ag.* 228–47) likewise couples the literally unspeakable nature of what is being done with the perverted communication between man and god: verbal communication and ritual communication are isomorphic. As we have seen, Heracles' bestial roaring at
Cenaeum in *The Trachiniae* reflects the distorted communication between man and god in the rite, but it also has its origins in the non-
communication between husband and wife symbolized by the gift
of the robe that passes between them in lieu of the words they in
fact never address to each other.

Language per se is therefore a major concern of Greek tragedy.
Its dissolution parallels the shedding of kindred blood and the
crimes of incest in the familial code and the perversion of man/god
communication in the ritual code. All three codes meet, as we have
seen, in the sacrifice of Iphigeneia and the misunderstood prophecies of Cassandra in *Agamemnon*. Indeed, the whole *Oresteia* can be
read in terms of the dissolution and gradual reconstruction of
language, parallel to the destruction and reconstitution of ritual
forms. Language is a central theme in Sophocles' *Electra*, *Philoctetes*, and two Oedipus plays. Instead of clarity, tragic language creates ambiguity (*Oedipus Tyrannos*). Instead of communication it en-
forces deception, even on the part of those whose natures incline to
heroic truth and straight-speaking (*Electra*, *Philoctetes*, the "Tru-
grede" of *Ajax* 646–92). Instead of separating man from beast, it
obscures the boundary between them as the heroes roar, bark, or
wail like bulls, dogs, or birds.

8

Greek tragedy is remarkable for its ability to face the disintegration
of the cosmic, social, or psychological order without thereby losing
all sense of coherence. Tragedy in Greece was rooted in mythical

paradigms that gave a certain unity and shared intelligibility to experience but still remained open to radical questioning and undog-
matic speculation. It could thus combine a sense of the sacred, the
numinous, the mysterious entering human life with a belief in the
power of human intelligence to plumb fearlessly the deepest questions of existence. For this reason, perhaps, it could step beyond
the terms of conventional morality and confront the unjust suffering of an Oedipus, a Hippolytus, a Philoctetes while not losing
touch with its own imaginative abilities to shape new forms of
order: the power of the city to create law in the *Oresteia*; man's capacity for spiritual strength, compassion, friendship, loyalty in the
midst of chaos and destruction in Sophocles' Oedipus plays and
Philoctetes and Euripides' *Heracles* and *Hippolytus*; the restorative
vitality of language and myth in tragedy itself, implicit in Euripides' *Helen* and the finales of Sophocles' *Philoctetes* and *Oedipus at
Colonus*.

From a structuralist perspective the complexity of Greek tragedy
lies both in its full utilization of the highly coded structures of the
social order and the dissolution of those structures. For these reasons any structuralist analysis of tragedy is engaged in the paradoxical activity of elucidating structures that are deliberated, questioned, negated, inverted, or on the verge of dissolving into chaos.
Whereas the structural analysis of myth can be normative and descriptive—viewing the infrastructure of the society's values through
the relationships composed and varied in their metaphorical and
symbolic equivalents in the language of the myths—the structural
analysis of tragedy is forced in just the opposite direction. It highlights those infrastructures of the society, only to see them strained
to the breaking point or beyond.

At some point, therefore, the analytic rigidity of constructing
parallel sequences of homologies must pass into the flexibilities of
ironic deconstruction. The structuralist literary critic, at least of
tragedy, may begin as the reassembler of *bricolage* ("structural man
takes the real, decomposes it and then recomposes it . . ."),[31] but he
is soon confronted with the systematic disassembly going on beneath the logical structures, a *basso ostinato* moving ever farther
away from the dominant. Like the tragic work itself, he is continu-

31. Barthes, "Structuralist Activity," p. 149.

ally forced away from the logic of non-contradiction into the area of paradox and the coexistence of opposites.

Roland Barthes has defined structuralism as an "activity" (as opposed to a subject-matter) concerned with reconstructing the mental processes through which man makes his world intelligible:

Creation or reflection are not, here, an original "impression" of the world, but a veritable fabrication of a world which resembles the first one, not in order to copy it but to render it intelligible. Hence one might say that structuralism is essentially an *activity of imitation*, which is also why there is, strictly speaking, no *technical* difference between structuralism as an intellectual activity on the one hand and literature in particular, art in general on the other: both derive from a *mimēsis*, based not on the analogy of substances (as in so-called realist art), but on the analogy of functions (what Lévi-Strauss calls *homology*).[32]

Yet the structuralist study of tragedy must take special account of the structured deconstruction of those patterns, for that process constitutes part of the uniqueness of the tragic form. Tragedy maintains and even intensifies the systems of homologies and the analogies of functions on which the social order, like the aesthetic order of a work of art, depends. But even as it utilizes and through its interlocking metaphors clarifies the codes of normative values, it is always simultaneously pulling in tension against the normative, the mediated realm of social life, towards the abnormal, the unmediated, the liminal.

32. Ibid., p. 150.

Chapter Three

Polis and Monarch in Early Attic Tragedy

Anthony J. Podlecki

The mutual interdependence of Greek drama and Greek political life is not a new topic;[1] but neither is it one that has been thoroughly exploited, let alone exhausted, by critics. In spite of the fact that some of what follows has received at least passing recognition in the critical literature, it has seemed worthwhile to restate the case, and to give greater emphasis to certain themes that have been either overlooked or undervalued in the commentaries and handbooks. The present study may also serve as a corrective to the tendency, discernible in the most recent work on Greek drama, to ignore its political aspects entirely.

At a fairly obvious level, Athenian drama could address itself directly to a contemporary, or near-contemporary, event. Thus *The Capture of Miletus* by Phrynichus, an older contemporary of Aeschylus's, was presented probably very soon after the occurrence to which its title refers, the destruction of Miletus by the Persians and the enslavement of its populace after an unsuccessful, five-year revolt lasting from 499 to 494 B.C. The impact of the production on the Athenian theater audience was enormous. Here is how Herodotus, our oldest source of information about the event, describes it: "the audience in the theatre burst into tears, the author was fined a thousand drachmae for reminding them of a disaster which touched them so closely, and they forbade anybody ever to put the play on

1. See, for example, V. Ehrenberg, *Sophocles and Pericles* (Oxford: Basil Blackwell, 1954); G. Zuntz, *The Political Plays of Euripides* (Manchester: Manchester University Press, 1955); A. J. Podlecki, *The Political Background of Aeschylean Tragedy* (Ann Arbor, Mich.: University of Michigan Press, 1966); K. Hermassi, *Polity and Theatre in Historical Perspective* (Berkeley and Los Angeles: University of California Press, 1977), pp. 3–86; C. Meier, *Die Entstehung des Politischen bei den Griechen* (Frankfurt am Main: Suhrkamp, 1980), pp. 144–272.

the stage again."[2] Later in his career Phrynichus turned again to current events for dramatic material when he made the battle of Salamis the subject of his play *The Phoenician Women*. Although the date of the production is not quite certain, it was probably the Great Dionysia in spring of 476 B.C., for Plutarch records an inscription commemorating a victory in that year by Phrynichus, the *choregus*, or financial sponsor, being Themistocles, who would have had a keen interest in supporting an enterprise that brought before an Athenian audience events in whose successful outcome he had played so large a role.[3]

Aeschylus's first surviving play, *The Persians*, also dealt with the Athenian defeat of Xerxes at Salamis, and there is an ancient scholarly note to the effect that Aeschylus "borrowed" or "adapted" much of the material for it from his predecessor Phrynichus's play.[4] But it is to rather different and less obvious reflections of contemporary political concerns in Aeschylus's dramas that I wish here to direct attention. I shall argue in what follows that several themes that can be called "political" in the strict sense emerge from a close reading of Aeschylean tragedy. The first is a tendency by the author to "democratize" the *polis* of the mythical period. An Aeschylean monarch, although technically possessed of "autocratic" power, may feel that he cannot reach decisions independently of the *dēmos*, the citizen-body, especially if the issue is a critical one, such as the waging of a war, where the collective support of the citizens may be indispensable. Again, the *dēmos* itself, if not so outspokenly captious as Thersites in book 2 of the *Iliad*, may obtrude on the monarch's consciousness to the extent of either inhibiting his freedom of action or at least making him feel uneasy about failing to take its wishes and welfare adequately into account. We may, if we wish, fault this unrealistically (for the mythical period) high profile of the Aeschylean *dēmos*, and call it merely "anachronistic." But this would, I believe, be to misinterpret both the dramatist's and his audience's way of thinking. Better say that these are thought-patterns

2. Herodotus 6.21.2, quoted in the translation of A. de Selincourt (Harmondsworth, England: Penguin Books, 1972), p. 395.

3. See Plutarch, *Life of Themistocles* 5.5 for the inscription, with F. J. Frost's comments on pp. 77 and 89 of his *Plutarch's Themistocles: A Historical Commentary* (Princeton, N.J.: Princeton University Press, 1980).

4. The ancient "Hypothesis," or Prefatory Note, to *The Persians;* see the introduction to my translation, *"The Persians" by Aeschylus* (Englewood Cliffs, N.J.: Prentice-Hall, 1970), pp. 10–20.

that would have been natural and almost inevitable for a writer whose career coincided with the flowering of the Athenian constitution into its fully democratic form. Conversely, spectators, especially if they were Athenian, could not have appreciated the problem if it had been posed in any other terms, and neither would Aeschylus have been prepared to cast his kings in artificially "realistic" authoritarian roles.

Another theme is more difficult to track, perhaps because it may have been still inchoate in the dramatist's creative mind. There is a tendency to politicize the army by emphasizing its close relationship and essential identity of interest with the bulk of the population left at home. Together, these form one unit,. the *polis*, and they are but two complementary parts of a unified whole; neither can function completely successfully without the other. There is an immediate corollary: to be successful and respected the Aeschylean leader must be able to lead both in the field and in the political assembly, and his performance in one sphere cannot be judged separately from his actions in the other. The citizens of Susa and Argos expect their commanders to succeed in their military ventures, and when they do not, their ability to govern at home cannot help but be impaired.

We may now turn to the evidence of the plays. It is clear that by 472 B.C., when *The Persians* was produced, the Athenians must have begun to ask themselves, How do political groups function? What turns a mass of individuals into a cohesive, aware, governable unit? Evidence for this kind of speculation can be found in the play itself, for besides being a story of the defeat of the Persians by the Greeks, especially the Athenians, it is also an analysis of how political groups function vis-à-vis different kinds of leaders. Early in the play, Atossa, Xerxes' mother and widow of King Darius of Persia, asks the chorus of Persian elders about their Athenian adversaries, "Who is set as shepherd or as lord to oversee the host?" and the chorus-leader replies, "Slaves of no man are they called, nor in subjection to any man."[5] I would be surprised if the original audience did not react like one of which I was a part in the summer of 1965 in the Odeion of Herodes Atticus in Athens, which rose to its feet en masse and interrupted the actors' dialogue with cheers. For here was a striking difference, as the Athenian patriots loved to be

5. Lines 241–42. This and the following quotations are from my translation (see preceding note).

reminded, between themselves and their barbarian opponents. The Athenians are "not slaves or subject to any man"; by contrast, Xerxes' rule over Persia is absolute: he is the "Great King" and the commanders of the various contingents catalogued in the chorus's entrance-song, though called "kings" in their own right, are also his "servants" (24). More to the point, the troops who represent, at least in terms of dramatic exaggeration, the population of the whole Asian continent over which the Persian king rules (56–57, 61–62), are described in terms such as "numberless" (40), a "throng" (42, 53), from "teeming Asia" (73). Their attack is as irresistible as that of a "raging flood" (88). They advance "like a swarm of bees" (128).

Xerxes' rule over this vast, somewhat amorphous, horde appears to be absolute, as Atossa makes clear when, after narrating the ominous dream she has had in which Xerxes' chariot is overturned by an unruly horse symbolically representing Greece, she comments: "If my son fare . . . ill—he owes the city no explanations; if [he is] safe, he's ruler of the land just as he was" (212–14). The Queen Mother uses a word, *hypeuthunos*, which for an Athenian audience would have pointed the contrast between Xerxes' position and that of their own elected or appointed leaders—generals, administrative officials, financial officers—who were very much *hypeuthunos*, "accountable," to the citizens for their actions while in office.

One of the lessons the playwright no doubt intended his audience to take away from this performance in the theater of Dionysus was that vast numbers do not of themselves spell success. For when the messenger opens his narration of the defeat at Salamis, he repeats that "the whole barbarian troop is lost" (255), "the entire force perished" thanks to the Greek ships (278–79). "In a matter of sheer numbers," he assures the queen, "the ships on our side would have conquered" (337–38), for Aeschylus has the messenger record what was to become the traditional, though perhaps exaggerated, figures of 1,207 Persian ships to 310 Greek. The vast size of the Persian armament is emphasized again in the last part of the play when the queen tells the ghost of her dead husband, whom the chorus have conjured up to give them aid and comfort at this time of disaster, how total was the defeat. "All the city-sacking Persian nation has itself been sacked," she tells him (714); Xerxes has "emptied out the whole, broad-stretching continent" (718) and "all of Susa groans for its emptiness of men" (730). Darius for his part remarks that his son has "brought to this citadel of Susa—emptiness" (761; at 533 the chorus has lamented the "masses of men" Zeus destroyed). When the tattered Xerxes appears at the close, the chorus ask him, reprovingly, "Where is the rest of the throng of friends?" (956), and the king later refers to the blow, which he himself feels, against "so huge an army" (1015).

Xerxes' ambitious venture was doomed to fail. His was an act of *hybris*, an attempt to equate himself with the gods, or at least intrude himself into a plane of activity that the gods reserved for themselves. His vast numbers gave him a false sense of invincibility: in their opening song, the chorus proceed from comments that the Persian hordes are "irresistible" and "cannot be withstood" to a reflection on the deception the gods often practice on men, coaxing them into "the net of ruin" (87–100, where I retain the manuscript ordering of the stanzas). Furthermore, Xerxes had offended against the gods' own sensibilities. He bridged the Hellespont (130–32, 722–25), an act of presumption for which his father's ghost reproves him: "Mortal that he was, he foolishly thought that he could master all gods, among them Poseidon" (749–50). Nor did he stop there; the army, on entering Greece, overthrew the gods' images and set fire to their altars and temples (810–12). The gods, then, had good reason to chasten Xerxes to teach him the lesson "that mortal man should not think more than mortal thoughts" (820). In the world viewed through Greek eyes, "whenever a man himself goes rushing in, God speeds him on" (742), as Xerxes learned to his cost.[6] But the converse also held good: the gods' plan to punish Xerxes depended, for its fulfillment, on the human determination of Xerxes' intended victims to resist his attack. And here, for a Greek audience, was an even more powerful lesson to be learned: what human effort could accomplish with divine approval. The vast numerical superiority of Xerxes' forces was neutralized, disparity reduced to equality, by two factors, the second of which is relevant to the present discussion. The first was the ruse by which Themistocles sent a false message to lure the enemy into the cramped and confining straits of Salamis. A second and even more important factor was the organization, good order, and obedience to command (the more effective for being voluntary rather than enforced) that any Greek army could be expected to manifest, and that the combined fleet at Salamis did exemplify to a very high de-

6. The version given by Aeschylus at *Pers.* 354–60 is substantiated by Herodotus's more historical account (8.75).

gree. This aspect of the Greek reaction to the Persians' inroads into the straits comes through very clearly in the messenger's narrative: with the dawn's light, as the Persian ships came funneling into the Salamis channel, the Greeks raised the sacred Paean and "rushed into battle with daring confidence" (394). Their response was instantaneous and "from one command" (397), the squadron's right wing appearing first, "in order just as they had been arranged" (399–400). As more and more enemy ships crowded into the straits, the Greeks encircled them "with perfect plan and order" (417). Although the Persian side had begun its attack in orderly enough fashion (374), the end result was utter chaos and confusion. Xerxes, who had watched from a vantage point on neighboring Mt. Aegaleos, tore his robes and "rushed away in disordered flight" (470), and the Persian ships that survived the disaster "raised their sails in haste and fled in disarray wherever the wind might lead" (480–81).

A disaster of such magnitude might be expected to leave an aftershock, and, at least as viewed through Greek eyes, this would be felt most strongly in the political sphere. If the masses have been led off both unwillingly and to ultimate defeat, some challenge to Persian rule would be only natural.[7] Atossa has already, in a rather cryptic passage, satisfied herself that as long as Xerxes himself returned, his own personal power would suffer no loss.[8] In their lament for the disaster the chorus envision the break-up of the empire and perhaps even a threat to Xerxes himself:

Those throughout Asia's land are ruled no longer by Persian laws.
They carry their tribute no longer, by a master's necessity fixed,
Nor prostrate themselves to the ground and adore: for the royal strength
    is destroyed.
The tongues of men are no longer kept in check, for the mass of men
Went loose and free in their speech when the yoke of strength was
    loosened.

(584–94)[9]

7. Some interpreters have seen a personal challenge to Xerxes' leadership already hinted at early in the play at line 13, where there seems to be a reference to the massed army "barking that the man [i.e., their leader] is young," but the meaning of the phrase is uncertain.

8. Lines 166–67. When he learns of the magnitude of the disaster Darius laments that "the vast wealth I labored for is gone, overturned, left for the taking of anyone who comes along" (751–52).

9. In the third choral song (852–908) the chorus give substance to their fears by listing in a long catalogue the places in the eastern Mediterranean and Asia Minor won by Darius that are now, in effect, open to the taking (of Athens, as it turned out,

All this is, of course, typically Greek. It is what a Greek *polis* (especially one like Athens, with an empire in the making) might well have worried about after having suffered so decisive a setback to her expansionist designs. If there were any such repercussions in the great monolith that was the Persian empire, our sources are totally silent about it. On the personal level the suggestion, barely hinted at earlier, that the loss might somehow impair Xerxes' own prestige and give an opportunity for disaffection among his immediate subjects, is given no play in the final scene. The dirty and tattered Xerxes returns, and he and his "aged counsellors" join in a lengthy jeremiad about the vast losses they have suffered. Xerxes' own authority has somehow survived, apparently unscathed, and in this he parts company with his hypothetical Greek counterpart. It turns out that his mother's reading of the situation at v. 213 was correct: unlike a Greek commander or political leader in similar circumstances, Xerxes is "not accountable to the city."

In Aeschylus's somewhat later drama, *The Suppliants*, produced probably in 463 B.C.,[10] we see the strange sight of a king in the mythical period, who in theory possesses absolute power, nevertheless choosing to restrict himself to acting only within what might be called "constitutional" bounds. The fifty daughters of Danaus, fleeing from the predatory marital designs of their cousins, the fifty sons of Egypt (who may or may not under Egyptian law have had a legal claim on marriage with their kinswomen),[11] turn up in Argos, their ancestral home, and demand that King Pelasgus give them asylum. Aeschylus devotes much attention to the agonizing dilemma confronting the king: if he accedes to the girls' importunate requests, he risks involving the Argive *polis* in war with Egyptian invaders, whose arrival to press their suit is imminent; if he rejects them, they will commit suicide—and so sacri-

---

since many of the places had by 472 B.C. joined Athens's maritime league, the "Confederacy of Delos"). In tones reminiscent of their earlier song "ruled no longer by Persian laws" (*personomountai;* 585) they lament the loss of "the great honor of Persian rule" (*personomou timēs;* 919).

10. For the date of *The Suppliants,* which is not quite certain, see A. F. Garvie, *Aeschylus' Supplices: Play and Trilogy* (London: Cambridge University Press, 1969), pp. 1–28.

11. The king in fact remarks, "If Egyptus's sons rule you by customs native to your city, claiming nearest of kin, who would wish in that to oppose them?" (387–89). But the legal issue is unclear; cf. G. Thomson, *Aeschylus and Athens* (New York: Haskell House, 1968), 289–91; S. Ireland, "The Problem of Motivation in the Supplices of Aeschylus," *Rheinisches Museum,* n.s., 117 (1974):25–26 with n. 23.

lege—at the altars of the city's gods. In spite of the girls' insistence
that he give them an answer at once, Pelasgus defers a decision until he has consulted the Argive *dēmos*. It is not a casual or uncon-
sidered deferral, nor are the suppliants (or, for that matter, the audience) in any real doubt about his authority to decide on his own
initiative. For one thing, at his first encounter with the newcomers,
Pelasgus is made by Aeschylus to emphasize the totality of the
sway which he holds in Argos. He refers to himself as *"archēgetēs* of
this land,"[12] its *anax* (252: both of these terms denote absolute rule),
over which he "exercises power" (*kratō*, 255, 259). We are therefore
unprepared for the turn the dialogue takes later on, when the
women finally and quite bluntly put their request for protection,
and Pelasgus replies:

> You are not suppliants at my own hearth.
> If the city stains the commonweal,
> In common let the people work a cure.
> But I would make no promises until
> I share with all the citizens.[13]

The women immediately call the king's bluff, as it were, by pointing
out that

> You are, yes, the city, the people,
> A prince is not judged.
> The land, the hearth, the altar you rule
> With the single vote and scepter;
> Enthroned you command,
> And fill every need.
>
> (370–75)

After some additional exchanges, he gives further voice to his painful dilemma:

> The choice is not easy: choose me not as judge.
> I said before that never would I act
> Alone, apart from the people, though I am ruler;
> So never may people say, if evil comes,
> "Respecting aliens the city you destroyed."
>
> (396–401)

12. Line 251, also 184; cf. *Seven Against Thebes* 999 and Sophocles, *Oedipus Tyran-*
nos 751.

13. Lines 365–69, in the translation by S. G. Benardete (D. Grene and R. Lattimore, eds., *The Complete Greek Tragedies* [Chicago: University of Chicago Press,
1956]); all the following citations from *The Suppliants* are from this translation, unless otherwise indicated.

Pelasgus's refusal to act without consulting the *dēmos* is similar to Athene's refusal in *The Eumenides* (470–72) to judge Orestes' case on her own authority alone, and both seem to have similar motives for hesitating: a just decision is likelier to be arrived at collectively and—even more important—any negative effects such a decision may have will to some extent be mitigated if the responsibility is shared.

The resolution, when it comes, has an interesting twist. At the very end of this central scene, after the king has sent the girls' father Danaus off with suppliant boughs to win the sympathies of the citizens of Argos, he tells them that he will "assemble all the native people [and] make the commons well disposed, and teach your father all that he must say" (517–19). When Danaus returns to tell his daughters the results of the city's deliberations, his account contains this significant difference: it was not he who addressed the Argive assembly, but King Pelasgus himself, who, in a persuasive harangue, brought the Argive *dēmos* to vote unanimously ("so bristled thick the air with hands," 607–8) that the Danaids be given not only asylum but resident-alien status (609); any Argive who does not come to their assistance against any attempt, by citizen or foreigner, to remove them from Argive soil will lose his citizen rights (be declared *atimos*) and be punished with exile by vote of the people (613–14).

The oddity of all of this has often been remarked on.[14] The repeated emphasis on the *dēmos* (607, 614, 623; cf. 621 *leōs*); the details of procedure, including technical terms like *dēmou dedoktai* (601) and *edoxen* (605), both meaning "it was decreed";[15] mention of the herald, if only to say that the assembly's enthusiasm made his services unnecessary (622), who was a regular feature at Athenian assembly meetings—all this has suggested that Aeschylus very much had in mind the procedure for handling this sort of problem in the Athens of his own day. But if that is so, then it tends to cast Pelasgus in a different light; he is not so much the absolute ruler he had made himself out to be in his opening speech, but something like a *dēmagōgos* in the technical sense, a political leader who has to put his ideas across by compellingly persuasive rhetoric. In fact, Danaus comes close to describing the king's performance in just

---

14. Cf. my comments in *Political Background* (see n. 1 above), pp. 45–52.
15. Similar technical-sounding language occurs in the impugned final scene of the play, 1005, 1025; cf. 1036 and 1040.

these terms: "The *dēmos* of the Pelasgians hearkened to the persuasive [rhetorical] turns addressed to the *dēmos*." [16]

This transference of responsibility away from the king and to the people of Argos has two effects, one immediate and verifiable within the present play, the other hypothetically posited for a plot-development later in the trilogy, of which *The Suppliants* was the opening piece. As an immediate result of the news they receive, the girls break into a hymn in which they express their intense relief and gratitude to the Argives for benefits of which, as they believe, they have been assured. The choral song soon develops into a prayer for reciprocal blessings from Zeus upon the Argive *polis*. Although the manuscripts are considered by editors to be defective in verse 698, where there seems to be a reference to "protection of privileges" (perhaps "for the citizens"), the reading in the next two lines has not been impugned: "the *dēmos* [Aeschylus uses a formulation from the adjective, *to dēmion*], which rules over the *polis*, a government that takes forethought and plans for the public weal." [17] It does not seem to me accidental that Aeschylus uses a word for the rule exercised by the people, *kratunei*, that is reminiscent of the way that King Pelasgus describes his own power earlier (*kratō* at 255 and 259). At a more remote distance, it has been suggested that, as the trilogy developed, King Pelasgus was slain in battle with the Egyptian invaders, and more and more the responsibility for deciding the validity of the latter's marriage-claims on their cousins fell to the Argive assembly, which may even have elected Danaus to succeed to the royal power. [18]

However that may be, I have analyzed the passages of this, the extant play, in sufficient detail to support the conclusion I wish to draw—that this is no ordinary, heroic-age monarchy. Nor can I accept the suggestion that the prominence given to the Argive people in the decision to accept the Danaids, and perhaps in later decisions about their situation, crept in almost by oversight on Aeschylus's part, or as an almost inevitable anachronism. I suggest, rather, that he is consciously transferring to the mythical past a very real

16. My literal translation of 623–24. The word *dēmēgoros* in other contexts denotes a speaker in the popular assembly.

17. Lines 699–700, again in my over-literal translation.

18. For such and other suggestions (mostly hypothetical) of how the action may have developed, cf. Garvie, *Aeschylus' Supplices* (see n. 10 above), pp. 163–233; R. P. Winnington-Ingram, "The Danaid Trilogy of Aeschylus," *Journal of Hellenic Studies* 81 (1961):141–52; and my paper, "Reconstructing an Aeschylean Trilogy," *Bulletin of the Institute of Classical Studies, University of London* 22 (1975):2–8.

problem that may have been vexing contemporary Athenians: how are decisions arrived at in matters when it is crucial to have the support of a whole citizen body? What, in short, is the nature of effective leadership in a society of free, and often independent-minded, individuals?

The question of leadership arises again, but in a less obviously perceptible way, in Aeschylus's late great trilogy, the *Oresteia*, produced at the Great Dionysia in the spring of 458 B.C. Here we have an interesting new development: Argos is seen as artificially and unnaturally divided between its noncombatants, mostly the old and the women who have been left behind, and the army that has sailed to Troy to recover Helen. Agamemnon, who levies the expedition, is to be measured as a leader in both spheres, the military and the political, which are interconnected: Agamemnon's failure, when it occurs—his tragedy—is a double one, for the loss of life at Troy cannot be justified by the essentially selfish aims of the expedition, and Agamemnon's ten-year absence has left a hiatus in the political leadership at home, which allows the usurpation of power by his scheming wife and her stay-at-home lover. Once again the contemporary Athenian political situation seems to be affecting the way Aeschylus brings this matter to the stage. If it is unlikely that he would have forced Agamemnon into the mold of the latter's Homeric exemplar (and even in Homer, Agamemnon feels constrained to consult his "council" of Greek chiefs), it would have been almost impossible to ignore the fact that Athens's army, certainly after 480 and through the turbulent period during which the foundations of her empire were being laid by continuing anti-Persian, and often anti-Greek, military operations, had developed a corporate sense. In time of war, an army's views are important, even more so when the economic well-being of an expanding *polis* depends on the continued success of that army. Let me cite two examples from recent (in 458 B.C.) Athenian history. Plutarch tells the story of how Cimon and his fellow generals, fresh from a military victory, were given the signal honor of being allowed to supersede the regularly allotted panel of judges from the tribes for the dramatic competitions at the Dionysia held in spring 468 B.C. "The reputation of the judges," Plutarch comments, "heightened the rivalry of the contest," in which Sophocles, competing for the first time, was awarded first place (to Aeschylus's chagrin, Plutarch adds—but that is another story). Whether or not this victory was, as some scholars argue, that against the combined Persian land and sea forces at the Eurymedon River in Pamphylia does not matter; what is important is Plutarch's report that with the vast profits realized from the sale of the Persian spoils from the Eurymedon victory "the Athenians were enabled to meet various public expenses and in particular to construct the southern wall of the Acropolis" (*Life of Cimon* 13.5, trans. Scott-Kilvert). Such were the domestic fruits of the army's successes. The converse case is, if anything, even more illlustrative. Some time in the 460s—the ancient authorities disagree about the exact date—the Spartan territory suffered a series of severe earthquakes. When the subject population of Messenia, the so-called "helots," took this opportunity to revolt, the future of the Spartan state was threatened. A protracted siege of the rebels at Mt. Ithome in Messenia availed nothing, so the Spartans called in their allies, including the Athenians. Cimon, whose friendship with Sparta was notorious (he had named one of his sons "Lakedaimonios"), urged strenuously that Athens could not abandon her "yoke mate," but his political opponents, led by a certain Ephialtes, argued that this was a good opportunity to let Sparta's pride be humbled. Cimon's advice prevailed and a large Athenian force was sent with him as general to aid the Spartans. For reasons that are not entirely clear, this force was sent back by the Spartans even before the siege was ended and their services fully utilized. This constituted a personal insult to Cimon and was taken as a national affront by the Athenians at home, who, again under the instigation of Ephialtes and probably also Pericles, used Cimon's Messenian fiasco to discredit him altogether; a reform of the Athenian judiciary was carried through which involved a reduction in the powers of the revered and venerable court of the Areopagus; in addition, in about 461 B.C., Cimon himself was ostracized. Several lessons are to be learned from all of this: how important the influence of the Athenian army's successes (or failures) upon internal domestic politics had become; how necessary it was that a general present an unblemished record of continuing successes if he were to survive personally, let alone play a leading role in shaping domestic policy; and, finally, and most bitterly for Cimon himself, how short the memory of the Athenian *dēmos* was.

Let us turn to the opening play of the *Oresteia*, the *Agamemnon*, at a point where the action of the play is already well advanced. Clytemnestra's ingenious, if rather extravagant, device for having the news of Troy's capture relayed to Argos by a series of beacon signals is shown to be not only effective but truthful, for all the chorus's incredulity: an advance runner, his coating of dust betokening the urgency of his mission, has arrived to report that Troy has indeed been captured. After the first of his three long, beautifully varied, perfectly diplomatic speeches, he and the chorus leader engage in a dialogue. He has touched his native soil and so will die happy, he announces. The chorus leader expresses surprise, with an admixture of pleasure, at the love, *erōs*, of his fatherland which the messenger displays.

> Chorus: A sweet illness, then, that you were afflicted with.
> Messenger: I'll be master of your meaning when you explain it to me.
> Chorus: You were struck by a desire for those who loved you in turn.
> Messenger: Do you mean that this country longed for an army that was
>   longing for it?
> Chorus: So that it often let out a sigh from a gloomy heart.
>
> (*Ag.* 542–46)[19]

What could better illustrate the sense of incompleteness felt by both components of the single political entity that is Argos, unnaturally and, as it turns out, disastrously rent by Agamemnon's mad expedition to Troy? The army's messenger is bringing evil news: the commander himself has survived and is returning, but that does not in itself spell success for the venture. In the ode the chorus sang just before the messenger arrived, the audience has heard the old men of Argos tell of Helen's flight with Paris, "leaving behind her for the citizens throngs of infantry and sailors under arms" (403–5). The war against Troy (like Xerxes' hybristic attempt to conquer Greece) has drained off men of fighting age not only from Argos, but from other cities: "for the generality of those who set out together from the land of Hellas there is grief" (430),[20] and the chorus go on to describe very touchingly the effect on numerous households of receiving back not the vigorous soldier, the one "skilled in battle" that each had hailed forth, but a small cremation urn, filled with a dead man's ashes, and "for the sake of someone else's wife" (448).

---

19. The translation of this and the subsequent passages from *Agamemnon* is my own.

20. Earlier, the chorus had called Agamemnon and Menelaus "like-minded leaders of the youth of Hellas" (109–11).

This, then, is the messenger's unhappy task. And this is why he is both so reticent and so roundabout and wordy: the news he brings is, as far as the city is concerned, of unmitigated disaster. So far from being a glorious venture, it was one racked by discomfort and toil (555–66). Troy has been taken, true, and her plundered riches are to be nailed up in the gods' temples to "give eulogizing witness to city and commanders" (580–81). But what of the men? Are they to come safely home? The messenger can no longer put off his dreadful news. The chorus-leader asks bluntly about the fate of Menelaus, and the man must admit that no one has any knowledge of his whereabouts, or, for that matter, of the fate of the rest of the fleet, for the expedition has been struck by a heaven-sent calamity, a disastrous storm on the homeward voyage. Even after the chorus-leader has asked straightforwardly for details of the storm, the messenger must preface his account in the last of his three speeches with an apologetic and shamefaced introduction.

A day of good omen should not be spoiled with news of evils. . . . When the messenger with gloomy visage brings to the city news it had prayed never to hear, that the army has fallen, this is a wound to the body of the city, and multiple is the loss felt by the numerous homes that have lost men . . . but when he comes to a city rejoicing in her good luck, how can I mix good with bad?

(636–48)

All this is very roundabout, for the messenger seems not to know to which category he really belongs: the Trojan campaign was nominally a success, as the aforementioned spoils attest, but a storm-bred conspiracy of fire and water "destroyed the miserable army of the Argives" (652). The view that awaited the survivors when the sun rose on the morning following the storm was "the Aegean Sea blossoming with corpses of Greek men, and with wreckages of ships" (659–60); again, we are reminded of the carnage in the straits of Salamis (*The Persians* 424–32). A small verbal detail in his description confirms the poet's intention to present the storm as a continuation, or even fulfillment, of the evils experienced by the army at Troy. The messenger in his narrative refers to the "fresh disaster to the army, afflicted and evilly ground to dust" (*spodoumenou*, 670). Earlier the chorus had used this term of the cruelly deceived hopes of the relatives of the men who had died at Troy: "Instead of men, urns and dust [*spodos*] come to the homes of each" (434–36);

"Ares . . . sends to their families from Troy's pyres a sorrowful weight of ashes, loading urns easily stowed, full of dust [spodou] replacing a man" (440–44).

Here is a damning incrimination of Agamemnon's leadership. To the loss of life in the fighting and the grinding discomfort of the bivouac at Troy is added this final humiliation: he didn't even bring the remnants of his army home safe. The storm had been heaven-sent, true,[21] but this does not absolve Agamemnon of personal responsibility. If anything, in an Aeschylean world in which events are "over-determined," it compounds it. Agamemnon is judged by the gods as unfit to lead an army as he is shown by the action of the play to be unfit, or at least unable, to rule his city. (Once Agamemnon has been murdered, the moral strictures against the Trojan expedition are forgotten and the whole venture is subject to some revisionism. In the next play, The Libation Bearers, Orestes, Agamemnon's son and would-be avenger, will lament the fact that "the most celebrated citizens in the world, overthrowers of Troy with honorable intent," are now subjects of the tyrannous Clytemnestra and Aegisthus [302–4], and it is an irony of which the poet may not himself have been conscious that Orestes should express the wish that his father had been slain at Troy, "thus leaving fair fame at home and enviable life for your children" [345–53, although Electra dissociates herself from this wish at 363–66].)

In the central paradox of Agamemnon, repeatedly noted by critics, the expedition to Troy has been undertaken at Zeus's behest, but the discharge of Zeus's command lays upon Agamemnon a heavy burden of sacrilege: first the slaying of his daughter Iphigeneia, then the pillage of Troy's temples. Clytemnestra in her eerie vision of the captured city early in the play warns that the army's safe return is conditional upon an observance of piety toward Troy's civic gods and shrines (338–42) but the messenger's opening speech makes it clear that Agamemnon's attitude was in fact the opposite: he "overturned Troy with the spade of Zeus's justice and razed it to the ground, the gods' altars and shrines obliterated" (525–27). We can now appreciate the full import of the chorus's warning earlier, "the gods do not fail to observe those who slay many" (461–62), where their surface reference is to the numerous deaths of Greeks,

21. The text of 649, though doubtful, seems to refer to the "wrath of the gods against the Greeks."

since they have just commented on the grieving households that received cinerary urns instead of their loved menfolk. But the indiscriminate slaughter at Troy must also be included in their warning. Troy as a *polis* has been annihilated,[22] and of that crime Agamemnon cannot, will not, be exonerated.

The chorus's reaction to the news that Agamemnon's ship (and probably also Menelaus's)[23] survived the storm might be expected to be one of unalloyed joy that their king is returning. In fact, they launch into a lengthy lament about the evils wrought by Helen. They make marvelous play with Helen's name by calling her *helandros* ("man-destroyer") and *heleptolis* ("city-destroyer"); but two cities are involved in the destruction that the venture to recover her has unleashed, Troy and Argos. Toward the end of the song they descant upon the dangers of prosperity, *olbos*, when it engenders arrogance, *hybris*: "Justice shines in smoke-darkened houses . . . but averts her gaze as she leaves gold-spangled halls where hands are filthy" (772–78). As they utter these words, Agamemnon is seen entering, and the chorus turn to address him formally as their king. It is therefore difficult not to take their strictures against *hybris* and injustice as pertaining to him;[24] a subtle shift has occurred in the course of their song, from disapproval of Helen as city-destroyer to sympathy for her city, which has been destroyed— it cannot be fortuitous that, after the chorus's reference to justice "shining in smoke-darkened [*dyskapnois*] houses," Agamemnon should be made to gloat over a Troy "captured and even now conspicuous by her smoke (*kapnōi*, 818)—to a corresponding disapproval of the destroyer. After a roundabout introduction in which they seem to be trying to warn him, albeit somewhat obscurely, that the joyousness of Clytemnestra's greeting will be insincere, they tell him: "At the time when you launched the expedition to Troy, for

22. The terms *polis* and *politai* are used far more often with reference to Troy than to Argos: 29, 127, 267, 278, 321, 338, 532, 710, 715, 739, 812, 818, 824, 1065, 1167, 1171, 1200, 1210, 1287, 1288, 1335; cf. H. G. Edinger, *Index analyticus Graecitatis Aeschyleae* (New York: Hildesheim, 1981), p. 258.

23. After avoiding the chorus leader's direct question about Menelaus's whereabouts, the messenger closes his account by telling the chorus to "expect first and foremost that Menelaus has returned" (674–75): so much was required by the myth.

24. As H. Lloyd-Jones remarks, "the stasimon closes on an ominous note for Agamemnon, whose entry immediately follows its conclusion" (note on line 781 of his translation, *The Agamemnon of Aeschylus* [Englewood Cliffs, N.J.: Prentice-Hall, 1970], p. 59). Cf. B. Knox, *Word and Action* (Baltimore: Johns Hopkins University Press, 1979), pp. 30–33.

Helen's sake, I shall not conceal it, you were painted by me very unattractively as one who had lost control of his senses." [25] In a sense they are just owning up to the criticisms they had leveled at him earlier for bringing so much grief to Greece's womenfolk " 'for the sake of someone else's wife'—someone will mutter this quietly as resentful grief begins to spread against Atreus's sons. . . . Dangerous is the angry utterance of the citizens, and it pays a debt exacted by the people's curses." [26]

Agamemnon for his part seems to be aware, but only vaguely, that something is wrong, that some threat to his rule may be brewing, but when, in the course of his opening speech, he says "about the other matters which concern the city and the gods, we shall summon communal gatherings and deliberate in assembly" (844–46; the Greek for the last phrase is *en panēgyrei bouleusomestha*), this seems to be no more than a token recognition of his need to secure the citizens' support. Contrast the pompous tone of his opening lines in the great debate with his wife: "It is right to address first Argos and the country's gods" (810–11) with Clytemnestra's direct appeal to "citizens, elders of the Argives here" (855). Commentators have noted the ambiguous phrasing used by Clytemnestra when she tells her husband the reason their son Orestes is not present: a Phocian ally, Strophios, had suggested that the boy be lodged with him for security, citing "danger to your person at Troy and if anarchy noised about by the people should overthrow deliberation" (882–84). Clytemnestra's use of such seemingly technical terms as *dēmothrous anarchia*, which clearly recalls the chorus's warning earlier about *"dēmos-validated curses,"* [27] and *boulē*, which can mean either "deliberation" or "deliberative council," has laid Aeschylus open to the charge of using language more appropriate to the Athens of his own day than to prehistoric Argos. [28] However

25. Lines 799–802. How they continued is unfortunately unclear. E. Fraenkel, who marks 803 as unsound, takes the "dying men" of 804 as referring to "the gigantic losses to be expected in the field" at Troy (*Aeschylus: Agamemnon* [Oxford: Clarendon Press, 1962], vol. 2, p. 365).

26. Lines 456–58. Fraenkel draws attention to the ambiguity of the expression: is it Agamemnon or the "citizens' utterance" that "pays the debt"? I note the similarity of formulation "validated by the people" (*dēmokrantou*) to the phrase in *The Suppliants* (604) describing a vote in the assembly as *dēmou kratousa* (*cheir*).

27. The two expressions, *dēmokrantou aras* (458) and *dēmothrous anarchia* (383), in a sense coalesce later, when after the murder the chorus warn Clytemnestra that she will be the subject of "curses uttered by the people" (*dēmothrous aras*; 1409, 1413).

28. See, for example, the note on lines 883–84 in the edition of J. D. Denniston and D. L. Page (London: Oxford University Press, 1957), p. 146, and Fraenkel's long

that may be, it is obvious that the *dēmos*, the citizen body, are a presence whose importance, in political terms, both Clytemnestra and Agamemnon acknowledge,[29] although neither gives the impression of taking the people's influence seriously into account as a determinant of his or her own actions. For Agamemnon this becomes clear in that part of their great contest, or *agōn*, which has come to be known as the "carpet scene." Clytemnestra has ordered gorgeous and expensive tapestries, such as are fit for worship of the gods (922; perhaps reminiscent of the robe woven specially for Athene's statue in the four-yearly Great Panathenaia), to be strewn along Agamemnon's triumphal path into the palace. She tries various weapons against the not very thick armor of her husband's resistance.

> Clyt. What do you think Priam [an ill-omened comparison, this, of an Oriental monarch, lately slain, with a Greek commander] would have done, if he had accomplished feats like yours?
> Agam. I suppose he would be quick to step on the woven cloths.
> Clyt. Do you feel scruples, then, at merely human reproaches?
> Agam. Yes, for what the people say [*phēmē . . . dēmothrous*] is very strong.
> Clyt. But the man beyond envy is also beyond emulation.
>
> (935-39)

Agamemnon, then, does not resist. He enters the palace, to the warm bath that is the prerogative of dusty travelers,[30] and is there murdered by his faithless wife and her lover, who is in fact Agamemnon's own cousin, Aegisthus. The chorus, who represent the political entity that is Argos, the "ruled," may have grumbled under their breaths about the inadequacy of Agamemnon's rule, self-centered and disastrously militaristic as it was, but once he has been murdered, their sympathies take a sudden swerve in his direction. They cannot, after all, acquiesce in this usurpation of legitimate authority. They had tried, somewhat feebly perhaps, to warn him of the crucial importance of distinguishing "that citizen who is a just housekeeper of the city from the one who does so

---

discussion of 884 in his *Commentary* (see n. 25 above), vol. 2, 398-99; also E. R. Dodds, "Morals and Politics in the Oresteia," *Proceedings of the Cambridge Philological Society* 186 (1960): 19-20 (= *The Ancient Concept of Progress* [Oxford: Clarendon Press, 1973], p. 46).

29. Note Dodds's remark in "Morals and Politics": "Argos is not yet a democracy, as it will be in 458 [B.C.], but the opinions of the *dēmos* are already important" (p. 20 [= p. 46]).

30. Compare *Choephoroi* 670; the fatal bath is referred to again in line 491 of that play and in *The Eumenides* 633.

inopportunely,"[31] but their warnings went unheeded. Now, as Agamemnon is in his death throes (his cry is heard from within, 1343 and 1345), they stand helpless and start to canvass various possible courses of action. One member of the chorus comments, "It's clear to see: their actions are a prelude and a sign of tyranny" (1354–55), and another, a few lines later, "To die is a milder fate than to endure tyranny" (1364–65).

Aegisthus for his part does not take the trouble to deny the charges. When he appears, he struts about and blusters very much in the manner of the stage-tyrant, whom we shall recognize again in the character of Creon in Sophocles' *Antigone*. The chorus's criticisms he brutally tries to silence by "pulling rank": they are merely "seated at the oars below," whereas "those who hold power [*kratountōn*] aboard ship are the ones in the steersman's bench" (1617–18). "Using this man's riches," he proclaims, "I shall try to rule the citizens, and the one who disobeys shall find himself in a heavy yoke."[32] He then threatens imprisonment and starvation against any recalcitrance to his command, and remarks caustically, "It shows lack of prudent judgement to [? abuse—the text is defective] the one who holds power" (*kratounta*, 1664). Aegisthus for his part sees the murder not as a necessary step to legitimizing his union with Clytemnestra but as satisfaction for an old family debt: in the preceding generation, Aegisthus's father, Thyestes, and Atreus, father of Agamemnon and Menelaus, had disputed the rule of Argos, and Atreus had driven Thyestes from the city into exile (1585–86). As if this were not enough, Thyestes' children were later butchered and served up in a meal by his brother, a horror recounted both by Aegisthus (1590ff.) and by Cassandra in her visionary trance (1095–97); according to her, "the whole city cries aloud" the crime (1106). If the chorus had anything to say in the matter, the guilty pair would be publicly banished:[33] "You will be city-less," they threaten Clytemnestra, "crushed by the hatred of the people" (1410–11), where the reference seems to be to the

---

31. *Ag.* 808–9. We see where the rather odd metaphor, *oikourounta* (literally, to "be a house-keeper, stay-at-home"), is leading when first Cassandra and then the chorus apply the term insultingly to Aegisthus (1225, 1626).

32. Lines 1638–39. The tone and phraseology, especially *ton mē peithanora* ("disobedient"), are reminiscent of Eteocles' pompous formulation "Obedience to Rule [*peitharchia*] is mother of Success and wife of Safety" (*Seven Against Thebes* 224–25) and will be heard again in Creon's comment: "When men are successful, what saves them for the most part is *peitharchia*" (*Ant.* 675–76).

33. See n. 27 above.

regular practice of public execution by stoning, a threat the chorus later make in more explicit terms to Aegisthus.[34]

At the end of the play the chorus warn of a vindication at Orestes' hands (1646, 1667), and in fact in the succeeding play, *Choephoroi (The Libation Bearers)*, Orestes' return is seen as a restoration of legitimate rule and his blow against Clytemnestra and Aegisthus as a liberation from tyranny. Orestes expresses his sense of outrage that "the citizens, most celebrated of men, who overturned Troy . . . should be thus subject to two women" (*Cho.* 302–4), and the chorus, composed of serving women in the palace but not unrepresentative of the city's views as a whole, express their approval of the impending tyrannicide. In the course of the ode they sing when the nurse has gone to fetch Aegisthus they comment, "These matters go well for the city,"[35] and just after he enters the palace, unsuspecting that death awaits him there, they rejoice that Orestes will recover "the right to rule and administer laws for the city."[36] Toward the close of the play, when Clytemnestra's corpse has been added to that of Aegisthus, they congratulate Orestes: "You did well . . . you set free the whole city of Argos by neatly cutting off the snake with two heads" (*Cho.* 104–47). Indeed, in the final play, *The Eumenides* (*Wellwishers*, a euphemistic title of the Furies), Orestes manifests a newfound confidence and assurance. After his acquittal by the Athenian court of the Areopagus, which Athene has instituted precisely to hear his case, he promises that, upon his return home, he and his people will be everlasting allies of Athens: "If [the Argives] constantly honor this city of Pallas by an armed alliance, we shall be kindly disposed to them" (*Eum.* 772–74). Orestes has, in truth, not only entered into his patrimony, he has assumed the mantle of true leadership that sat so uncomfortably on his father's shoulders. He speaks now with an authoritative voice, committing his people to a course of action whose effects will be felt even into the fifth century.[37] What is more, he is sure that he has the support of the whole Argive people behind him.

34. Lines 1615–16. Again, the language echoes earlier phrases: *dēmorripheis . . . leusimous aras*, literally, "curses consisting-in-stones hurled by the people" (this was a standard form of capital punishment: *Seven Against Thebes* 199).

35. *Cho.* 824. As often in this play, the text is not above suspicion.

36. *Cho.* 864. The phrase is marked as corrupt by Page in his edition (*Aeschyli septem . . . tragoedias* [Oxford: Clarendon Press, 1972]), but clearly some such sense is demanded of the words *archas te polissonomous* (most editors, like Murray, merely accept Porson's alteration to the dative case).

37. For the significance of these allusions to the treaty concluded between Athens and Argos in about 461 B.C., see my *Political Background* (cited in n. 1 above), pp. 82–83.

The Aeschylean hero, then, and the *polis* he rules, are shown in the throes of a crisis of leadership and, although the problem is cast in a mythical age, it really reflects a situation made familiar to Aeschylus's audience by contemporary Athenian history. Was it reasonable to expect the same man to function both as a successful military strategist and as an efficient marshaler of public opinion in the assembly of citizens? In a way, there was no alternative once the Athenians had taken the step of turning their chief magistracy into an allotted office, while leaving the office of general an elective one, with no restrictions on the number of times a man might be reelected.[38] The transference of power, its devolution, so to speak, from the military to the political sphere, must have proceeded fairly quickly in these decades when Athens, first for self-defense against the Persians and then for her own expansionist ambitions, kept her forces almost constantly in the field. As a character in Sophocles' *Philoctetes*, much later and in a different context, puts it: "A city, and an army too, are entirely dependent on the leaders."[39]

What means of marshaling public opinion were open to the successful general who now aspired to political leadership? There was only one sure method: he must have a consistent policy and, even more important, be able to persuade a majority of the voters in the assembly that this was the correct course to be followed on each and every occasion that the matter came up for debate. It is no accident that the outstanding fact remembered about Pericles was his ability to charm an audience.[40]

At times, this must have seemed intolerably restricting for a leader. A general might expect unquestioning obedience from his troops; why did the *dēmos* in assembly have to be persuaded? Led and not marshaled? Thucydides reports a debate in the Athenian assembly held in 427 B.C. in which the Athenian politician Cleon castigated the *dēmos* for its eagerness to be "spectators of arguments, an audience [rather than participants] for deeds . . . experts at being deceived by novelty in debate . . . slaves of the unusual . . ." (3.38). And in fact we find characters on the Athenian stage who betray a

38. The year was 487–486 as we know from the *Constitution of Athens* ascribed to Aristotle (22.5) and the man behind the change was probably Themistocles (see my study *The Life of Themistocles* [Montreal: McGill-Queen's University Press, 1975], p. 10), although this has been disputed.

39. *Phil.* 386–87, with Jebb's note justifying the above translation (Jebb remarks on the contrast presented by *Ant.* 738, to be discussed below).

40. "A kind of persuasion sat upon his lips, so he could cast a spell and alone of the orators left his sting in the hearers" (Eupolis, *The Demes*, fr. 98 Edmonds, 5–8).

certain impatience with the rough and tumble of open debate and who sound as if they would really be happier if they could bark military commands to citizens in strictly civilian contexts. *Seven against Thebes* by Aeschylus (467 B.C.) focuses, at least in its early part, on a military commander, Oedipus's son Eteocles, who insists on trying to impose military discipline on a civilian chorus composed of women in the city of Thebes, which is under siege by Argive invaders. The women are in a state of utter panic; their entrance song consists in frenzied appeals to the city's protector gods, individually and en masse. Eteocles for his part wants to impose on them a strict military discipline:

> Here now running wild among the citizenry
> You have roared them into spiritless cowardice.
> So, outside of our gates, gains strength the enemy
> While we are by ourselves, within, undone . . .
>
> . . . .
>
> What is outside is a man's province: let no
> Woman debate it: within doors do no mischief!
>
> (191–94; 200–201)[41]

In an early, extended example of the "ship of state" figure, he asks sarcastically: "What, shall the sailor, then, leave the stern and run to the prow and find device for safety when his vessel is foundering in the sea waves?" (208–10). He wishes he could impose on them the *peitharchia*, obedience to authority, that he expects from his troops (224). As it turns out, Eteocles' view is dangerously one-sided, and it is his failure to heed the chorus's remonstrances to improve his relationship with the gods that will later destroy him.

The overlap between the spheres of military and civil authority is taken up again by Sophocles in two plays that perhaps date from the decade 450–440 B.C. Menelaus struts about in the last scene of *Ajax*, charging insubordination against the hero, Ajax, who has committed suicide out of disgrace at his failure to be awarded Achilles' armor and because of his humiliation at his having slaughtered the army's sheep and cattle in the crazed belief that they were the Greek commanders, his former colleagues, now his deadly enemies. "It is the mark of a base man [Menelaus expounds] for an ordinary citizen [*dēmotēs*] not to deign to obey those set in authority over him. For neither would the laws have a prosperous voyage in a city where fear was not firmly established, nor would an army be

41. This and the following translation are by David Grene (see n. 13 above).

prudently led if it did not have fear and respect as a protection"
(*Ajax* 1071–76). (The relevance of this argument to the play's action
does not here concern us; in fact, as the hero's half-brother Teucer is
quick to point out, Ajax was not an "ordinary citizen," bound to
respect "the authorities," Agamemnon and Menelaus. He came to
Troy of his own volition, as a commander of an independent contingent from Salamis.) This assimilation of the civil to the military
mode of authority is also at the heart of Creon's rather pedantic exposition to his son in *Antigone*, when he tries to justify his insistence that his edict must not be disobeyed, even by his niece and
his son's fiancée, Antigone. "Whoever the city appoints, that man
must be obeyed, in small matters and great, in just causes and the
opposite. I would feel confident that this man would be a good
ruler and would be willing to be ruled, and that in the storm of
battle he would keep his appointed place as a just and noble comrade" (*Ant.* 666–71). He then goes on to excoriate *anarchia*, disobedience to rule, which "destroys cities, ruins homes, makes allied
armies break and run" (672–75). Creon does not understand why
he cannot command the same unquestioning loyalty and obedience
from the citizens as he would be entitled to if he were a general in
the field.[42] In insisting on this kind of quasi-military obedience,
Creon shows that he is indeed unable to brook any challenge to his
authority: he is not a true leader of free citizens, but a tyrant, and
his son tells him so: "Your face causes fear to the citizen (*dēmotēs*)
who might speak words which you would not enjoy hearing"
(690–91). To the boy's repeated insistence that the city of Thebes is
on Antigone's side and approves her pious attempt to bury her
brother, even if he was, in Creon's terms, a "criminal," Creon can
only bluster,

Creon:	Will the city tell me what commands I should give?
Haemon:	Don't you see you're talking like an impetuous youth?
Creon:	Should someone besides me rule this land?
Haemon:	It is not a *polis* if it is the possession of one man.
Creon:	Isn't the city held to belong to the one who exercises power [*kratountos*]?
Haemon:	You'd make a fine single ruler—of a desert!

(731–39)

---

42. In fact, in what almost seems to be an unconscious slip, Sophocles has Antigone refer to Creon earlier as "general" (*Ant.* 8); for a more politically loaded interpretation, see V. Ehrenberg, *Sophocles and Pericles* (cited in n. 1 above), pp. 105–12.

Taken to its limits, the treating of citizens as if they were troops is tyranny. The Aeschylean Xerxes is the direct ancestor of Sophocles' Creon.[43]

I conclude on a more speculative note. It is just possible that, when political theorizing took its rightful place as a legitimate field of ancient philosophical investigations—when, that is, the seeds planted by Protagoras, Antiphon, and Hippias of Elis bore fruit in the writings of Plato and Aristotle—there existed documentary evidence for the origin and development of tyranny in archaic Greece: possible, but unlikely. Instead, the philosophers probably relied on oral tradition, written constitutions of a later period and whatever other material they could find, and from this extrapolated a schematic development of early forms of government. Both Plato and Aristotle espoused the view that a close relationship existed between successful generalship and tyranny. Plato makes the connection in his discussion of the evolution and devolution of political structures in the latter part of *The Republic*. The man who sets himself up as the champion of the *dēmos* becomes, through the working of forces easily recognizable as "demagogic," a tyrant. Thenceforward, after he has assumed his new role, "he must continually stir up war against outside enemies, so that the people would be in need of a leader [*hēgemōn*]" (*Rep.* 566e). The theory was taken up and developed by Aristotle, who dubs the tyrant *polemopoios*, a "maker of war," so that the people may be kept busy fighting and in constant need of him as *hēgemōn* (*Politics* 1313b28). Even if he neglects all the other virtues, he must cultivate "the warlike virtue" (*tēs polemikēs* [*aretēs*]) and take care to develop for himself a reputation in this sphere (1314b22). The clever tyrant will be careful in the way he administers the taxes and other income he needs for "occasions for war" (*polemikous kairous*), and will behave like a "guardian and steward" of public funds rather than of his own private property (1314b16–18).

This hypothetical connection between tyranny and war making is also used by Aristotle to explain how tyranny arises. Men who are "bold by nature" and have been entrusted by monarchs with the administration of war (*timēn . . . polemikēn*) often attempt to depose their superiors (1312a18). "In ancient times, when the same

43. For a development of Creon as tyrant, see my article "Creon and Herodotus," *Transactions of the American Philological Association* 97 (1966):359–71; D. Lanza, *Il tiranno e il suo pubblico* (Turin: Einaudi, 1977), p. 149.

man was both good at leading the people [*dēmagōgos*] and a general, they changed to tyranny" (1305a7); "the champions of the people, when they became warlike, made an attempt at tyranny" (1305a21). To illustrate his point, Aristotle cites the cases of Cleisthenes of Sicyon who, because he was *polemikos*, had to be treated with respect (1315b17); the famous tyrant of Corinth, Periander, also was *polemikos* (1315b30). According to the *Constitution of Athens*, ascribed to Aristotle, Peisistratus set himself up as tyrant at Athens after having been "*dēmagōgos* and a general" (22.3).

What accounts for the prominence of war as an explanation of how tyrants arose and maintained themselves in power in the archaic age? I suggest that the thinking of Plato and Aristotle on this matter may have been influenced in part by the portrayals in fifth-century tragedy that we have been examining, where leaders stand or fall at home on the basis of what they have achieved against foreign enemies, and where we often see military men—Agamemnon, Menelaus, Creon—behaving inappropriately in civilian contexts, trying to impose their will against manifest opposition. The developing *polis* of the fifth century was pondering the question, What makes a good leader? The charisma of military success could be expected to carry over into the purely political assembly of citizens, especially if the *polis* were regularly at war or under threat of war; this no doubt accounts for the long, and on the whole untroubled, careers of such leaders as Cimon and Pericles. Failing such an automatic transfer of loyalty, a less-than-charismatic politician might well have asked himself how he could duplicate conditions on the battlefield, which required instantaneous, unquestioning response to commands, *peitharchia*. One course open to him was to inflame the bellicose instincts of the citizens, to keep the *polis* always in a state of war-alert. If that was not feasible, he might still try to exact a quasi-military respect for his authority, even from unwilling "subjects." If he chose that course, he would have crossed the boundary into a mode of behavior which, in the fifth century, had acquired a harsh name, tyranny. And to this the prescribed antidote was tyrannicide, literal slaying of tyrants in the archaic age and, for their democratic counterparts in the classical period, removal from office and sometimes the imposition of a fine or exile, penalties which, in one form or another, had been inflicted on Miltiades, Themistocles, Cimon, and Pericles himself.

Chapter Four

Thebes: Theater of Self and Society in Athenian Drama

Froma I. Zeitlin

1.

THE TOPOS OF THEBES

The city I am calling Thebes occupies a very small territory, no larger than the extent of the stage in the theater of Dionysus under the shadow of the Acropolis at Athens. In keeping with the conventions of Attic tragedy, no special scenery or stage set identifies it and no particular props are necessary for its representation. The typical façade of the *skēnē*, the stage building, that normally stands for the front of a house or palace serves just as well for Thebes as for any other location where dramas are supposed to take place.

And yet we know the city once the play has begun, or better, we ought to recognize the place—not only from its being named as Thebes or as the city of Cadmus, not only from verbal references to its walls with the seven gates that are its most distinctive architectural feature, but from what over and over again the tragic poets cause to transpire there as they treat the different myths that share a common terrain in Thebes. We think immediately of the saga of the house of Laius that situates Oedipus at its center and extends beyond him to the dramas of his children—his sons, Eteocles and Polyneices, and his daughters, Antigone and Ismene. But there is

An earlier and shorter version of this paper was delivered at the Convegno internazionale di studi, "Oedipo: Il teatro greco e la cultura europea," held in November 1982 at Urbino. This essay forms part of a more extensive study concerning the representation of Thebes in Athenian drama. The foundations have been laid in my recent book, *Under the Sign of the Shield: Semiotics and Aeschylus' Seven Against Thebes* (Rome: Edizioni dell'Ateneo, 1982). The notes have necessarily been kept to a minimum, and in the case of Aeschylus's *Seven*, fuller discussion of the issues I raise can be found in the study mentioned above.

also the prior story of Cadmus, the Spartoi, or Sown Men, and the founding of the city through autochthony (birth from the earth) and fratricide, as the Sown Men fight one another to their mutual destruction with the exception of five who survive to inaugurate the history of the city. And, thirdly, we must include the myth of the god Dionysus himself, the son of Zeus and Semele, who, reputedly born at Thebes, returns home to claim recognition of his divinity and to establish the cult of his worship in his native city.

In proposing that there is some conceptual category in the Athenian theater named "Thebes" and that some underlying "unity of place" organizes these disparate stories and their treatment in the work of all three Athenian tragic poets, I am, in effect, suggesting that we look at Thebes as a *topos* in both senses of the word: as a designated place, a geographical locale, and figuratively, as a recurrent concept or formula, or what we call a "commonplace." That is, through the specific myths associated with Thebes on the Athenian stage, certain clusters of ideas, themes, and problems recur that can be identified as proper to Thebes—or rather to Athenian tragedy's representation of Thebes as a *mise en scène*. Additionally, certain formal structures underlie the variety of different plots—similar types of scenes, character portrayals, semantic fields, and so on. All these elements attest to a certain unifying tendency that allows each myth and each version of that myth its own autonomy, but brings them all together as a coherent and complex ensemble. This wide-angle lens that brings the background into the sharper focus can extend our conceptions of what constitute formal conventions in the theater and can show how these might interact together at their different levels for a larger design. Better still, this same lens can also illuminate the ideological uses of the theater in Athens as it portrays a city on stage that is meant to be dramatically "other" than itself. Thebes, I will argue, provides the negative model to Athens's manifest image of itself with regard to its notions of the proper management of city, society, and self. As the site of displacement, therefore, Thebes consistently supplies the radical tragic terrain where there can be no escape from the tragic in the resolution of conflict. There the most serious questions can be raised concerning the fundamental relations of man to his universe, particularly in respect to the nature of rule over others and of rule over self.

The program I have outlined above is, of course, too vast for the brief visit we can pay to Thebes in this preliminary essay. The matters we would need to consider in detail are far-ranging, involving issues of form, content, language, character, and structure, while the plays in question run the gamut from Aeschylus's early drama *Seven Against Thebes* to *The Bacchae* of Euripides, not produced until after the poet's death. In between, there are three plays by Sophocles—*Antigone, Oedipus Tyrannos,* and *Oedipus at Colonus,* as well as two further plays by Euripides—*The Suppliant Women* and *The Phoenissae.* This last play, for example, is an excellent witness to the general hypothesis, since it most fully combines the three myths I have mentioned above; dividing its attention between the sons of Oedipus and the last survivor of the Spartoi, it also organizes its metaphorical center around Dionysus in his negative and positive aspects.

But even with a limited tour that can stop at these individual dramas only to exemplify one or more points of the exposition, it will be possible, I hope, to sketch out what Thebes is and what it might mean in its dialogue with the city of Athens, whose theater invents its imaginary space. Oedipus is our best guide, I propose, for examining the challenges that Thebes will be seen to offer to relations between self, family, city, and cosmos. For is he not the most familiar representative of Thebes, and yet the only one who in the later dramatic tradition is permitted to make his way from Thebes to Athens? Part 1 of this essay, therefore, using Oedipus as its point of departure, will suggest some of the more significant structural and thematic parallels between plays of very different sorts. Part 2 will raise the issue of Thebes as an "anti-Athens" and will map out the territory, as it were, of this "other" city. Part 3 will confront Thebes more directly with Athens through the figure of Oedipus to suggest how the two cities are radically contraposed, especially with regard to their views and uses of time and history.

Oedipus and Thebes. In one sense, we might describe the career of Oedipus as a search for a home. More precisely, a place where he might be at home, where he might truly belong. Viewed from this perspective, Oedipus immediately presents us with an extraordinary paradox. For once Oedipus discovers that he has found his true home in Thebes, he also discovers to his or our horror that he has been only too much "at home." The strange territory to which he had come when, to contravene the oracle of Apollo at Delphi, he had turned away from the road to Corinth in favor of the road to Thebes, proves to be none other than the place where he was born.

Thus his subsequent sojourn in the city turns out to be not his first, as all had thought, but his second. Here the dramatic tradition diverges: in two extant plays reference is made to his death at Thebes at some indeterminate time (Aesch. *Seven* 914–1004, Soph. *Ant.* 899–902), while later theatrical works revive Oedipus, we might say, in order to expel him once again from Thebes, this time never to find his way back there again.[1]

The moment of this last exile is not fixed. Sophocles prepares the way when, at the end of *Oedipus Tyrannos*, Oedipus longs to go at once into exile (*OT* 1436–50, 1518–19), fulfilling the edict he had imposed upon the unknown murderer before he knew that the other he sought was in truth himself (*OT* 224–54; cf. 815–24). But in *Oedipus at Colonus* he tells us that in fact he had first remained in Thebes. Only much later, he says, long after his grief and anger had modulated into acceptance and when his truest desire was to stay at home, only then did Creon and his sons cruelly expel him against his will and sentence him to years of homeless wandering (*OC* 425–44, 765–71, 1354–59). Euripides' *The Phoenissae* marks yet another shift in the temporal ordering of events in Oedipus's life. Here, where the drama belongs to the next generation, as it treats the sequel to Oedipus's own story, we discover that the aged father is still present after all in Thebes, kept inside the house like a hidden ghost, a pale shadow of a dream (*Phoe.* 63–66, 1539–45). But he is not to remain there. At the very end of this panoramic play, when Oedipus has lived to see the curses he had laid upon his sons accomplished in their death at each other's hands, Creon belatedly drives him out to embark on the path that will lead him, as he seems to know in advance, to Colonus and to death there away from Thebes (*Phoe.* 1705–7).[2] Sophocles in his version also, of course, brings the aged king to the same precinct in Attica and sets the stage there for the last act of his story, which is entirely concerned with finding a permanent home for Oedipus—first as suppliant stranger, and then as hero for the city once he vanishes into the sacred tomb. But Oedipus cannot reach this last resting place until he first confronts Thebes again and successfully resists the temptation he is offered to return home.

1. I omit here discussion of the epic tradition.
2. It is generally agreed that Euripides' drama precedes that of Sophocles, although the passages in *The Phoenissae* relevant to the place of Oedipus's exile have sometimes been suspected of being interpolations.

The true terms of that offer, however, tell us why he will refuse. No one who comes from Thebes to fetch him in *Oedipus at Colonus* has the power or the desire to promise him a place at home in the house or in the city, despite their pretenses to the contrary. Rather they will offer him only a site betwixt and between, on the border of the city's territory, where he will be home and not home, returned and not returned (*OC* 299–400, 784–86; cf. 1342–43). For Oedipus the man, who demands the dignity of his human status, the supplications of Creon, the current ruler, and of Polyneices, Oedipus's son, are a sham, since they desire only to gain domination over his person and this for their own political ends. On ritual grounds, it may also be true, as Creon claims, that the patricide can never be repatriated (*OC* 406–7). But in a larger sense, Thebes's spatial designation of Oedipus's position in its land at this date only spells out more explicitly the underlying rules of the system in this city whose own ambiguities are matched by those of its most exemplary native son.

Thebes is the place, I will argue, that makes problematic every inclusion and exclusion, every conjunction and disjunction, every relation between near and far, high and low, inside and outside, stranger and kin. Thus Oedipus is only perhaps the crystallization in purest form of the city of Thebes itself. And by that same logic, we might say that Thebes is therefore the only possible birthplace for Oedipus. In the last Sophoclean play, Oedipus will finally rupture the symbiotic relationship between himself and his city on the new territory of Athens to which both his destiny and his own choice have assigned him. But in the prior stages of his life story, what happens to the figure of Oedipus is emblematic of the larger concerns associated with Thebes. When he fluctuates between a fixed imprisonment in the house and an unstable wandering too far from home, or when, in a different vein, he alternates between a condition of solipsistic autonomy and involvement in too dense a network of relations, Oedipus personifies in himself the characteristics that Thebes manifests in all its dramatic variants, through all its other myths, and through the extant work of all the tragic poets of Athens.

I propose then first to play the roles of both Creon and Polyneices. My purpose, like theirs, is heuristic—to seek to bring Oedipus home again to the place where his story truly belongs as its place of origin and as its point of departure. And, like them, I want to bring

him back not for his intrinsic value and interest as a human character but for an instrumental aim. That is, I want to refocus the question of Oedipus as a question about Thebes. This means that I want
to resituate Oedipus in Thebes, not only in his Sophoclean representations, but through those of Aeschylus and Euripides as well.

This terrain, first of all, Oedipus must share with others. His
story is predicated on the two oracles given in advance, first to his
father and then to himself, but its terms extend beyond him to affect those whom he engenders as children of an incestuous marriage. Oedipus would seem to occupy a special position in extant
Greek drama as the middle term that faces two ways as the child of
his father and as the father of his children, whose interdependence
is emphasized, even exaggerated by the fact that he shares a double
kinship with his progeny—that of father and brother. Thus his
story can only be completed with the third act—the sequel to
Oedipus at Thebes—both as regards the drama of his children's
lives and in the retrospection that an aged Oedipus can bring to
bear on the interpretation of the entire network of relations.

We should not wonder then if there are striking similarities in the
structures of plot and thematic concerns in Sophocles' three Theban
plays (*Oedipus Tyrannos, Oedipus at Colonus, Antigone*), Aeschylus's
Seven Against Thebes (the last and sole survivor of his Labdacid trilogy), and Euripides' *The Phoenissae*. Nor should we omit Euripides'
The Suppliant Women, which is set not in Thebes but in Eleusis near
Athens, and concerns not only the family of Oedipus but the Argive women who come to claim burial for their own sons who have
fallen before Thebes. That play looks back for its pattern to Sophocles' *Antigone* and ahead to that other burial, that of Oedipus himself, in Sophocles' *Oedipus at Colonus*.

All these plays share a common point of reference, since they
each treat some event, directly or indirectly, that can be traced back
to the house of Laius. But it may be less apparent how Dionysus
and the myth associated with him can and should be integrated
into this theatrical space. Let us turn then to Euripides' *The Bacchae*
to see whether we can find a relation between Oedipus the king
and Dionysus the god and to look for a common ground upon
which both might stand.

Oedipus Tyrannos and *The Bacchae*.   Is not Dionysus at Thebes, like
Oedipus, both at home and not at home? Is he not also the stranger

who comes from elsewhere—this time not from another Greek city like Corinth but from the more distant spaces of barbarian Asia? Yet he, too, is a child of Thebes returning home to the place of his birth in order to assert his identity and claim his patrimony. The critical difference, of course, resides in the fact that he is a god, the son of Semele and Zeus, and it is this honor, rather than political kingship, that he claims. Thus, while confusion of origins and problems of legitimacy are common threads that link Oedipus and Dionysus, the gap between mortal and immortal status ensures entirely opposite outcomes. Moreover, as a result, Dionysus is called upon to assume two contrasting roles that are typical in Thebes. Like Oedipus, he is the *xenos* (stranger) who is also native born (*suggenēs*); like him, he is the unacknowledged offspring of the royal dynasty who will come to reveal his true identity to the city. But if Dionysus compels mortals to discover the incontrovertible truth of his identity, he also brings the king of the city to discover the limits of his own. Thus, when *The Bacchae* replicates the conflict between human and divine knowledge that Oedipus and Teiresias acted out in *Oedipus Tyrannos*, Dionysus necessarily aligns himself with the familiar role of the seer. And like Teiresias, the agent of Apollo in the Sophoclean play, Dionysus has the power through his enigmatic words to question the identity of the ruling king in Thebes: "you do not know what life you lead, nor what you do, nor who you are" (*Bach.* 506; cf. *OT* 413–15).

Pentheus is not the child of Laius, nor even, of course, a child of Oedipus. Rather he is sprung from Echion, as he states in reply to the god's challenge (507), one of the descendants of the autochthonous Sown Men. But Dionysus's echo in *The Bacchae* of Teiresias's taunt in *Oedipus Tyrannos* might forewarn us that Pentheus, too, is liable to manifest in himself the Oedipal conflicts so typical at Thebes. And indeed he does. In thematic terms, Pentheus has already attacked the paternal figure in the hostile verbal exchange he undertakes with his grandfather Cadmus (*Bach.* 330–46), and the climax of the plot confirms that he is irresistibly drawn to join his mother. His hidden desire is to see her participate in the sexual activities he imagines the women are engaged in, and he longs both to assert his phallic power and to be cradled in her arms again like a child (*Bach.* 964–69). Like Oedipus, he, too, turns out to be a voyeur, seeking without his conscious knowledge to see and know those secrets that are forbidden to him in the domain of the mother.

In structural terms, Pentheus's joint meeting with Cadmus, the
father of the family, and Teiresias, the seer of Apollo, condenses the
two sequential encounters that occur for Oedipus in Sophocles'
play—first, with Creon, his uncle and an older male in the family,
and next, with Teiresias himself. But the symmetrical conflict between the two cousins, Pentheus and Dionysus, puts us also and
perhaps more directly in line of the conflict of enemy brothers,
Eteocles and Polyneices, and the correspondences between *The
Bacchae* and Aeschylus's *Seven Against Thebes* are even more pervasive than the parallels with *Oedipus Tyrannos* noted above. A comparison between these two plays may serve, in fact, to demonstrate
best of all the common elements of the Theban scenario, since they
recount apparently very different *mythoi* in the history of Thebes
and the dates of their composition stand at the furthest remove
from each other in the history of the theater: *Seven* is an early speci-
men of extant Aeschylean drama, the last in Aeschylus's lost trilogy, whose first two plays treated the earlier generations of Laius
and Oedipus, whereas *The Bacchae*, although referring back to what
we might take as the founding myth of the theater itself, is one of
the last plays in Euripides' dramatic repertory.

The Bacchae and *Seven Against Thebes*.   As we examine these two
dramas, we observe first of all that both sets of doubles are engaged
in a conflict, which is that of war. Eteocles and Polyneices will meet
directly in armed warrior combat at the gates of Thebes in the context of the Argives' expedition against the city. Although Pentheus's
situation is more complex, and the circumstances provoking his
desire for armed intervention are far more problematic, this king is
also portrayed as a military leader. Ranged against Dionysus, the
leader of the Asiatic troops of maenads (*Bach.* 50–52), Pentheus is,
at the same time, ready to lead out his army against the Theban
women of the city who themselves have gone as maenads to the
mountains. Dionysus, like Polyneices, the exiled brother, demands
the right to return and claim what is his own, and like him, may be
said to come with a foreign force against his native city.

Secondly, both Eteocles and Pentheus must confront on stage a
chorus of insubordinate women, and their responses in each play
are antagonistic and violent. Like the chorus of Asiatic maenads
whom Pentheus would lock up and put away in the house, Eteocles' first anger is directed against *his* unruly chorus—the women

of Thebes. In his case, the women have come out of the house to the city's ramparts, unbidden and in maddened fear at the enemy's approach, to pray at the public altars in this time of crisis. Eteocles, too, would shut them away in the house, and he further accuses them of helping the enemy against the city's interests with their subversive piety (*Seven* 77–263).

In *The Bacchae*, however, the conflict between male and female is more pervasive and more complex than the limited catalytic role afforded to the Theban women in Eteocles' city. The conflict here takes place with two female groups—the chorus of Asiatic women in the city and the Theban women outside it. The women's ritual challenge (both foreign and domestic) to male authority is not a reaction of terror to an impending disaster in which they fear they will be its most helpless victims, but rather itself constitutes the crisis in the city—its symptom and major cause. Offstage, as the drama progresses, the Theban women will also prove to be Pentheus's true antagonists, once the god works his seductive spell over his adversary and Pentheus in his madness makes common cause with Dionysus. The women are the ones who, having already defeated men in a clash of spear against thyrsus, as the messenger tells us (*Bach.* 761–63), will also defeat Pentheus in an unequal contest now of many against one.

Pentheus leaves the stage for the last time disguised in bacchant costume, and Eteocles departs arrayed in warrior dress. One is on the way to the mountains, the other to the city's gate where he is to face his enemy brother. But even here there are grounds for comparison between them in that both are impelled by irrational forces—one in a state of Dionysiac possession and the other in the grip of his father's Erinys, reminding us once again that, as figurations of madness, bacchant and Erinys are often interchangeable in tragic diction.[3] And, finally, in both cases, these two hoplite figures, Pentheus and Eteocles, go forth to murderous confrontations with the closest members of their own family, whether masculine (brother) or feminine (mother).[4]

---

3. See J.-P. Guépin, *The Tragic Paradox* (Amsterdam: Adolf M. Hakkert, 1968), p. 21; William Whallon, "Maenadism in the Oresteia," *Harvard Studies in Classical Philology* 68 (1946): 321; and, for Eteocles, my *Under the Sign of the Shield*, p. 96.

4. It is worth observing here that Thebes is the setting for yet another Dionysiac scenario in Euripides' play *Heracles Mainomenos*, where Hercules kills his wife and children (although stopping short, through Athene's intervention, of killing his father) and is himself imaged as a bacchant of Hades (cf. 892–99, 965–67, 1142).

Nevertheless in keeping to the specifics of gender that are established in each play, we can observe that despite the different
emphases, a battle is taking place on two fronts for both Eteocles
and Pentheus, one with an enemy brother and a foreign force
and one with the women inside the city who escape out of the
house, whether into public places (*Seven*) or outside the city altogether into the mountain wilds (*Bacchae*). Eteocles meets the
Theban women in the first part of the play and Pentheus finds them
in the last. Both feminine groups, albeit for different reasons, exhibit the same passionate and uncivic forms of religious worship,
and their behavior in each case triggers the intemperate reaction
from the ruler that will shift the issue of his control over them to
that of his problematic and precarious control over self.[5]

On the other hand, male antagonism to male is the central and
most dramatic element of each play and the representation of this
conflict each time calls the very notion of the self into question as it
arranges the terms as those of doubling identity. *Seven* postpones
as long as possible the confrontation of Eteocles and Polyneices,
who never even meet on stage, but whose pairing at the seventh
gate caps the extensive shield scene where Eteocles matches Theban
against Argive at each of the preceding gates. They do meet even-
tually, as the messenger reports, after Eteocles has made his exit in
order to face his brother in combat, and the opposites cancel each
other out as their identities collapse into one through their mutual
slaughter. Pentheus and Dionysus meet three times on stage in
their struggle for control over the other. But for them, of course, the
enemy doubles diverge at their widest point of difference precisely
when Pentheus comes under the power of the god, as Dionysus is
the son of Olympian Zeus and the king is the son of Echion, the
gēgenēs, the earthborn. At the same time, Dionysus works precisely
by transforming Pentheus into a double of himself.[6] He dresses the

---

5. The *Bacchae* is obvious in this regard. In *Seven Against Thebes*, however, the
matter is more subtle, since Eteocles' final response to calm the women's anxiety and
to show that he is in charge is to promise them that he will stand as the seventh
champion in the line of defenders (*Seven* 282–86). He thus prepares the way for the
confrontation with his brother, even as Pentheus will meet his double, Dionysus
(discussed below).

6. On Pentheus and Dionysus as doubles, see, first, Francis Cornford, *The Ori-
gins of Attic Comedy* (Cambridge, 1914; repr. Garden City, N.Y.: Doubleday, Anchor
Books, 1961), pp. 130–31, 183; Robert Rogers, *A Psychoanalytical Study of the Double
in Literature* (Detroit: Wayne State University Press, 1970), pp. 64–66; and René
Girard, *La Violence et le sacré* (Paris: B. Grasset, 1972), pp. 182–83. See also Charles
Segal, *Dionysiac Poetics and Euripides' Bacchae* (Princeton, N.J.: Princeton University
Press, 1982), p. 29 and passim.

king and arranges his coiffure so that in his female disguise, he, too, resembles the god in his own maenadic disguise, thereby merging his identity with that of the god and his worshippers. Moreover, it is through the power of Dionysus that Pentheus acquires the fateful capacity to see double. He sees two suns, two cities of Thebes (*Bach.* 918–19), and in his female dress, he himself is doubled, or, we might say, divided with his masculine self.

The Identity of the Self. It is time now after following all these permutations to come back to a correspondence with Oedipus himself in the light of an endemic problem in Thebes—that of the unstable arithmetic of the self. In his search for the murderer Oedipus at first can also be said to see double: he imagines that there is an other, a stranger, but discovers that the other was only a fugitive phantom of the self—that is, there was only one when he believed there might have been two. On the other hand, numbers continue to play an essential role in Sophocles' play in yet another way. As a last resort, Oedipus had pinned his hopes on the two different versions of the murder of the man at the crossroads. Killed by many, says the servant (*OT* 118–25, 842); killed by one, Oedipus knows (*OT* 811–13). The text, oddly enough, never clears up this discrepancy, but a closer inspection of the underlying issues suggests that on a more symbolic level, it need not ever do so. Once we know the identity of the slayer as the incestuous Oedipus and consider in formal terms what that implies, a literal reading of the "many versus the one" proves to have been a false signpost on the road to truth. Rather it can be construed retrospectively as yet another riddle, which is presented now in current dramatic time and to which the appropriate answer is none other than Oedipus himself. That is, Oedipus turns out to be both one and many, doubled in his role of son and father with his self-same mother and doubled as brother to the double progeny he has engendered from that single source.[7]

In the sequel to Oedipus's story, we can see that a similar logic operates for his sons by a simple reversal of terms. For Oedipus is one where the social system dictates there must be two (father, son), while the two sons he begets represent a surplus, since for son to replace father, there is need of only one. Thus significantly, Eteocles in *Seven* also evinces a curious interest in numeration.

---

7. See also Charles Segal, *Tragedy and Civilization: An Interpretation of Sophocles* (Cambridge, Mass.: Harvard University Press, 1981), pp. 215–16, who sees the implications of the "one and the many" but not its aspects as a riddle.

Naming himself as a singular (*heis*) in the first lines of the play
(*Seven* 6) with reference, as he thinks, to his position of ruler in
Thebes, he will find out that this statement is both true and false.[8]
On the political level, he is truly one among the many, since as citizens of Cadmus's city, they can invoke their autochthonous ancestry, while he is the cursed child of the cursed Oedipus. On the level
of the family, however, his identity is not singular but will finally be
doubled and linguistically fused with that of his brother: the choral
lament that follows the fatal duel repeatedly refers to the two under
the single grammatical form of the dual (*Seven* 811, 816, 863, 922,
932) and Eteocles loses his name to the pluralizing force of the
other's—*Poly-neikeis* (829–30).

The brothers collapse distinctions in yet another way, as they
take up their legacy as Oedipus's sons with regard to their father's
twofold transgression. For Oedipus himself, the patricide and incest were two separate and sequential events, each directed in turn
toward the family members of the appropriate gender. But for the
next generation, these two actions merge into one as the brothers in their passionate desire for mutual confrontation (*erōs*, 688;
himeros, 692), are radically divided against each other as hostile antagonists, but at the same time are drastically fused into one in
their reflexive and mutual fratricide.

Moreover, the quarrel between Eteocles and Polyneices ramifies
more widely the implications of Oedipus's twin actions for the
larger society as the brothers' desire to possess the father's house
and goods has nothing now to do with the desire for the biological
mother (long dead) but is rather displaced and diffused as a claim
for political hegemony. In *The Bacchae*, by contrast, the quarrel between Pentheus and Dionysus is focused precisely on who is to
have power over the women of Thebes, most especially, over the
maternal figure of Agave. This play, therefore, directly poses a confrontation between mother and son and more openly dramatizes
the dilemma of a self as a family member, divided between contradictory impulses of attraction and hostility.

What I am suggesting then in this comparison between *Seven
Against Thebes* and *The Bacchae* is that Pentheus, the child of the

---

8. On this issue, see further the discussion in my *Under the Sign of the Shield*,
pp. 37–41. In line 6, the text juxtaposes *heis* (the one) with *polus*, which in its immediate context means "much," but the phrase clearly anticipates the more general
problem of singular and plural as well as the specific force of the name Poly-neikes.

earthborn, and Eteocles, the child of an incestuous union, seem to share a kindred bond that links them together as friendly doubles of one another. They are *semblables, frères,* on the territory of Thebes, exchanging places, as it were, for their mutual elucidation. Pentheus in *The Bacchae* brings to light what remains implicit and displaced in the Oedipal struggle between Eteocles and his brother in *Seven.* The dilemma of Eteocles, on the other hand, as developed in the language and structure of *Seven,* urges us to focus on the opposite, but complementary, relations between the history of the house of Laius and the autochthonous prehistory of the city that more directly concerns Pentheus. And this in two ways. First, by identifying himself with the autochthons of the city rather than with the destiny reserved for him by his father, Eteocles looks to autochthony as the positive myth of the city's political solidarity. But fratricide, the culminating act of *Seven,* finds its model not only through its hypostasis of Oedipus's previous transgressions against the family but also through the negative aspect of autochthony that is manifested on the political level in the internecine conflict of that warrior band, the Sown Men.

Foundations: Incest and Autochthony. With autochthony, we have reached the third in the cluster of myths that are central to the representation of Thebes on the tragic stage (in addition to Dionysus and the house of Laius), a myth that brings us back a long distance from Oedipus to the very foundation of the city. Cadmus slew the dragon of Ares and sowed the crop of Spartoi from the dragon's teeth. They in turn slew one another, except for five who survived as the first autochthonous inhabitants of the city. Cadmus, for his part, married Harmonia, the daughter of Ares and Aphrodite, finally giving his own daughter Agave to Echion, one of the earthborn, and another daughter, Semele, to Olympian Zeus.

The troubles in Thebes started at the very beginning, it seems, both for the stability of the city and for that of the self, where autochthony, Dionysus, and, ultimately, Oedipus rule. Harmonia, as her name indicates, is the logical outcome of a union between the two antithetical principles of Ares and Aphrodite and serves as the idealized emblem of marriage that joins together the opposite genders. But in Thebes, Harmonia is rather a euphemistic and finally illusory hope. How can it be otherwise in a place where both War (Ares) and Love (Aphrodite) operate as illegal factors in both the city and the family, leading not to domestic or political tranquillity but to internal strife and incestuous origins?[9]

These issues, needless to say, require further discussion. For the moment, I wish only to point out that autochthony is an underlying theme in *The Bacchae* that comes to the fore when Pentheus, the son of the Spartos, falls under the power of his cousin Dionysus,[10] whereas *Seven Against Thebes*, as remarked above, invokes it as both a contrast to and a paradigm of the fratricidal combat undertaken by the sons of Oedipus. But autochthony is a far more prominent element in Euripides' far-ranging drama, *The Phoenissae*, which beyond any other extant play best exemplifies the complex interweaving of all three Theban *mythoi*.

The Phoenissae. Here in his version of the Aeschylean *Seven*, Euripides through his characters and his choral odes situates the struggle between the sons of Oedipus in the widest context of the city's history.[11] On stage he contraposes the sons of the incestuous union against Menoiceus, Creon's son, the last surviving descendant of the Spartoi, sown from the teeth of the dragon of Ares. Despite the negative evaluation of Oedipus's progeny in this play and the positive idealizing of noble Menoiceus, the two sides cannot wholly be separated, one for the family and the other for the city, since Euripides also insists on their interrelations. The sons of Oedipus and the earthborn's seed must equally meet their deaths, each expiating an anterior fault of another generation (the curse of the family, the wrath of the·dragon). Second, they are drawn together into an intimate association through the figure of Jocasta,

9. Autochthony as a myth of origins in Thebes has two stages. In the first, it has affinities with incest, given the analogy that obtains between mother and earth. In the second, it leads to violence among kin (fratricide most directly, but patricide can be included by extension). On these issues, see my discussion in *Under the Sign of the Shield*, pp. 29–36. On the relations between autochthony and incest, see now also Lowell Edmunds, who, starting from a very different viewpoint, arrives at a similar conclusion in his "The Cults and Legends of Oedipus," *Harvard Studies in Classical Philology* 85 (1981):235, and see too Jean Rudhardt, "De l'inceste à la mythologie grecque," *Revue française de psychanalyse* 46 (1982):753–57.

10. On the chiastic relations between Pentheus, the son of the earthborn, and Dionysus, the son of the Olympian, see Segal, *Tragedy and Civilization* (cited above, n. 7), pp. 180–84 and passim.

11. For an excellent discussion of *The Phoenissae* as a general overview of Theban history, see Marylin B. Arthur, "The Curse of Civilization: The Choral Odes of the *Phoenissae*," *Harvard Studies in Classical Philology* 81 (1977):163–85. The scope of this play extends far beyond the geographical boundaries of Thebes as it seeks to situate the struggle at Thebes in the most extended frame of reference. Its complexities cannot be discussed here.

who in this play is mother to her sons as well as foster mother to Menoiceus (*Phoe.* 986–89). Additionally, the play establishes yet another set of affinities by persistently making parallels between the dragon of Ares in the generation of Cadmus and the monstrous Sphinx in the generation of Oedipus.

As for Dionysus, he is included as the drama's metaphorical point of reference that shapes the underlying rhythms of the play. Dionysus has a double function as the emblem of joyous festivity in the city's life and also as the model for maddened strife. The chorus, recalling the birth of Dionysus at a promising moment in the early history of the city, at first suppress the violence of his engendering in their song (*Phoe.* 645–56). But as the pressure of events in the present increases, that latent force returns to the surface when we reach the third stasimon. At the moment when the city and sons of Oedipus prepare for deadly battle, Dionysus faces, we might say, his ambiguous opposite in Thebes in the figure of the god Ares, and the dividing line between them falters as Ares assimilates the language and gestures of Dionysiac celebration. That martial power is preparing an anti-fête of blood and war by contrast to peaceful Bacchic pleasures and yet it also converts Dionysiac elements for its own use so as to draw them into unholy alliance with the destructive forces of strife (*Phoe.* 784–800).

Even those happy pleasures, however, have their sinister side, as we learn from the prologue, in that Dionysus had a prior role to play in the misfortunes of Thebes. The god, in a sense, presided over the very begetting of Oedipus; it was at a Dionysiac revel that Laius, having indulged in too much wine, coupled with his wife and thus transgressed the prohibition of Apollo's oracle that forbade him to engender children (*Phoe.* 17–22). And if Dionysus ruled over the beginning he also proves to rule over the end of the play. For the aftermath of the battle that takes place in the drama between the enemy brothers, and more largely between Thebes and Argos, ends by transforming Antigone, the shy virginal maiden of the play's prologue, into a bacchant of corpses (*Phoe.* 1489–90). In fact, she makes her valedictory to Thebes by exchanging the happy rites of the god in whose honor she had formerly danced to take up rites of mourning and to depart for exile and ultimately her death (*Phoe.* 1753–57).

Thus Euripides' late contribution to the Theban tradition in the history of the Athenian theater draws all the various strands to-

gether and plays them off one another in ways that are distinctively
his own, but that reveal in fullest form the kindred relations of
these seemingly disparate elements in Thebes. It is a minor but significant detail in the play that Teiresias makes his predictable entry
on the Theban scene by informing us that he has come not, as is his
wont, from the nearby altars, but, strangely enough, from Athens,
where he has been procuring the success of that city in its battle
against Eumolpus and the men of Eleusis (*Phoe.* 852–57). Yet the
reason for Teiresias's curious excursion abroad is not difficult to discern, if we consider that his prophecy no longer concerns the house
of Laius but rather demands the patriotic sacrifice of Menoiceus to
save the city. This new message, we might say, is one that Teiresias
cannot bring from within the territory of Thebes. Instead, to find
his model, he must travel to Athens, where just lately the daughters of autochthonous Erechtheus have sacrificed themselves for the
common good, an event Euripides himself represented in an earlier
play.[12] Only in this way can Teiresias import a pure and disinterested
civic act into a place whose nature, no matter what proper political
sentiments its leaders at first profess, seems to preclude the kind
of noble voluntary offering for the city that Menoiceus decides
to make.

And with this important distinction, we come now to the heart
of the matter.

2.

THEBES AS THE ANTI-ATHENS

What then does Thebes as a *topos* represent for Athens on the dramatic stage in the theater of Dionysus? I propose that Thebes functions in the theater as an anti-Athens, an other place. If we say that
theater in general functions as an "other scene" where the city puts
itself and its values into question by projecting itself upon the stage
to confront the present with the past through its ancient myths,[13]
then Thebes, I suggest, is the "other scene" of the "other scene"

12. This play is *Erechtheus,* which is dated to about 423 B.C. The fragments can
be found in Colin Austin, *Nova Fragmenta Euripidea in Papyris Reperta* (Berlin: De
Gruyter, 1968), pp. 22–40.
13. See the splendid piece of Jean-Pierre Vernant, "Tensions et ambigüités dans la
tragédie grecque," in *Mythe et tragédie en Grèce ancienne* (Paris: Maspero, 1973),
pp. 25–27. Translated by Janet Lloyd in *Tragedy and Myth in Ancient Greece* (Brighton,
Sussex, and Atlantic Highlands, N.J.: Humanities Press, 1981), pp. 9–10.

that is the theater itself. Thebes, we might say, is the quintessential "other scene," as Oedipus is the paradigm of tragic man and Dionysus is the god of the theater. There Athens acts out questions crucial to the *polis*, to the self, the family, and society, but these are displaced upon a city that is imagined as the mirror opposite of Athens.[14]

The dramatic relation of Athens is twofold. First, within the theater, Athens is not the tragic space. Rather it is the scene where theater can and does escape the tragic, and where reconciliation and transformation are made possible. Thebes and Athens are, in fact, specifically contrasted to one another in several plays, such as Sophocles' *Oedipus at Colonus* and Euripides' *The Suppliant Women*, and implicitly juxtaposed in Euripides' *Heracles* when Theseus comes to lead the broken hero away to sanctuary and protection in Athens.[15] But Thebes is also the obverse side of Athens, the shadow self, we might say, of the idealized city on whose other terrain the tragic action may be pushed to its furthest limits of contradiction and impasse. As such, it also furnishes the territory for exploring the most radical implications of the tragic.

In other words, Thebes, the other, provides Athens, the self, with a place where it can play with and discharge both terror of and attraction to the irreconcilable, the inexpiable, and the unredeemable, where it can experiment with the dangerous heights of self-assertion that transgression of fixed boundaries inevitably entails. Events in Thebes and the characters who enact them both fascinate and repel the Athenian audience, finally instructing the spectators as to how their city might refrain from imitating the other's negative example. There where Thebes holds the stage, both Dionysus and Oedipus, each from opposite corners (of the "irra-

14. Dario Sabbatucci, in his *Il mito, il rito, e la storia* (Rome: Bulzoni, 1978), pp. 117–41, also argues for the position I have indicated Thebes occupies on the stage of Athens. He makes many interesting and suggestive remarks, but his general theoretical approach and his treatment of the literary texts require a far more extensive critique than space permits here. I note only that, in my opinion, his a priori scheme of *genos* and *polis* leads him astray in assessing the function of Thebes for Athens.

15. I have not included Heracles among the significant personages at Thebes because he has many other associations and never remains for long in that city. Nevertheless, the situation in *Heracles* is demonstrably appropriate to Thebes (see above, n. 5). Even in Sophocles' *The Trachiniae*, which takes place in Trachis and not in Thebes, since Heracles and his family are in exile, the Theban paradigm still seems to operate. For at the end of the drama, Heracles shocks and offends his son when he insists that Hyllus commit the two Oedipal transgressions—put an end to his father's life and marry his father's bride (*Trach.* 1204–51).

tional" and "rational") tempt the self to play roles that can only lead
to disaster. And both Dionysus and Oedipus end by confounding
identity, their own and others', establishing hopeless antitheses
and hopeless mixtures. They do this at different moments in the
mythic history of Thebes and by different dramatic means throughout the history of the Athenian theater.

The Middle Term: Argos. In this schematic structure, Argos occupies
the middle space between the two extremes that Athens and Thebes
represent. As its mythic repertory demonstrates—most notably, in
the story of the house of Atreus and the saga of the Danaids—
Argos, too, is a city of conflict, and it has erred grievously in sending the expedition of the Seven as foreign invaders against the sovereign city of Thebes. But the city, or more precisely, its characters,
can be saved—Orestes primarily at Athens and the Danaids probably in Argos itself. In *The Suppliants* of Aeschylus, the first and only
surviving play of his Danaid trilogy, we find a model king, Pelasgus, just like Theseus, and a democratic city that closely resembles
the Athenian ideal. There the Danaids slay their husbands on their
wedding night with the exception of one, Hypermestra. But there
are reasons to suppose that Argos in the last play will have fur-
nished a solution in its own city to the dilemma raised by the collective crime of the maidens. And the means most probably are not
unlike those deployed to save the Argive Orestes in the third play of
Aeschylus's other trilogy, the *Oresteia*.[16] In this last act of the house
of Atreus, Orestes, of course, is exonerated from matricide and his
redemption is ratified when Athene allows him to return as legitimate ruler in Argos (*Eum.* 754–61). Euripides never goes as far as
Aeschylus. Quite the contrary: his three plays that treat the story of
Orestes (*Electra, Iphigeneia in Tauris, Orestes*) introduce disturbing
ironies that critically challenge the validity of their Aeschylean
model. Yet all these dramas agree in one way or another that Orestes may finally be redeemed.

Argos, Athens, Thebes. *The Suppliant Women* of Euripides furnishes
the most instructive example of how the conventions of the theater

16. That is, a trial before a tribunal and the establishment of a new ritual. For a
summary of the various hypotheses, see A. F. Garvie, *Aeschylus, Supplices: Play and
Trilogy* (London: Cambridge University Press, 1969), pp. 163–233, and see also R. P.
Winnington-Ingram, "The Danaid Trilogy of Aeschylus," *Journal of Hellenic Studies*
81 (1961): 141–52.

assign to each city a specific identity as it schematically arranges a triangular relationship on stage between Athens, Thebes, and Argos. In this frankly ideological play set in the sanctuary of Demeter at Eleusis, the Argive women, together with the general Adrastus, have come as suppliants to beg the assistance of Theseus, king of Athens, in their grievance against Thebes. In the aftermath of a successful defense of their city against the expedition of the Argive Seven, the Thebans have refused to allow the mothers and wives to take up the fallen warriors for burial. In effect, Athens is being asked to risk the lives of its own citizens in a conflict with Thebes, not for some cause of its own, but to support a general humanitarian principle, which is additionally encumbered with the fact that the Argive expedition was no just enterprise. Theseus at first refuses the appeal of Adrastus, taking the opportunity to vent his righteous indignation at the misguided political conduct of this leader (e.g., *Suppl. Women* 214–49). But yielding to the intervention of his mother, Aithra, who, responding to the women's desperate sorrow, speaks in the name of compassion and a higher political justice, the Athenian king agrees to honor the request of the repentant Adrastus to procure the burial of the Argive dead, even at the cost of armed battle that is to follow. Adrastus may be admonished and admit the error of his ways and be finally linked, therefore, to the side of the Athenians. Indeed, the rapprochement is successful enough to allow him the right to speak like an Athenian over the Argive dead, in the form of miniature *epitaphioi*, those funeral orations normally delivered annually over Athenians who died nobly for their country in battle.[17] But the contrast between Athens and Thebes is posed at its most extreme. There is an implicit reversal of the Theban terms we have come to recognize, in that Athens respects and heeds the independent ritual activity of the women despite the irregularity of a suppliant rite at this particular altar, and in that the Athenian king can accept the counsel of a woman and grant his mother a mediating function denied to women in Thebes, as especially in the case of Jocasta in *The Phoenissae*. Explicitly, however, Thebes, as represented on stage through its herald, takes on its most negative colors, going so far as

17. These orations are not without their ironies, and scholars are still sharply divided as to their interpretation. For the most recent discussion with bibliography, see Nicole Loraux, *L'Invention d'Athènes* (Paris and The Hague: Mouton, 1981), pp. 107–8.

to launch an open attack against Athenian democracy. Whatever suggestive ironies this critique may include, Thebes is shown as beyond redemption, offering a bleak and bitter portrait of the tyrant and the tyrannical city, which respects no laws or institutions and knows only violence and wrath (*Suppl. Women* 399–597).

Mapping the Territory of Thebes: Self and Society. Looking back now over this brief survey, we might characterize Thebes as the place either of imprisonment or exile, as the city of negation and death. There Oedipus, after all his arithmetic of the one and the many, is addressed by the chorus as self-cancelling, equal to nothing (*OT* 1186–88). In his parallel story in *Antigone*, Creon similarly discovers for himself that he is no longer a regent, no longer a self, but a nothing (*Ant.* 1321). And, perhaps on the most literal level, Pentheus demonstrates the furthest stages of the deconstruction of the self through the physical *sparagmos* he undergoes. There are survivors but no heirs. Creon remains alone in the city at the end of *Antigone*, his son, his wife, and Antigone, the last of the line of Oedipus, all gone. Cadmus and Agave leave together at the close of *The Bacchae*, Oedipus and Antigone at the end of *The Phoenissae*. Oedipus, however, is the only one who can be redeemed—but only in Athens and through his conscious choosing of Athens over Thebes. Even so, let us remember how late is the moment of his salvation—only and properly at the point of his crossing from life into death.

In the version of the oracle given to Laius in Aeschylus, the problem of Oedipus is posed as a choice between the fate of the ruling dynasty and that of the city. "Dying without issue," Apollo declared, "you will save the city" (*Seven* 745–49). This prophecy only comes to fulfillment in the third generation, with the death of the two brothers in *Seven* and the final expulsion of Oedipus and Antigone at the end of *The Phoenissae* (along with the last of the descendants of the Sown Men, who, we might say, inherits a version of that prophecy to Laius). When all these plays conclude, the outer walls of Thebes are still standing and the foreign enemy is invariably beaten back or driven out. In *The Bacchae*, Dionysus himself does not remain, but, as he tells us in the prologue, will continue his journey to other cities in order to reveal his rites (*Bach.* 48–50). If these are the terms on which the city continues to be rescued, we are entitled to ask for what purpose and for whom? And, in our context, we might well reply: for Athens and its tragic stage. It is essential for Athens that Thebes remain intact as a theatrical enclosure so that within its closed confines yet another play may be staged that reenacts in some way these same intricate and inextricable conflicts that can never be resolved.

For the tragic poets Thebes represents the paradigm of the closed system that vigorously protects its psychological, social, and political boundaries, even as its towering walls and circular ramparts close off and protect its physical space. Once we grasp the import of autochthony and incest as the underlying patterns at Thebes, we can diagnose the malaise of this city, which has no means of establishing a viable system of relations and differences, either within the city or without, or between the self and any other. Unable to incorporate outsiders into its system and locked into the priority of blood relations of the *genos*, Thebes endlessly shuttles between the extremes of rigid inclusions and exclusions on the one hand and radical confusions of difference on the other. Eteocles (and Pentheus), for example, are intent on not letting the women *inside* come outside[18] but fail in their attempts, and Dionysus and Polyneices are the outsiders who press their claim to being insiders, with destructive results. The most conspicuous symptom of this maladaptive system is the problem of marriage in this city, the institution that normally regulates relations between non-kin and circulates women as signs to be exchanged between men. When it is not refused altogether (as by Antigone in her play or Eteocles in his), marriage brings danger from two different directions, either as excessive endogamy in the form of incest or as its contrary, when Polyneices' search for a bride *outside*—too far from home—instigates the expedition of the Argive Seven against his native city.

Autochthony, as the political myth of collective solidarity, and incest in the domestic domain might suggest a fundamental cleavage between city and family. And in one sense they do. In *Seven Against Thebes*, a fundamental opposition opens up between Eteocles and the true autochthonous defenders who found and anchor the system of Thebes in the first triad of champions (Melanippus, Megareus). In *The Phoenissae*, the division is even sharper. Menoiceus must choose to die for the city without the knowledge of his father, who, despite Teiresias's unequivocal assertion of its political neces-

18. Helen Bacon in "The Shield of Eteocles," *Arion* 3 (1964):27–38, has excellent remarks on this topic.

sity, has refused to sacrifice his son.[19] But a hidden analogy connects family and city, since each reproductive model (autochthony, incest) looks back to a single undifferentiated origin and each holds out the ideal of a self-refere.itial autonomy.

A typical Theban scenario shows us a king who at first governs, as he imagines, wholly in the city's interests, relying solely on his powers of reason and judgment to maintain civic order. But the pressure of events reveals him as one who has confused the relationship between ruler and city, identifying the state, in fact, with himself. In each case, the true imperative is the desire to rule, to exercise single hegemony over others and to claim all power for himself.[20] Yet once confronted with the limitations he has never acknowledged, this ruler discovers that he cannot rule himself, cannot maintain an unequivocal identity. And in this surrender to hidden constraints, he must surrender the political kingship he has craved. That Thebes is the paradigmatic home of tyrants, as even Oedipus is liable to become when at home, can be attributed perhaps to the fact that incest and patricide are seen as the typical tyrannical crimes (cf. Plato *Rep.* 9.571b4–d3).[21] But the desire on the political level to rule alone in autonomy is also equivalent in the family domain to the desire for an autonomous self-engendering, which the acts of patricide and incest imply. Such a desire finally crosses the last boundary in demanding equivalence for the self

19. One must beware, however, of treating autochthony as a unitary phenomenon, since it can take many different forms in different locales. Athens's comparable myth follows very different lines and, unlike the Theban version of the Sown Men, does not include the ingredients for internal strife among its inhabitants or the same equation with incest. On Athens's myth see particularly J. J. Peradotto "Oedipus and Erichthonius: Some Observations on Paradigmatic and Syntagmatic Order," *Arethusa* 10 (1977):85–101, and Nicole Loraux, "L'Autochtonie: Une topique athénienne," in *Les Enfants d'Athéna* (Paris: Maspero, 1981), pp. 35–73. On the political implications of the Theban myth, see Zoë Petre, "Thèmes dominants et attitudes politiques dans *les Sept contre Thèbes* d'Eschyle," *Studii classici* 13 (1971):15–28.

20. The desire for *kratos* and *archē* is a prominent motif in every Theban play. Both Oedipus in *OT* (628–30) and Creon in *Antigone* (733–39) are brought to the point where they openly declare that they must rule at any cost and that the city belongs, in fact, to the ruler. Creon in *OT* stresses in his argument with Oedipus the precise opposite, that he has no desire to rule and is content to wield only informal power (*OT* 583–602). But once he comes to the regency in Thebes, after the sons of Oedipus both die in their bid for power, he offers the same rationale in his argument with Haemon. Although Creon's play precedes that of Oedipus in the Sophoclean corpus, the point is that whoever fills the role of king (or regent) succumbs to the same political error.

21. The phrasing of Eteocles' rebuke to the unruly women in *Seven* is very suggestive in this regard: Obedience to rule (*Peitharchia*) is Good Luck's *mother* (*tēs eupraxias mētēr*), *wedded* to Salvation (*gynē Sōtēros*), they say (*Seven* 224–25). The son of Oedipus says more than he knows.

with the gods and taking their power for its own. Thebes therefore shows us the self playing for the highest stakes, only to succumb inevitably to the triple force of the restrictions that *polis*, family, and gods impose. *The Bacchae*, which best represents the workings of the tragic process, since there the god of the theater is an actor in his own drama, also most overtly represents the way these three elements are intertwined. For there, in the conflict between Dionysus and Pentheus, the religious, political, and familial issues all unequivocally converge at the same point. Yet all the Theban dramas offer their own distinctive but comparable variations on the same set of themes.

3.
THE ETERNAL RETURN

Antigone. From its breakdown of all these differences that result from the complex interplay of incest, autochthony, patricide/fratricide, and tyranny, Thebes bestows a continuing legacy upon all the characters in its city who predictably act out their allotted roles. Sophocles' *Antigone* provides an excellent case in point, since Creon himself, a collateral and secondary member of the dynasty, has not directly participated in the muddled and accursed history of the family of Laius. Yet he and Antigone, the two antagonists of the play, divide between them the marked features of the Oedipal family, both masculine and feminine.

Antigone, on the one hand, proves her lineage as her father's daughter (cf. *Ant.* 471). By refusing to accept differentiation between the two brothers, one who was loyal to the city and the other who was not, she manifests in a feminine version that Oedipal equalization of everything that is one's own, and insists on the absolute principle of family union even, and especially, in death. Creon, for his part, looks back most of all to Oedipus's son Eteocles in Aeschylus's *Seven Against Thebes* and continues in his own drama to play out yet another version of the self-destructive impulses of the very family to whose place he has succeeded. He, too, insists on rigid antitheses and lives by military standards of absolute obedience to the city, only to find, like Eteocles, that the balance will shift to his detriment from the public to the private sphere. Taking over in Thebes after the death of Eteocles, he only repeats, now on different grounds, the patterns both of Oedipus's children and of Oedipus himself. For the women of the chorus whom Eteocles had tried to suppress in *Seven Against Thebes,* Creon substitutes the single figure of Antigone. He also renews the Oedipal hostility between kin in his conflict with Antigone and with Haemon, the child in his immediate family. Within the compass of the dramatic time of the play, events seem to echo (or anticipate) different moments in Sophocles' later treatment of Oedipus's story, whose features, however, are already given by the myth. Creon tempts his son to repeat Oedipus's patricidal crime against his father and drives his wife, Eurydice, to imitate Jocasta's solution of suicide. Creon, in his own right, we might say, paradoxically also insists on the absolute unity of the family, denying to any of its members the right to differ from himself, denying Haemon in fact the right to make the generational passage into adulthood. He thereby doubles the disaster by simultaneously cancelling out the future of the family of Oedipus as well as that of his own.[22]

In his initial zeal to distinguish conclusively between friend and foe, insider and outsider,[23] Creon first blurs distinctions between family and city by demanding from his son the obedience due to ruler from subject (*Ant.* 659–78). But in the process, he also proves to confound the most significant difference of all—namely, that between life and death—when he entombs Antigone alive and keeps the dead unburied above the earth (cf. *Ant.* 1068–71). When he reverses his previous position on the burial of Polyneices after the visit of Teiresias, he moves too far in the other direction (that is, by attending now first to the dead [Polyneices] before the living [Antigone]), and thereby brings the cumulative disaster upon himself (*Ant.* 1196–1205). In initially undervaluing the meaning of death, he proves to undervalue the meaning of life. Hence Creon brings death to those around him and himself remains, as the messenger says, no longer truly alive, but only a breathing corpse (*Ant.* 1166–67).[24]

But there is more, and here the particular issues raised by *An-*

22. See also the fine discussion of Segal, *Tragedy and Civilization* (cited above, n. 7), pp. 184–90. He does not, however, note the close parallels with Aeschylus's *Seven Against Thebes.*

23. The problem that the burial of Polyneices poses is how to incorporate an insider who has made himself an outsider to the community.

24. On Creon's relation to death and its meanings, see Charles Segal, "Sophocles' Praise of Man and the Conflicts of the *Antigone*," repr. in *Sophocles: A Collection of Critical Essays,* edited by T. Woodard (Englewood Cliffs, N.J.: Prentice-Hall, 1966), p. 83. In general, see the very useful work of Vincent Rosivach, "The Two Worlds of the *Antigone*," *Illinois Classical Studies* 4 (1979):16–26.

tigone exemplify in clearest form another and wider aspect of the distinctive situation in Thebes. Creon's refusal to honor the rights of the dead offends against the entire cultural order, against the gods as well as against persons and the collective of the city.[25] But it can also be construed as an offense against time itself. Both in refusing to bury the dead and then in giving temporal priority to the dead Polyneices over the living Antigone, Creon has failed to observe the critical distinction that separates the dead from the living precisely by an irreversible point on the line of time that marks the moment of their demise.

To Antigone, *death* is the timeless eternity, the absolute principle to which she gives her undivided allegiance, and she therefore privileges it over mortal life since she understands the perfected meaning of death (*Ant.* 74–76), even to the extent of going to meet it before her time. The opposite holds true for Creon. Living, as he thinks, in the all-absorbing present of the political moment, he takes a stand that paradoxically suggests that mortal life has no finitude. Or better, we might say that for Creon, life and death comprise an uninterrupted continuum by which principle the unrelenting hostility that existed during life is prolonged indefinitely in death.

The issue of burial is central to Thebes, whether here in *Antigone* or in *The Suppliant Women* of Euripides or, of course, in *Oedipus at Colonus*. It is the focal point at which the two coordinates of space and time converge and whose symbolic value refers us back to the critical problems raised by incest and autochthony. The dead are buried outside the city; they are also buried beneath the earth. Thus *inside* and *outside, above* and *below,* are factors that come to determine the most important boundary of all, that between *before* and *after.* Death in this city partakes of both dimensions, as it must always face both ways—as an end, but also as a return, even as Antigone's longing for death before her time is also a regression back to the hidden sources of the family from which she springs.

The conclusion to *Antigone* makes it clear that no future time opens out in Thebes. *Genos* (family) and *gonē* (generation) have become a contradiction in terms, although they share the same root.

---

25. Creon's refusal of funerary rites to the dead enemy/traitor had its legal precedents in contemporary Athenian practice. But literary precedents, such as the end of the *Iliad* and, even more, Sophocles' own play *Ajax,* show that such a narrow political outlook cannot prevail within the larger scheme of things.

The city's young have made a marriage only in death; Antigone's name has been appropriately glossed as "antigeneration." [26] Creon's undervaluation of death and Antigone's parallel overvaluation of it both direct our attention to the most recurrent and most negative feature of Thebes, which manifests itself in the dimension of time.

Repeating the Past. Thebes is opposed to time as it passes through subsequent phases that ordinarily would lead to change, reconciliation, development, and transformation, whether through a genetic model or through the formation of new institutions in the city. In Thebes the linear advance of the narrative events turns out in the end to be fundamentally circular, as closed back upon itself as the circular walls that are the city's most distinctive architectural feature in space. Time in Thebes returns always and again to its point of departure, since it can never generate new structures and new progeny that can escape the paradigmatic patterns of the beginning. What this means is that Thebes is a place where the past inevitably rules, continually repeating and renewing itself so that each new generation, each new episode in the story, looks backward to its ruin even as it offers a new variation on the theme. This is the city, after all, where Laius was bidden to die without issue, a prophecy that indeed finally comes to pass in the third generation.

From this perspective, we may say that Thebes is a world that obeys the law of the Eternal Return in contrast to one where history can unfold into differential narrative for the future, a history that is supported by the paradigm of its founding myths as a point of origin but is not subject to the tyranny of their domination over all its representative figures and events. The autocratic prestige of both autochthony and incest in Thebes claims power over each character in turn. More specifically, failure to inaugurate a viable line of time for the individual actor produces two negative patterns for the self—doubling of one figure with another at the same moment of time, whether father and son or brother and brother, and compulsive repetition of actions from past time.

There are many different dimensions in which this phenomenon manifests itself in Thebes. We can point here only to a small repre-

---

26. See Seth Benardete, "A Reading of Sophocles' *Antigone:* I," *Interpretation* 4 (1975):156: "Her name, whose meaning—'generated in place of another'—bears witness to success, proves to mean 'antigeneration.'" See also his further discussion, pp. 156–57.

sentative selection. First, in the house of Cadmus, the regressive mode is made literal at the end of *The Bacchae*. Pentheus, as we have seen, both returns to the mother when he makes his way to the mountains where the maenads are, and simultaneously discovers his true identity as the son of the autochthon, Echion. But Dionysus, as the deus ex machina at the end of the play, goes still further in his predictions for the future by sending Cadmus and his wife back to the beginning, or, more accurately, to a stage before the beginning. They are to regress back to a state and a form that preceded the very foundation of the city. In fact, they will be turned into serpents like the serpent of Ares whom Cadmus slew in order to establish Thebes, sowing the dragon's teeth from which the autochthons sprang. And Cadmus, the Phoenician and bringer of culture, will revert back to the negative side of his barbarian origins, since he is destined in the future to bring a foreign army to invade Greek territory (*Bach.* 1330–37). In *The Phoenissae*, the dragon of Ares lives in still another more dramatic way, since Ares' wrath over the blood of his dragon had never been put to rest, but returns to demand the sacrifice of the last surviving autochthon, whose blood must be shed in turn in order to expiate the primordial crime of the city (*Phoe.* 930–44).[27] In this play, too, it is the chorus, consisting of Phoenician maidens who have come from the ancestral home of Cadmus, that takes us back to a time before Thebes even existed.

But more significant still are the workings of time for the house of Laius, where, given the dominant and continuing role of oracles in its history, the future can and must fulfill an end already predicted in the past. Repetition and reenactment for the sons of Oedipus will bring them to the very effacement of identity in their doubling, back to a time before the beginning and the foundation of the family, which was under the sign of negation at its very inception. Thus every new *logos* in Thebes proves in one way or another to be yet another version of the *archaios logos*.

On the narrative level, the structure of Sophocles' *Oedipus Tyran-*

27. Strictly speaking, Creon is the last of the pure autochthons (*Phoe.* 942–43), and he has two sons, Menoiceus and Haemon. Menoiceus is chosen because Haemon is already betrothed to Antigone and hence no longer an *ëitheos*, the male equivalent of *parthenos*. (*parthenos* = virgin girl, normally the preferred sacrificial victim.) By the end of the play, however, when Antigone refuses to consider marriage with Haemon but rather opts for both burying her brother, Polyneices, and exile with her father (*Phoe.* 1672–82), the future of Haemon, whose existence in the theater depends entirely on Antigone, seems very dim.

nos itself brilliantly demonstrates the general principle. Every advance that Oedipus makes toward uncovering the identity of Laius's murderer, every new figure who enters upon the stage in the forward movement of the plot only leads him further back in a retrograde direction, until, with the last and critical entry of the old herdsman, he returns to the very moment of his birth as the infant with the pierced feet who was given over to that very herdsman to carry off to Mount Cithaeron. With this revelation of his origins, Oedipus simultaneously realizes another regression—namely, that he had returned to seed the mother's womb from which he was engendered. Is not incest, after all, the quintessential act of return? Is not incest the paradigmatic act that destroys time by collapsing the necessary temporal distinctions between generations?

From this point of view, the riddle of the Sphinx can be read in two ways. On the one hand, the riddle suppresses the dimension of time, since the enigma resides in the fact that it makes synchronic the three phases of human life by uniting them under the single form (or voice) that is Man. As such, Oedipus's unique ability on the intellectual level to solve the riddle is commensurate on the familial level with his singular acts of patricide and incest. On the other hand, the full interpretation of the riddle would seem to require that Man must properly be defined in his diachronic dimension. Man is to be measured by the sum total of his life, which can only be known as he passes through time. Hence, each of his multiple *aspects* (four-footed, two-footed, and three-footed) will be construed as a sequential phase of orderly human development.[28] For Oedipus at Thebes, time is out of joint, not only because he has effaced generational difference, but because his act of reversing time in returning to seed the womb from which he was born is predicated on the earlier act of patricide that speeded up the temporal process by giving him his father's place too soon.

City of Myth vs. City of History.   Oedipus at Colonus. Let us now look back to consider again the question that in good Theban fashion returns us to the beginning of this essay: why can Oedipus find a last resting place in Athens and what is the significance of his re-

---

28. For a discussion of these two aspects that the riddle can suggest, see also J.-P. Vernant, "From Oedipus to Periander: Lameness, Tyranny, Incest in Legend and History," *Arethusa* 15 (1982) [*Texts and Contexts: American Classical Studies in Honor of J.-P. Vernant*]: 24–26.

fusal to return, as earlier tradition would have it, to Thebes? The answer to the first part of the question can be phrased in spatial terms as marking the fundamental, even defining, difference between the two cities, since Athens represents itself on more than one occasion as capable of incorporating the outsider into its midst. But the moment at which Oedipus arrives at his new destination and the ways in which he must win acceptance invite us to focus here on the issue of time. Thus we might answer the second part of the question by proposing the following: Oedipus has finally discovered time as process because he has now lived sequentially through all the terms of the riddle.

In the act of self-blinding, as many have observed, Oedipus has prematurely aged himself. He has entered upon the third stage of life before his time and must go forth into the world on "three feet." Oedipus's act of self-mutilation therefore continues to accelerate the pace he has forced upon the temporal process as I outlined it above. At the same time, the very nature of the existence he has thereby fashioned for himself insures that henceforth he will walk slowly for a long time, too long, as he journeys through the rest of his life. Moreover, wandering on foot, to which exile now condemns him, means that each day he must again and yet again translate the metaphor of his existence into literal steps on his journey.

But in *Oedipus at Colonus*, his situation is finally commensurate with his chronological age. He has caught up with himself, we might say, and the stories he can tell about past, present, and future are made contingent on his own extended experience with time as his teacher and constant companion (*OC* 7).[29] His previous acts made the son structurally equivalent to his father and the sons structurally equivalent to himself. But all concerned have also been

29. Imagery of the wanderer and the road is of central importance in the play, which ends, we may recall, with Oedipus's last journey into the grove of the Furies. See Helen Bacon, "Woman's Two Faces: Sophocles' View of the Tragedy of Oedipus and his Family," in *Science and Psychoanalysis: Decennial Memorial Volume* (New York: 1966), pp. 10–24, and see the further discussion of Segal, *Tragedy and Civilization* (cited above, n. 7), pp. 365–69, 402, 406, who integrates the images into the structure of the drama. Edmunds, "Cults and Legends of Oedipus" (cited above, n. 9) makes the interesting suggestion that the wandering is a sign of Oedipus's status as a revenant, and his arguments are convincing (pp. 229–31). As a motif in Sophocles' play, wandering is integrally connected to the representation of Oedipus's career. It is worth noting that the Sphinx (and the riddle) is never mentioned during the play (unlike in *The Phoenissae*, where it receives remarkable emphasis) despite the appropriateness of its recall now in the context of Oedipus's interpretative gifts. The terms of the riddle require no exposition, however, since Oedipus himself acts them out.

individual actors in their own stories along the narrative line of the family's history. This means that Oedipus can now profit from a temporal perspective that marks his mediate (and now differential) position as the son of his father and the father of his sons. Thus in this late and novel play by the aged poet concerning his now aged hero, which concludes with the conclusion of its protagonist's life, the question of time is of the essence. Bringing Oedipus back on stage allows him to assume a double retrospective—first, as a fictional character who reviews and reevaluates the events of his own life, and second, as one who does so through the dramatic tradition that precedes him, which includes all three models—Thebes, Athens, and Argos—and whose varied echoes resonate at different levels throughout the play.

On the one hand, Oedipus seems to repeat the ancient patterns. He trespasses again, as has been observed, on forbidden female spaces,[30] this time in the sacred grove of the Furies, and the fact that he is admitted to the city but chooses to remain on its borders confirms the irreducible ambiguity of his status.[31] He also seems to continue the two original impulses to excessive violence and excessive intimacy in his relations with his kin, angrily cursing his sons and just as tenderly embracing his daughters. Moreover, the fratricidal destiny he is led to predict for his sons will ratify the traditional conclusion to the story of the house of Laius. These repetitions of acts and attitudes in a play that is haunted by the past reconfirm the essential identity of Oedipus and maintain the obdurate constancy of a willful self whose power, after death, will bring a *kerdos*, a gain to the community that receives him. But enacted on a different territory at a different time, these repetitions also indicate transformations.

More particularly, the specific change of venue is essential. For only in Athens is Oedipus, the paradigm of tragic man,[32] ideally situated to confront and resolve the tragic problematic of time that his

30. See Cedric Whitman, *Sophocles: A Study of Heroic Humanism* (Cambridge, Mass.: Harvard University Press, 1951), p. 200; Bacon, "Woman's Two Faces" (cited above, n. 29), pp. 17–18; and Barbara Lefcowitz, "The Inviolate Grove," *Literature and Psychology* 17 (1967):78–86.

31. On the significance of Oedipus's preference for the "marginal space of the grove" over "the ruler's palace," see Segal, "Tragedy and Civilization" (cited above, n. 7), p. 381.

32. The chorus in the *OT*, we may recall, address Oedipus as their *paradeigma* of mortal men (1163); on this point, see Bernard Knox, *The Heroic Temper* (Berkeley and Los Angeles: University of California Press, 1964), pp. 146–47.

story exemplifies. That is, how is one to establish relations between old and new, same and different, constancy and change, and, even more broadly, between tradition and innovation? This feat Theban Oedipus can accomplish on his own terms now that he has found his way to Colonus. When Oedipus solved the riddle the first time, he invoked a capacity for abstract intellection that led him only to erase distinctions in such a way that he became an anomalous riddle himself. Now time, which has brought his wanderings to an end in Athens, has also brought him to establish critical distinctions in his own life on the basis of what he has undergone. Now, from his vantage point of knowledge and experience, he can confidently reinterpret the past and evaluate present and future—but only through creative interplay with what Athens represents.

To this end, the verdict he brings in upon himself of "not guilty" by reason of self-defense and ignorance of the stranger's identity modifies his own continuing sense of pollution without dismissing it altogether (*OC* 270–74, 505–58, 969–99). In effect, he has evolved a set of juridical principles that distinguish between legal and religious responsibility and between act and intention, appropriately voicing these on Attic land. For Oedipus has entered into the frame of reference that in the last play of Aeschylus's *Oresteia* had provided an escape within the city from the endless repetition of the past by establishing the authority of a law court that judges each case on its particulars.[33] But what in *The Eumenides* required the elaborate apparatus of the gods' intervention is won here by Oedipus himself as a result of his objective experience. In this sense, we might say that he finds his way to Colonus precisely because the proper moment has arrived, a moment in which, as Oedipus's interpretation of the new oracles tells us, the gods also concur. Now is the time when this figure, who best embodies the combination of will, passion, intellect, and the urge to autonomy that always proves so destructive to rulers at Thebes, can demonstrate that on his own initiative he has already shifted the paradigm for himself from Thebes to Athens.

33. The last time Oedipus defends himself, the Areopagus is specifically mentioned (*OC* 947–49). Many have, of course, noticed the significance of the *Oresteia* as an important influence in *Oedipus at Colonus* (although none in any systematic way nor with regard to the differing structures of Athens and Thebes). See the discussions of R. P. Winnington-Ingram, "A Religious Function of Greek Tragedy: A Study in the *Oedipus Coloneus* and the Oresteia," *Journal of Hellenic Studies* 74 (1954): 16–24, and *Sophocles: An Interpretation* (Cambridge: Cambridge University Press, 1980), pp. 264–78 and 324–26.

In creating his own destiny on his own terms, he does far more
than follow in the footsteps of Argive Orestes, who preceded him.
Rather, where Oedipus is, the question must inevitably turn on
power (*kratos*) over self and over others, and this power the play
now vindicates in a number of different ways. First, the drama
allows Oedipus the right not only to defend but to judge himself as
well as others. Second, it specifies as the determining factor in
Oedipus's decision about his future the right he claims to retain
control over his own body. These are the grounds, in fact, on which
he can resist returning to Thebes precisely because there others will
exercise control over him. And finally, the play justifies this demand for power over the self by investing that self with a perennial
power that Oedipus can transmit for all time to the city that will
possess his body and burial place.[34]

This power will be a political asset for the city in which, as it
turns out, Oedipus finds a permanent home, but Oedipus's transformation into a cult hero at Colonus is not achieved, as critics
often suggest, through his renouncing the *genos*. It is true that he
repudiates his sons, going so far as to declare that Polyneices has
no father (*apatōr; OC* 1383), and he bars his daughters from their
proper familial function of attending to his burial rites. Indeed, his
new home in Attica and his new status in cult, signified by the
mysterious manner of his passing, separates him from the *genos* he
has doomed to extinction in Thebes. But he by no means abjures
the principle of the *genos* as a category. Quite the contrary. Such a
strategy would only replicate the destructive policy in Thebes of
choosing either the *polis* or the *genos* to the exclusion of the other or
confusing the separate domains of the two, as both Creon and Polyneices do in their desire to use the *genos* for furthering their ambitions in the *polis*.

On the one hand, Oedipus upholds the archaic law of the family,
and, in his paternal role, insists on laying down the law of the father that decrees that children return their *trophē*, the price of their

34. References to *kratos* are numerous: *OC* 392, 399–400, 404–5, 408, 644, 646,
1207, 1332, 1380–81. The concern with *kratos* is characteristic of Sophoclean drama,
which concentrates on the self-definition of the tragic hero. It can be said of all his
principal figures that "they will not be ruled, no one shall have power over them, or
treat them as a slave, they are free" (Knox, *Heroic Temper* [cited above, n. 32], p. 40).
But in Thebes, in Sophocles as elsewhere (as, e.g., in *Seven Against Thebes*), the
matter is more specific. The issue of *kratos* is both political and individual, power
over others and power over the self (as discussed earlier). See also the discussion in
Winnington-Ingram, *Sophocles* (cited above, n. 33), p. 251, who correctly sees the
connections of Oedipus's *kratos* with the theme in *OT*; and see the remarks of Segal,
Tragedy and Civilization (cited above, n. 7), p. 386.

nurture, to their parents. The curse itself for the neglect of that *trophē* also belongs to the past: it has an essential role to play in the traditional destiny of Oedipus's sons and, more generally, is allied with the archaic power of the Erinyes. On the other hand, there is an important parallel between the new distinctions Oedipus has made between absolute guilt and contingent circumstances in his own case, and these principles he now applies to the larger question of the family. The *genos* is no longer an inviolable and indivisible unity, as Antigone continues to believe (e.g., *OC* 1181–91). It is first of all a lived relation among its members of shared reciprocities and obligations, so that entitlement to its privileges depends upon actions each individual knowingly and voluntarily undertakes. Thus Oedipus reserves his love for the daughters who have tended him in spite of the social conventions that would have them stay safely at home and repudiates his sons who have intentionally behaved contrary to family rules in refusing the nurture they owe to their father (*OC* 337–60, 421–44).

In this sense, the focus on *trophē* as a given element of the myth serves a double function. Paradoxically *trophē* both joins with and separates itself from the inherited curse on the family. As connected with the curse, the offense against *trophē* is yet another manifestation of a recurrent feature in the family of Oedipus, which revolves around the continuing treatment of kin as non-kin. As such, the issue of *trophē* bears implications for the self of a collective familial *physis* that predetermines the behavior of each actor. But if we consider that *trophē* in itself concerns not the circumstances of birth but rather the continuing process of nurture, then *trophē* furnishes the appropriate motivation by which to hold the individual responsible for conduct that is based on deliberate and conscious choices.

The structure of the second part of the play confirms the new orientation that Oedipus has brought to the old features of the myth, and hence to the general question of the family, since it postpones the father's definitive curse upon his sons until the hostilities between the brothers have already begun and Polyneices himself arrives upon the scene to reveal himself in person before his father and the spectators.[35] As a younger doublet of his father, the sup-

---

35. I agree here with those who read Oedipus's curse in this scene as the definitive and formal bestowal of the curse. See especially, Winnington-Ingram, *Sophocles* (cited above, n. 33), n. 49 and pp. 266–74. We, of course, know more than Polyneices and so read the earlier cues as echoes rather than previews.

pliant and exile, Polyneices, too, has the opportunity to review the past. In his case, retrospection has led him to regret his earlier treatment of his father. But his true purpose in enlisting his father's assistance so as to win political power from his brother undercuts his sincerity[36] and more generally demonstrates how fully he subscribes to the typical terms that operate at Thebes with regard to the interrelations between *genos* and *polis*. It is significant, too, that his rhetorical strategy for persuading his father to join him involves an appeal to their common experience, since beyond its general appropriateness as a tactic of persuasion, it reminds us how characteristic it is for a child of Theban Oedipus to stress the sameness between son and father without regard for their differences. This strategy fails, not only because Polyneices is too late—his father is no longer either a suppliant or an exile[37]—but because it runs exactly counter to how Oedipus now treats relations within the family. His task is to make distinctions rather than efface them and he does so between his sons and daughters of the same generation and, above all, between himself and his sons.[38]

In Oedipus's unrelenting anger at his sons, critics have seen a parallel between him and the Erinyes in *The Eumenides*, and one scholar, in fact, has called him an "unpersuaded Erinys."[39] But we are faced here with an "unpersuasive" Polyneices, who, unlike Orestes in the counterpart of this scene, shows us he cannot win

36. The authenticity of Polyneices' regret is much disputed (as is the interpretation of the scene itself). Here I would remark only that Polyneices' statement to Antigone that he will not tell the Argive army the truth about his father's curse (on the grounds that one does not report ill tidings; *OC* 1429–30) does nothing to enhance our opinion of his general integrity.

37. On this point, see Winnington-Ingram, *Sophocles* (cited above, n. 33), p. 277. For the interrelation between the two suppliant scenes (Oedipus, Polyneices) and its importance for the structure of the drama, see Peter Burian, "Suppliant and Savior: *Oedipus at Colonus*," *Phoenix* 28 (1974):408–29.

38. The fact that Theseus grants acceptance to Oedipus on the grounds of their common experience as strangers and exiles and as more generally sharing the common human condition (*OC* 562–68) while Oedipus refuses Polyneices' similar plea (*OC* 1335–39) has often been noted, either to Oedipus's discredit or with the observation of his new daimonic power: "Oedipus' curse stands outside the boundaries of ordinary moral judgment," says Burian ("Suppliant and Savior" [cited above, n. 37], p. 427). Without entering into a larger discussion here on the complementary, but contrasting, roles of Oedipus and Theseus, let me simply point out the significance of Oedipus's shift from the more universal principle established by Theseus to the emphasis he lays on knowledge and intention. In this regard, we might contrast Artemis's absolution of Theseus at the end of Euripides' *Hippolytus*: "You appear in my eyes to be base . . . but as far as your *hamartia* is concerned, your ignorance [*to mē eidenai*] releases you completely [*ekluei*] from the charge" (1320, 1334–35).

39. Winnington-Ingram, *Sophocles* (cited in n. 33 above), p. 275. Cf. also George Gellie, *Sophocles: A Reading* (Melbourne: Melbourne University Press, 1972), p. 168.

exoneration from the faults of the past. Quite the contrary, he is only driven to repeat it. There is, in fact, a curious inversion that operates between the two filial representatives. The gravity of Orestes' act in slaying his mother is *diminished* and is made expiable precisely through the arguments that make the mother no blood kin to him. Conversely, Polyneices' offense in neglecting his father's *trophē* is *magnified* into the charge of patricide (*OC* 1361), thereby providing Oedipus with the grounds for declaring that his sons are no longer kin to him (*OC* 1369, 1383).[40]

If Oedipus therefore transcends the family, as he must, of course, as an outsider in Athens, he also defends it while importing into it juridical evaluations that belong to the city. In this he combines in himself the opposing roles of *both* Apollo/Athene and the Furies, his divine counterparts in *The Eumenides*.[41] Like the Olympians, he lowers the prestige of blood ties as an inalienable bond and subjects the family to a law outside itself. And if, like the Furies, he upholds the law of the family for his sons, he does so, however, on the same judicial basis by which he abrogates it for his own act of patricide. Finally, he also follows the next phase of the Aeschylean pattern by following the path that leads to the grove of the Eumenides, for like those Erinyes, Oedipus, too, will transfer his power to bless and to curse from the sphere of the family to that of the city. In demonstrating his capacity for judgment in the domain of the family, Oedipus therefore qualifies himself to gain a place as an adopted stranger who will protect the city, since he will distinguish for the future between insider and outsider on the basis of particular actions and intentions. Thus the city and the family interpenetrate, each offering a model to the other, and each finding their terms of interaction through Oedipus himself.[42]

40. From this perspective, we may also recall the arguments in *The Eumenides* claiming that the father is the only true parent of the child, while the mother is reduced to the status of *trophos* (*Eum.* 657–61). Origins, not *trophē*, is the issue in the *Oresteia*, where responsibility cannot turn on the question of ignorance vs. knowledge, as it does in *Oedipus at Colonus*, since Orestes explicitly acts under Apollo's orders. Orestes can be redeemed, however, for although he continues the family patterns, he does so in a very different spirit.

We might note parenthetically that both trilogies nonetheless arrive at the same point from these two widely divergent positions, in that both agree on the primacy of paternal power.

41. In the *Oresteia*, Athene introduces the juridical principle into the family through the establishment of the law court, and the Erinyes import the awe associated with blood ties into the city.

42. For the ways in which *The Eumenides* accommodates the old and the new, see my essay, "The Dynamics of Misogyny: Myth and Mythmaking in the *Oresteia*," *Arethusa* 11 (1978): 164–73, reprinted in *Women in the Ancient World*, ed. J. Peradotto and J. P. Sullivan (Albany, N.Y.: State University of New York Press, 1984), pp. 159–94.

On these grounds, there is one more distinction to be made in the family, this time between Oedipus and all his children, since he has elected to remain in Athens, while both Polyneices and Antigone freely choose to return to Thebes. The moment arranged for the meeting between father and son is one where Polyneices might still return to Argos rather than marshal his host against Thebes, while Antigone has the firm offer of a refuge in Athens, which is reiterated for emphasis at the end of the play (*OC* 1739–41).[43] But each is locked into the family pattern of repeating the past as they face the future, repetitions we recognize through the echoes of the earlier dramatic tradition that pervade their discourse.

The interchange between Polyneices and Antigone is especially revealing because it takes us back all the way to Aeschylus's *Seven Against Thebes*. Now the siblings replicate the terms by which the chorus of women there attempt and fail to dissuade Eteocles from going to meet his brother at a comparable moment in his drama, just when he, too, has acknowledged the power of the father's curse.[44] The aim of *Seven Against Thebes*, as remarked earlier, is to collapse distinctions between the brothers when they meet in their fratricidal duel. Here in Sophocles' version, where Polyneices, as the elder brother, claims a more legitimate right to the throne, Poly-

---

43. We must not minimize for either Polyneices or Antigone the effects of that double determination by which action is predicated on both internal and external agency. Though Oedipus declares that Polyneices will not live to take power (*kratos*) over his native land with sword or to make his return (*nostos*) to Argos, Polyneices chooses not to go back to Argos (cf. *palin*; 1347, 1398, 1403, 1418). The text is also careful to leave the question of Antigone's return open (if there will be a *nostos* for you, says Polyneices at *OC* 1408) and to give us her decision as her own.

44. Critics have seen general Sophoclean echoes in this scene, but have strangely missed the more precise referent in Aeschylus. The stage for *Seven* is already set in Polyneices' speech to his father enumerating the seven warriors according to Aeschylus (rather than according to Euripides, although not in the same order, *OC* 1313–22), where he significantly ends the list with a reference to the eponymy of Parthenopaios, a critical feature of the shield scene in *Seven* (*Seven* 536–37, 662, and 670). See also my discussion in *Under the Sign of the Shield*, pp. 98–105, 142–44.

Just before, Polyneices echoes the thoughts Aeschylus gives him in the scout's report: he first offers the alternative of dying in his just cause or repaying in kind the one who has driven him out (cf. *Seven* 636–38 and *OC* 1305–08), and then follows his statement of intent with prayers (*litai*) to the paternal authority (in Aeschylus, to the gods of the *genos*, *genethlioi* and of the fatherland, *patrōoi*). Cf. *Seven* 639–40 and *OC* 1309.

But in the dialogue with Antigone, Polyneices speaks with the voice of his brother Eteocles. He refuses the pleas of the female to desist from this *thumos*, to take cognizance of the curse, and to give up his murderous project against his brother. Like Eteocles, he puts his warrior honor first and, in refusing to yield his position, yields to the power of the curse. Cf., generally, *OC* 1414–38 and *Seven* 676–719.

neices' repetition of his brother's Aeschylean response already signifies in a wonderfully subtle way that there is and will be no real difference between them.

As for Antigone, this same scene prepares her for her future, when she will shift her allegiance from father to brother on the very issue of burial that her own play, *Antigone*, has already dramatized. At the close of *Oedipus at Colonus*, she will already have made this transfer when, forbidden to bury Oedipus, she chooses to follow her perennial vocation of burying her own by making the choice of Thebes over Athens. It is a small but immensely significant point that at the end, in despite of prohibitions to the contrary, she desires nothing more than to violate them, and in a typically Oedipal way. That is, she yearns to look upon a forbidden sight in a domain she may not enter, now that of her father's secret tomb. Let us turn back (*palin*), she says to her sister, to see the dark hearth (*OC* 1726), and Ismene must remind her that it is not *themis* to look upon it (*OC* 1729). Still she returns again to her desire a second time, this time before Theseus, whom she now supplicates on her own, and again her wish must be refused, as the tomb is not *themiton* to behold (*OC* 1754–77). On this level of analysis, looking back and going back become equivalent terms. Repetition is for Antigone her mode of action and her proper terrain is therefore Thebes.[45]

Oedipus, on the other hand, has become the master of time—of past, present and future, precisely because he acknowledges the

45. Looking back is a term that Antigone herself uses with regard to her father. In urging him to yield to her request to give the suppliant son a hearing, she advises him not to regard the present but to look back (*aposkopei*) to the past (*eis ekeina*) at what he himself has suffered in his relations with his father and mother. Then he will know what evil end awaits evil wrath. She is proposing a break in the chain of action and reaction, offense and retaliation, as she specifically says a few lines earlier: "You begot him [*ephusas*], so that even if he were to do [*drônta*] the most impious of all evils to you, o father, it is not *themis* for you to do him harm in return [*antidran*]" (*OC* 1190–91). The moment is still open, as she thinks, at least on the level of supplication, a request that, when granted by Oedipus in just requital to her, only leads, as we know, to the empowering of the ancient curse. Yet the moment remains open for her, since she is ready to reenact her role once again as the one who tries to reconcile the antagonistic males in her family. This is the explicit reason she gives for her return to Thebes ("send us to ancient [*ôgugious*] Thebes, if somehow we may prevent the coming bloodshed among kin"; *OC* 1768–69) and it recalls the function she is asked to perform by and with her mother Jocasta in *The Phoenissae* (*Phoe.* 1264–79). The issue of burial, only ironically implicit in this play (since she has neither promised Polyneices that she will undertake the task for him nor is the outcome of fratricide certain if, as she thinks, she might succeed with the brothers where she has failed here) is, of course, the furthest extension of the reconciling principle she represents. On Antigone here, see also Segal, *Tragedy and Civilization* (cited above, n. 7), pp. 403–4.

power of linear time over him and over human affairs. He can distinguish between the time of the gods, which is ageless and deathless forever, and all-mastering time that turns everything upside down. Subject to the timelessness of eternal return that incest implies, he has also known time in its purely human dimension of flux and reversal. In the case of Oedipus's children, the acts of repetition and return lead to the cancellation of the family line, this time aided by Oedipus's prophetic word and their own choice to return to Thebes. But Oedipus has known both absolutes and relatives. He has lived, in effect, in the two dimensions of synchrony and diachrony and is therefore truly in a position to stand betwixt and between, not in the cruel ambiguities of the insider-outsider on the border of Thebes but as one intermediate in status between mortal and immortal—namely, in the category of the hero.

As a result, if the children of Oedipus return to the past, Oedipus himself is empowered to look to the future, especially in the message he brings to Athens as the reason why his body will bring them benefit. In larger terms, what he brings them is the general lesson on time that tragedy itself can teach. The means, of course, are those most associated with Thebes—that is, the use of prophecy to control the future from the past, but there are significant differences now. This prophecy is closely linked with the vision Oedipus now has of time, and he chooses to deliver it at the perfect moment in the narrative structure of the play. It comes just after Theseus has first received him on the grounds of the common experience of exile they as non-kin share, and prepares the way for Theseus's promise to receive him as a suppliant and enroll him as a citizen in the land.

Here are Oedipus's own words:

Time, the all-mastering [*pagkratēs*], confounds all things. The strength of the earth withers away [*phthinei*], and that of the body withers away too [*phthinei*]. Faith [*Pistis*] dies [*thnēskei*] and distrust [*apistia*] burgeons forth [*blastanei*], and the same spirit [*pneuma*] is never steadfast either among friends [*philois*] or between city and city. For to some at once and to others in later time, the sweet becomes [*gignetai*] bitter and then again becomes dear [*phila*]. And if it is a fair day between you and Thebes, then uncountable time [*murios chronos*] will give birth [*teknoutai*] to countless, myriad nights and days as it proceeds, in which for a small word, they will scatter with the spear the pledges of concord today, there where my slumbering and buried corpse, grown cold, will one day drink their warm blood, if Zeus is still Zeus and Phoebus the son of Zeus is manifest.

(*OC* 609–23)

Metaphors of time and meditations on time itself are common-places of Greek tragic poetry, but Oedipus more than any other fig-ure invests this language with its fullest resonance and strengthens the general gnomic wisdom whose significance he is best qualified to expound. Peripeteia, the rule of reversal that governs the struc-ture of drama, is also the principle that rules the structure of his own life. This is peripeteia in its most complete form, since only Oedipus will undergo the full cycle of tragic process in its double and opposite movement from high to low and then again from low to high.[46] The length of his days as well as perhaps his exile from Thebes now suggest a view of time that reaches out far beyond a single lifetime and beyond the triadic span of generational time.

Many others have observed the significance of this speech and its relation to Oedipus and tragic notions of time.[47] What I wish to stress, however, is the purpose it serves in sharpening the dialectic between Thebes and Athens.[48] For there are further signs that Oedipus has confronted the dilemmas that characterize Thebes so as to entitle him to claim a rightful place in Athens. Conversely, these also suggest why Athens would wish to appropriate for its benefit what Oedipus possesses and in his person represents.

46. The text specifically invokes the formal principle of reversal with respect to Oedipus just after the departure of Polyneices and before the first clap of thunder (*OC* 1449–56). The chorus are responding to the "new ills of a heavy doom that come from the *blind* stranger" who has cursed his son, but their reference to "time [*chronos*] that always [*aei*] sees these things" and regulates reversals prepares the way at this pivotal point of the play for Oedipus's coming vindication by time.

47. These mostly center on the notion of reversal or of endurance through time: See, e.g., C. M. Bowra, *Sophoclean Tragedy* (Oxford: Clarendon Press, 1944), pp. 334–35 (with good citation of ancient texts); Whitman, *Sophocles* (cited above, n. 30), pp. 198–99; and Gellie, *Sophocles* (cited above, n. 39), p. 169.

It is tempting to read Oedipus, the paradigm of tragic man, as the incarnation, even allegorization, of the tragic process itself. See, for example, the remarks of Whitman, *Sophocles*, p. 210, and Segal, *Tragedy and Civilization* (cited above, n. 7), pp. 406–8. In addition to embodying the pattern of reversal in his own history, he exemplifies the principle of the *lex talionis* (the doer must suffer: the sufferer must "do" in return [*antidran*]), "the very formula for tragedy," as Winnington-Ingram observes (*Sophocles* [cited above, n. 33], p. 264). Moreover, if we consider the tragic slogan of *pathei mathos* through the workings of time (*Aeschylus Agamemnon* 177), then Oedipus himself more than fulfills its premises in his own person. He does this not only through the emphasis laid upon knowledge in the play as the guide to action, but by a rather remarkable rewriting of his own story. He claims that, because of his ignorance, he was not the doer as regards his transgressions against the family, but rather the sufferer: *peponthot' esti mallon ē dedrakota* (*OC* 266–67). Thus he redoubles his role as the sufferer (through parents, through sons), and makes himself, as it were, the exemplary sufferer. As such, and through the long workings of time, he can therefore personify tragic wisdom as well as tragic time.

48. Segal, *Tragedy and Civilization* (cited above, n. 7), pp. 376–77 and passim, gives an excellent reading of the relations between Thebes and Athens in this play but does not recognize the larger schematic principles informing them.

First, Oedipus invokes those stages of the life cycle that are heavy with negative significance for the family of Laius—birth, nurture, and death—and creatively integrates them with nature on the one hand and abstract general values on the other. The strength of the land withers and so does that of the body, while trust and distrust alternate through phases of growth and death. Above all, he links generation and time itself by transferring to a higher metaphorical plane the physical act of begetting and endows time itself with reproductive power.[49]

Second, the lessons that Oedipus has learned from his own experience can be now shifted appropriately to the political level and to the relations between cities. These comprise the substance of Oedipus's message to Theseus, so as to naturalize, we might say, and make organic the realities of Greek political life in which shifting allegiances lead now to friendship and again to enmity. Oedipus's body and tomb will be a defense to Athens against Thebes, but so will the knowledge of the cosmic laws of alternation and reversal that Oedipus now embodies.

Theseus knows (*exoida*) the principle of reversal in human affairs at the level of individual experience, being a man like other men, as he says (*OC* 566–68), and on this basis, he is willing to receive Oedipus and to grant his request. But in his prophecy, Oedipus brings surprising news to Theseus concerning an invasion of Attica by Theban forces, news that Theseus does not know and will never know with certainty since the event that Oedipus predicts no longer belongs to the time of myth but rather to some unspecified moment of historical time. The reference, as the ancient scholion suggests, may recall a minor skirmish with Theban cavalry that took place near Colonus in 407 B.C., or it may generally serve as an open prediction for the future. But the point is clear. Oedipus finally crosses the boundary of time beyond the synchrony that marks the eternal return of the mythic patterns in Thebes and beyond the narrative of the family history to a new zone of futurity where no one at Thebes has ever ventured before.[50] And it is precisely on the terms of this

49. Polyneices, on the other hand, uses the metaphorical language of house, family, and nurture, within the family circle, when he first addresses his father (*OC* 1259–60, 1262–63), thereby "pointing up," as Segal remarks (*Tragedy and Civilization* [cited above, n. 7], p. 388), "his failure as a son in an *oikos* to whose ruin he has contributed."

50. In contrast to Euripides' fondness for contemporary political allusions, this is the only extant Sophoclean play to make reference within the text to a historical event.

prophecy that he claims the right to cross the spatial boundary into Athens.

On the other hand, only in Athens, where the outsider may enter a new state through rites of supplication and political bestowal of resident rights, can Oedipus himself transcend human time as he crosses the boundary between the living and the dead to make permanent his value to the city in the institution of cult. In the perennial existence to be granted him, issues of space and time coincide in a characteristically Oedipal way. For in entering the grove of the Furies that it is forbidden for others to penetrate, Oedipus confirms the spatial equivalence between the body of the earth and that of the mother. At the same time, he verifies the positive temporal symbolism of incest with the mother as the gesture that raises intimations of immortality because it has effaced normative linear time. Oedipus at Thebes made literal the terrible deeds that other men only dream of in their sleep. In Athens he can transcend the physical body through metaphor and cult to be incorporated into this idealized territory for his longest sleep. Historical evidence may never make clear in what way Oedipus's prophecy about relations between Thebes and Athens comes to pass. Theseus, in fact, in the furthest extension of Oedipus's emphasis on individual responsibility, goes so far as to deny an intrinsic connection between Creon's behavior and the nurture he has received in his native city of Thebes (OC 919–23).[51] Here we know better than this kind and simple king of Athens, and so, I suggest, should the spectators. There is no cause for wonderment that Thebes should some time in the distant future turn hostile to Athens, if we consider the radical incompatibility between the dramatic representations of the two cities. From this point of view, the truth of Oedipus's prophecy is never in doubt, since it already rings true to the rules of the genre. The message of Oedipus therefore also assures us that his disappearance can only be temporary. After all, whenever Thebes returns to the tragic stage, Oedipus, too, must come back to life.

51. Theseus's "praise" of Thebes has puzzled many commentators, especially in view of the continuing political antagonism between Thebes and Athens during this period. See the discussion in Burian, "Suppliant and Savior" (cited above, n. 37), p. 420 n. 30. What I propose conforms to the underlying logic of the play and the role assigned to Theseus as the representative of a city free from prejudice.

Chapter Five

Politics and Madness

Michael Davis

Sophocles' *Ajax* is on the surface simple. Ajax is the big, strong, dependable, not very imaginative or bright, second-best warrior of the *Iliad*. His valor is unquestionable and unalterable. Ajax is not fickle; he is steady and steadfast, always there to defend when the Greeks are attacked. His trademark is his sevenfold shield. Ajax is a great defensive fighter. When Achilles dies it is not surprising that Ajax expects to be acknowledged as the best remaining warrior. He has fought Hektor to a standstill in hand-to-hand single combat. They have exchanged gifts in mutual admiration. Ajax's expectation is thwarted. He is angered, and resolves to gain his just honor by killing the army that denied him Achilles' armor, with especially brutal deaths for the leaders of the army, Agamemnon and Menelaus, and Odysseus, who has received Achilles' armor in his stead. Athene restrains Ajax (as she restrains Achilles in book 1 of the *Iliad*) by making him mistakenly see the Greek herds as the army. When Ajax discovers that he has slaughtered domesticated animals rather than warriors, he kills himself. The rest of the play concerns his burial. The Atreidae want to leave his corpse for the birds and dogs as punishment. His half brother, Teucer, insists that he be buried. Odysseus then intervenes to see that his former enemy is buried. While all of this is superficially clear, the heart of the play is extremely dark and closed to us. Its external simplicity hides its internal complexity from view. The event that would seem to make

Seth Benardete and I read *Ajax* together in the fall of 1980. He has also kindly made available to me his notes for the course he offered on *Ajax* in the summer of 1981. I am doubly grateful to him. A good deal of what is in this paper emerged first in conversation with him. He has especially helped me to understand the importance of enmity in the play, and the importance of Hades. The degree to which these two figure in the argument of what follows gives some small indication of the extent to which this essay is indebted to him.

sense of everything else, Ajax's attempt to slaughter the whole Greek army, does not itself make sense. To understand that event is to understand the peculiar character of Ajax's madness. But to understand Ajax we have to look first to Odysseus.

1

The play opens with the word "always," uttered by an invisible goddess. In light of Ajax's later claims about the etymology of his name (430) this first word, *aei*, is suggestive.[1] Ajax, the steady, is always there to defend the Greeks from their enemies. Here, however, the word is systematically ambiguous. It may mean that Athene is always looking at Odysseus, or it may mean that Odysseus is always hunting, trying to snatch some advantage from his enemies. If the latter, Athene would have characterized Odysseus as essentially an enemy, a man *always* at odds with other men. Later (77) Athene and Odysseus together will suggest that to be a man (*anēr*) means to be an enemy. What Odysseus is always doing in general, he is here doing in particular. Odysseus is tracking. The purpose of the tracking seems to be to determine whether Ajax is inside his tent, although it is hard to see why Odysseus doesn't simply look in the tent to see if Ajax is there. Odysseus either prefers, or is forced, to learn by signs (32) what Athene knows directly (13). Athene can not only see Odysseus; she can also see Ajax. That Athene can "see," without looking, that Ajax is in his tent, and that Odysseus chooses to track, when he might "see," suggests that looking inside the tent is not so easy as it at first appears. Athene apparently sees not only Odysseus's actions, the tracking, but also sees his intentions, his wish to find out whether Ajax is "within or not within." This phrase *"eit' endon eit' ouk endon"* can also mean that Odysseus is attempting to learn whether Ajax is sane or not, whether he is in his right mind.[2] What Odysseus cannot see and must learn by signs, what it takes a god to see, is the inside of Ajax. The action of *Ajax* is utterly unintelligible without this first scene. Without the gods we would never have been sure of Ajax's motives, and without his motives his actions might have appeared simply pathetic, the

1. Throughout I have used the Greek text of Jebb (Cambridge: Cambridge University Press, 1907). Numbers in parentheses refer to the line or lines of the text.

2. For this use of *endon*, see Aeschylus's *Choephoroe* 233 and Aristophanes' *Acharnians* 396. For the use of the opposite of *endon* in a way that suggests insanity, consider lines 639–40: *"ouketi suntrophois orgais empedos, all' ektos homilei."*

deeds of a once great man now hopelessly mad. Odysseus is reading signs at the beginning of the play because he has no other way
of getting at Ajax's motives, no other way of knowing for certain
that Ajax is an enemy. Had he looked inside the tent Odysseus
would have learned little more. That is confirmed by Tecmessa's account. She can see what Odysseus would have seen had he looked,
and she thinks Ajax is mad (239). Without Athene every attempt to
look inside Ajax would yield a new outside. To look at the inside of
a man is as hard as looking at the inside of a body. Once one has
opened it, its inside has become its outside. One does not learn a
man's motives by dissecting his corpse. Knowledge of motives apparently requires indirection, something like tracking or learning
by signs. Such knowledge will be imperfect; perfection requires the
intervention of a god. Athene will tell Odysseus what Ajax's motives for the slaughter were and also stage a conversation in which
those motives become clear. She will call Ajax out in such a way
that he reveals his inside to Odysseus; she will turn him inside out
without destroying the character of his inside.

    Odysseus can hear but not see Athene. He recognizes her from
her voice. Later Ajax will be seen by Odysseus, but will not see
him, and it is clear that were Odysseus to speak, Ajax would hear
him (87). Athene puts Odysseus in the position of a god with regard to Ajax. When Tecmessa gives her account of Ajax's madness,
she includes her version of Athene's conversation with Ajax. To her
it looks as though Ajax is talking with invisible shadows, and she
takes that as confirmation of his madness. Odysseus's behavior
would look like that as well if we were not also privy to the voice of
a goddess. Talking to gods looks like madness.

    The limits of human sight are emphasized by what Odysseus re-
lates to Athene. Odysseus knows that the herds have been slaughtered and the herdsmen as well. He suspects that Ajax did it, but is
puzzled because the deed is so unintelligible, literally invisible (21).
Everyone says that Ajax did it, and there is even a witness who saw
Ajax bounding alone across the plain. But Odysseus has his doubts.
They will be confirmed by what Athene tells him. The human *optēr*,
or witness, saw what could not have been the case. Odysseus can
tell from the confusion of tracks that Ajax did not return "alone,"
and it is unlikely that he "bounded" (30) across the plain with a
herd of sheep and cattle tethered (62) behind him. Odysseus's indirect knowledge turns out to be more reliable than human vision,

but it is flawed because it cannot lead to certainty about whether Ajax killed the animals, and if he did, why he did. Athene solves both problems rather quickly. Ajax did it, and he thought he was slaughtering the whole army.

Her description of the slaughter is peculiar in two ways. One might overtranslate Athene's remark to Odysseus at 39 to mean that "these deeds of this man are yours." And when Odysseus asks at 38 whether he toils (*ponō*) to some purpose, the *ponō* is soon to be echoed by *phonōi* (murder), used in describing Ajax's action at 43. In a general way it is clear that the whole description of Ajax's deed is paralleled by the deed with which the play begins and which is also cut short by Athene. Both Ajax and Odysseus move against their enemies in stealth. Both are like hounds. Both sneak up on tents and never quite make it to the door because Athene steps in. One is obviously led to wonder whether Odysseus and Ajax are up to the same thing. Was Odysseus about to murder Ajax? The *Ajax* begins with this strange ambiguity. We thought we knew what Odysseus was doing, but what he intends is not at all clear. Odysseus may have to rely on signs to know Ajax's inside, but we are in a similar position with regard to him. Athene restrains Odysseus with her voice, with speech. She had restrained Achilles with a combination of force and speech (*Iliad* 1.197–200). She had pulled him by the hair to prevent him from killing Agamemnon. Ajax apparently cannot be stopped by a speech but only by a vision. He cannot be stopped by his inside, but only by transforming the outside so that his action is not what he intended it to be.

There is another peculiarity of Athene's account. One can imagine Ajax's hatred for the Greeks expressed to himself in terms that portray his enemies as less than human, as sheep for example. Athene simply makes this internal metaphor of anger and enmity real. Ajax was about to treat the whole Greek army as though they were beasts. Athene turns beasts into his enemies. By turning him inside out, Athene makes Ajax's anger visible to all. When made visible it looks crazy, but when invisible it seems understandable. In a way, Athene has simply shown Odysseus that Ajax is really sane. Like Odysseus he was seeking to get the advantage of his enemy. Still, the character of Ajax's anger is peculiar. At first the significance of Athene's action seems to be that she has succeeded in showing that Ajax is incapable of distinguishing between men and beasts. That has something to do with his unwillingness to recog-

nize the gods. But his unwillingness to recognize the gods is rooted
in the fact that his own virtue is suspect so long as it depends upon
the gods for support (758–77). Of all the Greek heroes Ajax alone
scorns the help of the gods. It is this boast for which he is punished
by Athene. At second glance it is clear that there is something more
subtle about Ajax's inability to distinguish the human from the bestial. Since he slaughters the herdsmen as well as the herds, it is
clear that his madness consists in seeing everything as human. That
everything looks human to Ajax means that everything is seen as
having purposes or intentions. One could say that Ajax's world is
fully moral. Wherever he faces opposition of any sort he faces an
enemy. There is no chance in his world. That in part accounts for
the fact that he doesn't ever think of the possibility of trying again
once his first attempt to kill the army has failed. Having failed once
he has failed simply, for if there is no chance, he can have been defeated only because of his essential inferiority. Now, if all opposition means enmity, then the appropriate response to opposition is
anger. *Ajax* is therefore a play about the absolute character of enmity in a world that is entirely purposive.

All of this sets the stage for the appearance of Ajax himself.
Athene says she will show Odysseus Ajax's disease so as to make it
apparent "all around" (*periphanē*; 66), so that having "looked in"
(*eisidōn*) he will be able to tell all the Greeks.[3] Later (81) Athene
taunts him with the suggestion that he might be afraid to see a
madman all around (*periphanōs . . . idein*). Odysseus never does reveal the source of his knowledge to the Greeks. He tells them its
content, but allows them to think that in his usual wily way he has
deduced Ajax's intentions. He not only fails to mention Athene; he
also suppresses what she emphasizes, the *periphanēs* character of
the knowledge she supplies him with. That kind of knowledge is
supposed to enable Odysseus to laugh at his enemy—the sweetest
kind of laughter according to Athene. Why that should be the case
is at first hard to make out. It seems linked to the godlike perspective from which Odysseus is to be allowed to view his enemy. To
see Ajax's inside, and to see him all around while remaining unseen
himself saps enmity of its harshness. Odysseus seems to fear that
being thus sapped, he will lose himself. That is not a foolish fear,
given what will happen to Ajax in this play. It is only because a god

3. Compare *Oedipus at Colonus* 1370 and 1536–37.

contrives to give him a godlike perspective that Odysseus remains to observe Ajax. Otherwise he would wish to be *ektos*—that is, literally outside, or, in the context of *Ajax*, mad. The two alternatives to ordinary enmity seem to be madness and divinity.[4]

Ajax is called away from torturing the captured animals by Athene's call. He apparently sees her and hears her. Everything is visible to Ajax in human form. He tortures the animals in an attempt to get revenge. That is, he takes revenge on what he takes to be his enemies' bodies, their outsides. Athene, on the other hand, avenges herself through Ajax's mind. Ajax cannot be sure that, for all his torture, those he thinks he is torturing will regret what they have done, while Athene, by getting inside Ajax, can be sure that he will have regrets. Since he has not done what he thought himself to have done, when he regains his sanity he will be ashamed. He will be doubly ashamed; to become aware of Athene's deception is to become aware that her sort of battle is superior to his, that the mind is stronger than the body. But if that is so, if the inside is stronger than the outside, then Ajax was rightly denied Achilles' armor.

Ajax lost to the wily Odysseus in that contest even though he was by general agreement the stronger fighter. Odysseus's superior wisdom consists in knowing, even before Athene's demonstration of her power over Ajax, that the gods can do anything (86). That is tantamount to saying that the best man does not always win, that the invisible gods affect the outcome of human battles, that chance has its effect in human affairs. Ajax, on the other hand, can claim to be superior to Odysseus only if he is *pronousteros* (119). Since he is clearly not wise in any ordinary sense, let alone wiser than all others, his superior foresight must have some other meaning. There are two related ways to understand Athene's strange description of Ajax as having more foresight. Ajax seems the least likely of all the Greek heroes to earn this epithet. His steadiness in battle seems to have to do with his failure of imagination. Ajax is most dependable because of all the Greek warriors he comes closest to having no inside. He is least subject to panic and delusion, least inclined to shrink from imagined horrors or, having rashly underestimated the strength of an enemy, to be surprised and then de-

4. Greek lends itself to making a connection between enmity and being outside. In the fourth century *echthos* even becomes a variant of *ektos*, outside, and of course the Greek for hatred is *echthos*. The result is an almost perfect coincidence in a single word of the two major themes of *Ajax*, the inside/outside problem and the enmity problem.

feated by his enemy's real strength. Similarly, that Ajax cannot be inspired by a god means that he will never show greater strength than one might have expected. That Ajax is *pronousteros*, then, means that he is least subject to delusion with regard to himself. Athene seems to suggest that if even he has an inside, then having an inside must be a universal human trait. To say that Ajax is *pronousteros* means that his is the hardest case for the gods, the man who does not recognize the divine. That he talks to Athene, even calls her an ally, seems to belie this interpretation, but he treats Athene only a little better than he treats Tecmessa. She is his helper; she is *always* to him *symmachos* (117). It is a word the Athenians use to designate the smaller cities that assist them in their wars. For Ajax to talk to Athene as he does suggests that he considers her beneath him. That is tantamount to denying her divinity. Once again Ajax sees only the human. He sees beasts and gods as men.

Ajax can be understood to have foresight in another way. Because he sees only the human and does not acknowledge the power of chance, he sees only the intentional, the purposive. Ajax's world is one in which the best man always wins. That is what it means for him to say that Athene is *always* his ally. Ajax is admittedly the best man. That is something to which even Odysseus agrees with no hesitation at the end of the play (1336–41). Ajax's world is one in which the good prevail. Perfect foresight in such a world only requires knowing who the good are. He justly considers himself the best after Achilles, and so does not doubt himself at all. This lack of doubt is the necessary prerequisite for his lacking an inside. Ajax can be a superficial man because his world is a superficial world, one suited well for sight, but not at all for speech. It is a world in which there is no difference between being and seeming. Still, Ajax cannot be closed to the fact that it is a world in which there are conflicts, and so winners and losers. That there are conflicts means there are at least temporary disturbances of that perfect order. Ajax needs the possibility of such disturbances to justify his initial loss of the armor. But he needs it more significantly to justify war at all, and so to justify his excellence in war. His plan to punish the whole Greek army is therefore not simply the result of wounded pride. If there is no punishment beyond human punishment, his punishment of the Greeks is the necessary condition for the morality of the world. What Athene's trick has allowed us to see is that the substance of Ajax's madness is its excessive morality. Ajax treats men as though they were beasts not because he is immoral, but because he is too moral. To justify his anger he must consider his enemies all bad, just as he considers himself all good. That is almost to make them into a different species. Given his view of the world, an enemy is someone for whom Ajax could never feel pity. That is the source of his brutality.

Athene has forced Odysseus to see that brutality in Ajax. That is why this opening scene ends unexpectedly in Odysseus's expression of pity for his enemy (121). He sees his own nature in Ajax, and so concludes that we are nothing but images or shadows (126). The being of images and shadows consists in their pointing beyond themselves. They are not what they are. They are not superficial. Odysseus and Ajax are alike in that both are "always hunting to snatch some advantage against their enemies." The difference between them is that Odysseus sees the fragility of taking one's bearings by enmity. In various ways the remainder of the play is concerned with understanding why it is that Ajax takes his bearings by enmity. If we have thus far understood the character of his madness we have yet to understand the necessity for going mad.

2

The world in which the intentional, the moral, reigns supreme is the political world. Whether the City of God or the City of Man, a fully purposive world is one understood in essentially political terms. That Ajax sees only the human means that he sees only the city, the *polis*, but since there is more than the *polis* in the world, whether understood in terms of chance or of the divine, Ajax's view of the world is necessarily distorted. The distortion is instructive to us because it is peculiarly political. The political seems from its own perspective to be self-sufficient; it therefore confuses itself with the natural. The perennial danger of the *polis* is that it will take its view to be all-inclusive (*periphanēs*), and so take itself too seriously, thereby suffering something analogous to the fate of Ajax. It runs the risk of madness and brutality. What the Trojan War means for Sophocles is that at the very moment that Greeks come to think of themselves as Greeks, they run the risk of thinking of their enemies, the barbarians, as subhuman. It is no accident that in taunting Teucer as the offspring of a non-Greek mother, Menelaus calls him a slave. That non-Greeks are slaves by nature means that they

are not really men. They are subhuman. What unifies the Greeks
therefore threatens to brutalize them. That is the fundamental political problem. It is also the problem of Ajax.[5]

Ajax shares the goal of all Homeric heroes, "always to be the best
and to be preeminent above others." It is a goal, let us call it virtue,
that is intrinsically aristocratic and that the political order must encourage for its own survival. The Trojan War is the story of the dependence of the small on the great, and finally on the greatest of all,
Achilles. But Achilles, and Ajax after him, are problematically related to the *polis*. The goal collectively set for virtue is that the greatest man is the man who is a law unto himself, autonomous. When
Achilles reenters the fighting, he fights for his own purposes and
not for those of the Greeks.

Ajax is aware of this dependence of the small on the great, but he
is altogether unaware of its corollary, the dependence of the great
on the small. The chorus know all about this dependence (148–61).
They look to Ajax for protection, but at the same time they are
aware that he is in an awkward position because of the power of
rumor. The chorus imply that since the great alone are always subject to rumor, the "great kings" (188) Menelaus and Agamemnon
are as vulnerable to them as Ajax has proven to be to the rumors of
Odysseus. But rumor is simply the less pleasant consequence of
the honor Ajax demands (98). Far from being autonomous, Ajax
depends for what he most values on those whom he despises. The
chorus make it clear that thoughtless men cannot see this mutual
dependence. They have tacitly identified Ajax as thoughtless (162).
He is unaware of the consequences of a view of virtue that is essentially comparative. Achilles did not share Ajax's plight because he
never had to contest his position as best. Ajax is in the peculiar
position of wanting to prove that he is the best, where the best

5. One could imagine an alternative to this understanding. The Greeks, at war
for ten years, have been brutalized by so much fighting. In his madness Ajax may be
meant to represent not so much the city as a certain sort of city. Common sense,
after all, suggests that political life is not simply mad. Tragedy, however, does not
mean to be commonsensical. Rather than treating extreme situations in an everyday
way, it represents the everyday by the extreme at its core. When Athene says to
Odysseus of Ajax "These deeds of this man are yours" (39), we are meant to see that
there is something brutal at the heart of the *polis*. Ironically, Odysseus, by seeing
what happens to Ajax, i.e., by seeing that he is the same as Ajax, becomes different
from Ajax. In discovering the imperfectibility of the *polis*, he becomes better suited
to live in the *polis*. By becoming imperfectly political he becomes more civilized.
Seeing the fate of Ajax from a godlike perspective does for him what seeing *Ajax* is
meant to do for us.

means better than all the rest of the Greeks, and of wanting his own bestness acknowledged. Yet the only way to prove that he is best is to slaughter the very army on which he depends for the honor he seeks. Ajax is unaware of the extent to which he depends on the city. His suicide therefore may well be simply a self-aware version of the attempt to slaughter the army. Without knowing it, Ajax's initial action was also a kind of suicide.

Still, he is not entirely to blame. The city itself necessarily encourages a notion of virtue that points beyond the political altogether. That is why in Ajax's last speech he traces all of his problems back to the *monomachia* with Hektor (661–65). Accepting Hektor's sword now replaces slaying the animals as the primary reason for Ajax's suicide. Ajax begins the battle with Hektor for the honor of the Greeks, but the exchange of gifts when neither can defeat the other represents a crucial change. His admiration for Hektor means that Ajax has recognized that in some way he shares more with his greatest foe than he does with the Greeks for whom he is fighting. From the perspective of the *polis* that is the first sign that he is not entirely trustworthy. Accepting Hektor's sword is merely a milder version of his attempt to slaughter the whole army. Ajax now fights for his own ends to the exclusion of the common ends, but just as the attempted slaughter represents a kind of suicide, so does accepting the sword. Having taken Hektor's sword, Ajax has implicitly undermined the order that establishes Hektor as enemy and the Greeks as friends. Without that order the distinction between friend and enemy becomes confused, and with it Ajax's virtue. Ajax must have friends in order to have enemies. The problem is perhaps clearest at 441, where Ajax says that if Achilles still lived he would have awarded his armor to Ajax rather than to Odysseus. Of course if Achilles were alive no one would get his armor. So long as Achilles lived he was Ajax's competitor. Two cannot be "best and preeminent above all others." Only in death can there be a mutuality of interest between Ajax and Achilles.

The confusion of friendship and enmity is in some way the deepest issue of the play. Ajax first addresses the chorus as *philoi* (friends) and then asks them to kill him (349–61). Athene is a goddess who is particularly dear or friendly to Odysseus (14) and holds particular enmity toward Ajax. Tecmessa, who appeals to Ajax on the basis of those who are dear or friends to him, as his captive woman, was formerly his enemy. Odysseus, for whom Ajax holds the deepest enmity, treats him as a friend at the end of the play. Menelaus, for whom the Greeks came to Troy, and Agamemnon, who leads them, are at first the embodiments of what friendship seems to mean for Ajax (i.e., those for whom one will fight), but end by being almost the greatest of his enemies. His half brother Teucer and his son Eurysaces are more complicated cases. The other characters point to the instability of friendship and enmity in their movement from one to the other. Teucer, in whom Ajax places the most trust, and Eurysaces, about whom he seems to care the most, are both the offspring of non-Greek women—that is, of women who were once enemies. Teucer and Eurysaces are proofs of the falsity of the view that makes of enemies a different species. Common humanity makes itself visible in the phenomenon of the half-breed. That seems to be why half-breeds are particularly prone to the social ostracism rooted in the city's sense of its own naturalness.

Nowhere is the confusion of friendship and enmity that saturates this play more present than in the speeches of Ajax. Ajax's first speech of any length begins with his famous reflection on the etymology of his name (430–33). He makes a connection between *aiai* and *Aias*. It is appropriate that he who suffers so much should be named by the verb *aiazō*, which means to bemoan. Ajax begins with his characteristic mistake. He sees intention where there is only a chance. That mistake allows him to collapse the difference between a conventional name and a natural pathos. Ajax collapses the difference between convention (*nomos*) and nature (*physis*). That is, of course, the necessary condition for seeing one's own *polis* as natural, and so its enemies as natural enemies. The difficulties with it are made clear in Ajax's speech beginning at 545. Holding Eurysaces up to the sight of the animals he has just slain is designed by Ajax both as a proof that the boy's nature is like his father's and as a means of habituating him in the laws (*nomois*) of his father. That the latter is necessary at all seems to be a sign that nature and *nomos* are not simply the same. Ajax's difficulty is that he is now the enemy of the gods, hated by the Greek army, and hated (*echthei*) by all Troy (457–59). Ajax is hated by all humans, whether understood as divine, human, or bestial. He is consequently an enemy to all men. The consequence of his being *ektos*, outside or mad, is that he is an object of hate (*echthos*). For Ajax, the great defensive fighter, to act virtuously in this situation means for him to fight back. However, he cannot attack the Greeks without aiding the Trojans, and he cannot attack the Trojans without aiding the Greeks. He seems to be in a double bind. One cannot, it seems, have enemies without friends. What remains for him is to attack the third of the enemies listed in this speech, the gods. Ajax considers suicide as a means to strike back against the gods. It is his way of showing that it is not possible for the gods to delude him about himself the way Athene deluded him about the Greek army. Suicide cannot be an illusion. Ajax seems to contemplate it as an assertion of friendship to himself.

That Ajax should despair of the possibility of friends is not surprising. Those most "dear" to him, at least those who can talk, are remarkably self-centered in their reactions to his contemplated and actual suicide. The chorus worry about what will happen to them if he dies. Tecmessa worries about how she who has suffered so much as a captive woman, for which Ajax is of course responsible, will suffer as a captive woman after Ajax is dead. Teucer, after asking for Eurysaces, goes on to worry about what his father, Telemon, will say. In each of these cases, the characters rather naturally tend to do what Odysseus openly avows at the end of the play. They labor for themselves (1367). That is merely the predictable consequence of the view that there is no getting inside human beings, in other words, that our motives are necessarily hidden from view. Beings for whom there is no inside cannot have friendship because they lack self-awareness. Beings for whom there is an inside cannot have friendship because they lack awareness of others. Their friendships are necessarily partial.

Ajax's suicide does not run counter to his nature. It is the only defiance left open to him. In his most famous and most ambiguous speech (646–92), he makes that clear. However, it also becomes clear that even this defiance is not really open to him. The speech as a whole is ambiguous. The chorus take it to mean that Ajax has changed his mind, that he is one of those things that time changes, and so they conclude that he does not intend to kill himself. We assume in hindsight after his suicide that he had decided to kill himself. The only thing that seems initially certain is that Ajax has undergone some sort of change. In fact two things have changed. He has come to pity Tecmessa, and he will kill himself outside the tent rather than within it. There is an added ambiguity. Granted that the speech can be read either way—that is, granted that we do not really know what Ajax intends—we also do not know whether he intends the ambiguity. Does he wish to deceive the chorus and Tecmessa, or is the deception unintentional? That we do not know Ajax's intentions means that we cannot vouch for the truth of his initial claim that time changes everything. If we do not know and cannot know the inside of Ajax, we cannot know whether he has changed. This speech, which has been the source of so much scholarly debate, seems to be intentionally ambiguous; it is an example of the problem it describes.

The speech as a whole is Ajax's explanation of a change he has perceived in himself. He is surprised at the change. He seems to think that *Aias* and *aei* belong together. Ajax is most of all unchangeable. Athene can fool him with visions, but that he changes his mind is something of a shock, and for that reason it is something for which he feels impelled to provide an explanation. The change seems twofold. Ajax has come to pity Tecmessa and Eurysaces. The chorus take that to mean he will not kill himself. Ajax takes it as a revelation about himself. For Ajax to pity as Odysseus has pitied him (131) means for him to acknowledge that some fates are undeserved. That, of course, undermines his whole understanding of the world as completely human. Ajax has seen the power of chance. The second change in Ajax has to do with his resolve to kill himself. When he went inside at 583 there seemed no doubt about his intention to commit suicide immediately. What he sees inside the tent are, of course, the dead bodies of the animals he has slain. He must see that, were he to slay himself, he would be indistinguishable from them, one more piece of carrion. Ajax changes then, not in his resolve to kill himself, but with regard to the question of how to kill himself. Ajax simultaneously discovers chance, his need for the gods (and among them especially Hades), and his dependence on the Atreidae (and so on the *polis*). It remains to see how thoroughgoing this change is. Ajax may have decided to revere the Atreidae, but his death speech makes it clear that he hates them still (835–42). He seems only to have realized how limited his alternatives are, not to have forsaken them absolutely. His discovery of chance coincides with his discovery of Hades, or the invisible. Ajax can think of himself as revering the Atreidae only because he has discovered the intimate relation between friendship and enmity. Since he is what he is by virtue of his enemies, he must "love his enemies," but in a sense rather different from our customary understanding. Ajax has learned that he must love to hate. He has learned to speak ambiguously so that he might say the same thing.

The first word of the play is *aei*, always. Ajax considered that a fit description of himself until he discovered the way time has of bringing the unexpected—that is, the invisible—to light (646–49). But Ajax, who wishes to be always, must therefore hate time, and, insofar as he is changeable, hate himself. What he discovers here is that time, and the necessity for change, is itself eternal. But only what is eternal is worthy of love. That is confirmed by our ordinary experience of love or friendship. When we confide in a friend, the tacit assumption (however foolish), is that friendship is a lasting thing and what is said will therefore be kept *forever* in confidence. But if there is nothing eternal but enmity and hatred, then there is nothing to love but enmity and hatred. Ajax's discovery that one must be *sōphrōn*—that is, moderate or *sane*—is therefore merely the truth for which his mad slaughter of the animals is the metaphor. It is the true brutality. Ajax has apparently not changed at all. He remains a man whose morality is the root of his bestiality. He is the same sword with a new edge.

The difficulty with Ajax's final view becomes clear from his final speech. His meaningful suicide, in order to be meaningful, has to presuppose more than the indifference to chance and the invisible. The "unexpected" must be interpreted as "that which we hope against" (648) in order for Ajax to succeed in his last attempt at autonomy. His last speech therefore begins by personifying the sword given him by Hektor and the instrument of his death. It becomes the source of all his trouble. It must be the focus of his enmity. It is not accidental that Ajax's last speech has to do primarily with the gods, and especially with Hades. In order to love the eternity of enmity, Ajax must place himself in the position of Homer's Ajax in book 11 of the *Odyssey*. He must be a shade in Hades with the possibility of eternally refusing to speak to Odysseus. But that, of course, requires that there be Hades. To create the possibility of his own virtue, in the end Ajax is forced to create and turn to the very gods whose assistance he at first scorned. To rectify a world in which there is chance, Ajax has to make the chance character of his world intentional. That amounts to inventing a world beyond this world in which chance does not rule. Ajax invents Hades. Ajax who began by acknowledging only the visible, the outside, in the end can commit suicide only because he leaves the dead animals inside and discovers Hades on the outside. That is, Ajax who once saw only the outside now sees only the inside. But that is to turn the inside into the outside. Ajax has simply rediscovered in Hades the world he had renounced in his speech on time.

3

With the death of Ajax the *polis*, which had been implicitly present since the beginning of the play, comes in with a vengeance. The scholarly dispute about the unity of the play points to the problem of the play. The issue of the second part is the proper way to treat Ajax's body, his outside. By trying to prevent the burial of Ajax, Agamemnon and Menelaus treat his visible part as though it were his invisible part, and so run the risk of repeating Ajax's error. The second part of the play threatens to repeat the suicide of the first part, but this time on the level of the city. The suicide of the city seems to be prevented by the fact that its principles are embodied in different men. The city consists of the mutual dependence of the great and the small. It depends on the coincidence of the noble and the just. Menelaus seems to point to the dependence of the small on the great and Agamemnon to the dependence of the great on the small. The city is presented in its ambiguity, but because that ambiguity is not present in one soul, it does not lead to self-destruction. The city will be like Ajax in its madness, but unlike Ajax it will not be aware of its madness. It therefore runs the risk that its moralism will lead to a brutality of which it never becomes aware. Ajax treated his enemies as though they were beasts. In the name of the city Agamemnon and Menelaus treat Ajax as though he were a beast. The contest over Ajax's body is another version of the contest for Achilles' armor. It is a contest the ultimate issue of which is the nature of contesting. It is a contest over strife (1163).

Teucer's defense of Ajax's corpse falls into two parts. He first argues with Menelaus and then with Agamemnon. The two are separated by the chorus's reflection on the Trojan War (1185–1222). Menelaus warns Teucer not to bury Ajax. He makes it a question of political theory. For the *polis* to exist, rulers must be obeyed. They can only insure that they will be obeyed if they are feared, and they will not be feared if crimes such as Ajax's are not punished. Ajax was apparently fearless in life and so beyond rule, but even Ajax must die and depend on others to bury him. Menelaus's principle is that the small, because they are dependent upon the great, must obey the great. But if it is the great who are to be obeyed, it is clear that Ajax surpasses Menelaus. If superior virtue is the criterion for the great being obeyed, then the great are a law unto themselves. The implication of Menelaus's speech is that the law (*nomos*) by which he is constituted ruler is natural. Like Ajax he is forced to make the conventional and the natural one. Also like Ajax, in order for this final fear, fear of not being buried, to have the effect Menelaus claims it will have, the existence of Hades is presupposed. Menelaus points back to the problematic relation of Ajax to the gods. He needs them to support an argument that otherwise remains fully within the human. Menelaus presents the city as though it needed no justification. He presents it as having no inside, no invisible part, but his own argument requires the existence of Hades. Menelaus presents the city as an unselfconscious Ajax. The city's law, like Ajax's oath, is its own justification.

Teucer's reply points to this weakness of Menelaus's argument and at the same time shares the weakness. According to Teucer there is no city. Ajax came to Troy for his own reasons. His oath is reason enough. It is not an oath to the Atreidae; it is a self-imposed obligation. Ajax's manifest superiority to Menelaus is sufficient to undermine Menelaus's tacit identification of *nomos* and *physis*. The problem with this account is that if it were true Ajax never would have acknowledged the right of Agamemnon and Menelaus to award Achilles' armor; there would have been no slight to his honor, and hence no attempt to slaughter the Greek army. Teucer's position is self-contradictory. One cannot deny that the city exists and at the same time covet its honors. Menelaus and Teucer end by exchanging metaphorical insults (1142–58), but not content to leave them as metaphor, they interpret them. When *nomos* and *physis* perfectly coincide, nothing remains hidden. But in such a situation the city is everything and the city is nothing. When the political becomes everything, the political disappears.

Whereas Teucer had argued against Menelaus that there was no common good, against Agamemnon he argues that Ajax's deeds on behalf of the common good deserve gratitude. The change has to do with the change from Menelaus's monarchical principle, that the small depend on the great, to Agamemnon's democratic principle, that the great depend on the small (1243). The city not only demands that men strive to be best; it also demands that having so

strived, they be willing to submit to those who are admittedly inferior to them. But for a city to exist requires that it have some principle of unity. Agamemnon repeatedly emphasizes Teucer's birth.
Teucer is not Greek because born of a Phrygian mother. He is therefore by nature a slave. Conventional difference has been transformed into natural inferiority. Like his brother, Agamemnon is
forced to defend the perspective of the city by exaggerating its
scope. The two human events least politicizable are death and
birth. Menelaus has politicized the one, Agamemnon the other.
Agamemnon's two themes fit together. Being Greek means being
born of Greek parents. That alone is enough to make one by nature
superior. Greekness is both the lowest common denominator and
the limit placed on how high one can go. Ajax in the exchange of
gifts with Hektor tried to become more than Greek. That the city
cannot tolerate. But it presents this equality among its citizens as a
virtue. It can do that by comparing its citizens to others. With
Agamemnon barbarians become natural slaves, but as natural slaves
speaking an unintelligible tongue they cease to be thought of as human. The invention of barbarians runs the risk of making the
Greeks barbaric.

These two aspects of the perspective of the *polis* are separated by
the third stasimon, the chorus's reflection on the war (1185–1225).
It has a number of peculiarities. *Hellanōn* in the first strophe is in
the same position as *anthrōpous* in the first antistrophe. There is
also a suggested comparison of *polukoinon Haidan* at 1193 with
koinon Arē at 1196. Greeks are interchangeable with men and common Hades is opposed to common war. The second strophe shows
how much the chorus resent the common war. It is always and unceasing. They have therefore come to think of hatred and enmity as
a permanent condition. The result of that permanent war is that
"man" and "Greek" have become interchangeable for them. The
chorus pave the way for Agamemnon's introduction of the notion of
barbarians and his reduction of them to slaves. The chorus therefore point to the fact that Greeks have come to define themselves in
terms of what they are not. By defining themselves in terms of what
differentiates them from all others they gain unity, but at the expense of perpetual war, for strangers will of necessity be different
in a way perceived as essential difference. Agamemnon and Menelaus therefore point to the problem of the city as such. The city is a
community of men that discovers its unity in a common war, and

so requires the continuation of that war in order to remain a community. Its foundation is enmity. The Trojan War means the death of the dual meaning of *xenos*. After the theft of Helen, strangers must cease to be guest-friends and become enemies. This is, of course, the same as the problem of Ajax. Ajax discovers his own dependence on his enemies, and so discovers the priority of enmity. That is also what Odysseus realizes in his claim to labor only for himself (1367). The problem then is for the city to avoid the tragedy of Ajax. If the *polis* is allowed to recognize that it exists by chance and not by nature, then it will dissolve. If it does not recognize its non-natural character it will become cruel and brutal. If Ajax is buried the city dissolves, and if he is not buried the city is brutalized.

Not to bury Ajax is to say that there is nothing but the *polis*, nothing but the human. If there is nothing but the human, there is no chance. But if there were only chance there would be no intention, no morality, no providence. The solution to this problem, the problem of common war, is common Hades (1193). The play begins with an invisible goddess because invisibility is the essential characteristic of the gods. The presence of the gods assures a kind of providence, which because it is not fully human will not be fully intelligible or visible to humans. The experience of it will not be so very different from the experience of chance. The gods are therefore necessary within the *polis* to make possible the mixture of providence and chance that prevents the *polis* from sinking into bestiality. The world can be understood as providential as a whole while its parts remain inscrutable, and so contingent.

When Odysseus argues for the burial of Ajax, it looks as though he is making the same mistake that Ajax made. Having come to admire his enemy, he has come to prefer him to his friends. But Odysseus is cleverer than that. He does not argue that the live Ajax should be honored. He rather argues that the dead Ajax should be buried. In that way he provides a way out for Agamemnon and for the city. Agamemnon cannot honor Ajax openly, but he can be persuaded to allow him to be buried. Burial is meant to point to the limits of the political by providing a realm, Hades, in which Ajax and Hektor are equally honored. Burial moderates the common war by pointing to a realm beyond the city, the invisible Hades, which is completely moral in a way that this world is not. The invisibility of that realm and of the gods is crucial; otherwise it would undermine the claims made on us by this world and by particular cities. Its existence is equally crucial, however, in order to prevent the brutality of extreme moralism. Ajax would not have felt the same urgent need to punish his enemies had he thought that they would ultimately be punished in Hades.

Unlike the others, Odysseus seems to know that Hades, too, is a *Greek* god. Common Hades is an illusion of a particular *polis*, which serves to protect it against its own particularity. For that reason Odysseus is willing to honor Ajax in death and not simply bury him. If, as he has earlier suggested, we are all shades (126), then Hades *is* realized in this world. The invisible gods are the sign that we know that human beings have insides without knowing what is inside. The awareness that men have insides, like the belief in a general providence, prevents Odysseus from turning into Ajax, whose complete devotion to the human is only a hair's breadth from the attempt to annihilate the human altogether. Because Ajax is like the *polis* in his complete devotion to the human, he is finally not a political man. Political life requires incomplete devotion to the *polis*.

Political life requires the gods, but their presence tends to destroy the *polis*. The gods can be present only indirectly. Their presence, like Athene's, must be invisible. Hades is therefore the paradigmatic god. It is the limit within the city on the completeness of the city. Rituals of burial are the sign that it is present. But there is another sign within the city of the incompleteness of the political world. *Ajax* ends with the chorus's statement of the limits of human foresight.

> Many things are to be known to mortals by being seen;
> But before seeing, no one is a prophet of the things to
> come, what he will do.
>
> (1418–20)

Ajax was *pronousteros* because of his belief that, by doing his duty, he would necessarily prevail. His general belief that the good would triumph allowed him to foresee the future. The chorus end by telling us in general that foresight is unavailable to men. That, of course, is itself a general sort of foresight. In general it is prudent not to trust too strongly in one's predictive powers.

If *Ajax* is a play about the limits of human sight, about our inability to see the inside, it is also about a certain way by which we can see the inside. The play is itself an attempt to show us the limits of our vision by showing us the inside of Ajax. It begins with a scene setting in which Athene uses the word *skēnais* to refer to the tents of Ajax (3). But the word has another meaning as well. It may refer to the backdrop for a stage.[6] By setting the stage Sophocles enables us to see inside Ajax. He makes it possible for us to do the impossible in order for us to learn that it is impossible. Of course, to do that it is necessary for him to reproduce the error of Ajax. Everything in the world of tragedy is significant; it is a fully moral world. That is a necessary dramatic fiction. *Ajax* therefore points to tragedy as the vehicle for revealing the incompleteness of the city to itself. Tragedy can only do that by being like Hades. Because it is a fully purposive world, it can reveal the inside by the outside, but it does that in such a way that we are not tempted to reproduce its tragic fiction in our own lives. *Ajax* ends by pointing to the fact that what seems necessary in retrospect is always contingent in prospect. It is this fact, which tragedy points to, that makes politics necessary and that makes politics possible.

Ajax is a play about the nature of tragedy. Tragedy has as its goal the purging of certain dangerous moral passions. Insofar as tragedy is a solution to the problem of the presence of those passions, *Ajax* is a play about the solution to the problem of politics, and so is not simply tragic. This may account for why the action from which all others develop in the play, the slaying of the animals, is almost a caricature of a tragic action. Were the consequences slightly less severe the play could be a comedy. That Ajax cannot quite rise to the level of Achilles and that Ajax's nature runs parallel to the nature of the city point to the moral of the play: it is best for the second best not to try to be best.

6. Compare Plato's *Laws* 817c with 944a.

Chapter Six

The Politics of *Antigone*

Warren J. Lane and Ann M. Lane

1

The issues of justice and law evoked throughout *Antigone* and embodied in two such powerful characters as Creon and Antigone inevitably raise questions about the proportioning of right between
them. At least one eminent critic has concluded that Antigone is
someone "who does the right thing for the wrong reason."[1] Out of
"purely personal" love for her brother and "indifference to the
claims of the polis," she defies Creon as the hate-filled ruler of the
city. Though the gods ultimately vindicate her "championship
of the family" in their punishment of the king, they also refuse to
condone Antigone's defiant indifference to the *polis* and so permit
her death.

This essay argues, however, that Antigone acted rightly and for
the right reason. Our endeavor is to shift attention from an en-
trenched assumption evident in the above commentary, which lo-
cates in the drama significant struggle between family and *polis*.
Such a struggle as manifest in the antagonism between Antigone
and Creon is assumed to articulate itself through the interrelated
oppositions of nature/convention, female/male, Hades/Olympus,
intuition/reason, divine duties/human-made duties, and so on.
The chief protagonists are conceived as finally destroying one another through the exclusive pursuit of, and imperious attachment
to, the normative attributes of their respective spheres.

We believe that the postulate of family-*polis* conflict, centered on
what amounts to a gender specific division of human activities,
moral capacities, and cosmic dimensions, is highly misleading. It

1. Bernard Knox, *The Heroic Temper* (Berkeley and Los Angeles: University of
California Press, 1964), p. 116.

162

precludes a priori a consideration of Antigone as having political self-understanding of her relation to fellow citizens and as having salient views about proper versus corrupt rule. Moreover, this postulate precludes attention to the fatal flaws in Antigone's stance toward the citizenry, which is indissolubly linked to the politically marginal and subordinate position of women in the city-states. Given her female status, it is unfair to cite Antigone's lack of regard for the *polis* against her, especially when no indication is made of what such an expected positive regard might be. Censuring her without consideration for the more general issue of women's political position in the polity becomes the literary equivalent of the political practice of blaming the victim.

It is our view that while Antigone's aspirations arise from her acute comprehension of civic corruption, the excesses attributable to her must be related to her efforts to overcome the cultural limitations placed on her because of her womanhood. Her stature as political actress emerges through her struggle to face the challenges posed by Creon from the subordinate place to which she is assigned owing to her gender. The particularity of Antigone's situation suggests that her civic project may best be comprehended by distinguishing between two kinds of ideas and concerns in the play: those that are relatively gender specific (differentiated between women and men) and those that are gender indeterminate and sharable.

In *Antigone*, there are significant cultural conceptions of an ideal for men and women encouraging pride of lineage in the relationship of kin to one another[2] and of a further ideal of *philia*, meaning the attachment expressed in word and deed to those people and things held dear. These conceptions provide political and cultural background for understanding both Creon's edict denying burial to his nephew and Antigone's defiance of the corrupt regime settling in upon Thebes.[3]

2. We use "pride of lineage" to encompass the ways in which an awareness of shared forebears, spiritual and material legacies, and wider cultural values prompts respect, consideration, and trust among kin to a degree not expected among non-kin. "Lineage," here, refers not to the aristocratic *genos* but to the circle of kindred (see below). On the characteristics of kinship in relation to other modes of commonality, see Warren Lane, "Classical Moral Paradigms and the Meaning of Kinship," *Dialectical Anthropology* 5 (1980):193–214.

3. The central kin constellation of the play through which cultural understandings and pride of lineage are refracted is not a family but a more extensive network of persons—a kindred. It is precisely the kindred-based sense of right uniting uncle to nephew that Creon tries to ignore. On kindreds in general, see Roger Keesing,

The conflict of Antigone with Creon recapitulates the Homeric struggle between Achilles and Agamemnon over who is the "kinglier man."[4] In the democracy of fifth-century Athens this Homeric struggle could reappear with new cogency. If man was the measure of all things for a political culture that had begun to take the impress of Protagorean teachings, a further inescapable question arose: What was the specific kind of man that constituted that measure? The struggle between Antigone and Creon can be understood as the Sophoclean response to this further question.[5] In Sophocles' estimation, Antigone is the winner of this struggle; she is the exemplary human being who weaves the civic oath of fidelity to city, customs, and gods into the texture of daily life.[6] She thereby reaches the height of greatness, representing a measure to her fellow citizens for inserting the divine into human affairs. Above all others presented in the play, she recognizes the twin foundational principles of her culture and steadfastly and at mortal risk acts upon them.

Specifically, those principles imply that Creon has dishonored his lineage by corrupting the city and that Antigone has demonstrated *philia* by honoring the body of her dead comrade (and brother) Polyneices. Her "kingliness" in action is modeled on Homeric aristocratic patterns and their democratized fifth-century forms. Thus, she attempts to bury her brother in the spirit of a war comrade and condemns her uncle's corruption in the spirit of a political equal. Ismene warns in the first scene of the play that, "We must remember that we two are women / so not to fight men. . . . [but rather we must] obey the men in power" (61–67).[7] Antigone in no way responds to this separation of women from men in following out the foundational principles. She speaks of herself as the "doer" who dares the "crime of piety." She has no sympathy for

Kin Groups and Social Structure (New York: Holt, Rinehart and Winston, 1975), pp. 14–15, 96–99. On the Greek kindred (at Athens, the *Anchisteia*), see William Lacey, *The Family in Classical Greece* (Ithaca, N.Y.: Cornell University Press, 1968), pp. 28–29, 275 n. 21.

4. For a discussion of this question and its consequences in the *Iliad*, see Cedric Whitman, *Homer and the Homeric Tradition* (New York: W. W. Norton, 1958), pp. 183–87.

5. This suggestion is made by Cedric Whitman, *Sophocles* (Cambridge, Mass.: Harvard University Press, 1951), p. 99.

6. Consideration of the civic oath occurs on p. 180 below.

7. Throughout we use the translation of *Antigone* by Elizabeth Wyckoff in *The Complete Greek Tragedies*, ed. David Grene and Richmond Lattimore (Chicago: University of Chicago Press, 1951).

Ismene, who severs herself from the grounds on which the city and their house are based. Later in the play, Creon echoes Ismene's separation of roles for men and women: "I must . . . not let myself be beaten by a woman. / Better, if it must happen, that a man / should overset me. / I won't be called weaker than womankind" (676–80). While Ismene and Creon comprehend Antigone's action as a reflection on women in general, and therefore inappropriate, Antigone repeatedly explains herself in terms that account for the overriding principles of the city pertaining to *both* citizenship and kinship. For her, distinctions between the actions of men and those of women simply are illegitimate.

The play asks whether such distinctions really do need to be made. Although Antigone emerges as the "kinglier" person and Creon concedes defeat in the end, what does it mean that every other character in the play appears to be bound to distinguishing realms for men and women at the expense of principles of justice? Why does Antigone—who clearly acknowledges herself to be a woman, as in the comparison of herself to Niobe—never seem to perceive herself as acting outside the boundaries appropriate for women? She follows the principles of justice at the expense of obliviousness to her fellow citizens' incapacity to take seriously her example of civic excellence because she is a woman.

Although it may be that Sophocles creates Antigone for ironic purposes to show that *even* a woman may be better able to comprehend civic principles than corrupt men, it is also true that the play thematizes the difficulties Antigone encounters because she acts within a political context that recognizes only male actors. Men and women around her cannot conceive of a woman issuing the summons to protest. They cannot comprehend a political *actress.* The conventional, masculine biases of the culture are evident not only in the exaggerated manly conceit of Creon's despotism but in the response of the elders, Ismene, and even Haemon.

This woman's action is invisible to them because they differentiate domestic (familial) and public spheres in terms of gender polarities. And, following from that split, each sphere and corresponding gender is understood to have its own moral basis. Thus even Antigone's most ardent supporters view her as stepping beyond the limits of suitable female behavior. They concentrate on her courageous fulfillment of familial obligations (of burial) customary to women's sphere. Her violation of the feminine proprieties of obedience and silence appear to be the exceptional steps necessary to defend the norms of that womanly domain. Nonetheless, they are seen as violations. Antigone appears to her fellows to have taken on a masculine role. Sophocles shows us that the other characters do not *hear* what Antigone tells them. Her public speech does not reach ears attuned only to male actors. Her words have no public audience. Not even her sister, the first person to whom she turns, treats her as a peer. Ismene instead accuses her of "wild and futile action." For Ismene, Antigone appears mad as soon as she dares speak aloud about Creon's corruption. Thus, Antigone is left alone in her pursuit of civic excellence. She is autonomous, outside of conventions, singular in her passion for the twofold moral principles of the city. Demanding the utmost of herself, she is intolerant of the human weakness around her. When the Thebans fail to respond to her call for civic virtue, she comes to assume an almost divine remoteness to the human world. The purity of her devotion, Sophocles suggests, verges on madness: *erōs* haunts her love of virtue and drives her to excess and distraction.[8]

In the absence of fellow citizens, Antigone has no choice but to sustain herself alone—to become autonomous. Such pursuit of *philia* without others is a kind of madness. *Philia* binds friends, kin, and citizens together. Antigone is denied that crucial involvement with others not only because she lives amidst the fearful and corrupt, but also because she is a woman. And being a woman, silenced and housed, she needs a demonic eros strong enough to bridge the gap between her gender-determined limits and her knowledge of civic possibilities. Ismene, driven by no such passion, views Antigone from within the confines of her gender. Hence she is horrified by the public (to Ismene, male) nature of Antigone's intention to proclaim her deed of burial: "You crave what can't be done" (90). Antigone strives to achieve the seemingly impossible against the regal authority that drives the city toward corruption and, more importantly, against the masculine conventions that define her place as a woman.

Antigone's self-consciousness of membership in her lineage and regard for its leadership in the city animates her invitation to Ismene at the opening of the play. She urges her sister to act in partnership to honor their dead brother Polyneices with full burial. Though even the token burial Antigone finally succeeds in giving the body demonstrates a human regard that renders Polyneices re-

---

8. "Who has you [*erōs*] within him is mad" (790).

spectable in the netherworld,[9] it signifies even more to Antigone. By the deed, she endeavors to dissociate herself and her kin from Creon, his regime, and the shame he has cast upon their lineage.

Antigone's pride in her house provides her with the moral basis to defy Creon's edict. Disobedience restores the honor of her lineage, tarnished by Creon. In refusing to join with Antigone, Ismene not only fails to live up to her heritage but further degrades herself—in her sister's eyes—by not even attempting to reclaim the prestige of their kin group.

A moral gulf separates the two sisters. Ismene lacks Antigone's driving commitment to their house and its status and thus lacks any basis other than obedience to male power on which to plan and to act. Segregated by her gender from the imperatives of honor common to Antigone and their brothers, she wishes to enclose her sister within the silence of those who passively obey. Antigone is outraged by this secrecy. She denounces Ismene's fear of disobeying Creon as a political crime—as rendering her a traitor. And she denounces Ismene's promise of silence as behavior worthy of a foe. For Antigone, the force of her act is dependent on its *public* nature; whether that jeopardizes her life is irrelevant. Only the proclamation of her deed will make clear the connection between her womanly duty to bury the dead and the genderless imperative to honor one's kin in life and death. Ismene's offer of silence would sever the act of burial from principle and meaning. Obedience—and hence survival—are the ultimate values for Ismene.

Grieved by her brother's death, horrified at Polyneices' fate, outraged by Creon's tyranny, and morally abandoned by Ismene, Antigone declares that her only path of response to the burial prohibition leads to death. To die committing a noble crime is preferable to living in humiliated submission. From the time of her dialogue with Ismene, she knows death is inevitable. The theme of her impending end recurs with increasing intensity through the drama. She is not so much obsessed with dying[10] as she is dissociated from

9. Complete burial was a means of assuring to Polyneices that he, like Eteocles, would "have full honor with the dead below" (26). A denial of burial, Knox observes (*Heroic Temper*, p. 92), would mean that as a ghost, Polyneices would "suffer the contempt of his fellow ghosts. . . . Even in death's kingdom the Greek is obsessed with . . . the respect of his fellow men."

10. That Antigone is a woman genuinely obsessed with death is a theme stressed by R. P. Winnington-Ingram, *Sophocles* (Cambridge: Cambridge University Press, 1980), pp. 131–33, 315; and also Charles Segal, *Tragedy and Civilization* (Cambridge, Mass.: Harvard University Press, 1981), pp. 183, 186.

the living beings around her. Grief, anger, and shame radically separate her from the reticent and conventionally minded populace.

The moral distance that separates Antigone and Creon is epitomized in her comment to Ismene: "Further he has the matter so at heart / that anyone who dares attempt the act / will die by public stoning in the town" (35–37). What preoccupies the king is not pride in and loyalty to kin but the vicious penalty by which to command obedience. Throughout the play, Antigone refers to the edict as a decree (*kērygma*) rather than a law (*nomos*), thereby indicating its injustice and immorality.[11] In her eyes, the edict manifests Creon's unworthiness to rule.

To Antigone, the immorality of the decree transcends all other practical political considerations surrounding its formulation. She never mentions the recent war with Argos that proceeded right to the city gates. Nor does she refer to the rivalry of Eteocles and Polyneices for the throne. And she is silent about the mutual slaying of the brothers outside the city walls. It is Ismene who relates this information to the audience. Antigone also ignores the issue of whether Polyneices was provoked to treachery by Eteocles, which would have qualified the certainties about Polyneices' treachery and Eteocles' honor. Many of these considerations preoccupy Ismene. As a woman, she feels such issues remain outside her influence and power. "We'll perish terribly if we . . . try to cross the royal vote and power" (59–60) is her summary comment on the prior events in Thebes. Antigone refrains altogether from pursuing these considerations; her concentrated focus on the morality of the decree shifts attention from matters pertaining to accountability for the war.

By her defiant burial of her brother, Antigone seeks to preclude extraneous issues from emerging, while ensuring that the unjustness of the decree itself looms paramount in her challenge to Creon's authority and moral fitness to rule. The gender boundaries so crucial to Ismene are irrelevant to Antigone. She foresees that Creon's edict, at the inauguration of his reign, augers well neither for their house nor for the city, and that gives her the courage to cross the boundary of customary gender behavior. She comprehends that the principles underlying both kinship and civic life are at stake.

11. The unjust nature of the decree and its implications are discussed on pp. 169–71 below.

Sophocles reveals that Creon is not wholly wrong in realizing that times of crisis may require emergency measures on the part of the city's leadership. Thebes is at a point where its recovery from the recent invasion and loss of its king could require an inescapably dangerous, nonconstitutional endeavor, such as evidenced historically in the radical reforms of Cleisthenes and Ephialtes. It is in the character of politics in times of extremity to demand the exercise of unprecedented powers and to test the moral, intellectual, and political resources of citizens to the utmost. But Creon is oblivious to the manner in which genuine power, civic morality, and clarifying common deliberation are inseparably related. Thus, while the situation of Thebes may prompt a new ruler to unprecedented general edicts, Creon's own particular reliance on intimidation and moral coercion to marshal his people to special effort behind his rule makes him highly suspect as the person best suited to steer the city at its present critical juncture.

The edict is formulated by Creon to alleviate the instability he fears as successor to Eteocles and to consolidate his newly gained position. Since Creon lacks any record of political accomplishment or fighting prowess, is aged, and has not visibly proved himself against the Argive invaders, he wishes now to impress on his fellow countrymen evidence of his warlike spirit. He takes the symbolic path of ensuring the desecration of Polyneices' corpse. Creon can seemingly inflict as great an injury as Eteocles on their common foe and thereby can share in the aura of reverence for Eteocles as savior of the city. Creon thereby seeks personally to assert a legitimacy as successor to reinforce morally the formal entitlements to office he publicly announces.

Creon's unjust decree displays his tyrannical nature. First, the decree is excessive in its objective. The prohibition on burial and mourning is total. It bans burial not only within the boundaries of Thebes, a legitimate restriction, but by implication forbids it outside these bounds as well. Creon seeks to shut the dead man completely off from any signs of respect he might have expected to receive from those of his city of birth and early manhood.[12]

<hr>

12. On the immorality of Creon's treatment of Polyneices' body one may consult the following: C. M. Bowra, *Sophoclean Tragedy* (Oxford: Oxford University Press, 1944), pp. 71–72; Albin Lesky, *A History of Greek Literature* (London: Methuen, 1966), p. 280; and Victor Ehrenberg, *Sophocles and Pericles* (Oxford: Basil Blackwell, 1954), pp. 29–30. Though it might be argued that the obligation of giving burial to the war dead of one's bitterest enemies—as the Greeks did for the Persians at Marathon and

Second, the edict is cruel in the penalty imposed. It exacts a lingering, ignominious death by public stoning. This capital penalty was customarily assigned to traitors.[13] To make disobedience equivalent to treachery and to reject other penalties for disobedience— fine, exile, even enslavement abroad—foreshadows the merciless-ness to be expected from Creon's rule.

Third, the ban is abhorrent and impious in its effects. Creon stresses that the exposed corpse will be despoiled by birds and dogs (29–30, 206–7). As Antigone tells Ismene, exposure of the body is an unholy deed and an affront to the gods. Teiresias sharply denounces Creon for the impiety of interfering with the passage of the dead Polyneices to the netherworld and, by his living entomb-ment of Antigone, preventing the living from remaining with their own kind in the upperworld. Through his ban, Creon not only in-vades the prerogative of Hades' realm but violates the justice of Zeus, which governs the proper relations within and between all spheres of the cosmos. Creon thus incurs the punishing wrath of the Erinyes "sent by Hades and by all gods" (1076–77).

Finally, the prohibition is arbitrary in its foundation. The decree lacks the usual community sanction of the advice and consent of the city elders. Creon speaks of himself as a governor who listens and then "holds to the best plans of all" presented to him (179). But the elders, uneasy about the ban and afraid of Creon, state at the conclusion of his speech that the decree is his responsibility alone.[14]

Many of the stereotypical features Athenians imputed to tyrants appear in Creon. He is quick to anger, inordinately proud, sus-picious, capricious, violent, and vulgar. A traditionalist in his ex-pectations of obedience from his household, he breaks political tra-ditions of consultation with the elders and religious traditions of attentiveness to the oracles.

His latent, but now kindled, ambitiousness is revealed even in the form of his speech, with its overuse of the first person singular,

---

the Persians for the Greeks at Thermopylae—did not apply in the case of traitors, it must be recalled that to Sophocles even the traitorous Ajax deserved proper burial, and the kings who wished to deny it and punish a dead man after his death were censured for it.

13. See Joan O'Brien, *Guide to Sophocles' Antigone* (Carbondale, Ill.: Southern Illi-nois University Press, 1978), p. 12.

14. Thus even an emergency power context for a decree should be interpreted to have required consultation and a measure of deliberation between ruler and elders. If this were not the case there would have been no need for Creon to have publicly dissembled the elder's participation in his decision.

and in the gloating contemplation of the seeming sovereignty of his authority.[15] Despite his immediate contentment with his position as ruler, Creon is deeply uneasy about the firmness of his new-found power. Catapulted by events at a late stage of an undistinguished life into the kingship he covets, he is not about to permit any occurrence that will again thrust him into the background of public life.

2

Antigone can find no partners for her action, and Creon is determined to exclude anyone from joint participation in the governance of the city. There is not only a moral gulf between the protagonists in their separate views of kinship obligations, but also in their different understandings of the foundation of public life. Antigone's burial of her brother and Creon's edict each manifest those divergent conceptions.

Against her uncle's atomizing, hierarchic ideal of rule, Antigone emerges as the champion of *philia*. She condenses in her person, and dramatizes by her conduct in a demoralized society, three modes of *philia*, bearing on kinship, friendship, and rootedness in city and homeland.

For the Greeks, *philos* referred to that which is dear, loved, or liked, including kin, friends, allies, or any object cherished. *Philia*, the relationship of affection and commitment among persons, contrasts with hostility (*echthros*) on the one hand and is differentiated from charity (*agapē*) on the other. The Greek sense of *philia* in friendship and community carries the idea of genuine regard and loyalty and further implies a mutual knowledge of character, the sharing of words and deeds, and the responsible actions and emulation of virtue that sustain bonds of association.

Given Creon's narrow understanding of people, his plodding factual mindedness, and his superficial piety, there is no room for *philia*. Because of this his subjects are all potential enemies. Thus he

15. Especially repugnant to Antigone would be Creon's remark in the preamble referring to himself as closest in connection or kinship to the dead brothers. While Creon means to refer to his standing as eldest surviving male of the royal house, his words would actually remind Antigone that far from being most akin to her brothers, the king is actually in spirit most removed from them, herself, and their parents. See Winnington-Ingram's remarks on Creon's language of this speech (*Sophocles*, pp. 123–24). On the customary Athenian view of the tyrant, see Anthony Podlecki, "Creon and Herodotus," *Transactions of the American Philological Association*, 97 (1966):359–71.

seeks to use the edict to force his opponents to reveal themselves, as well as to insinuate himself into the public reverence for Eteocles. The decree constitutes a loyalty test[16] and is, in short, Creon's clever "snare" or "net," in whose "twisted mesh" he hopes to capture those whom he suspects of secret disaffection with him as Thebes' ruler before they can threaten his position.

The proclamation of the decree makes it part of the law of the *polis*. To Creon the ban's incorporation into city law means that the "well mindedness" of citizens toward the polity can now be appraised by reference to this newly instituted, ostensibly state-enhancing, rule. The stance of citizens toward the edict, as revealed in their obedience or disobedience, can be interpreted as symptomatic of their moral condition as "just" or "wicked." The edict is therein transformed by Creon into a test of his fellow countrymen's loyalty.

The edict's assimilation into law at the termination of Creon's speech retroactively affects the meaning of his prefatory declarations. The decree as test amplifies the king's statement that one "cannot learn of any man the soul, / the mind, and the intent until he shows / his practice of the government and law" (175–77). While chiefly self-referential, the comment also reminds others that their conduct is under surveillance. It implies: "I am this—and what [my chief advisors and citizens] are you?" [17]

Moreover, the decree converts Creon's statement that the polity constitutes one's highest attachment into a warning that insubordination through word or deed renders less than is due the polity. Those committing disobedience forfeit friendship and merit punishment. It is even hinted that those who do not denounce the disaffected in their midst are themselves traitors (185). Thus, the burial prohibition is not merely symptomatic of a tyrannical nature or simply an expression of blind hate for a dead man; it is a device to draw out concealed attitudes toward the king himself.

In his conversation with the elders immediately following the prohibition's announcement, Creon requests them to serve as "sen-

16. The following discussion is an elaboration of highly suggestive comments by Karl Reinhardt (*Sophocles*, trans. H. Harvey and D. Harvey [Oxford: Basil Blackwell, 1979], pp. 69–70). Though Reinhardt clearly identifies the way in which the edict functions as a loyalty test, he neglects the background of Creon's rule: the newness of the regime and his long years of obscurity. As a consequence Reinhardt tries to locate the need for the test in an alleged factional dispute of Creon's with the supposed Theban supporters of Polyneices as an exiled faction head.

17. Ibid., p. 70.

tinels" of the decree. Disquieted by the measure but too fearful to speak up, the elders delicately refuse to spy for the king by misunderstanding his intent as a desire for watchers over the corpse itself. This, they plead, is too arduous a task for them. Creon, sensing their moral reservations, assigns them a less active but more complicitous task in his plans—not to side with anyone who disobeys the ban. This they readily accept (219). Having won their assent to remain silent about their reservations, Creon astutely implicates the elders ever more thoroughly as supporters of the decree (576, 632). He does this in a manner consistent with his initial lie about their inclusion in the decree's formulation. Fearful of disloyalty even among the docile elders, Creon everywhere sees the presence of hostile aristocrats offering bribes to others to act in ways discrediting to him and identifying him as a weak, supplantable ruler (222, 236, 462, 1061, 1326).

Murmurings in the city against Creon for his unjust and impious decree have come to his attention even prior to the edict's second proclamation (290). Filled with anxiety and anger, he is blind to the self-destructiveness of his own cunning. Through distrust of his fellow citizens, Creon unwittingly stimulates precisely the disloyalty he sought to detect and quell. His reliance on the decree as a loyalty test illustrates one of the underlying insights in the Ode to Man. The craft by which men seek to control their environment results in ruin if not undergirded by a deeper, principled understanding of the world they inhabit. Creon comes to this realization too late (1261–69). When the king presents his prohibition as a state-strengthening measure and stifles criticism by wrapping himself in a mantle of civic loyalty, equating disagreement with treason, Antigone cannot countenance the arrogance.

The spirit of the edict, his use of the ban as a loyalty test, and the additional repugnant aspects of his inaugural speech furnish Antigone with abundant evidence of Creon's moral and political unworthiness to rule the city. His speech exhibits powerful corroboration of her initial resolve to bury her brother, to vindicate her lineage's honor, and to publicize the unjustness of the decree.

Antigone's later return to the burial site signifies forethought and unshakeable determination to disavow the decree and the king's authority, but it is also a reproof to the citizenry of Thebes and, in particular, to the respected elders. Her return to the corpse occurs significantly after the official announcement of the ban to the assembled citizenry, when all stand in the silent acceptance prefigured by Ismene. Though neither an elder nor even a male, Antigone ventures to undertake the lonely initiative of reburial that challenges Creon's merits as ruler and the populace's demeaning acquiescence to the edict. She exemplifies the cultural understanding that *philia* not only cuts across the distinction between kin and non-kin, but traverses gender and generational distinctions, while moreover setting the standard for what should be considered best in forms of association.

In Antigone's relationship to Polyneices, a quality beyond kinship is evident. She addresses him as her "dearest brother" in the prologue and as "the brother of my heart" in her last justificatory speech. This relationship has less to do with kinship than with heightened friendship. Neither Eteocles, her other brother, nor Ismene has such a privileged place in her thoughts. In the "hyperbole of her claim"[18] that she would not have risked her life in defiance of the edict for a husband or child but only for a brother, she declares to Polyneices the all-surpassing nature of her love for him.

The statement is not meant to contrast sibling with non-sibling ties. Rather she resorts to kinship idiom to highlight the incomparable bond of friendship existing between her and Polyneices. Her words to Ismene in the prologue also indicate that her brother stands closer to Antigone in friendship than even kinship permits. Antigone declares that dying for her act means that she can lie with Polyneices as "friend with friend," or, in another translation, "as loved one with loved one" (73). In Greek terms the language here is appropriate to those who consider themselves close friends and comrades in arms. Like a Homeric hero or citizen soldier, Antigone will dare a noble death in the defense of the body of her slain friend against possible despoilment by the enemy. She vows to succeed or die beside him in the effort. Antigone conceives of her burial of Polyneices as a glorious engagement in battle; it is a heroism that resonates with her embattled sense of herself as the last heir and only defender of her lineage (941). Antigone's stance strikingly contrasts with Creon's own self-serving use of Polyneices' corpse to demonstrate military prowess of a violent and destructive kind.

This self-identification as guardian of her kinspeople and as friend and warrior comrade to Polyneices also reveals her embed-

18. Knox, *Heroic Temper*, p. 106.

dedness in the polity—another aspect of *philia*. Rather than a "woman essentially indifferent to the city,"[19] Antigone is so attached to it that she feels free to call upon Thebes—in its long-established physical presence—to bear witness to the unjust sufferings its current generation of inhabitants are only too ready to countenance (937–43). The city itself is rooted in the land, and the cherished and enduring landscape features of her homeland— Dirce's spring, Thebes's grove, and its plain—are invoked as guarantors of Antigone's uprightness. For Antigone, her homeland will in its very configuration record for all time the shamefulness of the law casting her to an undeserved death (840–45). Her remarks are a special rebuke to the council of elders, whose age and experience should have ensured a sensitivity to the claims of kinship and *philia* she asserts.

Antigone's adherence to *philia* is the positive counterpart to her disavowal of Creon's corrupt authority and the complicitous citizenry. *Philia*, ultimately grounded in the cosmic order of justice founded by Zeus, is overseen by the retributive power of the Erinyes. When Creon accuses Antigone of "overstepping" the law, she counters by accusing him of seeking to "outrun" the divine ordinance itself. However, a contrast of man-made law with a higher law of the gods is not at issue in the struggle between the two protagonists. A simple hierarchy of kinds of law is not how divine and human interaction is presented in the play. For Antigone, the divine is immanent in human *philia*,[20] which is understood to be nourished by the traditional ways discarded by Creon's decree. Hence there are two forms of *human* law in conflict in the drama, and only that law represented by Antigone can claim participation in the unwritten, immortal ways of the divine.

Antigone acts against a prevalent atmosphere in Thebes of fear and silence. In upbraiding the docile Theban citizenry, especially its leadership, and denying recognition to Creon as king, Antigone draws attention to the civic corruption around her. More than that, she tries to recall her countrymen to an eclipsed standard of dignity and worth. Only this standard of divinely sanctioned *philia*, substantiated in words and deeds, can return Thebes to the path of justice. Antigone fails, however, to communicate the

19. Winnington-Ingram, *Sophocles*, pp. 127, 129, 141.
20. As Ehrenberg rightly observes (*Sophocles and Pericles*, p. 31), *philia* is "one of the forces active in the unwritten laws." See, too, O'Brien, *Guide*, p. 66.

full civic dimension of this exemplary project. Her people never adequately comprehend what she shows them of their situation and possibilities.

By her insistent repudiation of Creon's authority, Antigone establishes her right to call herself the last genuine heir of the royal line (941). She redeems the honor of the house from the disgrace into which the edict and loyalty test plunge it. However, her rebuke to the citizenry for their meek compliance with the ban goes unheeded. Her exemplary questioning of Creon's fitness to rule is ignored. The path of *philia* Antigone offers the polity as a means to reverse its decline into corruption and regain its divinely endorsed moral foundation is neither taken nor acknowledged.

The only genuine outbreak of political indignation in Thebes over the nature of the edict and its implications for the tenor of Creon's rule appears early in the play (290–95). The disaffection is irately noted by the king in his remarks to the guard. These sparks of political resistance are, however, random and short-lived.[21] The real outcry in the city (690–95, 733) occurs only after Antigone is snared by the guards, and the populace sees that it is indeed the daughter of Oedipus and sister of the dead men who is bound over for execution. Popular discontent is not directed at the civic issues posed by Antigone's defiance, however, but arises out of sheer sympathy for the victim. The penalty of public stoning is shameful and agonizing; the entire city "grieves for this girl unjustly doomed if ever woman was" (694). What so moves people is the cruelty of the punishment inflicted on a young woman who was only performing her religious and familial duties of burial. The force of the phrase "if ever woman was" highlights the traditional character of the tasks Antigone carries out, for which it is patently wrong to punish someone. She is seen by the populace not as a political actress on behalf of house and city, but merely as a woman with traditional, gender-defined tasks to perform. While the affections of Antigone's fiancé Haemon and of Ismene are with her and mingle with those of the citizenry, no one who supports her adequately comprehends the civic import of her acts or statements.

21. Creon characteristically misconstrues the nascent opposition to his rule that his decree and treatment of Antigone elicit as a symptom of an underlying anarchic temper of the city's populace that he must henceforth control singlehandedly. Of lines 672–73 A. A. Long observes that here occurs the "earliest known example of *anarchia* meaning 'unruliness' or 'anarchy' in an absolute sense. (Hitherto) in most 5th century writers the word means literally 'absence of rule'" (*Language and Thought in Sophocles* [London: Athlone Press, 1968], p. 54).

Vacillating elders condemn Antigone on the grounds on which she is justified by her partisans. The elders see her as pursuing her duties in a rash and assertive fashion unbecoming to a woman. Thus, while it is the spirit of Antigone's acts that the elders censure, they—like her partisans—focus on the traditional and religious dutifulness of her conduct, ignoring the public repudiation of Creon expressed by her words and deeds.

Antigone does not expect this incomprehension and announces to Creon that public opinion would undoubtedly favor her were people not silenced by fear (504–5). At this point she does not know of the outcry over her impending execution, and we learn of it through Haemon's report to his father of what is happening in the city. But Antigone would be surprised by the traditionalist cast of the defense emerging among her countrymen. Just as she approaches Ismene in anticipation of her support, so she expects support from the citizenry. She feels she is approaching them as an advocate of the traditional ways of *philia* and of a successor to the kingship worthy of his lineage, skilled in the weaving of friendship into the life of the polity. Antigone's expectations of those around her are unrealizable.

3

Antigone's commitments are single-minded and total. She is intolerant of all moral failings or hesitancies in action engendered by circumstances and upbringing. Behind the elders' misunderstanding of Antigone as a woman of willful independence is the imperiousness of a temper animated by demonic eros. She is indeed a person of terrible (*deinos*) righteousness, and she expects others to respond to the requirements of virtue in the same way. Ismene's accusation that her sister is a lover of the impossible (90) alludes not only to disregard for practical considerations but also to the ferocity of her pursuit of justice. In succumbing to this demonic eros— most conspicuously in her implacable repudiation of Ismene— Antigone transgresses the limits between the human and the divine.[22] And for this offense, the gods punish her by luring her to a precipitate suicide in the rocky cave.

22. Antigone is, after all, as the elders remark, the "unhappy Oedipus's" child (379–80, 471–72). Richard Braun sees in the etymology of her name the meaning "born to oppose" (*Antigone* [New York: Oxford University Press, 1973], p. 7). She is the one compelled to contest with resolute integrity the fate of her kin and the cor-

The divine powers ultimately vindicate Antigone's civic stance, humble her chief enemy, and punish the city that failed to understand and support her. But they also punish Antigone for her inhuman pursuit of a virtue that exceeds the bounds proper to mortal excellence. The gods permit her to commit suicide in violent haste just before the now troubled Creon recants and orders her release. Antigone fails in her civic endeavor, and the consequences for her homeland are disastrous. In the apocalyptic end of the play, one encounters the exposure of the hollowness of Creon's pretensions to rule, the suicides of his son and wife, the consignment of Creon and Ismene to their own forms of living death, and the sinister presence of Dionysus over the city, which the deluded chorus take as a sign of salvation rather than of the foreign invasion foretold by Teiresias.[23]

The ambiguity of the chorus's final comprehension of what has transpired in Thebes is foreshadowed by the Ode to Man.[24] The ode seems to set out an evolutionary view of political community and the development of the arts attributable to rational mastery of the environment. But at its conclusion this power is seen to be ambiguous at best. The chorus perceive that when human powers lack intelligent moral direction, these capacities and designs recoil and destroy their agents. Although "clever man" subjugates all things on the earth and in the heavens, he may lack proper insight, becoming the victim of his own endowments and achievements, and thus be trapped and overpowered in the "tangled mesh of his nets." There is here an ominous allusion to Creon as the potential victim of his own cunningly contrived loyalty test. But at a more significant level, the words can be understood to introduce Antigone as the genuine embodiment of the daunting though wondrous creature—"man."[25]

In the light of the ode, Antigone's is the eloquent "speech" that amid the silence of the city admonishes those around her. It is her "wind-swift thought" that confronts the crisis created by Creon's

---

ruption of her city. But as a consequence of her womanly status and the intensity of her commitments she must succumb to the doom awaiting her house.

23. On the ominous meaning of the last choral ode, see Winnington-Ingram, *Sophocles,* pp. 111–16.

24. Some of the ambiguities of the ode are helpfully explored by C. Segal's "Sophocles' Praise of Man and the Conflicts of the Antigone," in *Sophocles,* ed. Thomas Woodward (Englewood Cliffs, N.J.: Prentice-Hall, 1966) pp. 62–85.

25. O'Brien, *Guide,* pp. 46–62, has an informative discussion of this point.

ban. She alone thinks and speaks as the guardian of the *philia*, or "feelings that make the town." Not rationalist statecraft (more properly belonging to Creon) but the distinctly non-rationalist, formative impulse of *philia* is identified by the chorus as drawing together and sustaining people and polity.[26]

The ode's concluding lines reinforce this view and focus attention on Antigone. Among all the people of Thebes, and in special contrast to its male citizenry, only Antigone "weaves" into "the laws of the land the gods' sworn right," a genuine concern for loyalty to others—*philia*.[27] Because *philia* is the human element in closest touch with the unwritten, divine law to which mortals are "sworn," only *philia* can keep humans from moral ruin and in touch with honor for self and city.

The ode further elaborates the interlacing of divine and human through the double meaning of those "laws of the land" meant to be leavened by *philia* (369). On one hand, the phrase refers simply to the laws of the polity; but on the other, it identifies the ways of the earth (*chthōn*). The ways of the earth are those of the Erinyes as emissaries of Zeus. His justice governs all things and can be brought into the affairs of the polity only through the promotion of *philia*. The justice-protecting Erinyes always lurk in the background as sanctions for Antigone's acts. Zeus and the Erinyes stand as the guarantors of the quality of workmanship with which *philia* is woven into the fabric of *polis* life. The harsh yoke and harnesses to which Creon turns to organize, or rather confine, political life must give way to the new model for citizenship and rule Antigone represents: the intelligent weaving of firm friendship.[28]

The juxtaposition of Antigone's entrance as a political criminal with the culminating lines of the chorus's condemnation of lawbreakers is jarring. Having sung the praises of civic "man," they are confronted with civic woman. Sophocles shows a woman precluded from taking the sworn civic oath—similar to that administered at Athens—to be most sensitive to the implications of the "gods' sworn right." This oath, taken by free-born young men (*ephēboi*) on the assumption of full citizenship, was intended to

26. On the *astynomous orgas*, or city-shaping temper of Antigone, see ibid., p. 56.

27. Discussion of the controversies surrounding the reading of lines 368–69 as an active "inserting" or "weaving-in" rather than the more reticent "honoring" is to be found in Knox, *Heroic Temper*, pp. 185–86, and in O'Brien, *Guide*, p. 60.

28. The last lines of the ode seem to both echo the Solonic concept of *eunomia* and prefigure the weaver of Plato's *Statesman*.

sustain the ways of the polity. Central to these ways were considerations that dominate Antigone: loyalty to comrades, protection of
the homeland, and readiness to vindicate sacred and public institutions and established customs against external and internal enemies.[29] A leadership or citizenry that permitted the corruption of
civic morale violated its pledge.

Only her enemy Creon, preoccupied with the need to ensure his
newly won power, is sensitive to the political implications of Antigone's repudiation of his authority. The substantial moral under-
pinnings of her challenge naturally escape him. But Creon's enmity
toward his niece is all the more intense because his challenger is
a woman. He is outraged and humiliated at being opposed and
scornfully addressed by a woman (525, 578, 680, 746). Not to punish Antigone would unman him (484), he imagines, and unleash
anarchy in the city (672). Hence the king's male conceits quicken his
desire to rid himself of Antigone and the seeming threat her presence poses to his continued secure reign. Antigone, for her part,
fails to appreciate the full danger to her from the hidden snares of
masculine prejudice in which her struggle to overcome civic corruption finally entraps her. As a consequence of these prejudices,
the thrust of her heroism is turned aside and the full honor that is
rightfully hers as sponsor of the city is denied. Animated by a radical understanding of her situation and loyalties, she ironically dies
a martyr to traditionalism in the eyes of her fellow citizens.

4

As she is led away to entombment, Antigone acknowledges the aspects of her existence as a woman she has hitherto ignored. She
neither regrets the deed leading to her death nor dwells on her impending suffering. Rather, she laments two promises of her life
now denied: marriage and motherhood. "No marriage-bed, no
marriage-song for me, / and since no wedding, so no child to rear"
(917–18).[30] It seems strange for this courageous woman to linger re-

29. On this oath at Athens and the allusions to it in fifth-century literature, see
P. Siewart, "The Ephebic Oath in Fifth-Century Athens," *Journal of the Hellenic Society*
97 (1977): 102–11. Such an oath could provide an important internal point of reference for political debates about the spirit of the Athenian polity in the late fifth and
fourth centuries that looked to the character of the "ancestral constitution."

30. These words evoke the important theme of Antigone's impending marriage to
Haemon. This theme was announced by Ismene (568, 570), touched upon thereafter

gretfully over deprivation of these ordinary womanly experiences. Such judgments, however, fail to give adequate heed to Antigone's demonic eros, which empowers her to break through conventional gender-based limitations and to champion the civic principles of lineage pride and *philia*. Eros so captivates her that she becomes oblivious in important respects to the fact that she performs her heroic act as a woman. In her ferocious righteousness, Antigone denies herself any sympathy with the difficult situation of women like Ismene, who are unable to take unconventional initiatives without understanding and encouragement. Antigone also remains unaware of how her challenge to Creon and remonstrance to the citizenry will be received by those socialized into perceiving her as only a second-class citizen.

When Antigone is brought from the palace by the guards on her "last journey," she knows she has lost all connection to the living. Released from the enormous strain of acting amid human corruption, she can suddenly contemplate the aspects of womanly existence that have been eclipsed by her heroic task. Rather than betraying weakness, the scene of Antigone's misery at her unwed and childless state points to the many-faceted woman she might have been had she lived in a more just polity.

But this contemplative mood is brief. Having revealed her despair, Antigone walks to her death still reproving her accusers and claiming the justness of her action: "Look, leaders of Thebes / I am last of your royal line. / Look what I suffer, at whose command, / because I respected the right" (940–43). To say that Antigone ignores important aspects of her gender-defined situation is not, therefore, to assert that she conducts herself like a man, though such is the narrow-minded view of Creon. Her womanly identity is not exhausted by the husband and children denied her. Indeed, her womanhood is vitally implicated in her civic struggle: she is the loyal sister and loving friend of Polyneices, the last worthy daugh-

---

by the chorus (630), Haemon (637), and Creon (760), and now finally is acknowledged by Antigone herself. Thoughts of her relationship to Haemon now resurface in a shadowy, abstracted manner. Haemon is never mentioned by Antigone. Despite the prewar quality of their relationship—noted by Ismene for its "closeness"— her current meditative language conveys Antigone's own remoteness from her passionately devoted, but never fully comprehending, lover. Indeed, the very belatedness of Antigone's admission of these conjugal longings highlights the emotional distance that has grown up between her and Haemon with the unfolding of her city's civic crisis.

ter and heir to her house, and the preserver of the established ways
of her city.

By thus presenting Antigone as the weaver of *philia* into the texture of the polity, Sophocles makes striking political use of the masculine stereotype of his culture. The play transforms the typical
male understanding of the feminine as the repository of domestic
traditions, such as burial. Sophocles endows this woman with
guardianship of traditions not restricted to the domestic sphere
but inclusive of the entire *polis*. Antigone, as the epitome of responsible citizenship, acts from the basis of her womanly identity.

By forcing upon Antigone the necessity of adhering to certain
facets of her womanhood at the expense of its other significant aspects, Sophocles indicates the gender impasse in which the *polis* is
enmeshed. Antigone's subjection to a painful "choice" among her
possible involvements as a woman should never have occurred.
That it does is symptomatic of a peculiar frailty of the *polis*. Her
forced choice symbolizes the ultimately oppressive situation of
women at Athens, and her actual fate is emblematic of the effect of
such a situation: death in life.

Sophocles shows this deforming situation and impoverished fate
of women to be indissolubly joined to the ways of the *polis*. The
doom-laden atmosphere of the play's conclusion, with its grim
prospects for Antigone's survivors and the city as a whole, implies
the precariousness of the *polis* as a form of life. Inasmuch as the
city harbors within itself a blatantly unjust condition where half
the free citizens suffer at the hands of its free men, the very continued existence of the *polis* becomes questionable. The endemic li-
abilities of masculine preconceptions lie both in their pervasive op-
eration and in the insidious, fatal alliances they forge with those
ordinary forces of corruption latent in collective life. Sophocles
leads us to ask not merely whether a polity so unjustly structured
can survive but whether it deserves to.

Chapter Seven

Human Action and Political Action in *Oedipus Tyrannos*

Joel D. Schwartz

The Athenians are the most politically free and free-thinking people in all Greece, and "they fight as though their bodies were not their own." Such is the penetrating assessment of Athenian character made by the Corinthians early in Thucydides' *History*.[1] Later in the *History*, Pericles' Funeral Oration, delivered in memory of the war dead, proclaims the same remarkable Athenian freedom, one that extends from the city's "government" to its "ordinary life." While the Spartans live under a "painful discipline" from the moment of birth, Pericles says, "we live exactly as we please and yet are just as ready to encounter every legitimate danger."[2] Freest of all peoples, yet their bodies are not their own; a citizenry that lives exactly as it pleases, yet its loyalty to law and ancestral wisdom and its willingness to die in their defense are unmatched in all Hellas— how are we to make sense out of these apparently paradoxical characterizations?

Much has been written about the high value placed by the fifth-century Greeks on public action, especially as it contrasts with modern man's preference, sanctioned by the liberal tradition, for private accumulation. Less, however, has been said about exactly what public action meant to the Greeks. Action, above all else, implied freedom. But if we take freedom to mean "absence of external impediments," in Hobbes's phrase,[3] then the apotheosis of free hu-

1. 1.70. Richard Crawley renders this: "Their bodies they spend ungrudgingly in their country's cause" (*The Peloponnesian War* [New York: Modern Library, 1951], p. 40).
2. 2.37, 39.
3. Thomas Hobbes, *Leviathan; or, The Matter, Forme and Power of a Commonwealth Ecclesiasticall and Civil* (Oxford: Basil Blackwell, 1960), p. 84.

man action that is voiced so frequently by fifth-century authors is indeed paradoxical. Were the Greeks simply sloppy thinkers when they maintained, as Sophocles maintains, that freedom of the will is compatible with a belief that the gods routinely intervene in human affairs?—when they maintained, as Thucydides maintains, that political freedom is compatible with an allegiance to a profoundly authoritative community? Since men, it seems, were confronted with "impediments" at every turn, what could the Corinthians and Pericles have meant?

If we are to make any headway toward answering this question, we must discard the liberal lexicon, and in particular the liberal understanding of the vocabulary of human action ("freedom," "necessity," "authority," "rationality," "participation," and so on), and place the words of fifth-century authors in their proper context, the world view of the Late Archaic mind. These authors turned to tragedy and to a distinctly tragic kind of history, of which there is no better example than Thucydides' *History*, to clarify the nature of human action. Tragedy, I shall argue, in an analysis of *Oedipus Tyrannos*, was uniquely suited as a genre to present an ambiguous, or, more precisely, ironic, understanding of the human condition. Tragedy turns on irony: no tragedy can be "tragic" if man is viewed either as a tyrant over his destiny or as a plaything of the gods. The traditional debate over whether *Oedipus* is a "tragedy of character" or a "tragedy of fate" only serves to divide Sophocles' drama precisely where it is least divisible, at the point where character and fate, autonomy and "impediment" join, as we shall see, in what from the liberal point of view can only appear to be an untidy overdetermination of the action. My thesis is that by clarifying the action of the play, we are in a position to clarify what action itself meant to Sophocles and his audience.

Men, it seems, have always asked whether they are free. They have posed this as a religious question, as a philosophical question, and as a political question. Today, it is often posed as a debate in the philosophy of the social sciences waged between behavioralists, who portray action as an "effect" that logically must have a "cause," and Wittgensteinians and other "humanists" who maintain that action is characteristically purposive and intentional—in a word, "free."[4] Some have talked about different levels of explana-

4. For a useful analysis and bibliography of this debate, as well as an explication of variations within each camp, see J. Donald Moon, "The Logic of Political Inquiry:

tion in an attempt to stake out a compromise position that is no doubt unsatisfactory to both sides.[5] Unlike the fifth-century Greeks, we lack a genre like tragedy that can present the complexities of the human condition in a single voice—a genre that can make sense out of a creature that, as Aristotle puts it, is neither an animal nor a god, neither simply a creature of necessity nor an absolute master of necessity. Tragedy did not flourish until the fifth century, and it did not long survive the fifth century. It was born with the political culture of the age of Pericles, it both reflected and constituted that culture, and it matured, grew old, and died with that culture. Tragedy was not just a theatrical or literary form to Sophocles, one genre among the many he may have selected in which to make his argument. He wrote tragedy because there was no other genre that could both teach and "imitate," in Aristotle's sense, the tragic form of life of the classical *polis*.

In the first three sections of this essay I shall examine the ironic conception of "human freedom" (freedom of the will) in Sophocles' *Oedipus*. In the final section I shall extend this analysis in an effort to clarify the ironic "political freedom" of the Athenian citizen.

GNÔTHI SAUTON

While it is a mistake to read the great Athenian dramas as strict allegories, as though one could reliably expect a precise correspondence between dramatic action and historical event, it is also a mistake to interpret them solely according to aesthetic criteria and to underestimate their various didactic missions.[6] The festivals of Dionysus at which the plays were performed were above all religious and patriotic events, occasions to seek insight into the words and deeds of the day by holding them up against the constantly

A Synthesis of Opposed Perspectives," in *Handbook of Political Science*, edited by Fred I. Greestein and Nelson W. Polsby (Reading, Mass.: Addison-Wesley, 1975), vol. 1, pp. 131–238.

5. This is the position of Moon, "The Logic of Political Inquiry"; and of Georg Henrik von Wright, *Explanation and Understanding* (Ithaca, N.Y.: Cornell University Press, 1971). For a critique, see John G. Gunnell, "Political Theory and Political Action," *Western Political Quarterly* 34 (September, 1981): 341–58.

6. Two useful but overly allegorical readings of the *Oedipus* are Victor Ehrenberg, *Sophocles and Pericles* (Oxford: Oxford University Press, 1954), and Bernard Knox, *Oedipus at Thebes* (New Haven: Yale University Press, 1957). For an insightful discussion of the didactic dimension in ancient drama, see Peter Walcot, *Greek Drama in its Theatrical and Social Context* (Cardiff: University of Wales Press, 1976), pp. 94–103.

reinterpreted truths embedded in myth and religion. It is impossible to understand Plato's determined attack on the political consequences of drama if we forget that the dramatists, like the Sophists, competed with Socrates and Plato as teachers of men. When the chorus calls Oedipus a model or example—a *paradeigma* (1193)[7]— there can be no doubt that Sophocles means that Oedipus's terrible discovery is a lesson that the Athenians should bear in mind when they leave the theater to conduct their lives and the life of their city. The distinction between aesthetics and pedagogy, so central to much modern criticism, would just not have been meaningful to Sophocles.

But what does Sophocles teach in *Oedipus Tyrannos*? To begin with, he teaches that knowledge is to be preferred to ignorance. Oedipus, like Socrates, is the paradigmatic seeker after knowledge. When first approached by the plague-stricken citizenry of Thebes, he tells them "I already know" (58) your miseries; and faced with difficulties in the inquiry, he says "I shall start anew and make all clear" (132). When he has nearly brought the terrible truth to light, the cadence of his words becomes ever more insistent: "It cannot be . . . that I shall fail to reveal" (1058–59); "I will not be prevailed upon not to learn the truth" (1065); "Break forth what will . . . I am determined to know" (1076–77). In contrast to Genesis, where God forbids man to partake of the fruit of the tree of knowledge, the action of *Oedipus* begins with the god's command to identify and punish the slayer of Laius. Apollo himself was a riddler. But while he seldom revealed knowledge in all its clarity, he frequently commanded man to take action in its pursuit. Socrates, too, understood himself to be under such a command.[8] *Gnôthi sauton*—Know thyself—was the inscription on the wall of Apollo's temple at Delphi. The god commands action, however difficult, in the pursuit of knowledge, however awful.

But it would be incorrect to conclude that the most basic teach-

7. The reference numbers in the text are standard line numbers as found, for instance, in the Loeb edition. I have found the following translations the most useful: *Sophocles*, trans. F. Storr (Cambridge, Mass.: Harvard University Press, Loeb Classical Library, 1968); *The Oedipus Cycle*, trans. Dudley Fitts and Robert Fitzgerald (New York: Harcourt, Brace, Jovanovich, 1977); and *The Oedipus Tyrannus*, part 1 of *Sophocles: The Plays and Fragments*, trans. R. C. Jebb (Cambridge: Cambridge University Press, 1893). Jebb's notes are indispensable.

8. Delphi told Socrates that no man was wiser than he (*Apology* 21a). But Socrates understood this to be a "riddle" (*Apology* 21b), and he set out to discover its meaning. On the significance of Apollo's "riddles," see below, pp. 000–00.

ing of *Oedipus* is that knowledge is preferable to ignorance—that "the unexamined life," in Socrates' words, "is not worth living." Apollo's command is rather the axiom that precedes and motivates the search, the driving force in Oedipus's character that pushes the action forward and leads him to his discovery. But what does Oedipus learn? What is the content of this self-discovery? *Gnôthi sauton* was, of course, a gnomic saying long before Sophocles wrote, and its meaning was a subject of great debate by the 420s, when his play was probably performed. To the conservative poets of the Archaic period, it had been a call for restraint and piety. Know thy station as dictated by the gods; practice *sōphrosynē*,[9] humility and cautious prudence, for the fate of man, creature of a day, is in the hands of the gods. Know thy limits. Success, Pindar wrote, "does not lie within the control of men; it is a god [*daimōn*] that gives it, tossing now one man now another on high, and then bringing him below the level of his hands."[10] But to the Sophists and the humanistic historical and medical writers that flourished in the second half of the fifth century, the epigram's meaning had virtually reversed. When Hippocrates and Thucydides looked into their souls, they saw power, not limits—the power to diagnose the natural causes of disease and war and the purely human ingenuity to cure them. "Man," said Protagoras, "is the measure of all things."[11] As Heraclitus, an Ionian forerunner of the fifth-century humanists, had argued, no *daimōn* leaps upon man to shape his character, for "character is man's *daimōn*."[12] Sophocles' position on this debate,

9. The relationship between *sōphrosynē* and "self-knowledge" is discussed in Plato, *Charmides* 164d–165a. For an analysis of this interpretation of the *gnōmē*, see Alister Cameron, *The Identity of Oedipus the King: Five Essays on the Oedipus Tyrannus* (New York: New York University Press, 1968), pp. 16–17. See also Helen North, *Sophrosyne: Self-knowledge and Self-restraint in Greek Literature* (Ithaca, N.Y.: Cornell University Press, 1966), chs. 1–3 (pp. 50–68 focus on Sophocles).

10. *Pythian* 8. This is Pindar's last dated epinician ode, written in 446 for the winner of the wrestling prize at the Pythian games. For an analysis, see Hermann Fränkel, *Early Greek Poetry and Philosophy: A History of Greek Epic, Lyric, and Prose to the Middle of the Fifth Century*, trans. Moses Hadas and James Willis (New York: Harcourt, Brace, Jovanovich, 1975), pp. 497–504.

11. H. Diels and W. Kranz, *Die Fragmente der Vorsokratiker*[7] (Berlin: Weidmann, 1954), Protagoras B1. For a discussion of the fragment's problematic meaning, see Kathleen Freeman, *Companion to the Pre-Socratic Philosophers* (Oxford: Oxford University Press, 1946), p. 342. On the relationship between the fragment and the *Oedipus*, see Knox, *Oedipus at Thebes*, ch. 4.

12. *Heraclitus of Ephesus*, edited by Lewis A. Richards (Chicago: Argonaut, 1969), fr. 121. For the context of Heraclitus's fragment, see Frankel, *Early Greek Poetry and Philosophy*, pp. 370–98. Frankel argues (pp. 397–98) that the stark dialectical conflicts in Sophocles have their origin in Heraclitus.

his conjugation of the relationship between character and destiny, the hand of Oedipus and the hand of Apollo, is at the heart of his teaching in the drama.

The interpretations of this central issue in the play have of course been legion. Perhaps because of the very greatness of the drama, seldom questioned since Aristotle declared it the model for all tragedies in his *Poetics*, generation upon generation of philosophers and critics, Aristotle included, have achieved legitimacy for their own views by "discovering" them, however problematically, in Sophocles' text. In the end, however, these interpretations can usefully be divided into two camps. According to the first camp, Sophocles should be associated with his humanist contemporaries; Oedipus, it is maintained, is a free actor, causally, if not morally, responsible for the action of the play. To the second camp, Sophocles is numbered among the religious conservatives, and Oedipus is transformed into a pathetic pawn of the gods, his tale a remonstrance directed at the naturalists and a call for a return to piety.[13]

The argument of this essay is that both of these approaches, even in their most sophisticated forms, are incorrect, in part because each fails to take seriously the insights of the other. But the dual agency or over-determination that appears to result from a careful reading of the play is not simply an irrational mystery, at least not unless we are to give Plato and his philosophical successors absolute hegemony over the concept of "rationality." Oedipus is an active participant in his fate, an "ally," as he says,[14] of the gods. His discovery is that both his hand and the hand of god have been active from the beginning. When action is construed in this way as "participation," this dual or merged agency is not only tolerable but logically necessary (rational). Like the critics, Oedipus himself

13. For a useful bibliography of both "camps," see William Chase Greene, *Moira: Fate, Good and Evil in Greek Thought* (Cambridge, Mass.: Harvard University Press, 1944), p. 406. The "humanist" or "free will" school has been dominant in recent years. In particular, see Knox, *Oedipus at Thebes*, and Abby Leach, "Fate and Free Will in Greek Literature," in *The Greek Genius and Its Influence*, edited by Lane Cooper (Ithaca, N.Y.: Cornell University Press, 1952). The interpretations that I have found the most illuminating, all of which refuse to find a simple solution to the "free will" problem, are: Cameron, *Identity of Oedipus the King*; Laszlo Versenyi, *Man's Measure: A Study of the Greek Image of Man from Homer to Sophocles* (Albany: State University of New York Press, 1974), ch. 8; R. P. Winnington-Ingram, *Sophocles: An Interpretation* (Cambridge: Cambridge University Press, 1980); and G. M. Kirkwood, *A Study of Sophoclean Drama* (Ithaca, N.Y.: Cornell University Press, 1958).

14. See p. 204, below.

at times entertains the possibility that he is a pawn of fate or, alternatively, a tyrant over his destiny. But in the end he discovers the same truth that Pericles proclaims in the Funeral Oration, that authority and freedom are not only compatible, but that neither, at least for humans, is possible without the other. This is the position that Sophocles takes on the intellectual disputes of his day, the lesson that he advances by example (action) rather than by proposition (philsophy) to his ritually assembled Athenian audience.

THE HAND OF OEDIPUS

The evidence that the tragic hero of Sophocles' *Oedipus* is a free actor is impressive indeed, however much it must ultimately be reinterpreted in light of the equally impressive evidence to the contrary. Perhaps the strongest evidence for a humanist reading emerges from a comparison of Sophocles' treatment of the story with earlier treatments that certainly were on his mind as he wrote.[15] The basic plot of the story precedes Homer, and while several elements in this plot vary considerably from one version to the next, a single commanding theme had taken shape by the time Aeschylus wrote his Theban trilogy in the early decades of the fifth century. *Oedipus* was the second play in Aeschylus's trilogy, only the last of which, *Seven Against Thebes*, has survived. The summary of the plot that appears in the second stasimon of the latter play indicates that the focus of the dramas, like the focus of the *Oresteia*, was on the history of a cursed race, the house of Labdacus. Laius, so the old story goes, was cursed by Pelops for the rape of Chrysippus.[16] The curse was seconded by Apollo, who told Laius that *if* he had a son (the conditionality is important), the boy would murder his father and have children by his mother. Laius violated the command and the doom on the house was sealed. Oedipus's fall, then, is determined by the sins of an earlier generation, his deeds the result of the *miasma*, the ritual pollution, that infects his blood from birth. Just how Oedipus's *miasma* was brought to light is unclear in *Seven Against Thebes*, but it is perhaps likely that Aeschylus followed the

15. This comparison is masterfully drawn by Cameron, *Identity of Oedipus the King*, ch. 1.
16. C. M. Bowra, *Sophoclean Tragedy* (Oxford: Oxford University Press, 1944), p. 162; W. C. Helmbold, "The Paradox of Oedipus," *American Journal of Philology* 72 (1951): 294; and Cameron, *Identity of Oedipus the King*, p. 9.

brief story line in the *Odyssey*: "And thereupon," Homer writes, "the gods made these things well known to men."[17]

Aristotle says that there is no need for the poet to remain absolutely loyal to "the received myths,"[18] and it is clear that Sophocles shifted the focus of the story considerably to accommodate it to his purposes. Though we lack the first two plays in Aeschylus's trilogy, we can assume that Laius was the primary figure in the trilogy as a whole. The very conditionality of Apollo's oracle indicates that Laius's willing disobedience was the cause not only of his own death but of all the misery to follow. In Sophocles' version, the oracle is transformed into a simple statement of fact: "It was fated [*moira*]," Jocasta says, "that he [Laius] should perish by the hand of his own son, / a child that should be born to him from me" (713–14). But if the cause of the *miasma* is removed from the field of scrutiny, so is its fulfillment. All of the deeds stipulated in Apollo's prophecy to Laius have transpired before Sophocles' play begins. The father is dead, the mother is married, the pathetic children have been sired. These are all brute facts, according to the "free will" interpretation, all outside the action of the play.

Oedipus Tyrannos begins with a plague and a new oracle, both unprecedented in the history of the *mythos*. Delphi commands that vengeance be taken on the murderer of Laius: the god's concern, that is, is with Oedipus's crimes and not with the dark deeds of his ancestors. Moreover, unlike the Homeric version, in which the gods reveal the culprit, the burden of the inquiry is now placed squarely on Oedipus. "In this land," says the god, "who seeks shall find; / who sits with folded hands or sleeps is blind" (109–10). Oedipus sends Creon to Delphi to determine "How I might save the city by deed or word" (72), by temperament expecting from the first that the inquiry will fall to him. What we think of today as *the* story of Oedipus is almost completely Sophocles' invention. The concentration is not on the polluted house or the fulfillment of the accursed deeds, but on Oedipus's insistent investigation and ultimate self-discovery. By visiting the plague upon the city, Apollo has perhaps established the field of action, the conditions under

17. For Homer's remarks on Oedipus, see *Odyssey* 2.271–80. Aeschylus's Theban trilogy is reconstructed in G. R. Manton, "The Second Stasimon of the *Seven Against Thebes*," *University of London Institute of Classical Studies Bulletin* 8 (1961):77–84.

18. *Poetics* 51b27.

which Oedipus must undertake his task; and the god is certainly omniscient, at least insofar as Oedipus's guilt is concerned. But the curse on the culprit is pronounced by Oedipus himself (236–37). No god predicts that the investigation will be successful and no god predicts Jocasta's suicide and Oedipus's self-blinding and banishment. (The *Iliad* seems to say that Oedipus dies in battle.)[19] The conclusion, then, is that while the suicide and the incestuous marriage were not Sophoclean innovations, neither are they the subject of his play. "For in the play which Sophocles wrote the hero's will is absolutely free and he is fully responsible for the catastrophe."[20]

Only the trilogy provided sufficient scope for Aeschylus's purposes, to trace the *miasma* through successive generations of Theban royal blood. Sophocles compresses the drama into one play, one day, one man. According to the humanist reading of the play, this concentration of the action and focus on a single man was Sophocles' greatest invention, accomplishing for drama what the invention of the freestanding human statue accomplished for art.[21] Oedipus's *historein* (literally, his search or inquiry) and his *anagnōrisis* (discovery), which Aristotle makes essential to all tragedy, are undertaken in awesome isolation. (*Deinon,* a favorite Sophoclean word, ironically means both awesome and awful.) Similarly, Antigone is set apart by her character and literally entombed by Creon; Philoctetes is abandoned on a desert island; Aias is isolated by his madness. Oedipus conducts the investigation by himself and discovers only himself at its conclusion. Cast out as a baby and self-willed as an adult, he is self-banished at the play's conclusion, cut off entirely from the visible world by his self-mutilation. This entombment of the self, the "free will" interpretation concludes, is accomplished for a single humanistic purpose: only once Sophocles has completely isolated the hero from the traditional interventions of the gods and family and has scrutinized his inner machinery from every possible angle, can the author reliably ascribe the events of this world to the character of its greatest human inhabitants. Sophocles isolates the self the way Hippocrates isolates the cause of disease and Thucydides isolates the cause of war. If the focus of the epic was on the race and the focus of Aeschylus was on the family,

19. *Iliad* 23.679.
20. Knox, *Oedipus at Thebes,* p. 5. See also Greene, *Moira,* p. 138.
21. Versenyi, *Man's Measure,* p. 249.

Sophocles concentrates his lens on the individual, thus inventing the tragedy of character.[22]

In Aeschylus there is little difference between the stature of the protagonist and that of the other characters, but Sophocles uses the hesitancy of his minor characters and the pious pessimism of the chorus to underscore the transcendent *aretē* of his hero.[23] In contrast to the single-mindedness of Oedipus's resolve, Jocasta urges that a life without forethought may be "the easiest to bear" (983). "Alas," says Teiresias, "how dreadful it is to think when wisdom profits nothing" (316–17). Four times Oedipus is advised to drop the investigation and be content with inaction and ignorance, once by the shepherd (1165), once by Teiresias (320–21), and twice by Jocasta (848, 1060–61). Even in the pathetic final scene Oedipus's firm resolve is held in sharp relief against Creon's persistent cautiousness.[24] Above all, however, it is the chorus who echo the conservative fatalism of Pindar, Archilochus, and Sappho. In the lyric language of Archaic theology, the chorus consistently attribute both Oedipus's deeds and his discovery to the gods. "All-seeing Time," they conclude, "has found you out against your will" (1212–13). According to the humanist interpretation, the chorus are, of course, mistaken: Oedipus himself makes the discovery and this discovery is a direct expression of his will. "And this is precisely the dramatic function of minor actors and chorus alike. As representatives of the common measure, they counterpoint the uncommon measure, the extraordinary paradigm of humanity, that Oedipus represents."[25]

The investigation is commanded by Apollo, but the god, in his wisdom, has selected the proper actor for the task. Oedipus has used his energy, inquisitiveness, and intelligence to save the city once before, and when a plague ominously similar to the one visited upon the city by the Sphinx baffles everyone once again, it is only natural that the citizens should turn to their king for a remedy. The images associated with Oedipus—tracker, hunter, seeker, pi-

---

22. Greene (*Moira*, p. 138) goes so far as to call it "commonplace" that Sophocles wrote "tragedies of character."

23. In *Oedipus Tyrannos*, in contrast, for instance, to the *Antigone*, there can be no debate as to which character is "the" tragic hero.

24. See Knox's important remarks on the "recovery of Oedipus" in the final scene, in *Oedipus at Thebes*, ch. 5.

25. Versenyi, *Man's Measure*, p. 236.

lot, and so on[26]—are all characteristically active. Indeed, there are 199 questions in the play, 123 posed by Oedipus. As he takes command, he uses the word "I" (*egō*) more than thirty times. Small wonder that the chorus say that while Oedipus is not a god, he is nevertheless "the man surest in mortal ways" (33). When the Sphinx vexed the city, where was Teiresias with his famed powers of augury? "But I came by, know-nothing Oedipus—I thought it out for myself, no birds helped me" (396–97). He is, of course, thinking it out once again: he sets the penalty, calls the witnesses, conducts the questioning, and executes the punishment. Oedipus, in short, is the cause of the action of the play, not the other characters and not the gods. As he says time and again, "I will do everything" (145). His every word, moreover, flows ineluctably from a consistent character. "Being born such as I am," Oedipus says, "I could never prove to be some other sort of man, so as not to search out my birth to the end" (1084–85).

It would be incorrect, of course, to see Oedipus as a cool, detached rationalist. Like Plato's philosopher kings, he has an *erōs*, an all-consuming passion, for knowledge that is not at all inconsistent with his violent temper (his *atē* and his *thymos*).[27] When the chorus say that "Violence and pride [*hybris*] engender the tyrant" (872), it is the character of Oedipus upon which they are reflecting.[28] The ode is preceded in rapid succession by three events that cumulatively shock the chorus and lead them to issue their dire warning. First, Oedipus vents his rage, born of paranoid suspicions, at Teiresias. Second, obsessed with the same suspicions, he threatens to kill Creon. In the very next scene he describes to Jocasta how he met a company of men that blocked his passage at a place where three roads meet: "I struck with anger [*orgēs*] . . . and I killed the

26. For a discussion of the central images in the play, see Herbert Musurillo, "Sunken Images in Sophocles' *Oedipus*," *American Journal of Philology* 78 (1957): 36–51, and Versenyi, *Man's Measure*, pp. 242–43. Musurillo has some useful remarks on the problems that arise when modern critical techniques are applied to the study of the ancient poetic image.

27. On this "violent" aspect of Oedipus's character, see Greene, *Moira*, p. 157; Versenyi, *Man's Measure*, p. 224; and Cameron, *Identity of Oedipus the King*, pp. 125–33.

28. The word *tyrannos* can imply either an unscrupulous "bad" ruler or a "good" ruler (as Oedipus clearly is); but in either case he is a man who has come to power by his own devices (not a hereditary king—a *basileus*). See Bernard Knox, *Word and Action: Essays on the Ancient Theater* (Baltimore: Johns Hopkins University Press, 1979), ch. 9. *Tyrannos* is a post-Aristotelian addition to the play's title.

whole lot of them" (804–9). Events from the past recur in the present: we do not, of course, see the meeting at the crossroads, but given Oedipus's unwarranted temper within the action of the play, we are permitted only one interpretation of what must have happened. It is not sufficient, then, simply to conclude that only the events within the play are caused by Oedipus: by retelling the events of the past in close juxtaposition to the self-willed events of the present, Sophocles brings the whole of Oedipus's life within the ambit of his character.

When Oedipus describes his adventure at the crossroads, he says that with "one swift blow from the staff in this hand (*cheiros*)" the old man "was rolled right out of the carriage, on his back" (811–13). This remark contains a stage direction: when delivered, the actor of necessity must physically exhibit "this hand" to Jocasta and to the chorus. Ten lines later Oedipus says that if the old man should prove to be Laius, "I pollute the bed of the slain man with the hands by which he perished" (821). In all, the word "hand" appears twenty-five times in the drama, and the physical display of Oedipus's hand is surely one of the compelling visual images in any competent production.[29] Apollo's command was to "expel with a punishing hand [*cheiri timōrein*]" the slayer of Laius (107). But the murderer, too, had a punishing hand (140). Ironically, Oedipus is commanded to have a hand in the discovery of the hand that killed the old king. Over and over, Oedipus and the chorus refer both to the hand of the investigator and the hand, the blood red hand (465), of the *autocheir*, the villain whose own hand spilled the blood (231, 266). Slowly, inevitably, tragically, the equation is drawn. The same god that commands Oedipus to expel the *miasma* with a punishing hand once told him "that I was doomed to mate with my mother, and shed with my own hand my father's blood" (966). The two hands in the end are one.

In the imagistic universe of *Oedipus Tyrannos* a man's hand is the instrument of his action, the outward token of his voluntary and responsible acts. When, in the end, Oedipus asks Creon to care for

29. It is crucial to bear in mind that *Oedipus* is, after all, a play, and that its meaning emerges out of visual effects as well as the spoken word. This is especially important for Sophocles, whose concern for the visual aspects of drama led him to be the (probable) inventor of scene painting. See T. B. L. Webster, *An Introduction to Sophocles* (Oxford: Oxford University Press, 1969), p. 9. Sight images, moreover, are central to the language of the play: Teiresias is blind but sees the truth, and Oedipus can see metaphysically only after he has quenched his physical sight. The importance of sight images in the drama is the theme of Helmbold, "Paradox of Oedipus."

his daughters, he says "Signify your promise . . . by the touch
of your hand" (1510). Apollo has been active in his life, the sight-
less Oedipus concludes, but "it was none other's hand that struck
the blow; it was I [*autocheir*]" (1331). Three hundred lines follow
Oedipus's discovery that he is an incestuous parricide—three hundred lines during which he further discovers that his hand has
been the agent of these deeds. He has scrutinized his hands before,
but now they rival his gory eyes as the focus of his attention. Awe-
struck, he displays them one final time to Antigone and Ismene:

> Let me clasp you with these hands.
> A brother's hands, a father's;
> hands that made lackluster sockets of his once bright eyes;
> hands of a man who blindly, recklessly, became your sire
>   by her from whom he sprang.

> (1480–83)

The conclusion could not be more explicit. His hands, now blood red
once again, have been the agents of his life from the start—not the
sins of the father, not the will of the gods, but the hands of Oedipus.

THE HAND OF THE GOD

Unlike in *The Eumenides*, there are, of course, no epiphanies in
Oedipus. But the argument that Oedipus is the cause of the events
of the play—that his character "explains" the movement of the
plot—nevertheless has an air of unreality about it in view of the
relentless unfolding of Oedipus's prophesied fate. The evidence
that he is a free actor is an important corrective to the view that
he is merely a marionette jerked through the tragedy by leading
strings that descend from Olympus. But Oedipus does not have
complete control over the action. Apollo, from the prologue to the
exodus, is active as well.[30]

Since Apollo does not physically appear, he must be brought

30. The role of religion in *Oedipus* is a matter of great debate. At one extreme,
"humanists" like Knox (*Oedipus at Thebes*, pp. 5–6), while not questioning Sophocles' piety, deny that the gods intervene in the action. At the other extreme, the so-
called "Cambridge school" (Fraser, Cornford, Harrison, Murray, and so on) argued
earlier this century that all of Greek drama must be read as religious ritual. This
view is subjected to a "humanist" critique in J. T. Sheppard, *The Oedipus Tyrannus of
Sophocles* (Cambridge: Cambridge University Press, 1920), pp. xxix–xl. Cameron is
surely correct when he says that, while Greek dramas are not *just* ritual enactment
(like, for instance, much medieval drama), "anybody who overlooks the religious
factor, or deals with it by rationalizing it, is in my opinion not dealing with the
plays" (*Identity of Oedipus the King*, pp. x–xi).

into the action by emissaries and surrogates. The prologue opens
with the chorus, made up of representative Thebans of all ages,
gathered as suppliants before the altar at the entrance to the royal
palace. The chorus do not just make reference to a theoretical
plague that rages offstage, a state of affairs external or antecedent
to the play's action. Like Oedipus's hand, the terrible symptoms are
physically displayed to the king and to the audience. "Oedipus, my
sovereign lord, / you see how both extremes of age besiege thy altars. . . . For, as you see yourself, our ship of state, / sore buffeted,
can no more lift her head, / foundered beneath a weltering surge of
blood" (14–15, 22–24). The plague, then, is dramatized well within
the action of the play. And with the plague enters the god. At least
since the *Iliad*, Apollo had been the god who sends pestilence.[31]
When the play was produced, Athens herself had just suffered
from a plague that was popularly attributed to Apollo, whose
oracle at Delphi had promised support for the Spartans.[32] It is the
hand of Apollo on the countenance of the chorus, then, that moves
Oedipus—to pity and to action. This action is directed to the investigation of Laius's murder when Creon, literally Apollo's emissary,
returns from Delphia and reports Apollo's exact words: "Drive out
the *miasma* that has been nourished in this land" (96–7). The events
of the drama are initiated, then, not by the chorus and not by
Oedipus, but by the god.

Apollo enters the drama with the plague and the oracle not to
manipulate Oedipus so much as to spur him on, to commission his
search for knowledge. As Oedipus says, the inquiry is "a god-sent
business" (255). After Jocasta hears the story of the massacre at the
crossroads, she prays directly to Apollo's image: "To you O Lycean
Apollo, for you are nearest, / I have come as a suppliant with this
my prayer, / that you will bring to us a cleansing deliverance"
(919–21). Immediately, the Corinthian messenger appears, the
same man who, as a herdsman, delivered the crippled boy to his
king years earlier. To Voltaire, this arrival was an atrocious coincidence, a deus ex machina inserted into a failed plot. But there is, of
course, a simpler and more likely explanation: Jocasta's prayers
have been answered. The investigation has stalled, and Apollo, the
god who is "nearest," has acted again to help bring knowledge to
light. There are many coincidences in the play, and they collectively

31. *Iliad* 1.52.
32. Thucydides *Peloponnesian War* 2.54.

sustain a feeling of doom and divine power over the tragedy.[33] The humanist interpretation that maintains that the plot flows naturally from the character of the human actors cannot account for the arrival of the Corinthian or for these other coincidences. Put differently, the audience does not experience the entrance of the Corinthian precisely as a coincidence at all, as it flows naturally from the character of Apollo, the god of self-knowledge, a character introduced in the prologue and developed throughout. In the traditional story it was the Furies who prosecuted the curse on Oedipus. In Sophocles' play it is Apollo who "leaps upon him with the blazing thunderbolt" (469–70).[34]

No character plays a more ominous, "coincidental," role than the Theban shepherd, another novelty in Sophocles' version. It was he who was chosen to expose the infant but who, high on Mount Cithaeron, took pity on it and gave it to his Corinthian friend. It was he who was the lone survivor at the crossroads and who begged to be sent away when he saw the face of the new king. It is he, finally, who delivers the final piece in the terrible puzzle. He was present, then, when the baby was banished and then saved, present when the father was murdered and the mother married. Whenever Apollo's oracles have been enacted in the world, the herdsman has been present. Now his specific task, his final intervention as Apollo's tool, is to aid in the discovery, the only divine command that remains unfulfilled. Apollo may have originated as a god of shepherds in wild places,[35] and when the two herdsmen appear simultaneously on the stage, the conclusion is inescapable: the god who is now active in Oedipus's discovery has been active in his life from the start. The shepherds bring Apollo into the action.

But Apollo enters most explicitly in the person of Teiresias, the god's priest, "the lord who sees most / like the lord Phoebus" (284–85). Oedipus sent for Teiresias for the same reason that he sent Creon to Delphi, to get divine help in the investigation. But the prophet's words are slanderous and elusive: "Everything you say is too riddling and obscure" (439). Oedipus had heard both the

33. For a masterful discussion of the function of "coincidence" in the play, see Cameron, *Identity of Oedipus the King*, pp. 71–78. See also Greene, *Moira*, p. 154. Knox is aware that the Corinthian messenger raises problems for his reading (*Oedipus at Thebes*, p. 13).

34. The Furies traditionally pursue vengeance for the dead. Sophocles replaces them with Apollo, then, in part because he drops the "family curse" theme.

35. Sir William Smith, *Smaller Classical Dictionary* (New York: E. P. Dutton, 1958), p. 32.

dire predictions and the riddles once before, when he traveled to Delphi as a youth to question the god concerning his parentage (787–88). Certainly his quick temper with Teiresias in part reflects his gnawing memory of the oracle's haughty obtuseness. Where, Oedipus proudly asks, were the emissaries of Apollo when the city needed them most? "When the riddling Sphinx was here," he asks, "why had you no deliverance for this people?" (390–91).

Teiresias, then, reminds Oedipus of yet another riddler, one that the king believes he conquered years earlier. Unlike Gorgons and Harpies, the Sphinx is an "intellectual monster" who stymies men with logical questions.[36] Her relation to Apollo in Sophocles' play is unmistakable: both pose riddles and both enforce a plague until the riddle is solved. Who is the four-footed creature that is also two-footed and three-footed? Man, said Oedipus. But was his answer sufficiently precise? Who after all was the creature that was exposed on all fours as a baby and that walked proudly on two feet as a king? Who was it that was soon to feel his way with a cane as a blind outcast? As Teiresias puts it, in language that brings the Sphinx's riddle into the play, Oedipus will soon become, "A blind man from one who sees, / a beggar from one who is rich, / he shall make his way to a strange country feeling the ground with his staff" (454–56). The full answer, then, is Oedipus. *Gnôthi sauton.* Unsatisfied with partial knowledge, busy to the end with Oedipus's fate, Apollo has returned with another plague and another vexing riddle to push the search to its final conclusion.[37] "It is not your lot [*moira*] to fall by my hand," Teiresias says. "Apollo is enough to carry this out as it is his concern" (376–77).

Just as Oedipus's hand is a visible sign of his agency in the drama, his feet, the subject of the Sphinx's riddle, are a sign of the agency of the god. From his first entrance, Oedipus's limp contrasts ironically with his otherwise commanding presence. His feet are literally a sore subject: when the Corinthian reminds him of his old affliction, he asks "why do you speak of that old trouble?" (1033). But Jocasta has already spoken of it (717–19) and so, prophetically, have the chorus. The murderer of Laius, they say early in the play,

36. Cameron, *Identity of Oedipus the King*, p. 20.

37. Several authors have noted the "riddle/plague" parallel between the Sphinx and Apollo. Sheppard is surely incorrect, however, when he argues that "Oedipus showed he recognized himself in the [Sphinx's] riddle" (*Oedipus Tyrannus*, p. xvii–xviii). As Cameron says, "it is just Sophocles' point that he did not recognize himself" (*Identity of Oedipus the King*, p. 31).

must "ply in flight a foot / stronger than the feet of storm-swift steeds: / for the son of Zeus / is springing upon him" (469–72). No human foot is sufficiently strong—certainly not Oedipus's. Like Achilles' heel, Oedipus's feet are a reminder of his limits and mortality, a token ultimately of his fated condition. When prideful man "has scaled the topmost ramparts," the chorus say in a nearly untranslatable remark, he will be "hurled to a dire doom, / wherein no service of the feet can serve" (878–80)—wherein there will be no footholds to prevent his headlong fall to destruction.[38]

Oedipus discovers, then, not just that he is the object of his own investigation, but that the son of Zeus has had a hand in his fate all along. "Oedipus" ("Swollen-foot") gains self-knowledge, knowledge of his limits, his mortality, his fate. "O Zeus," he asks, "what is it that you mean to do with me?" (738). And again: "Would he who judged these things that came upon this man from some cruel daimon / not have the right understanding?" (828–29). In the imagery of the play, it may be Oedipus who "tracked" the criminal. But it was also Apollo: "Whatever the god / has need to track," Jocasta says, "that he will bring to light himself easily" (724–25).

THE JOINING OF HANDS: THE ARCHAIC CONCEPT OF PARTICIPATION

Any adequate interpretation of the play, then, must account for at least two stubborn facts: first, that while the immediate focus is on the discovery of Oedipus's identity, the play is constructed in such a way as to bring the axial events of his earlier life into the action; and second, that Oedipus's ultimate discovery is that both he and Apollo have been the agents both of the discovery and of these earlier events. The action is doubly willed. In *Antigone* the debate between the conservative view that the gods rule in all matters and the humanistic view that "man is the measure of all things" is carried out as an *agōn* between the two leading characters, Antigone, the criminal, and Creon, the prosecutor. Oedipus, however, plays a stunning variety of roles: he is both criminal and prosecutor, plague and doctor, problem and problem solver, son and husband, brother and father, hereditary king (*basileus*) and political newcomer (*tyrannos*). The great fifth-century debate, then, rages within the charac-

---

38. For the gloss here, see Jebb, *Oedipus Tyrannus*, p. 119.

ter of Oedipus; and neither voice in this debate is in the end dis-
proven. Oedipus does nothing that does not flow both from his
character and from the will of the god. Both Oedipus and Apollo
command the search and set the criminal's penalty (101–2, 216–17).
And both, when all is revealed, quench Oedipus's sight. Horrified
by the blinding, the chorus ask Oedipus, "What madness came
upon you? Who was the *daimōn* that leapt, with a bound exceeding
the extreme, upon that *moira* of yours that was already a *daimōn's*
evil work?" (1327–28). Oedipus by this point knows all, but both
the "free will" and "determinism" interpretations, as we have seen,
require ignoring half of his answer. "It was Apollo, my friends, it
was Apollo that was bringing these sufferings of mine [including
the blinding] to completion. But it was none other's hand that
struck the blow: it was I" (1329–31).[39]

What *daimōn* made him do it? It is unusual for us today to distinguish between such concepts as "fate," "destiny," "providence,"
and "necessity." Partly as a result of the influence of Plato and
Christianity, we assume that there is one Archimedean problem of
"free will," the same for all times and all cultures. When modern
commentators ask whether Oedipus is free, what they are often in
fact asking is whether he is "free" from this post-Platonic, supposedly Archimedean point of view. Sophocles, in contrast, has a
rich and intricate vocabulary of fate with many subtle differentia-
tions that are difficult to recover outside of the Greek of his day.[40]
He attributes human suffering to a wide range of cosmic forces—to
necessity (*anankē*), to chance (*tychē*), and to a personified Time
(*Chronos*). There is, however, a distinct cycle of related concepts
that have a special importance in the *Oedipus*. What, the Greeks
asked from the time of Homer, is man's part—his share, lot, portion, or measure (*moira, moros, aisa, heimarmenē*, etc.)? "*Daimōn*" or

39. The chorus's question and Oedipus's response are extremely difficult to translate, a fact that has led to many inadequate translations that seek a simple solution to
the problem of Oedipus's freedom. See *Oedipus Tyrannus*, trans. Jebb, pp. 174–75;
and R. P. Winnington-Ingram, "Tragedy and Greek Archaic Thought," in *Classical Drama and Its Influence*, edited by M. J. Anderson (London: Methuen, 1965),
pp. 34–35, from which I borrow the loose expansion of the chorus's question.

40. Our "fate" does not exactly correspond with any Greek term. See Knox,
Oedipus at Thebes, p. 33. I cannot, however, agree with Knox (p. 38) that Oedipus's
actions are at best only predicted by Apollo. On the Greek vocabulary of fate, see
W. C. Greene, "Fate, Good and Evil in Pre-Socratic Philosophy," *Historical Studies in
Classical Philology* 47 (1936):85–129, and *Moira*, ch. 8.

"*daimonion*," with its root *da-* (to share), belongs etymologically to this cycle. A *daimōn* is a sharer or apportioner of fates among men.[41]

It is not completely clear in Homer what the "whole" is of which each man is allotted a "part," but the relationship is illuminated in the *Iliad* when Achilles tells Priam of the two urns of Fate at Zeus's door from which the god dispenses men's *daimōns* (portions, destinies).[42] One urn contains blessings (good *daimōns*) and the other evils (bad *daimōns*), but no man can hope for more than a mixture of the two. Death (*moira thanatou*), for instance, we learn elsewhere in the *Iliad*,[43] is a lot that all men must accept. We can see, then, the religious origins of the classical "*eudaimōn*" ("happy": "attended by a kindly *daimōn*") and "*dysdaimōn*" ("unhappy"), although only the latter appears in Homer. Achilles' theme is that it is Zeus who allots the fates of mortals; that only the gods receive an uncontaminated measure of blessings; and that man must accept his mixed allotment and endure. "There is not an advantage to be won from grim lamentation."

The issue of freedom is complex in Homer, but Achilles' council of resignation rose to the fore as the dominant theme of the archaic lyric. "Few are the mortal men," says Bacchylides, "whom god [*daimōn*] has granted to be so fortunate all their days as to reach the time of grey temples without meeting woe."[44] "Happy the man on whom god [*theos*] has bestowed a portion of honors. . . . For no man on earth is fortunate in all things."[45] Just when man is most prideful, Bacchylides says, an "irresistible *daimōn*" will leap upon him to return him to his mortal place.[46] The gods, the distant pitiless gods, dispense the lots, and man must be stoic. "We must endure what the gods give mortal men," says Theognis, "and bear patiently either lot."[47]

41. On the etymology and connotations of *daimōn* and related words before Sophocles, see Fränkel, *Early Greek Poetry and Philosophy*, ch. 2; Greene, *Moira*, pp. 12–13; and E. R. Dodds, *The Greeks and the Irrational* (Berkeley and Los Angeles: University of California Press, 1951), pp. 39–43.

42. *Iliad* 24.525–33.

43. *Iliad* 21.83.

44. *Bacchylides: The Poems and Fragments,* trans. R. C. Jebb (Cambridge: Cambridge University Press, 1905), fr. 21, p. 421. Jebb's introduction (pp. 1–78) includes some useful remarks on preclassical Greek poetry.

45. Bacchylides *Epinikia* 5.50–55, trans. Jebb, pp. 274–77.

46. Bacchylides *Dithyrambs* 15.23–35, ibid., pp. 372–73. The reference here is to the evil *daimōn* in the story of Heracles and Deianeira.

47. In *Elegy and Iambus*, trans. J. M. Edmonds (London: William Heinemann, Loeb Classical Library, 1931), vol. 1, pp. 591–92.

By the classical period, all this had dramatically changed. Only after the "discovery of mind," in Bruno Snell's phrase[48]—only after the individual soul was disentangled from divine and environmental interventions—could the Greeks imagine a fully autonomous will. The soul could not be tended (Socrates' *therapeia psychēs*) until there was a freestanding soul to tend. Only then was happiness within the reach of the individual's own ingenuity. Aristotle, in fact, distinguishes *eudaimōn* from *makarios* (blessed) and asserts that the former, now cut loose from its etymological origins, is strictly a human achievement.[49] Plato, of course, insisted that the gods are not responsible for human destinies. In the Myth of Er, in the *Republic*, he maintains that each man, exercising his rational will, chooses his own *daimōn* before rebirth. Lachesis, the allotting goddess, controls only the order in which men make their choices; and Ananke, necessity, only seals these choices once they are made. "It is not that a *daimōn* will get you by lot," Plato writes, "but that you will choose a *daimōn*. . . . Virtue owns no master. . . . The responsibility is the chooser's. God is not responsible."[50] The fated man has become the free agent, the dispenser of his own destiny.

The conceptual universe of *Oedipus Tyrannos* lies on the seam between these two worlds. To the earlier religious poets a man's *daimōn* was a distant and totally alien force that sprang from the blue and frustrated his intentions, his very personality. To Sophocles a man and his *daimon* are on much more intimate terms. It has attended him from birth and has from the beginning shared in constituting his personality: it does not "frustrate" his intentions because from childhood it has been active in shaping the entire range of characteristic responses from which his intentional acts derive.[51] Socrates, Sophocles' contemporary, had such a *daimōn*, the "inner voice" about which he speaks in the *Apology*.[52] It is not identical to his "self" or "conscience" (Snell's "mind"), but its existence is not wholly disentangled from his personality either. Was Socrates a free

48. Bruno Snell, *The Discovery of the Mind: The Greek Origins of European Thought,* trans. T. G. Rosenmeyer (Cambridge, Mass.: Harvard University Press, 1953).

49. *Nicomachean Ethics* 1098a18–19. See the note on this passage in *Nicomachean Ethics,* trans. Martin Ostwald (Indianapolis: Bobbs-Merrill, 1979), p. 18.

50. *Republic* 617d–e.

51. Kirkwood, *A Study of Sophoclean Drama,* ch. 6, and especially pp. 283–87, on *daimōn* in Sophocles. On this subject, see Sheppard, *Oedipus Tyrannus,* pp. xxxiv–xl, and Winnington-Ingram, "Tragedy and Greek Archaic Thought," pp. 33–50.

52. *Apology* 31d–e. See also *Euthyphro* 3b.

actor when, obeying his *daimōn*, he rose to defend the Arginusae generals? When he refused to escape from prison?

"Oedipus's *daimōn*" is consistently the answer to the "from whence" question in the play, especially, however, when he acts impatiently, aggressively, passionately—in a word, characteristically. None of Apollo's prophecies—the murder, the incest, the discovery—could have been fulfilled were it not for Oedipus's characteristic acts. Yet, as we have seen, when he acts willfully and voluntarily, as in the self-blinding, he explains his deeds with reference to his *daimōn*, Apollo. If Oedipus must "endure," he must endure his own character. Character is man's destiny. If he is "free," he is free to obey the will of the god. Destiny is man's character. To the Sophists it was a man's nature (*physis*) from whence his deeds sprang. To Plato it was his rational soul. To Sophocles it was the hand of Apollo and the hand of Oedipus. The god and the mortal, joined since Oedipus's fateful birth, are doubles: both detest reticence and both are consumed with a passion for knowledge, driven to push the action through to its conclusion. Apollo "leaps" upon Oedipus (1300–1302); but Oedipus leaps too—upon Laius, upon Teiresias and Creon, upon Jocasta, and in the end upon himself. If Sophocles refuses to free Oedipus's "self" from daimonic interventions, he also refuses to make that "self" a pawn of nature or a prisoner of the transcendent, rational Forms.

Only in this context is it possible to understand the concept of heroic human action in Sophocles' play. Early in the drama the chorus prophetically says that Oedipus is "first in the visitations of the *daimōns*" (33–34). When Apollo commands, Oedipus takes action. "It is most fitting," he says, "that Apollo shows . . . this compunction for the dead. I also, as is proper, will lend my aid [*symmachon*: ally myself; participate] to avenge this wrong to Thebes and to the ·god" (132–36). When he repeats Apollo's curse on the criminal, he says: "Thus I ally myself [*symmachos*] with the *daimōn* and with the dead king" (244–45). Here, of course, he is merely participating in the fulfillment of Apollo's proximate command. But he ultimately discovers that he has been participating in his fate all along. Oedipus is not an autonomous actor, himself free to choose from Zeus's urns, but unlike the chorus and the other characters (and the Archaic conservatives) neither does he just "endure" his distantly apportioned destiny. His part is apportioned, but he "plays" his part—he participates—blindly and unwittingly at first and in the end with full knowledge of his alliance with the god. Oedipus's part, his *daimōn*, has in effect become a verb—it is something that he does, actively, passionately, heroically. If the god is the author of Oedipus's script, Oedipus is, so to speak, the method actor who has found himself in his part.[53] Heroic action to Sophocles, then, is not the endured part or the self-authored part, but the actively played part. The lower animals cannot be heroic actors because they are creatures of necessity (instinct), they have no hand in their *daimōn*. But the gods cannot be heroic actors either, precisely because they know no limits. They cannot be tragic heroes because they have no part (no *daimōn*) to play.

Tragedy was the ideal, perhaps the only, genre in which this understanding of human action could be expressed. The playwright, Aristotle says, is "a maker [*poietes*] of the stories [*mythos*]."[54] Sophocles, we have seen, did not invent plots ex nihilo: the "maker," to him, was a craftsman who worked with existing materials— existing "authorities."[55] But while the myth of Oedipus anteceded Sophocles' play, the poet shaped and molded it to accommodate it to his purposes. Oedipus's relation to his *daimōn*, then, recapitulates Sophocles' relation to the *mythos*. He was the "maker" of the *mythos* in precisely the same sense that Oedipus is the actor in his destiny. Sophocles "found" his theme in the ancient story just as Oedipus "finds" his character—his hand—in the allotted events of his life. It is not a coincidence that the first competitions between rhapsodes presenting Homeric poems at the Panathenaic festivals occurred just prior to the time that the earliest tragedies were produced in the city Dionysia (about 550 and 534, respectively). Unlike the traditional rhapsode, who merely recited Homer's words, the competitors at the festival began to dramatize the stories, im-

53. The greatest Greek actors were noted for similarly "finding themselves" in their "parts." It is said that Polus, the renowned actor who played Sophocles' *Oedipus* in the fourth century, once acted Sophocles' *Electra* not long after the death of his son. Polus used an urn containing his son's ashes in the scene where he, as Electra, is directed to lament over the remains of Orestes. Like Oedipus, he delivered his "scripted" lines, but at the same time, as Jebb says, he "suffered a natural grief." See Jebb, *Oedipus Tyrannus*, p. xxxi, for the ancient sources of this story. While the story may be apocryphal, its currency in the ancient world is significant, particularly in view of the common misconception that Greek actors mouthed their lines without emotion.

54. *Poetics* 51b27.

55. The Greeks did not easily believe that anything, including the physical universe, sprang up *ex nihilo*. Thus everything had an *archē*—an "origin" or "authority." Everything, in short, had a *daimōn*. From this point of view, the Platonic notion of an autonomous will is an "irrational" mystery.

personating the various interlocutors. "It was only a step to full im-personation [i.e., to drama], from the rhapsode who momentarily spoke in the person of Achilles or Odysseus to the 'actor' who presented himself as Achilles or Odysseus," G. F. Else observes.[56]

"Action," then, emerged simultaneously on many levels. Tragedy as a genre illuminates the ironic relationship between fate and character, and Greek tragedy in particular emerged as a dramatization—an "acting out"—of the traditional myths. Sophocles was the "maker" of the myth of Oedipus, and Oedipus was the "maker" of his destiny. Action, it is fair to say, was the central preoccupation of fifth-century authors, but on all of these levels it was inherently ironic—the played part. Like Oedipus himself, Sophocles' relationship to authority is one of participation.[57]

THE CITY AS *DAIMŌN:* HUMAN ACTION AND POLITICAL ACTION

Oedipus is a political man—his first impulse is to look for political intrigues, and his primary motivation, at least early in the play, is to save the city—but *Oedipus* is not a political drama. Sophocles' aim, in the end, is to portray the protagonist's relationship to the gods, not to Thebes. But since political authority emerged from religious authority in Greece, it is impossible to understand the Greek's relationship to his *polis* without first clarifying his relationship to Olympus. The concept of human action found in *Oedipus* emerged roughly from 750 to 500, side by side with the birth of the *polis* and the rise of the concept of political action enunciated in Pericles' Funeral Oration. The ironic political freedom of the Athenian citizen

56. G. F. Else, *The Origin and Early Form of Greek Tragedy* (Cambridge, Mass.: Harvard University Press, 1965), p. 69. See also Walcot, *Greek Drama in its Theatrical and Social Context,* pp. 28–29.

57. The "participatory" relationship between sacred and profane agents that obtains in *Oedipus* can also be seen at the heart of other Sophoclean dramas. In *Philoctetes,* for instance, Sophocles creates an almost oppressive tension between, on the one hand, the brute fact that Helenus, the seer, has prophesied that Troy will fall when Philoctetes and his bow return to battle, and, on the other hand, the sympathy that grows both in Neoptolemus and the audience for Philoctetes' case against the Atridae and his all-consuming desire to shun the battlefield and to return home. God and man, thus, appear to be at odds. In the end the gap between Olympus and earth is closed; the prophecy will be fulfilled, but in a manner consistent with the moral growth of Neoptolemus and with Philoctetes' passion to be reintegrated into a new Greek community governed by persuasion and friendship, and not by the deceit and violence that have been the hallmarks of the community over which Agamemnon and Odysseus preside. See P. E. Easterling, "*Philoctetes* and Modern Criticism," *Illinois Classical Studies* 3 (1978):27–39.

can only be illuminated in light of the ironic freedom of the Athenian will.

Writing during the second Messenian War (ca. 650–625), Tyrtaeus, the Spartan poet, says that the authority of the Spartan *polis* was established by Zeus, who bequeathed it to the sons of Heracles. It was Apollo, he adds, that gave the city its *politeia*—its constitution.[58] The same theme can be seen more than a century later in Aeschylus's *The Eumenides*, in which Athene passes the authority to determine justice to the Athenian jury. All the cities, in fact, sprang from mythological, divine foundings. Small wonder, then, that when Pindar contemplates the deeds of Athens during the Persian War, he calls her "holy," as if she were herself a goddess.

> Oh! shining and violet-crowned, famous in story
> champion of Hellas, illustrious Athens, city divine![59]

If the *polis*'s authority descended from the gods, it had also taken on a wide range of divine functions by the time Pericles spoke. Before the emergence of the *polis*, the good things of life—happiness and that measure of immortality attained when a hero was survived by the memory of his exploits—were dispensed by the gods, although a man's individual *aretē* on the battlefield was far from irrelevant. But Tyrtaeus has little admiration for the hero's exploits on his own behalf: it is the citizen who demonstrates steady courage in defense of the *polis* upon whom he lavishes praise. It is now the *polis*, with the aid of poets like Tyrtaeus, that bestows immortality and happiness upon its honored citizens. Herodotus describes an imaginary conversation between Solon and Croesus, the wealthy Lydian king, in which the great lawgiver is asked who among all the men he has met is the most happy. His answer is Tellus of Athens: "In a battle between the Athenians and their neighbors near Eleusis, he came to the assistance of his countrymen, routed the foe, and died upon the field most gallantly. The Athenians gave him a public funeral on the spot where he fell, and paid him the highest honors."[60]

Since the city is necessary for happiness, no man is more miserable, Aristotle says, than he who by nature or ill-luck has no city.[61]

---

58. *Elegy and Iambus,* trans. Edmonds, vol. 1, fr. 4.
59. Ibid., fr. 76.
60. Herodotus *History* 1.30.   61. *Politics* 1253a.

Banishment is the highest punishment. The *polis*, then, is not just a geographical entity, it is, in Werner Jaeger's words, "both an exalted ideal and a despotic power. As such it is something very like a god; and the Greeks always felt its divinity."[62] The dispenser of the greatest happiness and the greatest misery, the *polis* had become man's allotting *daimōn*, not replacing the gods, but duplicating the logic of their agency on a quasi-secular plane.

Just as Apollo "leapt" upon Oedipus from birth, shaping his personality, the city's *politeia*—its laws, customs, "culture"—exercised a decisive influence over the citizen's character. "Legislators," Aristotle says, "make the citizens good by forming habits in them, and this is the wish of every legislator, and those who do not effect it miss their mark."[63] It is important not to overlook the environmentalism that is implicit in Aristotle's political theory. Unlike the authors of the *Federalist Papers*, for instance, Aristotle maintains that the purpose of institutions is to mold and educate the citizen and not just to channel and regulate the egoistic proclivities with which man has been endowed by nature. Through experience in the properly crafted *polis*, man sheds his individual identity and is allotted a new measure—citizenship. Like Socrates' *daimōn*, the city's constitution whispers in a man's ear and urges him on to cooperation and to heroism in defense of the city's walls. Under the sway of this secular divinity, Tellus gladly sacrifices all, and his Athenian descendants "fight as though their bodies were not their own." The *polis* has "leapt" like Apollo and has its grasp upon their wills. "What *daimōn* made you do it?" Pericles might ask one of the courageous war dead. "It was Athens," he would respond. "But it was none other's hand that made the decision to fight; it was I."

How could this be? If the laws have quasi-divine authority and the citizen is "socialized," to use a modern term, into civic obedience, how can it be that he is at the same time a voluntary actor? How is political freedom compatible with political authority, individuality compatible with community? The answer, as a study of Sophocles' *Oedipus* shows, is only intelligible from within the Late Archaic point of view. The mystery that shrouds Solon's claim that Tellus is the most "happy" of men melts away when we understand

62. *Paideia*, trans. G. Highet (New York: Oxford University Press, 1945), vol. 1, p. 94.
63. *Nicomachean Ethics* 1103b.

that he is, in fact, the most *eudaimōn*. The Athenian, moreover, does not just "accept" or "endure" his civic measure, he plays his part, he actively participates in the *politeia* of the city. The war dead have been the "poets" (the "makers") of their own lives in the same ironic sense that Oedipus is the "poet" of his destiny and Sophocles is the "poet" of the *mythos*. Oedipus's relationship to his *daimōn* can best be understood as the culmination of a long process during which the distant gods approached and finally mingled (participated) with the character of man. Political authority, too, was distant and often tyrannical in the Homeric and pre-Homeric worlds. But when authority became vested in the city itself and man took up the persona of citizen, political authority and political man, author and actor, became equally intimate, their relationship equally participatory. The Athenian who obeys his daimonically allotted will is a free man because his *daimōn* and his "self" are joined inextricably together in his identity as citizen. His acts are not finally overdetermined at all, because his city and his soul are one.

The city has many "parts," as Aristotle says, but only the citizen "participates."[64] Those who exclusively play "household" parts (slaves, menials, women) are not free because they are slaves to the physical necessities inherent in the human condition. Like the lower animals, they "behave" but do not "act." Only the citizen can, like Oedipus, act his part. It is the *daimōn* of the citizen to be both ruler and ruled:[65] he is neither the tyrant who rules in all matters nor the slave who has no political part. Like Oedipus, the citizen has both a hand and a handicap. He alone can attain "happiness." He alone is capable of heroic action.

Classical tragedy, like the classical *polis*, required this conjugal merging of author and actor, theory and practice, and neither survived the wedge driven between the two by the influence of philosophy and the flow of events. To Plato, the gods, now returned to the heavens clothed as the Forms, dispense wisdom to the world of men from afar. The gods, says the Myth of Er, are innocent, but only because they have been replaced by the Logos as rational man's allotting *daimōn*. The particular may still "participate" in the universal, but the relationship is no longer either personal or reciprocal. The three "parts" of the Platonic city "participate" in justice, but, like the men in Achilles' parable of the two urns, they must "endure"

64. *Politics* 1289b–1290a.
65. *Politics* 1283b–1284a.

their lot as handed down from the distant, inscrutable Forms. Above all, justice is knowledge, not a human activity; it is attained by contemplation, not by action. Men can "participate" in justice, but "participation" is no longer something that men "do." And when men cease to be actors in their destiny, Sophocles teaches, they cease to be free.

Chapter Eight

Oedipus at Colonus: Exile and Integration

Laura Slatkin

> *Try now the Art of Oedipus.*
> *If a man with a keen axe-blade*
> *Lops the branches of a great oak,*
> *Defiling the beauty that men gazed at—*
> *Though its fruit has perished, yet it gives*
> *Witness of itself, when it comes at last*
> *In winter to the fire,*
> *Or rests on the upright pillars of a master,*
> *Doing sad labour in a stranger's house*
> *While its own land is desolate.*
> Pindar, *Pythian* 4.261–69[1]

In *Pythian* 4 Pindar appeals for the return of the exiled Damophilus by invoking the example of Oedipus in a remarkable double image. The first part of the metaphor of the oak suggests the persistent vitality and integrity of the outwardly shattered individual. Its second part expresses the exile's role in the achievement of a collective endeavor in which he, however alien, has a significant share.

This essay was originally conceived and written as part of a collective project in honor of John H. Finley, Jr. Because of publication exigencies, we came as collaborators to the decision to publish our work separately, but to record in each instance our tribute of esteem and gratitude to a beloved teacher and friend. His article "Politics and Early Attic Tragedy," *Harvard Studies in Classical Philology* 71 (1966): 1–12, has provided important bearings for the subject of the present volume.

This essay benefited from the unerring critical judgment of A. E. Johnson, one of the original collaborators; from the valuable advice of P. E. Easterling; and from the helpful editorial comments of R. Slatkin and S. L. Schein. I continue to mull over some challenging suggestions from S. Bercovitch.

1. From C. M. Bowra's translation in the Penguin edition of *The Odes of Pindar* (Oxford: Clarendon Press, 1964). All references to *Oedipus at Colonus* are to the text of A. C. Pearson (1924; reprint, Oxford: Clarendon Press, 1964).

The identity of the oak remains manifest not only in the ultimate trial of dissolution but in the modified "death" of transformation and subjugation. Yet the concept of integrity is linked, in both terms of the image, with that of service and utility. In its final elaboration, Pindar's image offers a vision of alienation and dispossession transcended in the paradoxical fulfillment of the oak, which the house elevates and by which it is crucially sustained. The double metaphor by which Pindar illustrates the "art" (*sophia*) of Oedipus indicates an approach to Sophocles' *Oedipus at Colonus*, where concern with the nature of the Athenian *polis* is contained within a dramatic action dominated by a sense of mystery and ineffable climax.

Critics of the play have tended to concentrate their discussions on its last half,[2] and particularly on the question of how the religious "solution" elucidates and encompasses what precedes it.[3] This essay has a different focus; it attempts to show, through attention to the opening of the play, that Sophocles is equally interested in political concerns and in their bearing on religious thought. A notable illustration of this interest is offered by one of the play's most suggestive elements, which has generally been read in connection with hero-cult; that is, with the end of the play and beyond: the recurrent reference to Oedipus as possessing a "benefit" to be-

2. See, for example, G. Meautis, *Sophocle: Essai sur le héros tragique* (1940; 2nd ed., Paris: A. Michel, 1957); C. M. Bowra, *Sophoclean Tragedy* (Oxford: Clarendon Press, 1944); and A. J. A. Waldock, *Sophocles the Dramatist* (Cambridge: Cambridge University Press, 1951). "This is the only work in which the miracle by which the main character is carried away becomes the purpose and the main significance of the action," writes K. Reinhardt, in his admirable *Sophokles* (1933), (Oxford: Basil Blackwell, 1979), p. 193.

3. More recently, P. Burian's treatment, "Suppliant and Saviour: Oedipus at Colonus," *Phoenix* 28 (1974):408–29, and T. G. Rosenmeyer's important article "The Wrath of Oedipus," *Phoenix* 6 (1952):92–112, in arguing convincingly, as both do, for its unity in terms of theme, characterization (esp. Rosenmeyer) and structure (esp. Burian), nevertheless emphasize the dominant significance of the end of the play. Burian writes: "Now, for the first time, it is clear that Oedipus' death will be part of the play itself, and not merely of his prophecy. What is, in retrospect, so clearly the central theme has been carefully prepared by being carefully subordinated to a series of confrontations" (428), and describes the final mystery as "transcending and transfiguring all that has come before" (429). Rosenmeyer writes "that everything in the play is oriented toward the heroization of Oedipus is clear" (104). Exceptions include the valuable contributions of P. E. Easterling, "Oedipus and Polyneices," *Proceedings of the Cambridge Philological Society* 13 (1967):1–13, and R. P. Winnington-Ingram, *Sophocles: An Interpretation* (Cambridge: Cambridge University Press, 1980), esp. 248–79, and the balanced chapter on *Oedipus at Colonus* in C. P. Segal, *Tragedy and Civilization: An Interpretation of Sophocles* (Cambridge, Mass.: Harvard University Press, 1981), pp. 362–408.

stow—*onēsis*[4]—a "benefit" that is never defined, yet whose meaning is central to the drama. Inexplicit as it is, this concept of benefit, potent early as well as late in the play, may help us to appreciate the relationship between the separate but overlapping contexts—political and religious—in which it is resonant.

Oedipus's enigmatic "benefit," as has been observed, serves to provide part of the aetiology for a cult of Oedipus, especially because it occurs in association with Ismene's report of the oracle's pronouncement of the power, benign to friends, hostile to enemies, that will emanate from Oedipus's tomb.[5] But her news of Oedipus's eventual power is only an echo of Oedipus's earlier promise of the "benefit" (*onēsis;* 288) he brings, which is first uttered in an entirely separate context. Sophocles' prior emphasis on Oedipus's potential beneficence in his presentation of himself to the chorus (258–91), independent of Ismene's subsequent revelation of his "service" (*ōphelēsis;* 401), requires us to see these terms as bearing distinct meanings, which ultimately converge. They come together not simply as the rationalization or invention of a hero-cult, but as a means of locating the hero within the definition of the *polis,* an issue anticipated, if not pursued, in *Oedipus Tyrannos.*

Oedipus conveys the offer of his benefactions at the very outset of the play, with utter conviction, yet cryptically. When asked to specify what benefit a blind man might provide, he replies, "In all that I say there will be sight" (*hos an legōmen panth' horōnta lexomen;* 74). Not surprisingly, his statement meets with a dubious response. The possibility that he could have anything helpful to offer is utterly unlooked for by the chorus of Athenian elders, as by the stranger who first finds him in the grove of the Eumenides. Initially, it is their pitying assistance that the blind wanderer calls forth, as they guard him against violating the sanctuary, then urge his confidence by guaranteeing him protection:

4. *Onēsis,* 288; *kerdos* ("advantage"), 92, 578, 579; *ōphelēsis* ("service"), 401; *arkesis* ("aid"), 73; *dōron* ("gift"), 577; *prosphora* ("profit"), 581; *dōrēma* ("present"), 647; *alkē* ("succor"), 1524, etc. It is noteworthy that *onēsis* recurs in an overtly political context at 452, where Oedipus accuses his sons of valuing power more than they value their own father, and predicts that they will gain no *onēsis* ("benefit") from ruling in Thebes. See also A. A. Long, *Language and Thought in Sophocles* (London: Athlone Press, 1968), pp. 148–49ff. on the techniques used "when Sophocles wants us to note a key-word," and p. 152 n. 15 on the variety of words meaning "help" in *OC.*

5. Lines 387–90; 401–2. See the introduction to *The Oedipus Coloneus,* part 2 of *Sophocles: The Plays and Fragments,* trans. R. C. Jebb (1928; reprint, Amsterdam: Hakkert, 1965); L. R. Farnell, *Greek Hero Cults and Ideas of Immortality* (1921; reprint, Oxford: Clarendon Press, 1970), pp. 333–34.

Never will anyone drive you against your will, old man, away from these seats.

(176–77)

Far less do they anticipate any advantage from him forty-five lines later when, his identity having been at last revealed, the chorus's terror of the pollution they suppose Oedipus to bear instantly outweighs their stated concern for his safety. At once they threaten him and attempt to drive him away, charging that their sympathetic commitment has been elicited by deception, and discrediting any association between him and themselves as inherently invalid because Oedipus is who he is—that is, a man who has been punished by the gods.

Punishment is not allotted to a man who requites deeds which he suffered first himself. One deceit matches the others, and in return gives pain, not favor.

(229–33)

Underlying their changed attitude toward him is the belief that Oedipus must have deserved his treatment from the gods, and that his suffering, for which they first pitied him, confirms as much; for them, it is the subjective aspect of his objective position in the universe.[6]

Thus the Athenian elders issue their commands—"Out of here— leave the country! Away from these seats! . . . Go back! Hurry out of my land, so that you do not attach some heavier burden to my city" (226; 234–36)[7]—apparently in a spirit of devout obedience to the gods who have visited punishment on the blind man. They condemn Oedipus expressly on behalf not only of themselves but of the entire *polis*, justifying themselves by the conviction that they clearly understand and righteously perform the gods' will toward

6. Cf. Aeolus's speech to Odysseus, *Od.* 10.72ff. From the chorus's standpoint, it is appropriate for Oedipus to live in exile. See E. Balogh, *Political Refugees in Ancient Greece* (Johannesburg: Witwatersrand University Press, 1943), whose discussion of the politics of exile as a punishment persisting "from tribal usage to city law" takes into account a psychological phenomenon: "the innate belief that the fate of the individual is directed by justice. The exile is not merely the victim of his political opponents. . . . The majority of the onlookers also, together with the victors, load him with moral guilt . . . and even friends will arrive at the conclusion that the refugee would never have been expelled without a just cause or at least without a compelling reason. His homeless wanderings are turned into a link in an awkward chain of causation" (p. 3).

7. The translation of this passage and the following one are closely based on that of Jebb.

Oedipus. Antigone's appeal to pity reinforces the chorus's collective sense of themselves as reverent, and their reiteration is uncompromisingly pious:

Know, child of Oedipus, that we pity you and him alike for your fortune; but fearing the judgement of the gods, we could not say anything beyond what has now been said to you.

(256–57)

Oedipus, however, responds to the chorus's assumptions about their community and him, not, as Antigone does, with a plea, but rather with a challenge, which promises, once more, his precious gift. Here we begin to be shown the role Oedipus must assume in the welfare and ideals of Athens—well before Ismene ever arrives on the scene to tell him the prophesied significance of his tomb. Oedipus challenges the chorus, by reconsidering his "case," to re-examine their own moral perspective. When he has finished his argument, they continue to invoke "reverence," but of a wholly new kind, reverence for the man himself.

Oedipus's speech is a forceful statement of the unity of moral and political realities:

What use, then, are noble fame and reputation idly spoken, if indeed people report that Athens is the most reverent of cities and uniquely able to rescue the suffering stranger, and to defend him? Where are these things in my case? You, having raised me from my seat, then drive me from the land, afraid of my name alone—not, certainly, afraid of my body or my actions. My actions were suffered rather than performed—if it were necessary to tell the story of my mother and father, on account of which you fear me; I know that well. And yet how was I evil in my nature? Having been wronged I repaid that wrong, so that even if I had acted knowingly, how would I have been evil?

(258–72)

Athens, he begins, illustrates the contradiction between reputation and true worth; the hostile actions of the previous scene belie her noble fame as "most reverent" (*theosebestatas*) and her traditional repute as a haven for the distressed stranger (*xenos*). Why should the Athenians shun Oedipus, if not out of an empty terror of his misleading reputation—"my name alone" (*onoma monon*)— in that, as he goes on to argue, he is innocent of any conscious crime. They cannot fear his actions, because these were "suffered rather than performed" (*peponthot' . . . mallon ē dedrakota*). The unspoken conclusion is that it is his sufferings they fear.

Oedipus thus signals the distinction between conscious intent and action, and the tension between one's nature and one's circumstances. His past acts are open to reinterpretation in the light of his "nature" (*phusis*)—which, however, is absolute and unchanged. He is now what he has always been, an innocent nature confronting dimly understood and inflexible events. He emphasizes, concentrating into a brief space the great theme of *Oedipus Tyrannos*, that his knowledge was incomplete. The problem is not one of moral deficiency but of imperfect comprehension, of flawed insight into the circumstances of his existence. Without acknowledging this limitation as the link between human nature and human suffering, society cannot begin to deal justly with the individual and his experience of life.

The speciousness of Athens's reputation is, then, not an analogue to Oedipus's own misrepresented fame but a corollary to it. Oedipus is using "reverent" (*theosebestatos*) in a new context—that of social relations—and, as a result, extending its meaning. To misunderstand Oedipus, and therefore to exclude him from society, is to be irreligious (*asebēs*), and the community of Athens stands in this danger. Rather than accusing the Athenians of being simply inhospitable (*axenoi*) or unjust (*adikoi*), Oedipus argues that to reject him from the community is to forfeit their own claim to reverence for the gods.

Now such would be the penalty for refusing help to any suppliant, and Jebb, for one,[8] notes this as the explanation of 275–78:

> For these reasons, strangers, I beseech you by the gods, just as you moved me from my seat, so protect me; and do not, while honoring the gods, deny those gods their due. Consider that they look on the righteous among men and on the profane, and that there never yet has been a means of escape for an impious mortal.

But Oedipus is not primarily concerned with ensuring that the chorus realize this as a general principle; it is clear enough from their initial reception of him that they do so. His concern is with the assumption underlying their reversal of attitude. Thus he asks them to reconsider "for these reasons" (*anth' hōn*), that is, on the basis of what he has attempted to illuminate for them about his own, specific experience.[9]

8. Jebb (cited above, n. 5) *ad* 278.
9. See the emphasis in T. P. Howe, "Taboo in the Oedipus Theme," *Transactions of the American Philological Association* 93 (1962): 124–43, on Sophocles' (and apparently

Oedipus argues (277–81) that by choosing not to accept him, this community usurps the discretion of the gods. It is up to the gods to judge whether or not he is pious; no man can escape divine scrutiny. It is not the function of the chorus to stigmatize as "polluted" a man who has suffered, or to punish him beyond what the gods and life itself have imposed. Oedipus knows himself to be "righteous" (*eusebēs*); the gods, in preserving his life, have confirmed this. The chorus can have no authority to condemn him with their parochial notions of "pollution." What appears to be a traditional, almost commonplace, statement about divine power becomes in the context of Oedipus's claims part of a radical critique of the failure of conventional social and religious sanctions to relate the gods' purpose to human experience.

As in *Antigone*, Sophocles' moral statement has political implications. While Oedipus challenges the community to reexamine their would-be religious orthodoxy in the light of their attitude toward him, he is, equally, testing their political integrity.

Do not cloud the happiness of Athens by ministering to unholy deeds; but just as you received the suppliant with your pledge, rescue me and guard me. Do not despise me when you look at this terrible face. For I have come to you as one sacred and righteous and bringing a benefit for these citizens.

(282–88)

For Athens as a state, the values she must protect are those by which she judges herself to be "happy" (*eudaimōn*). Not only her outward image (258–60), therefore, but her self-definition are at stake.

The sense of "happiness, well-being" (*eudaimonia*) the chorus endangers here derives from their approval of their state as an entity

---

Aeschylus's) presentation of Oedipus's "extraordinarily individual attitude toward his part in the taboo transgression" (p. 130) and on Oedipus's "feelings of profound individual engagement" in *OC* with the "immemorial prohibitions" he has violated. According to Howe, through their treatment of Oedipus, Sophocles and Aeschylus "denote a significant cultural change" from the treatments of Oedipus in the extant earlier literature, e.g., Homer. Cf. J.-P. Vernant's penetrating discussion of "La Personne dans la religion," vol. 2 of *Mythe et pensée chez les Grecs* (Paris: Gallimard, 1971), p. 90: "Mais la tragédie, alors même qu'elle s'alimente à la tradition héroïque, se situe sur un autre plan que le culte et les mythes des héros; elle les transforme en vue de sa propre enquête: cette mise en question par l'homme grec, à un moment de son histoire, de l'homme même: sa place devant le destin, sa responsabilité par rapport à des actes dont l'origine et la fin le dépassent, l'ambiguïté de toutes les valeurs proposées à son choix, la nécessité cependant d'une décision."

carrying out its functions "piously" (*hosiōs*).[10] (At this point Oedipus is not warning them against incurring a fate like that of Thebes, against jeopardizing their "prosperity"; he has not yet learned of his power to effect that.) The underlying assumption is of a sense of collective and individual well-being—comparable to that described in, and reflected by, Pericles' Funeral Oration—which comes from obtaining satisfaction from one's share of identification with the values and principles of the state. It is, moreover, the liberal ideal of an enlightened democracy, with which Oedipus's association with the Eumenides and the Areopagus has already allied him, that he is offering to safeguard for Athens. That association itself evokes the Aeschylean idea of democracy in the process of being created, and its need for continuous self-renewal.[11]

The very understanding of his particular identity and his exemplary nature as a man, which the exiled wanderer has come to and by which he knows himself to be "righteous" (*eusebēs*) and "sacred" (*hieros*), reveals him as "bringing a benefit for these citizens" (*pherōn onēsin astois*). Oedipus offers the Athenians the opportunity to make real their values by accepting him. They may prove themselves an open, inclusive, compassionate society by choosing to integrate a man who has acted and suffered, and to comprehend his moral vision. They may secure these values by accepting him not despite but because of his action and experience, by doing so not merely out of pity—for the pathetic failure of Antigone's appeal (237–53) demonstrates the inadequacy of any such foundation for a relationship—but in recognition of the power that derives from an individual's struggle with the condition of his own existence.

One hundred lines later Ismene arrives to bring news of the gods' acknowledgment of this power. Her message and its meaning, as mentioned above, have been appropriately viewed as having reference to a future hero-cult of Oedipus. His own crucial earlier claim to possess a "benefit," however, makes it clear that it is not simply something Oedipus will "bequeath" once dead: namely, the

10. See the commentary on *hosios* in A. W. H. Adkins, *Merit and Responsibility* (Oxford: Clarendon Press, 1960), 173ff.

11. Cf. the values expressed in the closing choruses of *The Eumenides*. See Winnington-Ingram (cited above, n. 3), esp. pp. 264–75, on the impact and echoes of the *Oresteia*, particularly *The Eumenides*. For a discussion of the nature of the Furies in their relationship to Athens, see esp. H. H. Bacon, "Aeschylus," in *Ancient Writers: Greece and Rome*, edited by T. J. Luce (New York: Charles Scribner's Sons, 1982), vol. 1, pp. 99–155, particularly pp. 149–52.

special protection of Attica—as though only with his death would his great power be released, then to be held in trust for Athens in his tomb. "Oedipus has certain benefits to bestow, but these will not be felt until after his decease," writes Jebb.[12] But it is the living Oedipus who is a dynamic force for the moral and political challenge to the *polis;* it is his life, his stamina for it and his own understanding of it, that the Athenians—in the play and in the audience—must measure their own against, much as Theseus does.

Ismene reports that he will be needed "dead and living" (*thanont' . . . zōnta t';* 389–90). That his corpse will be prized as sacred, Oedipus learns here for the first time; but it is his living being that has meaning for the Athenians. The concern of the tragic protagonist is, as everyone's must be, with his conscious existence: its potential, its significance, its place in the world—questions whose complex realities defy the simplicity and the abstraction of the old exchange between Oedipus and the Sphinx. Unlike Jocasta, Oedipus chose to live, admitting the consequences of having a given identity, with its limitations of family, history, context. Once such definitions for the self are recognized, it becomes—for the first time—intolerable to be a stranger, to live dispossessed, as Thebes compelled Oedipus to do. The Athenians, in restoring Oedipus to society, will themselves enforce the defining human ties his own discovery of these connections implied.

What Ismene announces as Oedipus' "service" (*ōphelēsis*) is not, then, a clarification or restatement of what Oedipus has neglected to make explicit about his potent gift to the Athenians; it is, rather, the divinely sanctioned extension of his offer and the response it meets with. If the Athenians are capable of accepting Oedipus, of sharing in a perspective that sees his nature as ultimately viable, even beneficent, they will be able, and will deserve, to inherit his spiritual power, his hard-won sense of "love" (*to philein;* 1617). It is not, finally, what happens to his corpse that matters. The dramatic illustration of this is that his mysterious end leaves no material remains. The treatment of a body is an issue in *Antigone.* Much like Creon in that play, the Thebans, who try to claim Oedipus physically, misunderstand what is involved here. If they cannot accept Oedipus alive, they do not participate, as Athens does, in that extension of spirit, and they cannot possess him dead.

12. Jebb (cited above, n. 5), p. xv.

Corresponding to this shift in focus from the material to the spiritual, from ritual practice to interpretation of divine meaning, is the play's overt concern with the value of language: the efficacy of argument, the power of reputation, the binding force of promise and of malediction. The extraordinary number of references to words and to speech, especially concentrated at critical confrontations but pervasive throughout the play, support close attention to the use of such individual terms as those riddling ones this essay began by considering, for which definition itself is an issue and a subject of inquiry within the very dialogue of the play.

Modes of verbal exchange constitute both theme and action in this play (what Polyneices and Oedipus *say* to each other replaces what Oedipus and Laius *did* to each other); and the process by which, through the first 550 lines of the play, Oedipus and the citizens of Athens arrive, as it were, on common ground, spells out Sophocles' interest in providing more than a static tableau contrasting Athens and Thebes, the enlightened society and its antitype. For this it would have been sufficient to contrast Theseus, who accepts Oedipus immediately, and Creon, who calls him "unholy" (*anagnon;* 945) to the last. But Theseus does not appear until the play is one-third over, and requires no discussion before offering his sympathetic protection, so that Oedipus replies to Theseus's first speech with

Theseus, your nobleness has in brief words shown such grace that for me it is necessary to say but little. You have rightly said who I am, and from what father, and from what land I have come; and so nothing remains except to speak my desire, and the story is told.

(569–74)[13]

Theseus does not question; Creon does not listen. The essential dialogue takes place between Oedipus and the chorus. It is their conception of him that he must address and win over, and their collective entity that must make a place for him. By the time Theseus arrives, Oedipus and the chorus have achieved that end; when Theseus has declared him "fellow-citizen" (*empolin;* 637), their choral praise is not for the leader but for the state.

Sophocles thus dramatizes the evolution of the Athenian community's moral perspective, and the challenge to, and enlargement

---

13. Translation based on Jebb's.

of, its values. Dating from a time, just before Arginusae, when Athens was critically oppressed by war, *Oedipus at Colonus* raises the possibility of an integrity that defies violation despite the shock of assault and the internal stresses of delusion, corruption, and doubt. It is possible for man and society to redeem each other, in an exchange of validation founded on what the trials of life have proved to be their elemental and irrevocable ties of mutual responsibility and interdependence. Attic tragedy's most ethereal and mystic resolution is revealed as both realistic and—according to a distinctively oracular pattern—practical in its social and political resonance. The theme of integrity—which Oedipus embodies, and which the Athenians first state and finally affirm—is not merely multiplied or made emphatic by its double enactment on the level of the isolated human being and then of the society capable of recognition. Rather, the dual expression illustrates that integrity exists as a potentiality of this dialectic between individual and society. The action is single and reciprocal.

The successful conclusion of this moral drama, which is the action of the first third of the play, sets into relief Thebes's failure to reintegrate Oedipus as the failure of the family. If the Athenian citizens have made a place for the stranger—for the man who is the limiting case of "outsider" to society—the Theban family, represented by the figure of Creon[14] as well as Oedipus' sons, is incapable of allowing Oedipus the place that is his as its innermost core. The Athenians, having taken Oedipus in, are portrayed as instantly united politically, as they, with Theseus, unanimously oppose Thebes's maneuver to repossess Oedipus. Not only can the Theban family not equal the model offered by the Athenian citizens, but by contrast, the family's calamitously destructive internal struggles are the community's greatest vulnerability, as the second half of the play depicts them. The family as an entity seems unable to coalesce with society; where they intersect, each undermines the other. The reality of political power annihilates family bonds;[15] family conflict outweighs or ignores the claims of community stability. Only in isolation, remote from society, can the family sustain itself; only in desolate wilderness can Antigone and Oedipus function as a family. By placing the opening and closing of the play in the grove of

14. For Creon's acknowledgment of this kinship, see lines 735–39.
15. P. E. Easterling (cited above, n. 3) has shown that Oedipus's recognition of this on the part of his sons underlies his rage against them; see esp. pp. 8–11.

the Eumenides at Colonus, Sophocles alludes to the harmonious end of the *Oresteia* so as to underscore at the same time the achievement of the inclusive, self-renewing community and, ironically, the dire inability of the family to share in that achievement—its inability either to integrate or to be integrated.

Pindar's metaphor dwells on the cost of integrity; the oak displays its power and value, but is consumed or enslaved. Sophocles incorporates a further dimension into the pragmatism of *Oedipus at Colonus.* Athena's imperative of reconciliation in the *Oresteia* has been wholly transposed into the human sphere, and the setting in which Oedipus and the chorus struggle toward it serves as the tangible emblem of their ultimate achievement: the actualization of the potential blessing chanted by the Eumenides.[16] The security and vitality of the blossoming grove represent the final beauty that emerges from the contradictions, resolves the transformations. Into this charged landscape Oedipus dissolves. If the gods have taken him, he belonged to them no less before, and his possession by Athens and by himself are unshaken. Nothing is lost. The "great oak" not only endures in essence, but gains its form again.

16. G. E. Dimock, Jr., has discussed the identification of the locations described in the play in his paper " 'Standing on Righteousness': Sophocles' *Oedipus at Colonus,*" presented at the Symposium on Greek Tragedy in honor of Helen H. Bacon, Barnard College, New York, April 7, 1984.

Chapter Nine

Political Corruption in Euripides' *Orestes*

J. Peter Euben

Euripides' *Orestes* is about political corruption.[1] That is the play's theme as well as the issue raised by the radical discontinuities that mark its plot and structure. In it, content and form conspire to provide an omnipresent atmosphere of political decay and disarray.[2]

The corrupt city on stage is Argos. But with a fully developed, apparently long-standing popular assembly and established public procedures for trying homicide, it is an Argos that looks very much like contemporary democratic Athens.[3] Indeed, no other Greek tragedy is so blatantly anachronistic,[4] so purposefully casual about sustaining the refracting guise myth had provided or maintaining a distance between audience and actors. Clearly the corruption that matters is that of the Athenian audience watching the play rather than of the city portrayed in it.

The situation on stage is irremediably bleak. Nothing in the play provides the slightest respite or hope except for a finale that I shall

1. Froma Zeitlin calls it "the most Euripidean of Euripidean plays, reflecting typical techniques, emphases, interests and outlook" ("The Closet of Masks: Role-Playing and Myth-Making in the *Orestes* of Euripides," *Ramus* 9, no. 1 [1980]:51).

2. In our society political corruption is usually understood as a matter of individual malfeasance. At certain times, as during Watergate, people said that our society as a whole was corrupt, though that usually meant it was full of corrupt individuals. But there is another understanding of corruption stemming from the Greeks and Romans (and implicit in the Latin *corrumpere*, from which our word *corruption* comes), which is systemic and structural in character. For a discussion of political corruption in these terms, see J. Peter Euben, "On Political Corruption," *Antioch Review* (Autumn 1978):103–18.

3. See A. W. Verrall's discussion of how this limits the public significance of Clytemnestra's crime and Orestes' matricide in his *Essays on Four Plays of Euripides* (Cambridge, England: Cambridge University Press, 1905), pp. 204–5.

4. This was William Arrowsmith's argument in his Bampton Lectures at Columbia University for 1984. I refer to the written version he has kindly made available to me. His argument on anachronization as a structural strategy in Euripides can be found in lecture 1, pp. 10–11.

argue offers neither. There is no consecration of a just city capable of integrating otherwise warring passions, principles, and forces into a whole that enhances the dignity of all, as there is in the *Oresteia*. Nor is there any Periclean vision of a city balancing passion, daring, and *erōs* with intellect, moderation, and deliberation in the freely chosen service of civic *aretē*. Nor does the *Orestes* contain anything resembling *Medea's* radiant ode to Athens, or the noble if flawed commitment to an idea as in *Hippolytus,* or the heroic endurance and trust in moral order in the face of crushing disaster that marks *Heracles*. All we see and all we get is the hollowness of ideals, the cynicism of the old, the violent instability of the young, and the poor judgment of all, singly and together.[5]

Since tragedy is an Athenian political institution, the disintegration the play portrays and imitates raises questions about the corruption of tragedy as genre and practice. In this sense a study of the play is a study of the city as context of performance, which is also a study of tragedy as part of that context. Thus an analysis of *Orestes'* violation of expectations[6] generated by myth, by Aeschylus's version of the Orestes legend, by the play's own surface logic, and by those institutional and literary traditions that define tragedy, reflects, and reflects on, a political culture fragmented by continual war, democratic excess, and the collapse of traditional values. The uncertainties about life and death, alliances and friendship, wisdom and destiny, victimizing and victimization, innocence and justice, power and action reflect on tragedy even as they are its thematic preoccupations.

In both cities and play[7] there is a breaking down and apart, a loss of identity and definition, and an erosion of common purpose and principle. With that erosion citizens no longer second one an-

5. See Charles Segal, *Dionysiac Poetics and Euripides' Bacchae* (Princeton, N.J.: Princeton University Press, 1982), pp. 56 and 213.

6. On the pattern of violated expectations, see Anne Pippin Burnett, *Catastrophe Survived: Euripides' Plays of Mixed Reversal* (Oxford: Clarendon Press, 1970), chs. 1, 8, and 9; E. R. Dodds, "Euripides the Irrationalist," *Classical Review* 43 (1929):97–104; Charles Rowan Beye, *Ancient Greek Literature and Society* (Garden City, N.Y.: Doubleday, Anchor Books, 1975), pp. 285–97; Christian Wolff, "Orestes," in *Greek Tragedy: Modern Essays in Criticism,* edited by Erich Segal (New York: Harper and Row, 1983), pp. 340–56; William Arrowsmith, "Introduction" to *Orestes,* in *The Complete Greek Tragedies,* edited by David Grene and Richmond Lattimore (Chicago: University of Chicago Press, 1958). I have relied on Arrowsmith's translation, with occasional emendations of my own.

7. On the relationship between the corruption in and of the play to the city that witnessed it, see William Arrowsmith, "A Greek Theater of Ideas," *Arion* 2 (1963): 32–56. Bernard Knox writes that Euripides produces by "dramatic means the same

other's moral, political, military, and intellectual power but go their own way, at best indifferent to one another, at worst destroying what Thucydides calls those "general laws to which all alike can look for salvation in adversity" (3.84). Collective action becomes impossible or perverse; collective thinking, whether deliberation in the assembly or tragedy in the theater, becomes problematic. Speech ceases to be an alternative to violence and a way of making known; instead it becomes a kind of violence that purposely obscures and misleads.[8]

As the disintegration and degeneration in the world of the characters and spectators intensifies, individuals are estranged horizontally from their living kin and compatriots, and vertically from ancestors and progeny.[9] But individual venality interests Euripides less in itself than as a symptom and sign of a structural or systemic corruption that is both political and intellectual in nature. That is why the play presents villainy rather than a single villain, and a pervasive lack of character rather than a single "flawed" character. The falsehoods, conceits, and reckless acts in the *Orestes* form a fabric of spiritual ailments that cloaks the stage in the self-righteous "dress of moralistic self-assertion."[10]

Euripides explores and presents this corruption in a number of

---

shattering effect Thucydides creates by taking us without a break from the Periclean Funeral Speech straight to the plague" (review of *Euripidean Drama*, by D. J. Conacher in *Word and Action: Essays on the Ancient Theater* [Baltimore: Johns Hopkins University Press, 1979], p. 328).

8. The corruption of meaning is suggested by the German "*Sinneskrise.*" See the discussion in H. P. Stahl, "On 'Extra-dramatic' Communication of Characters in Euripides," in *Yale Classical Studies*, vol. 25, ed. T. F. Gould and C. J. Herrington (Cambridge: Cambridge University Press, 1977), pp. 159–76, and Karl Reinhardt, "Die Sinneskrise bei Euripides," in *Tradition und Geist* (Göttingen: Vandenhoeck und Ruprecht, 1960). But Albert Cook (*Enactment in Greek Tragedy* [Chicago: Swallow Press, 1971], p. xiii), is right to warn against being content with "ascribing the profound disturbances of imaginative work to generating disturbances in the outside world." While the war provided the circumstances for the civic disintegrations in Euripides' plays, it "does not provide a full explanation for them."

9. Alexis de Tocqueville notes the consequences of this in his *Democracy in America* (trans. George Lawrence, ed. J. P. Mayer [Garden City, N.Y.: Doubleday, Anchor Books, 1969], p. 507): "The woof of time is ever being broken and the track of past generations lost. Those who have gone before are easily forgotten, and no one gives a thought to those who will follow. All a man's interests are limited to those near himself." Such men live for the moment, without larger sympathies or sustained principles (though with a common method unknown to be one).

10. Here is Reinhardt: "Schwäche, Mangel an Charakter, Lüge, Falscheit, Egoismus, Dunkel, Hemmungslosigkeit, Verknöcherung—der Maskenzug der seelischen Gebrechen schreitet über die Szene im pompösen Aufputz der moralischen Selbstbehauptung" ("Die Sinneskrise" [cited above, n. 8], p. 239).

ways. He parodies human aspirations to justice and mocks the sup-
position that men can understand, let alone control, their condition. The past offers neither solace nor sustenance. There are no
divine or human exemplars to provide inspiration for noble action
and character, and no firm demarcations or standards to provide
guidance for citizens and sons. Ancient moral strictures (at least as
embodied in the words and actions of Menelaus and Tyndareus)
are shriveled and irrelevant; present ones are a baffling maze that
draws the young especially into perverse error and violence.[11] In
The Eumenides the Athenians are road builders (*keleuthopoioi*) who
give human definition to what is otherwise untamed and wild.
Here, the barely disguised Athenians are destroying the very paths
that defined their achievement.

In such circumstances no literary form (even tragedy) can translate or transmit the past in a way that makes sense of, and offers
regenerative possibilities for, the present. The tragedian is in danger of becoming like Electra and Orestes who, cut off from a time
and culture in which their actions might perhaps have been meaningful and moral, exist in an alien time and world that immoralizes,
distorts, and trivializes what they say and do.[12]

Not only is the hope of realizing human intentions sheer vanity,
the cultural demarcations men take to be natural are in fact conventional (which does not preclude their necessity). The *Orestes* thus
collapses the distinction between free and slave, men and women,
heroes and cowards, and Greek and Barbarian. Various characters
in the play contrive forced marriages of contraries (as if to anticipate the contrived marriage of Hermione and Orestes that concludes the play). At one point or another beauty is called ugliness,
nobility criminality, and impiety pious. Courage becomes the cowardly murder of innocent women, *philia* a partnership in ludicrously
inept cruelty, and *sophia* a single-minded concern for power. In this
play, as in Thucydides' vivid portrait of civil war (*stasis*), words
have changed their meaning and everything has become its opposite, or something else, or nothing at all.

This corruption of language is exemplified and reiterated by the
play's effect of "*sparagmos*," its strained lexical resonances and arbitrary division of signifiers and signified.[13] Now *sparagmos* literally

11. Ibid., p. 238.
12. Arrowsmith, "Greek Theater of Ideas," p. 41.
13. Zeitlin, "Closet of Masks," pp. 56–57.

means pieces torn off, things shredded, violated, or fragmented. Usually referring to the mangling of corpses or convulsive, spasmodic behavior, it can indicate political as well as physical dismemberment. The connection between them, and to linguistic corruption, is made by Thucydides (though he does not use the word).

In his description of the plague that afflicted Athenian bodies and the body politic, but still more in his description of the *stasis* at Corcyra, Thucydides graphically portrays the ultimate character and result of political corruption. Especially at Corcyra, moral bankruptcy and social collapse pervert all human faculties and talents and so destroy the human community that made them possible. There reason and courage became animal cunning, the lust for power trampled all limits, and established institutions were transformed into instruments of private domination. Everything was a weapon, everyone a means, every act other than it seemed, all speech a ruse to distract a potential enemy from violent intentions. Since everyone was a potential enemy (not even party provided any limit), men lived in a continual state of war.

In this state nothing was stable or certain, everything was of, by, and for the moment. Disconnected from a past that was in any case reinterpreted to justify present excess, and from any care for the future, certain only of uncertainty and familiar only with unfamiliarity, men were no longer able to make sense to and for each other. "Words," Thucydides tells us, "were forced to change their ordinary meaning and to assume a significance that distorted the extraordinary deeds now undertaken." I quote his examples at length because they resonate with, and add political dimension to, the corruption in the *Orestes:*

Senseless audacity came to be considered the courage of a loyal ally; prudent hesitation specious cowardice; moderation was held to be a cloak for unmanliness; ability to see all sides of a question inaptness to act on any. Frantic violence and animal attacks became the attribute of manliness; cautious plotting, a justifiable means of self-defense. The advocate of extreme measures was always trustworthy; his opponent a man to be suspected. . . . [T]o forestall an evil or suggest the idea of a criminal deed where it was not yet entertained, was equally commended, until even blood became a weaker tie than party from the superior readiness of those united by the latter to dare everything without reserve; for such associations were joined not for purposes of enhancing the common good or in conformity with established laws, but by selfish ambitions to overthrow both.

(3.82)

It is worth remembering that Thucydides regarded Corcyra as a relatively restrained prelude to the greater excesses that later overwhelmed all Greece, which lends credence to Philip Vellacott's assertion that "Orestes is not merely Athens, but a whole war-crazed generation of Hellenes."[14]

There is a question as to how much the play itself exemplifies, or even contributes to, the political and linguistic corruption it thematizes. On one level, the disjointed speech and action of the characters in the play are part of the play's point. Here there is a contrast between the actions in the play and the play as action. But on another level, it remains uncertain how much the *Orestes* participates in the problem it depicts; how much the play as action is continuous with the action of the play.

All of this is related to the issue of whether the corruption of tragedy is Euripides' point or a point legitimately made in criticism of him. I suspect it is both, and that the way the play (perhaps purposely) participates in the disintegration it depicts is one reason why the *Orestes* provides such a textured understanding of political corruption.

1

Before turning to that understanding, a brief synopsis of this not very well known or often commented on play is in order.

It opens with the still-polluted Orestes fitfully asleep six days after the Apollo-commanded murder of his murdering mother. His sister Electra stands guard over him while explaining his condition and their joint fate to the audience. When her prologue ends, her aunt Helen appears, having just returned from Troy. With what turns out to be typical obliviousness, Helen castigates Electra for not being married and asks her niece (of all people), to go to Clytemnestra's grave and perform a libation since she, Helen, is in such disfavor with the Argives that she dare not go. Electra in turn curses her aunt's self-centeredness, symbolized by the tiny lock of hair Helen has given for the grave of her dead sister.

Orestes soon awakens, exhausted and bewildered, and has a moment of lucidity, but lapses back into madness when he hears the

names Clytemnestra and Helen. He pleads with Apollo to save him
from the Furies and turns on his sister, whom he now sees as one
of those gorgon-eyed bitches. But almost immediately he ceases his
imprecations and turns, with exquisite tenderness, to comfort his
comforter. This particular about-face is one of many, anticipating
the other actions of the play and the play as action.

Their despair is relieved by the news of their uncle's return.
Menelaus is their last hope, and so Orestes alternately argues,
cajoles, importunes, and remonstrates with him. Despite his rhetorical protestations Menelaus proves a false friend, whose resolve
quickly falters when Tyndareus, Clytemnestra's father and implacable enemy of his once-loved grandson, threatens the returning
king with loss of power in Sparta.

Almost as Menelaus exits, a true friend, Pylades, appears. Unlike their uncle, he insists on sharing their fate and prospects as he
has already shared in their crime. He proposes various stratagems
to reverse their fortunes and powerlessness, or if that is impossible,
to insure that they die a hero's death. His remark about good leaders (773) gives Orestes the preposterous idea (which Pylades then
encourages) of going before the Argive assembly and pleading for
his life and his power. The assembly grants him neither, and so
brother and sister must die. Pylades then urges the killing of Helen
to avenge themselves on Menelaus and to restore their good name
by punishing the woman whose infidelity has ruined Greece. At
the very least they will gain honor (*kalon*) by their deed. Electra
suggests in addition that they take her young cousin Hermione
hostage to forestall Menelaus's revenge. Orestes is delighted with
this suggestion on the part of his sister, a woman with a man's
heart.

Pylades and Orestes enter the house intending to carry out the
plot, but before they can, Helen magically vanishes. But Hermione
does not, and so they seize her, the one truly innocent character in
the play. When Menelaus enters he finds them all atop the house, a
sword held to his daughter's throat by his nephew, and the house
nearly aflame.

Amidst this chaos and threatened destruction, Apollo suddenly
appears. The action is frozen, and there is a total inversion of the
story's previous direction. Helen becomes a sailor-guiding star;
Menelaus will remarry and rule in Sparta; Orestes will marry
Hermione and rule in Argos after a one-year exile and acquittal by

a jury of gods at Athens; Pylades will marry Electra; and the god himself will reconcile the Argives to Orestes, now despised but in future their king. As with the ending of the *Oresteia*, mankind has at last found healing and release.

All such summaries are inadequate and misleading, but a summary of this play is especially so, given its theme, political corruption, and the way that theme is elaborated through incongruities of plot and structure. In it surface coherence obscures incoherent action and character, while conversely, surface incoherence makes a coherent point about incoherence. This is evident in the fact and nature of the *Orestes'* departure from the mythical heroic tradition, from Aeschylus, from its own seeming logic, and from the "pure" form of tragedy. The following sections deal with the fact and significance of these departures, taking each in turn.

2

The sense of corruption can be found in the play's departure from the mythical traditions that supply tragedy with its stories, characters, and themes. It is not the mere fact of departure that matters, but the extent of it. Aeschylus and Sophocles had also taken liberties with ancient legends, which were in any event multivocal. But their inventiveness was limited by the need for stable meaning lest the changes they made lose their impact and import. Too many violations of expectations would destroy the common understanding tragedy relied upon as a public institution in a still predominantly oral culture.[15] Indeed, it was precisely this conservatism that allowed it and them to be critical.[16]

The *Orestes* does more than depart from the mythical tradition

15. Which suggests that even the most radical critic presupposes a common language sufficient to make his critique intelligible to some groups within the culture. The sense in which Euripides is conservative is suggested by Helene Foley, who writes that, of the three tragic poets, "Euripides consistently comes closest to such dismantling of the divine superstructure, while simultaneously insisting on a restoration of ritual to a central place in the politically and socially unstable worlds he creates" (*Ritual Irony: Poetry and Sacrifice in Euripides* [Ithaca, N.Y.: Cornell University Press, 1985], p. 59; see also pp. 18–19 and passim).

16. If Albert Cook is right in insisting that myths are cultural givens that allow the playwright "to operate freely" (*Enactment in Greek Tragedy*, p. 16), what does it mean to problematize myth radically in the way Euripides does in *Orestes*? In one sense he is as constrained as his character Orestes is; or, to put it another way, Euripides shows what happens to freedom when myths are interpreted as the characters in the play interpret them.

and heroic ethic, it repudiates them. It is true that Aeschylus had dramatized the human cost of Agamemnon's commitment to far-flung glory and that Sophocles had depicted the destruction that attends a hero's unyielding sense of honor. But in Euripides' late plays, Aeschylus's unstable amalgam of citizen-hero is at best a contemporary failure, while Sophoclean heroes no longer achieve dignity amidst suffering. Whatever the appropriateness of heroism in the past—and the scope of Euripides' criticism makes us retrospectively skeptical of its moral validity and practical efficacy generally—it is now a vestigial remnant that is nevertheless an omnipresent, oppressive, and ominous force throughout the play (*perhaps* lifted by Apollo in the concluding scene).

The perverse power of the heroic tradition is made clear in the play's opening lines, in the utter helplessness of all the characters, in the slave scene, and in the ridiculous encomium to glory.

In the opening seventy lines Electra distances herself from the history of her house that she is recounting in detail: Tantalus was born of Zeus "or so they say"; the story of his fall from grace is a legend about which she does "not really know"; and of her father's fame she says, "if what he had was fame." These doubts (which appear in other plays of Euripides), here deprive her and us of any sense of secure interpretative context, and break the continuity of past and present. Since the story of the house includes the gods, her uncertainty extends to them and the deed Orestes has done at their behest.

Yet the efficacy of this uncertain legacy is evident in their present inheritance; madness for him, helplessness for her, isolation, vulnerability and hopelessness for them both. Electra's anguished description of the anguish men and women must bear reminds her of Tantalus, the "father" of their house. Born of Zeus and favored by the gods, he now writhes in terror at the rock overhead that always threatens to crush him. Cursed by pride and an unbridled tongue, this once luckiest of mortals now lives in perpetual torment, not only because of the rock but because, as another story goes, he is doomed to remain perpetually hungry and thirsty, with food and drink placed just beyond his reach. Together these two images suggest contradiction, doubtful and suspended action, men and women poised, as are Orestes, Electra, and Athens, between life and death, health and chaos, reaching for moral sustenance, political order, and the redemptive possibilities of ancient myths that lie just beyond their grasp. The children of a once-glorious Athens, like those of the once-glorious Tantalus, are no longer the chosen of the gods. They are, rather, unable to extricate themselves from the unceasing cannibalism of war, violation, and *pleonexia* (unceasing demands for disproportionate gain and advantage).

In *Orestes* men and women are victims rather than heroes. Repeatedly human exertion is blind and ineffectual at best, frequently sordid and contemptible, sometimes malevolent and cruel.[17] No character escapes victimization (except Apollo); no figure remains uncompromised (except Hermione but not excepting Apollo); no one has the intellectual and moral perspicuity to recognize the complexity of reality and the attendant difficulty of ethical judgment. Like Aristotle's slaves, these putative heroes are unable to accomplish any plan of their own. Orestes fails as a suppliant, rescuer, avenger, victim, and victimizer. He is an inept son, statesman, and thinker. His arguments fail to persuade, and his sword fails to draw blood. So much for the heroic ideal of being foremost in words and deeds.

The play not only reduces the heroic ethic to malevolent triviality, it parodies the greatness of the Trojan War.

While Orestes and Pylades are inside the house attempting to murder Helen, a Trojan slave runs out in terror for his life. The chorus are anxious for news of Helen, but he mourns for Troy. When he does answer, it is with attempted tragic diction and literary allusions.[18] Confronted by the pursuing Orestes, the cowering slave begs, deceives, and flatters to save his life. He succeeds because Orestes regards his plea that, "Slave man, free man, everybody likes to live" as "well spoken" and a life-saving piece of "wit" (*synesis*). Here at least persuasion is effective (in contrast to Orestes' failure to convince Menelaus, Tyndareus, or the assembly).

In another context the slave's response is banal: but not here and now. For one thing the slave is a reflection, even extension, of Orestes (who has already expressed his fear of dying like a slave). With uncharacteristic insight Orestes recognizes himself in the slave and the slave in himself. What he does to the slave is what has

17. Burnett, *Catastrophe Survived*, p. 14.
18. The richness of these allusions is elaborated by Zeitlin, who speaks of a "new type of literary consciousness" and claims that "no other characters in Greek drama are so bookish, so learned, although they themselves are marvelously unaware of their erudition" ("Closet of Masks," p. 53). The *Orestes'* violation of expectations is so intense precisely because of its rich allusions to the literary tradition.

been done to him by others, and so in a sense, what he does to him he is also doing to himself. He taunts the slave by dangling the lure of life before him as he himself has been taunted and harassed by "circumstances, gods, men and the impulses of his own mind."[19] The torture he inflicts on the slave by his indecision about whether to spare him or not is merely a further instance of the indecision that has tortured him.

For another thing, the "contest" between Agamemnon's son and a slave compatriot of Hector replays, as it ridicules, the heroism of the Trojan War. The ridicule serves to confirm Orestes' worst fears of insufficiency, insignificance, and impotence. Throughout the play he has been petrified of his own cowardice and inability to live up to his father's putative heroism. Against the ambiguous sexuality he shares with the eunuch slave stands the godlike power and uncompromised maleness of Agamemnon. Orestes asks: "Am I or am I not the son of Agamemnon, the man who ruled all Hellas . . . with godlike power?" to which he answers: "I shall not shame him by dying like a slave" (1166–69). Yet he slavishly clings to life. And, by using the same word (*synesis*) he has earlier given to his consciousness of guilt (for which he was willing to die) to the slave's cliché about wanting to live, Orestes trivializes his moment of glory and understanding.[20]

But there is another possible interpretation of this double use of *synesis* and of the identification of Trojan slave with putative Greek hero—that there is an equality of condition obscured by the conventional, if not illusory and vain, distinction between freeman and slave. But at least in this play, the force of this equality seems less the liberation of slaves or the empowerment of unheard victims than the enslaving of the free or, more radically, the abolishment of the categories of slave and free altogether. The collapse of familiar oppositions between slave and free, Greek and Barbarian, innocent and guilty, action and victimization, inside and outside, and male and female may demystify their "natural" status, but it also leaves the human landscape flat, homogeneous, and baffling.

This departure from the mythical tradition, parody of the heroic ethic, disjointed speech of a slave with whom the "heroic" Orestes identifies, impotence of the characters, and collapse of public discourse reflects back on the play itself. The abrupt changes in the

19. Wolff, "Orestes," p. 345.
20. Ibid.

drama mirror the abrupt changes in the drama's style; the parody of Homer and Troy is to some degree self-parody; the literary pretensions of the slave are to some degree the literary pretensions of the playwright, and the rejection of conventional categories and contrasts finds a parallel in Euripides' own amalgam of comedy and tragedy.

3

Euripides invites us to compare the theology, politics, and dramatic structure of the *Oresteia* to his *Orestes*. But that invitation only serves to create expectations that are disappointed and surface parallels that turn out not to be analogous. We look for actions and speeches that never occur, or occur in radically altered circumstances with opposite import. Each of the many echoes merely heightens the sense of dislocation, disquiet, and disharmony.

The *Oresteia* portrays the achievement of political justice at Athens through a joint effort of gods and men.[21] The final scenes of *The Eumenides* promise healing and relief from the suffering of the previous two plays, as the formerly warring divine and human forces become reconciled in a city that reflects divine *dikē*. The vehicle for this achievement is Orestes, a man who does what he must though he knows it to be a crime before and after he does it. Unlike his mother, he "knows not how this shall end" and so goes, at Apollo's behest, to Athens and Athene, where he will be acquitted of his crime.

Until Euripides' Apollo commands the characters to assume (more or less) the mythical role they have so far shown no inclination to accept on their own, the *Orestes* confounds the moral universe of the *Oresteia*.[22] Euripides' Orestes develops into (though does not begin as) a stalker of innocent women relatives. In fact his prospective killing of Hermione recalls Agamemnon's sacrifice of the innocent Iphigeneia, and so projects another brutal war and a further round in the cycle of vengeance that has plagued Atreus's

21. My interpretation draws on my essay "Justice and the Oresteia," *American Political Science Review* 76 (1982): 22–33.

22. In Aeschylus, moral complexities seem part of the way things are; in Euripides, "they appear as an aspect of human inconsistency and confusion. And Orestes' confusion is ours as well" (Deborah H. Roberts, *Apollo and His Oracle in the Oresteia*, Hypomnemata, vol. 78 [Göttingen: Vandenhoeck und Ruprecht, 1983], p. 113).

house. Nor is this Orestes driven by the same public motives that over-determined the matricide of Aeschylus's Orestes. There is no evidence that Clytemnestra and Aegisthus ruled as tyrants, and so Orestes cannot be a tyrannicide. (Argos is presented as being and as having been a democracy, and so the corruption we see in it is democratic corruption.) For these and other reasons Euripides' character cannot be a saving remnant on whose self-understanding gods and men build a jointly consecrated civic justice.

Not only does Orestes come to resemble his murdering father and the mother he murdered, he offers arguments drawn from Aeschylus's Apollo (in speaking to Tyndareus) and Furies (when before the assembly), even though in the *Oresteia* the latter seek his death. In fact we are never certain who is and who is not a Fury, any more than we are confident of who is enslaved and who is free.[23] In the first scene Orestes sees Electra as the Fury she will become, while the description of him by Menelaus and Tyndareus is reminiscent of how the Furies are described in the *Oresteia*. In the trilogy Cassandra sees the Furies atop the house of Atreus. In the *Orestes* Pylades, Electra, and Orestes are also found atop the house, as if to suggest that they have become their own Furies, doing to themselves what their enemies were unable to do in *The Eumenides*. That Orestes becomes an unwitting accomplice of those who wish him dead, and is, inadvertently, his own accuser, worst enemy, and executioner, suggests both a distressing affinity with his parents and a collapse of Aeschylus's vision of the world.

Given the *Oresteia*, any confusion about who is a Fury (or the implication that everyone is) confounds the opposition between male and female. In the trilogy men and women are in conflict: Apollo wishes to banish the Furies, Artemis demands perverse sacrifice when her father's eagles devour the unborn young of a pregnant hare, Zeus is at odds with *moira*, Agamemnon murders his daughter, Clytemnestra her husband, and Orestes his mother. However liberating and noble the male impulse toward heroism may be at times, it kills life and women. However essential the female values of hearth and home may be, their dominance is too confining. Justice therefore depends on establishing reciprocity between men and women such that each is a limit and complement to the other.

---

23. Nor are we certain that the Furies exist as anything other than the mad imaginings of a delirious Orestes. To be unsure about the existence, let alone moral place, of the Furies *and* Apollo is to undermine the divine boundaries of the *Oresteia*.

That is what a rightly ordered city means and what is achieved in *The Eumenides*.

But in *Orestes* the distinction between men and women is blurred much as it is in *Agamemnon* (with the mannish Clytemnestra and the womanish Aegisthus) but not in *The Eumenides*. Orestes is uncertain of his masculinity, Menelaus is introduced in terms that suggest effeminacy, and Electra pointedly alludes to her femininity in the very first lines of the play. Yet as the play progresses she becomes a mannish woman bent on violent revenge like her mother. When, after the messenger completes his description of the assembly she repeats the history of her house (and so the play's opening), she once more identifies herself as a woman. Soon afterward Orestes protests that her feminine lamentations, fears, and clinging to life will infect his courage. His expectations are unfounded, for this Electra, unlike Aeschylus's, is indeed her mother's child. (It is he that is fearful, clings to life, and lacks courage.) Soon Electra urges taking Hermione captive, is praised for having "the mind of a man," screams for Helen's blood, coaxes her cousin toward her death (as her mother had her father), and exhorts her cohorts to rest their sword on Hermione's throat in order to show Menelaus "what it means to fight with *men*, not cowards from Troy" (1353).[24] No more than Orestes is Electra a figure to lead men and women out of the moral chaos of *Agamemnon/Orestes*.

From one point of view the confounding of male and female, like the confounding of other oppositions (such as slave and free, Barbarian and Greek, inside and outside) is a liberating negation of the putative "naturalness" of Athenian categories and a demystifying of Aeschylean reciprocity between the sexes, which some regard as sustaining patriarchy. Certainly Euripides has been read this way and with justification. Still, on balance, his emphasis seems to be on the confusion of moral roles and the loss of identity such "liberation" portends, rather than the opportunities for reconstitution it provides.

"Freed" from the confines of an Aeschylean vision and world (and from faith in Apollo), Orestes deals with each situation in itself, living from moment to moment, changing who he is and what he says as circumstances seem to require. His positions and arguments are literally unprincipled. They are either self-contradictory

24. I emphasize *men* because *andras* here heightens the sense of masculinity (implying a "true man") and Electra seems to include herself in its denotation.

(as in his exchange with Tyndareus) or derive from incompatible principles (the Furies and Apollo). The irony is that his instrumental arguments designed for momentary success fail, as if self-interest narrowly understood makes one oblivious to context and others.[25]

If I am right, Euripides is not endorsing the emancipatory possibilities of freeing oneself from Aeschylean polarities. Still less does he reject them for some higher or fuller synthesis. *Orestes* pushes these polarities—between generations, male and female, persuasion and violence, speech and silence, corrupt death-dealing and life-giving sacrifice, necessity and freedom, gods and men— further, until they collapse into each other and into a claustrophobic whole that guarantees mutual destruction (barring the intervention of the god).

If Aeschylus's principles and polarities are confounded, undermined and negated, then so, too, is his hope of justice and what he means by it.[26] Indeed, the purposeful anachronism of a civic court that is already established but thoroughly corrupt plays havoc with the trilogy's closing scenes and establishes a chasm between them and contemporary reality.[27] There is no Athena, Areopagus, or majestic ceremony in the *Orestes* to consecrate the at least temporary resolution of Aeschylean tensions. Instead we have Apollo forcing Orestes to put down his sword and marry the woman he was about to murder in the name of honor. Such is the play's "resolution" of the opposition between men and women (or between what is male and female within men and women).

Justice as something other and more than a rhetorical façade for self-serving aggrandizement is of little concern to the characters in the play (which is not to say Euripides agrees with them). Orestes is tried by a corrupt Argive assembly rather than a divinely constituted Athenian court. As the messenger relates it, there were five speakers. The first, an old ally of Agamemnon now anxious to curry favor with the new power, gives a duplicitous speech claiming that Orestes' deed sets a precedent dangerous to parents. The second,

25. It is one of Hannah Arendt's arguments in *The Origins of Totalitarianism* (1951; reprint, New York: Harcourt Brace Jovanovich, 1973) that people preoccupied with self-interest are unable to protect either self or interests. That is also Socrates' argument against Thrasymachus in the *Republic*.

26. For Aeschylus's idea of justice as the reconciliation and reciprocity of otherwise disjunctive, if not warring, principles, see Euben, "Justice and the *Oresteia*," passim.

27. See the remarks of Elizabeth Rawson, "Aspects of Euripides' *Orestes*," *Arethusa* 5, no. 2 (1972): 155–56.

Diomedes, recommends banishment, but is ignored. The third is a professional rhetorician and demagogue. Reckless, glib, and easily bought, this new man joins with the old aristocrat Tyndareus to demand death by stoning, as if to suggest a conspiracy of violence between what is oldest and newest. The fourth speaker, a small farmer, is praised by the farmer-messenger as a true man, full of common sense and the backbone of the city. For him Orestes deserves a crown, since he killed a woman whose act of murder would have kept men from war and at home, worried about what might happen in their absence. Given the time when the play was produced, this praise of war compromises the praise accorded the speaker. So does the argument from precedent since, as the play makes clear, it speaks with equal force *against* what Orestes has done. Thus it is all the more significant that the fifth speech, which is made by Orestes, echoes these views (and incidentally those of his enemies in *The Eumenides*).

Justice goes unmentioned and unfulfilled in the speeches and assembly, silenced by narrow political self-seeking and rampant factionalism. There is no one here like Aeschylus's Athena to embody and extol justice while institutionalizing it in a divinely sanctioned human agency. Every speaker is corrupt and argues speciously (though similarly), except Diomedes, whose advice is ignored. Apollo's role in the matricide is also ignored, as if the gods, like justice, are useless in public life.[28] At the play's end he does indeed forecast Orestes' trial and acquittal at Athens. But it will be before a court of gods. Men are incapable of sharing divine authority, and we see why. If justice *is* achieved, it must be given to, or even forced on, recalcitrant human beings by gods who are themselves suspect provokers of matricide.

4

The *Orestes'* violation of its own surface consistency of plot and character adds another dimension to the fragmentation and dissonance established by the play's departure from the mythical tradition and from Aeschylus.

The plot develops with explosive shifts of mood and attitude. So discordant are the episodes in themselves and in relation to one an-

---

28. The messenger mentions him at 955–56, but that is the only reference between 591 and 1625 (except for one minor exception).

other, and so agitated are the speeches and speakers, that the play threatens to disintegrate entirely.

The chaotic shifts of mood are illustrated and paralleled by comparable shifts in the characters. None of the characters in the play, except for Hermione but including Apollo, are what they seem.[29] Each initially wins our sympathy through apparently noble words, deeds, and sufferings, only to reveal petty cruelty masked by hypocritical rhetoric.[30] We are drawn to them only to be pushed away until, finally chary, we withhold attachment to them as exemplary actors, and to the mythical tradition that celebrates them.[31] This is not only true of Electra and Orestes (as my remarks have already suggested) but of Menelaus, Tyndareus, Pylades, and Apollo as well.

Electra and Orestes regard Menelaus and his great power as their last hope.[32] But the hope is suspect even before the putative savior appears. This heroic king has smuggled his wife into Argos in the dead of night; that wife is so vain and penurious that she confirms Electra's earlier skepticism about the heroic dimensions of the victory at Troy and thus of the heroic stature of those who fought there; and the chorus introduce the Greek hero with *"habrosynē,"* which implies Asiatic splendor, barbarian excess, and effeminacy. Menelaus is the womanish man to Electra's mannish woman (which is how Aeschylus describes Clytemnestra), and Orestes doubts his own masculinity.

Nevertheless Orestes pleads with his paternal uncle to save him from death. He is answered with a string of questions, which come to focus on the issue of political power. Menelaus's persistence in asking whether the hated son will be allowed to take up his father's scepter is peculiar, given what Menelaus already knows, but is not peculiar given the true reason for his asking. As becomes clear after Tyndareus's interruption, Menelaus is less Orestes' savior than his rival.

29. Reinhardt ("Die Sinneskrise," p. 239) talks about the "unwillkürliche Selbstentlarvung" of the dominant characters.

30. See Seth Schein, "Mythical Illusion and Historical Reality in Euripides' *Orestes,"* *Wiener Studien: Zeitschrift für Klassische Philologie und Patristik,* n.s., 9 (1975):54, and D. J. Conacher, *Euripidean Drama: Myth, Theme and Structure* (Toronto: University of Toronto Press, 1967), p. 217.

31. Perhaps this explains why Euripides seems so distant from his characters (despite the lessened distance between tragedy and city).

32. On Menelaus, see Nathan A. Greenberg, "Euripides' *Orestes:* An Interpretation," *Harvard Studies in Classical Philology* 66 (1962):esp. pp. 168–70.

But initially he seems moved by Orestes' plight and persuaded of the primacy of kin obligations. But when Tyndareus threatens to bar Menelaus from power in Sparta, all noble protestations of honor collapse. At best Menelaus recognizes the existence of a moral issue he cannot understand and cannot summon up the courage to act upon. More likely his sophistic interrogation of Orestes and sparring with Tyndareus are stratagems to buy time and assess his own prospects. His decision not to honor Orestes, the suspect reason he gives for it (lack of power), and his un-fulfilled promise to aid his nephew with diplomacy and tact (he is silent in the assembly), suggest a man unmoved by principle. Per-haps Menelaus changes his mind. More likely he merely gives voice to what was on his mind from the beginning. But the difference may not much matter. Where resolve is so fragile there may as well be no resolve at all.

Like the other characters in this play, Tyndareus confounds our sense of what someone like him should say and do, acts inconsis-tently even in terms of these inverted values, and invokes the past (including reminders of the *Oresteia*) in ways that unsettle what is present and presented. As an old Spartan aristocrat, Tyndareus should be sympathetic to Orestes' arguments from kinship, and would be if this were the world of the *Oresteia*. But it isn't, and so he isn't. Not only do Orestes' arguments fail to win him over or even mollify his anger, they incite him to a vindictive fury that mocks his initial commitment to law, moderation, justice, and the ancestral practice of banishing murders instead of killing them. As he con-tradicts what he ostensibly admires and so perpetuates the cycle of vengeance he ostensibly abhors, his moral universe becomes that of Aeschylus's Furies. Tyndareus calls himself an avenging hound (as they did) and is immune to Orestes' plea of extenuating circum-stances (as they were). Refusing to accept the mediated sense of judgment his concept of justice requires, Tyndareus does not hear Orestes, though Orestes is at first sensitive to his grandfather's feel-ings and views. Refusing to listen, Tyndareus ignores his grand-son's dilemma, invocation of Apollo, and arguments, even when they mimic his own.

As older male relatives, Orestes' uncle and grandfather are prop-erly his exemplars and teachers. But what he learns from them is that seemingly plausible arguments are, in the end, as specious as the ideals they rest on; that elaborate protestations of principle are mere rhetorical façades, which collapse with the touch of interest. Menelaus hides behind *dynata* (doing what is practicable under the circumstances),[33] which is the principle the Athenian emissaries invoke at Melos when they reject the relevance of morality in politics; Tyndareus hides behind *nomos*, his major accusation being that Orestes took the law into his own hands. But in Tyndareus's hands the law becomes as impatient with complexity and as dismissive of extenuating circumstances as the Furies' view of vengeance in the *Oresteia*. Since one of the "extenuating circumstances" being dismissed is that Apollo commanded the matricide (not an appeal to a court), Orestes also learns impiety from precisely the man who should be, and who thinks of himself as being, most pious. Finally, but most importantly, Orestes learns that he is alone; that the man he loves most hates him most; that the man he looked on as savior has deserted him. Isolated with a remorse compounded by the indifference or vindictiveness of others, Orestes becomes a violent, but impotent, avenging fury.

The full extent of Orestes' isolation (and so his desperation) is suggested by the fact that these two male relatives span two generations and represent two cities. It is as if there were no time or place to which Orestes can look for understanding, sympathy, and moral enlightenment. The situation is all the worse if Orestes is seen not as a child of Agamemnon but of Athens; if Tyndareus and Menelaus are not Spartan and Argive elders but past generations of Athenians whose putative ideals have become self-serving, crippling, and corrupting. In these terms the frenetic aggressiveness of Orestes' subsequent actions are not so different from those that characterized the Athenians after the death of Pericles.

Of course, Orestes has Pylades, who appears to be, and in one sense is, everything Menelaus is not. He is the loyal friend to Menelaus's disloyal relative, willing to risk his life for his friend where Menelaus would risk nothing for his kin, as anxious to die with Orestes as Menelaus was anxious to detach himself from Orestes and so avoid danger. Where Menelaus cares about neither Orestes' salvation nor his name, Pylades is agreeable to any strategy that will either save his friend or ensure his glorious death.

Yet as with all the other characters in the play, Pylades is not what

---

33. Vellacott (*Ironic Drama*, p. 55) argues that Menelaus is in "an impossible position, in which he behaves with prudence and decency." Prudent for him certainly, but not for Orestes, and Menelaus's later silence is deafening.

he seems. It is he who reaffirms Orestes' idea of addressing the assembly in the insane hope that *"hoi polloi"* will either immediately accept Orestes' leadership, take pity on his high birth, be good citizens, and acquit him, or kill him and so save him from a coward's death. Pylades planned Clytemnestra's death and plans to reenact it by murdering Helen "in the name of all Hellas whose fathers and sons she murdered, whose wives she widowed" (1135). By the deed and this justification he believes they can avenge themselves on Menelaus, perhaps save their lives, or, if not their lives, then their good names. It is also this "loyal friend" who proposes that, if their other stratagems fail, they should burn down Atreus's house so that Menelaus will not have it and they will (again) have glory. Finally, it is Pylades who invokes Zeus to lead them in a heroic victory over a helpless woman (Helen) and her innocent child (Hermione).

Hidden inside this erstwhile friend and savior is a foe whose deadly counsel is a delight to Orestes' worst enemies. Instead of helping Orestes to speak, act, and think with honor and intelligence, Pylades speeds up the play's action until its manic rhythms signal total loss of control.[34] This saving friend, whose entrance promises all that was denied by the exiting kin, is an avenging Fury in disguise. No wonder Socrates finds Polemarchus's statement that justice is helping friends and harming enemies to be insufficient.

From one point of view, Apollo's miraculous appearance repeats the play's pattern of violated expectations, except that here, presumably, is an effective action by a god able to liberate human beings from their ineffectiveness, the play from its wayward pattern of destructive action, and the audience from their confusion. Earlier Electra has announced, "I have an answer; a way out for all of us"; to which Orestes replies, "That would take a god" (1179–80). Here now, finally, is the god, returning the characters and drama to something like their assigned place in a restored mythical order.[35]

But from another point of view this restoration and reassignment is suspect. For one thing, the preceding rhythm of promise and disappointment should make us leery of resolution, much as the cor-

34. Pylades, Reinhardt argues, "springt auf die Geschwister über und ergreift alle drei wie ein rasender Brand" ("Die Sinneskrise," p. 251).

35. On the nature of the restoration and reasons to be suspect about it, see Arrowsmith, "Introduction," pp. 108–11; Wolff, "Orestes"; Hugh Parry, "Euripides' *Orestes:* The Quest for Salvation," *Transactions and Proceedings of the American Philological Association* 100 (1969):337–53; and W. Burkert, "Die Absurdität der Gewalt und das Ende der Tragödie: Euripides," A 20 (1974), pp. 97–109.

ruption of *Agamemnon* shadows the concluding joy of the *Oresteia*. This unease is given substance by the abruptness of the anyway contrived rearrangement and by the parallels between the *Oresteia's* opening and the *Orestes'* ending. At the trilogy's outset we see a nightwatchman perched sleepless atop the house searching expectantly for a sign of Troy's defeat and his master's return. In *Orestes*, Pylades and Electra are atop the same house. But in Aeschylus the sign is a beacon fire and the returning master is Agamemnon; in Euripides the returning master is Apollo and the sign of his coming is a nearly consuming fire that signals not the triumph at Troy but the utter defeat of Atreus's house, Athenian greatness, Hellenic power, and human purpose.

For another thing the very arbitrariness of the ending, together with the idealized unity it contrives to establish, only emphasizes the impossibility of harmony and order. The ending's forced love and wisdom merely reaffirm the disparity between human community and what the play achieves, and suggest a god who mocks our insufficiencies rather than helps us compensate for or rectify them.

We do not know who Apollo is, or what he has intended, or now intends.[36] The *Oresteia* makes it clear that Apollo ordered Orestes to kill his mother. Whatever the justification of the matricide and however excessive Apollo's words and stance may be, his place in the trilogy is clear (though Aeschylus's judgment of him is not). Not so Apollo in the *Orestes*. We are uncertain about his role in the matricide (just as we are of who is and who is not a Fury), and whether this male-supporting god has the support of the exemplary male, Agamemnon. It is true that Electra says that "our father's ghost cried out against our mother; blood, blood" (192). But barely one hundred lines later Orestes contradicts his sister, accusing Apollo of deluding him into a gratuitous murder his father would have begged him not to do.

> I think now
> If I had asked my dead father at the time
> if I should kill her, he would have begged me,
> gone down on his knees before me, and pleaded,
> implored me not to take my mother's life.

36. The fact that, as Verrall argues (*Four Plays of Euripides*, p. 207), the oracular command is not regarded as authoritative by the play's characters (including Orestes) has implications for how authoritative we regard the ending as being.

What had we to gain by murdering her?
Her death could never bring him back to life
and I, by killing her, would have to suffer
as I suffer now.

(287–93)

The play's pattern of disappointed expectations, the arbitrariness of the concluding unity given the fragmentation that has dominated the characters and plot, and the uncertainty about where, or even whether, Apollo fits in the story, establishes a disparity between our experience of the play and the play's conclusion.[37] The disparity is so substantial that the inclusion of both strains our credulity. Not only are we asked to believe that Orestes suddenly embraces the woman he is about to kill, but the catty, overly elegant, vulgarly solicitous[38] Helen, whom Electra says the gods despise, is enthroned as an eternal star guiding sailors by her light.[39]

The implausibility of this transformation is emphasized by the importance of the often ironic and trite sea imagery in the play. Pylades is called a "helmsman"; Orestes' plight is compared to that of sailors battered by stormy seas; Menelaus compares sailing with politics; the chorus talk of unhappy lives in terms of the anguish of tattered sails whipped by wildly tossing seas and murderous winds that swamp all glory and joy; and the initial disaster that activates the curse of the Tantalids is the death of Mytilus, who is hurled into the sea from Pelops's chariot.

Given those disparities, the audience seems forced to choose between the play and Apollo, between the vagaries of action and their need for endings in literature and life. If we accept the "logic" of the plot and characters, then Apollo's intervention is, at the very least, as suspect as the resolution he brings about. Suspicion is increased when Orestes sees him as a Fury in disguise. It is further compounded by the possibility that the god may no more exist than the bow he gives Orestes, or that he may exist but remains indifferent

37. Froma Zeitlin argues that the deus ex machina "breaks the theatrical illusion of reality to inform us that this was only a play" ("Closet of Masks," p. 69). What happened on stage did not really happen. What was play is finished, the events no more substantial than the vaporized Helen. For this (and other reasons) the *Orestes* is a "truly self-reflective work of art . . . art in the process of reflecting on art." But if the breaking of theatrical illusion is also the breaking of the "illusion" of tragedy's institutional place and political aim; and if the art reflecting on art is not just art but also a form of political action; then Zeitlin's point needs qualification and extension.
38. The epithets are Beye's in his *Ancient Greek Literature and Society*, p. 295.
39. At 1377 the slave wishes for what the god grants Helen.

to human affairs except for sporadic interventions that force mortals to conform to a divine will at odds with their natural propensity for irrational violence. If he is not what he seems, then he is
like all the other characters in the drama and there is no reason to
suppose that his will is any less capricious than theirs, though his
divinity makes the consequences of such capriciousness more
drastic. If he does not exist, then the resolution he brings about is
no more real than Helen's vaporization. If he is indifferent to human fate until the point of conflagration, then all we can do is rely
on our impotence to save us from our perversity.

But as *Oedipus Tyrannos* suggests, to choose a play over Apollo is
to choose against tragedy. As Sophocles' drama unfolds, the skepticism of Jocasta and Oedipus reaches beyond prophets to Apollo
himself, and the chorus must choose between their savior king and
the god. In choosing the latter, they opt as much for the former's
sake as for their own, since it is better that Oedipus suffer more in a
god-filled world that gives suffering meaning than that he suffer less
in a godless world that leaves his pain random and meaningless. In
opting for Apollo and Oedipus, the chorus are also opting for tragedy, since tragedy is part of a religious festival honoring the gods.

Yet if we choose Apollo in the *Orestes,* we must accept the fact
that men and women can stave off suicide, moral bankruptcy, and
political corruption only because they are puppets of the gods.
Though the characters in Aeschylus and Sophocles are also victims, they are not just victims, but people whose lives are jointly
decided by their character and their destiny, by freedom and necessity. And even though the hero's stand against necessity or fate is
unavailing, his failure has restorative and cathartic power. But in
the *Orestes* men and women are denied joint ministry over a justice
jointly instituted.

Even worse, to choose the Apollo of the *Orestes* is also to choose
against tragedy, and so we are no better off than before. For insofar
as his appearance and actions compound the disjointedness that
already threatens the play's coherence, the god contributes to the
corruption of works performed in honor of the gods. If the presence of Apollo is as destructive of tragedy as repudiation of him,
tragedy has lost its place and point, except to suggest this fact.

There is a third possibility: that the choice between Apollo and
the play is illusory and a synthesis of god and drama is possible.
But this third alternative is no more attractive than the others in it-

self, or as an added possibility whose mere existence adds confusion to an ending designed to resolve confusion. In fact, this synthesis is, if anything, less attractive than having to choose between
the *Orestes* and the god. It is less attractive because it unites bad
myth and bad behavior in a murderous unity that intensifies the
bitter disillusionment that suffuses the play. Here is William Arrowsmith:

> Logos and ergon, apparently contradictory, are in fact complementary: de-
> praved, and immoral human action in the play is mirrored by, sanctioned
> by, the callous folly of heaven and the brutality of myth; Orestes and
> Apollo mutually create, mutually deserve, each other: murderers both.
> Man and god project each other; myth influences behavior, and behavior
> in turn shapes the myth in a vicious cycle of moral deterioration.[40]

In these terms the disparity between god and man, play and ending is a seeming rather than real one. In fact, each elaborates and
exposes the other and the moral abyss and political disarray into
which they have jointly fallen.

   It is this vision of powerlessness that makes *Orestes* so powerful.
Its form and content emphasize tragedy's tenuous ability to make
sense of, and compensate for, the systemic and systematic corruption of Athens. With Euripides, as with Apollo, the magic wand
leaves the nightmare unchecked, untouched, and undaunted.

5

By expressing skepticism toward stage conventions, parodying its
own style through juxtaposing realism and naturalism with lyric
extravagance, and fusing the "comic view of man's efficacy with a
tragic one of his responsibility," the *Orestes* violates expectations of
dramatic form.[41] Whereas Aristophanes shows deeds that are base
and inconsistent but generally successful, and the tragedians offer
heroic actions that are effective virtues or failures worthy of heavenly celebration or wrath, Euripides' characters are fully responsible for corrupt deeds that fail ridiculously. This heterogeneity of
tragic form represents both a bold attempt to expand tragedy as
genre, while reconstituting the educative role of the tragedian, and
a deformation of genre, which signifies the futility of tragedians as

40. Arrowsmith, "Greek Theater of Ideas," p. 46.
41. Burnett, *Catastrophe Survived*, p. 14.

political educators. It also mirrors, as it dramatizes, the heterogeneity of life and thought that made Athens great and plagued her
greatness.

By expansion I mean Euripides' effort to make tragedy a more
inclusive genre—alive to the "multiplicity of possible realities in
the texture of action"[42] and thought—that distinguished an Athenian social life now fragmented by war, empire, and sophistic
skepticism. But at some point the expansion of genre and the attempt at comprehensiveness, like the expansion of the *polis* itself,
brings a loss of identity and definition.

Euripides is sometimes accused of killing tragedy[43]—that, like
the Athenians whose daring created an empire that destroyed the
integrity of the *polis*, his dramatic inventiveness stretched tragedy
in ways that corrupted its shape and aim. The charge is too simple
in its assignment of responsibility. At a minimum, political corruption was as much a problem created for Euripides as one he created. He confronted a more factionalized audience than his prede-
cessors, and since Greek drama existed as public performance, any
radical dissociation of "the public" made the persistence of tragedy
as a communal experience problematic. Where there are audiences
instead of an audience, the tragedian is in danger of contributing to
the disintegration he warns against.

This is another way of saying that the corruption of the Athenians
as portrayed by Thucydides includes the corruption of the Athenian audience watching and judging the dramas before them. That
corruption is manifest in the dialectic between two seemingly incompatible sentiments and movements: expansion or distancing
(as in empire and skepticism) and contraction (as in a preoccupation with "self" and private interests). Together these developments signify a loss of center and balance, exactly what the *Oresteia*
warned against and what Euripides' experiment with tragic form
explores. The best example of this expansion and constriction is
the relationship between Orestes and Electra.

When Electra recounts her house's ills by including collateral family members going all the way back to Tantalus, the Orestes story is
expanded spatially and temporally. Yet, as Electra and Orestes be-

---

42. Arrowsmith, "Greek Theater of Ideas," p. 42f.
43. Most notably by Nietzsche (in *The Birth of Tragedy*) and Aristophanes (in *The
Frogs*).

come increasingly isolated, their world becomes increasingly claustrophobic and incestuous. Their manic imaginings, wild inconsistencies, and perverse moral proclamations remind us of Cleon, Alcibiades, Melos, the Sicilian debate, and Corcyra in Thucydides. In this world, like that of *Agamemnon*, there are so many meanings crowding in that one does not know where one stands. Yet this overfullness of meaning is accompanied by a constriction of space, possibility, and relationships.

To the degree that successful undestructive action is as impossible in the world as in the world of the play, the tragedian as political educator is as futile as Orestes' posings, except to dramatize that futility. Perhaps justice can be taught by philosophers in the *agora*; it can no longer be taught by tragedians in the theater. When the audience actually lives the myths of revenge portrayed on stage, then drama and life become one. As they do, tragedy and city disintegrate under the relentless pressure of centrifugal forces no leader can forestall and no dramatist contain. Or so the play suggests.

Though all this may be Euripides' point, the *Orestes* is on the verge of becoming part of the crisis it dramatizes, nearly a character in its own drama. This means an end to the separation of citizen-audience and stage actors, a separation that had afforded spectators a privileged position as knowing interpreters of action only partly understood by the characters on stage (except for blind seers or unheard prophetesses). Seeing the pattern of action and result from a vantage point denied the protagonists, the audience was able to achieve a balance of efficacy and limit: efficacy because of the confidence its superior knowledge instilled; limit because the knowledge was that, as mortals, they, too, were bound to imitate the partial blindness of the actors before them. But they had an advantage: they had seen the play, and so, like Socrates, knew their own ignorance. Knowing that, they could achieve a wisdom denied the characters and perhaps obviate the tragedy.

In these terms the convergence of tragedy and city signifies impotence and limitlessness, claims to knowledge that obscure ignorance, and ignorance that precludes wisdom. Removing the spectator's omniscience unites him with the principals in their baffled groping for meaning, puissance, and stature. It also unites the playwright with contemporary events in a way that calls the tragedy's prospects and possibility into question. For the corruption is not

only in the world of the play but the world in which the play is performed, and the collapse of the one into the other precludes the
distance understanding requires. The very capacity of tragedy to
order experience, to make sense of and make whole what appears
senseless and fragmented is now uncertain. This is not to deny that
on one level there is an ordered disorder in the *Orestes*. It is to
say that on another level the play works against itself in ways the
Oresteia and *Oedipus Tyrannos* do not.

It is true, of course, that Sophocles plays on the audience's knowledge of the outcome to invest a character's pronouncements with
tragic significance. The meaning of an action is often radically different from that supposed by the actor, whose understanding of
events always comes too late. That is what makes for Sophoclean
irony. But the design is not in doubt in the play or the world, and
the action is, after all, intelligible even if the ultimate pattern remains elusive. But in the *Orestes* the design itself is questioned
rather than being an unquestioned premise. And so any order that
comes into being does so despite the intentions, and behind the
backs, of the actors.

Indeed the gap between intent and achievement is so wide that
human will virtually disappears. Consequences wander aimlessly
and disembodied across the stage like orphaned children seeking
long dead parents, taking refuge in disappointment where and
with whom they can. When they reconnect with intentions, the resulting patterns seem as arbitrary as the momentary gestalts of a
rotating kaleidoscope. Under such circumstances men are victims
without recourse or remedy. In *Oedipus Tyrannos* various characters
possess bits of information that, when brought together, solve the
riddle of Oedipus. And two of them, Teiresias and the old shepherd, know everything from the beginning. There is nothing comparable in the *Orestes*. No one in the play (including Apollo) knows
what's going on and no human assembly or characters can solve, or
resolve, anything.

All this transforms Sophoclean irony into an irony of form that
counts on the audience's familiarity with the mythical tradition,
Aeschylus, conventional tragic plots, and tragedy as a genre to
ensure appreciation of the deformation of political and literary
norms. Given the corruption of practice and mind this demonstrates and portends, it is no wonder that Socrates was driven to
bring philosophy down from the heavens. It may even be that

Euripides anticipates the substance of that philosophy and its ultimate predicament even as he shows the need for it.[44]

At least that is so if his point in violating the audience's expectations is to make his fellow citizens self-conscious about their need
for formal and thematic structure no matter how contrived that
structure may be. In most Greek tragedies prophets or oracles predict a conclusion whose fulfillment ends the play and gives whole-
ness to its action. There are, of course, local deferments and momentary evasions of expectations that heighten the terror. But the
ultimate fact of closure and finality is not in doubt, if only because
plays have endings. But in the *Orestes* Apollo's imposition of a traditional ending on a radically untraditional plot is so blatantly contrived that the deferments and evasions somehow become permanent. More than that, the contrivance becomes a comment on, if
not a parody of, the audience's need to make endings out of moments, and images out of instants.[45] Even when men lose faith in
oracles, gods, laws, and tragedy, they create faith and closure in
spite of themselves *and* out of their deepest needs.

To confront both the fact of such creation and the need from
which it arises is profoundly disconcerting. Ideally such confrontations induce men and women to interrogate those political and dramatic forms whose fading efficacy has contributed to the corruption Euripides (and Socrates) disclose in and to Athens. It may even
push men, as citizens and individuals, to reflect on the possibilities
and ways of reconciling the dramatized disparity between the play's
reality and the idealized ending.[46] To put the matter this way emphasizes the similarities between Euripides and Socrates. It also
suggests a shared dilemma.

Socratic political philosophy requires that men accept their mortality, and so their partiality, in the dual sense of incompleteness

44. If Zeitlin is right (see note 37 above) in seeing the *Orestes* as a truly self-
reflective work, not just a mimesis of an action (except insofar as tragedy is a form of
action) but a mimesis of a mimesis; and if Foley is right (*Ritual Irony,* p. 61) that
Euripides' plays "deliberately hint at several incompatible views of human society
and divinity and close without definitely affirming any of them," we can see in tragedy an anticipation of Socratic political philosophy.

45. Speaking of the *Orestes'* conclusion, Roberts (*Apollo and His Oracle,* p. 119)
writes that Euripides is "satirizing a tradition that demands such endings and an
audience that desires and accepts them."

46. This is like and unlike the *Oresteia:* like because there, too, the audience
needs to reconcile the idealized Athens on stage with the factionalized one in the
world; unlike because that idealized world has religious and political substance and
plausibility.

and one-sidedness. Once they understand this they understand that no one can possess the truth (because they are only one person, because truth is not a possession like land or honor, and because given what we are, "the" truth can never be fully revealed even in dialogue), though all men can, and perhaps should at least on occasion, pursue it. The only way to pursue truth while remaining faithful to our partiality and consequent need for others is through dialogue.

But why should men and women care to pursue truth in their political, public, and private lives? What reasons can they have? What induces them to interrogate their fondest beliefs and rethink their deepest commitments? For Socrates, it is the recognition of ignorance that impels us toward knowledge. Once we become aware of, and so confused by, the existential contradictions in our lives, when we recognize how ignorant we are of the things that are most important to us, such as power, pleasure, or honor, we see the practical need to reexamine who we are and what we are doing (as individuals and members of a collectivity) to ourselves and to others. Once we realize that we do not know what we are convinced we do know, discover that what we do know is less important than what we do not know, or realize the discrepancy between what we say, believe, and intend, and what we do and accomplish, we cannot help but be philosophical or theoretical.

Tragedy in general, but particularly this tragedy, aims at, or at least does, something similar. The *Orestes'* repeated violation of expectations, which cease only with a bizarre fulfillment of them in a suspect final scene, forces the audience to confront the practical and intellectual contradictions in their public and private lives. At the very least the audience must make sense of them and decide how to live with them, whether by accepting their necessity or resolving them. What is clear is that a choice must be made and that the choice is up to the audience.[47] Not to make it, or to leave the choice to others, is to give up on democratic politics.

This interrogation of tradition and rejection of final harmony through parody of our need for it is part of the "Socratism" that has left Euripides open to the charge (also leveled at Socrates) of corrupting the youth. His response is implicit in the play (and re-

---

47. In his Bampton Lectures Arrowsmith argues that the chief object of the play is to put the onus of resolution upon the audience, to involve it intimately in the quandary of the culture as a way of interrogating and revitalizing the culture.

sembles Socrates' response in the *Apology*): the young (Orestes) are already corrupt, corrupted moreover by those (Menelaus and Tyndareus) responsible for teaching them justice. But the question, for Euripides as for Socrates, is whether interrogation is enough; whether, facing demagoguery, vapid ideals, hypertrophy of heroic virtues, growing privatism, and corrupt speech, Euripidean tragedy and Socratic political philosophy do not become part of the problem.

It is at least interesting that Euripides had less success among his contemporaries than did Aeschylus and Sophocles, that Socrates was found guilty by an Athenian jury, and that, in the *Republic*, Plato criticizes poetry and tragedy as he begins to distance himself from Socrates.

Chapter Ten

Myths and the Origins of Cities: Reflections on the Autochthony Theme in Euripides' *Ion*

Arlene W. Saxonhouse

> *When and for whom is it [the lie] also useful, so as not to deserve to be hated? Isn't it useful against enemies, and as a preventive, like a drug, for so-called friends when from madness or some folly they attempt to do something bad? And in the telling of the tales we were just now speaking about—those told because we don't know where the truth about ancient things lies—likening the lie to the truth as best we can, don't we also make it useful?*
>
> Plato *Republic* 2.382c–d[1]

1

At the end of book 3 of the *Republic* Socrates, in the process of creating his just city, presents his famed noble lie. It is a myth of autochthony. The members of the city he and his companions found in speech are not born of human mothers and fathers but fashioned in the earth. Before birth, the souls of these citizens are mixed with various metals that determine their station in the hierarchical structure of Socrates' city. The myth gives his city unity and order, cohesion and hierarchy. At the end of the previous book of the *Republic* Socrates explains that the gods do not need the lie, that deception is alien to their divine character, and that the tales of prevaricating divinities must be exorcised from the poetry of his city. At the same time, he suggests that mortals, lacking divine perfection, do need the lie.

---

1. *The Republic of Plato*, trans. Allan Bloom (New York: Basic Books, 1968).

The falsehoods used among mortals acknowledge the imperfection of their existence and the imperfection of what they may consider the best city, even in speech. It becomes apparent at the very beginning of the *Republic* that a lie among friends may be a necessity. Cephalus, wedded to a mercantile image of justice and thus insisting that truth-telling is justice, cannot understand. Or the lie may go beyond a small circle of friends and be transformed in the political realm into a myth where truth and falsity for citizens of the *polis* are no longer distinguished. The tale becomes true through the constant retelling of it, immune to the philosopher's or rationlist's critical standards.[2] It becomes part of the collective self-knowledge of the city and a basis for its moral and political standards. Such is the noble lie of book 3.

When Socrates founds his city in the *Republic* he is engaged in a process of myth (or story) building: "Come now," he says to his interlocutors as he begins his censorship of the old tales in considering the education of his warriors, "just as ones telling myths [*mythologountes*] in myth [*mythōi*] and ones having leisure, let us educate in speech the men" (2.376d). The poets depended on the muses for their stories and, as Hesiod has told us, we mortals cannot always know whether the daughters of memory tell us truth or falsehood (*Theogony* 27–28). Nevertheless, he sings and does not analyze. Socrates does not debate the truth of the poets' tales, only their use to the community. What is useful may not be true. At the end of book 3 (414b–c) Socrates sharply reminds us that this myth-building is based on a lie, albeit a noble one. He assures his companions in founding that in the process of lying (*pseudomenous*) they will be saying something noble (*gennaion ti hen*). The nobility of the lie is assured not by its use, but by its age; this particular lie is not something new (*kainon*), but a certain Phoenician thing (*ti*). It is a

2. By using the terms *myths* and *lies* I realize that I am entering, at the same time that I am trying to avoid, the vast literature on the topic. For the purposes of this essay I would like to refer the reader to G. S. Kirk's *Myth: Its Meaning and Functions in Ancient and Other Cultures* (Cambridge: Cambridge University Press, 1970), ch. 1, where he tries to distinguish myth, ritual, and folktale. When I use the term *myth* I am referring to a story (*muthos*) believed by a large portion of the population at whom it is directed that has implications for the political, moral, and social relations of that group. The noble lie as understood by Socrates in his position as the founder of a city is an untruth; it is one made to persuade "in the best case, even the rulers, but if not them, the rest of the city" (*Rep.* 3.414b–c). To the degree that it is believed by the members of Socrates' city, it is a myth. For a discussion of myth as political propaganda, see M. P. Nilsson, *Cults, Myths, Oracles and Politics in Ancient Greece* (Lund: G. W. K. Gleerup, 1951), ch. 3.

lie believed for a long time, transformed over time from a lie to a myth. In Socrates' city the tale is a lie because Socrates knows that it is not true, but this lie is spoken to the many in order to give the city a unity and stability it might otherwise lack. The untruth of birth from the earth becomes a truth—a civic and political truth.

On one level Euripides' play *Ion* confronts the issue of lies-become-myth that controls the Athenians' self-image of themselves.[3] Through the play's dramatic action and the poetic choruses, Euripides forces the citizens of Athens to look critically at the Athenian myth of autochthony, not so as to make them question whether their first ancestors were indeed born from Athenian soil, but rather to make them reflect on the implications of such a myth. Victor Ehrenberg has described the myths of the Greeks as "that peculiar mixture of saga, history, religion and poetical imagination . . . the element through which the poet was able to penetrate the minds of the people."[4] The autochthony myth as used in the *Ion* enables Euripides to present to the Athenians the foundations of their prejudices and their beliefs. At the end of the play, he allows those prejudices to stand; he does not deny that men can be born from the earth. It is the non-Athenian Xuthus who does this. Yet Euripides has given to the audience a greater sense of how a myth such as autochthony may limit the city and where the Athenians' political truths have left them. The prejudices have been revealed and their consequences dramatized. The political truths, though, may rest uneasily in the context of divine truths, a circumstance that perhaps accounts for the disquieting undertone to the successful and happy conclusion to the plot, a conclusion that explicitly confirms the necessity of the lie.

Bernard Knox has argued most persuasively that *Ion* is the first true comedy in a line extending through Menander to Molière and Oscar Wilde. Apart from the portrayal of mundane rather than heroic actions on stage, comedy, according to Knox, entails a restoration of normalcy, the reaffirmation of traditional values. "Comedy leaves us with a sense that the standards of this world, though not perfect, are sound: there is no flaw in the universe, only misunder-

3. As with any play by Euripides, this work confronts far broader questions concerning the purpose of human life in a possibly purposeless world. I have limited myself here to the political aspects, specifically the role and nature of political foundations.

4. *Sophocles and Pericles* (Oxford: Basil Blackwell, 1954), p. 20.

standings, maladjustments."[5] In many ways this statement does, as Knox intends it to, describe the situation at the end of *Ion*, but it also ignores the critical reflection on the theme of autochthony that runs, as Knox says, ad nauseam,[6] throughout the play. Autochthony is confronted, questioned, and then conditionally accepted as a political truth, though its limitations have been set before the audience.

When Socrates refers to a Phoenician tale in his discussion of the noble lie, he reminds us of Cadmus, who, after he has killed the dragon of Ares, accepts the advice of Athene and sows the dragon's teeth in the land that is to become Thebes. From these grow a crop of helmeted, armed heroes, who immediately set upon one another in battle. The five survivors of this conflict become the ancestors of Thebes's noble houses. The claim to nobility and to the Theban land found its origin in their autochthonous birth. But the tale that Socrates uses to make his citizens care more for one another and for the city (415d) was not only Phoenician, as he well knew, but was also incorporated in the mythology of Athens. At the base of Athens's early legends are a series of autochthonous characters. These characters, Kekrops, Erichthonius, and Erechtheus, are all associated with the snakes who emerge from the earth, and were portrayed as having the tails of serpents for legs. These heroes and the snakes associated with them appear repeatedly, as we shall see, in the story of *Ion*. They represent not only an underlying theme of the play, but a central part of its conceptual framework.

A mythologized autochthonous origin for a city—be it Athens, Thebes, or Callipolis—has important theoretical implications. First, it provides a unity, perhaps a false unity, but nevertheless one that differentiates this city from others. Second, it offers a world of cities whose boundaries are dictated by nature and not by human agreements. The city is created in opposition to nature, but an autochthonous origin gives it the appearance of being according to nature. The questioning that surrounds the legitimacy of the contemporary state, explicitly created in opposition to nature through the social contract, is silenced, and the city born from the earth itself is the natural unit for men's devotion and allegiance. The myth of autochthony eliminates another embarrassing question as well: To whom does, or did, the land belong? Who was con-

5. "Euripidean Comedy," in *Word and Action: Essays on the Ancient Theater* (Baltimore: Johns Hopkins University Press, 1979), p. 266.

6. Ibid., p. 267.

quered? Who was forced out in order for the city to arise? A city of autochthonous origins gives the appearance of peaceful origins. The violence at the beginning of cities is glossed over if a people inhabit the land from which their ancestors sprang.[7] There need never have been any conquest. The inherent injustice, the taking from others of what is theirs, entailed in the founding of cities is ignored.[8] And once again the nagging question of legitimacy is silenced. States founded in violence, conquest, or revolution are always subject to claims against them from those who would conquer and those who would revolt. If one group's legitimacy is based on conquest, why should another eager for conquest exercise restraint? If authority in the state is based on the rise to power of those who rejected previous authorities, why may their authority not be rejected by a younger generation?[9] The security of such states must always be tenuous. The security of the autochthonous state legitimized by birth from the earth is dependent in its turn on legitimate inheritance from those original earthborn creatures through the ages. Any break in the line of generation threatens to transform the city from one founded in nature to one based on the potentially uncertain conventions of conquest or agreement.

An autochthonous society, however, must also be xenophobic and aristocratic. The stranger not descended from the ancient line threatens the unity and hierarchy of the city. He does not have ancient ties or stature. The hostile attitude toward Xuthus throughout *Ion*, even on the part of his wife, emphasizes this point. The au-

7. There are many historical points we can describe as the "beginnings of cities"; one could talk about lawgivers, Theseus's *synoikismos*, or revolutions that overturned ancient kings or new tyrants. For the purposes of this essay, I am defining the "beginning" as the point at which a group of people come to identify themselves as united, as sharing in common a history and a land. As Aristotle says at the beginning of book 2 of the *Politics*: "A *politeia* is a certain community [*koinōnia*]; it is first necessary to share [to have in common (*koinōnein*)] a place [*topos*]" (1260b40–41). This first stage of acquiring a common place is the issue to which the myth of autochthony addresses itself.

8. *Dikē*, justice, originally meant to give what is due to each. Taking away from people what is theirs thus becomes injustice. A classic statement of this view is Polemarchus's quotation from Simonides at the beginning of the *Republic* (331e). Cf. the epigraph from Vergil's *Aeneid* that Rousseau placed on the title page of *The Social Contract*. Hobbes introduces a notion of justice that must come after the creation of the city (which means that there can be no injustice in creation of the city), but for the Greeks *dikē* was enforced by the divinities and thus not dependent on cities, i.e., it could exist before cities came into being to give it life.

9. Aeschylus's *Prometheus Bound* is concerned with just such a problem, inasmuch as Zeus, who has recently seized power for himself, now quakes in the knowledge that yet another may overthrow the regime he established after overthrowing his father's authority.

tochthony myths at the base of the Athenian *polis* created important tensions in a democratic community that prided itself on an openness not characteristic of its major opponent, Sparta,[10] and one based on sea rather than land power. The descent into the boats, the desertion of the land that was part of Themistocles' policy at Salamis, broke the religious ties to the land from which the ancestors were born, and forced the Athenians (and especially Euripides, as we shall see) to reevaluate the significance of the autochthonous beginnings of their city.[11] At *Ion* 278, for example, the land is equated with the city, which is also equated with the parent; to break with the land as the Athenians did at Salamis is to break with all that is old, legitimate, and aristocratic. Democratic Athens was based on the rejection of the autochthonous myths that gave legitimacy to the city.[12] A new source of unity and hierarchy needed to be developed; this gave rise to the various citizenship reforms that were instituted and debated during the mid–fifth century and that underlie much of the rhetoric of *Ion*.[13]

Despite the tension between the democracy and the aristocratic implications of the autochthony myth, the rhetoric of autochthony through reference to the children of Kekrops and Erechtheus continued through the fifth and well into the fourth century.[14] Thucydides avoids specific reference to the mythology of snake-footed men born directly from the earth and writes instead of the poverty of Attic soil that kept it free from invasion (1.2.5). The Athenians are children of the earth since they have lived there forever, rather than because of any miraculous birth. Thucydides has Pericles similarly recall the myth in the famed Funeral Oration, again without specific reference. Rather, Pericles says that he must begin with the ancestors, who, "always inhabiting the land handed it down in succession to the next generation" (2.36.1). The rationalism of

10. See especially Thucydides' rendition of Pericles' funeral oration, e.g., 2.36.4, 39.1.

11. J. Peter Euben, "The Battle of Salamis and the Origins of Political Theory," *Political Theory* 14, no. 3 (August 1986):359–60.

12. Nicole Loraux, "L'Autochthonie: Une topique athénienne, le mythe dans l'espace civique," *Annales Economies, Sociétés, Civilisations* 34, no. 2 (1979):3–26, discusses in considerable detail the different conceptions of the city that derive from the acropolis, from the field in which the army gathers, from the *agora* of commerce and discourse, and from the cemetery in which its soldiers are buried, each with an aristocratic, democratic, or in-between status. I am grateful to Marilyn Arthur for recommending this useful and provocative article.

13. See esp. George B. Walsh, "The Rhetoric of Birthright and Race in Euripides' *Ion*," *Hermes* 106, no. 2 (1978):301–15.

14. Specific citations can be found in Loraux, "L'Autochthonie," nn. 28 and 45.

Thucydides did not necessarily lead to a rejection of the conceptual significance of the myth.

In Plato's *Menexenus*, Pericles' Funeral Oration is parodied in a speech by Pericles' mistress, Aspasia; here the autochthony theme of Pericles' speech is especially articulated and the sexual implications of the myth openly addressed. Aspasia at Socrates' request recites a revised version of the Funeral Oration as she, a teacher of rhetoric, would have given it. In going back to the beginning, to the ancestors as Pericles had done, she states:

> And first as to their birth. Their ancestors were not strangers, nor are these their descendents sojourners only, whose fathers have come from another country, but they are the children of the soil, dwelling and living in their own land. And the country which brought them up is not like other countries, a stepmother to her children, but their own true mother; she bore them and nourished them and received them, and in her bosom they now repose. It is meet and right, therefore, that we should begin by praising the land which is their mother, and that will be a way of praising their noble birth.[15]

Aspasia's speech continues for a page more along these lines. But we should note a unique point here: Aspasia, a woman, emphasizes the earth as mother. The milk of the mother is like the fruit of the earth. Indeed the human mother appears only as an imitation of the earth, not the earth of the mother (238a). The autochthony myth does not traditionally emphasize the mother. Rather, unlike Aspasia's use of it, it serves to denigrate the female, to deny the origins of cities in heterosexual relations, and in turn to emphasize male potency without the female as intermediary.

This aspect of the myth is captured in Plato's other recitation of it in the *Politicus*, where the Eleatic Stranger describes the age of Cronos, an age when men sprang from the earth, when men possessed neither wives nor children, when women were unnecessary because there was no need for sexual reproduction. It is even unclear whether there were any women during the age of Cronos as described by the Stranger. They do enter, though, in the age of Zeus, when life deteriorates, when there must be heterosexual reproduction, and cities need to come into being in order for men to continue living. The age of sexual generation and birth with the female's presence required is an inferior age.

15. *Menexenus* 237b–c, trans. Benjamin Jowett, in Plato, *Collected Dialogues*, edited by Edith Hamilton and Huntington Cairns (New York: Bollingen Foundation, 1961).

The female is certainly excluded in the Theban autochthony myth of dragon's teeth, but the situation in Athens is somewhat more ambiguous. The myth prominent in *Ion* recalls Hephaestus's pursuit of Athene, the virgin goddess; as Athene escapes from Hephaestus, his sperm lands on Athenian soil. From that seed Erichthonius is born, and handed over by Ge to Athene, who in her turn puts the child in a covered chest. Women are involved and the earthborn here, unlike his Theban counterparts, is not one fully grown, but one still in need of nurture. However, the myth itself still finds the beginning of the Athenian line in a denial of hetero-sexual mutuality. Athene remains a virgin and Hephaestus drops his seed aimlessly.[16] Aspasia, as she tells the tale, ignores the role of the male god Hephaestus; there is no spilled seed. Earth creates the children of herself. It is the mother who interests her, and it is this interest that marks the difference between her speech and the one Pericles—or indeed any other Athenian orator—gave or could have given.

For the most part, a founding myth of autochthony suggests the exclusion of women from the origins of the city. The city and its public space is the realm of male warriors sprung from the earth. They are not to be divided by their ties to separate mothers, to sep-arate wives, returned to a private realm that may raise questions about the universality of the *polis* and its goals. The autochthony myth furthermore denies the uncertainty inherent in heterosexual procreation for the male. The question of the child's origins need never be raised. The city is peopled from a single source and not dependent on the diversity entailed in heterosexual creation.

Euripides' *Ion* as a play about autochthony is also a play about the exclusion of women from the foundations of cities; it is a play about the myths and legends that serve to unify the citizens of a community and what those myths determine about the society of which they are a part. The play calls the autochthony myth into question and forces us to see the violence at the beginnings of cities, as well as the heterosexual relations (and thus the female and not just the male) that lie there. And yet it is a play that relaxes at the end—that is, as Knox notes, a comedy. After it has revealed the phoniness and the pretensions at the base of the city's certainty, Euripides allows the protagonists of the play to live happily ever

16. Cf. Charles Segal, "The Menace of Dionysus: Sex Roles and Reversals in Euripides' *Bacchae*," *Arethusa* 11, no. 1–2 (Spring and Fall 1978): 191.

after—their deceptions accepted as necessary for the sake of the city and the role of Athens as the source of the Ionian race. However, at the same time that he has accepted the traditions of the past and returned us to a "condition of normalcy," he has also asserted a new vision, one that introduces the female into the origins of the cities and reveals the city's contradictory needs for mutuality and openness as well as for exclusiveness.[17]

In *Ion* Euripides has taken an unknown foundation myth as the basis for his play. The story is complex: Creusa, the daughter of Erechtheus, has been raped by Apollo. She reveals neither her pregnancy nor the birth of her child. Instead, she exposes the infant in the cave of Apollo. The child is taken by Hermes to Delphi, where he is raised by a priestess of Apollo and serves as a temple boy until the action of the play begins. Meanwhile Creusa marries Xuthus, a general from Euboea, but they remain childless. They go to Delphi to inquire of the god concerning their childlessness, Creusa secretly also eager to discover the fate of her baby. Apollo tells Xuthus that the first person he meets on leaving the temple will be his son; Xuthus meets Ion, claims him as his child, and plans to bring him back to Athens as the future king. Creusa is jealous of the child to be brought into her house and plans to murder Ion; she is encouraged in her vengeful plot by her old tutor, who cares about the line of descent from Creusa's autochthonous forebears. The murder is prevented, a recognition scene takes place, and Ion returns to Athens as the son of Creusa and Apollo, while Xuthus, the husband of Creusa, believes that Ion is his son by some Delphian maid he impregnated during a religious revel. The only source for this version of the myth is Euripides; in other words, it is very likely that Euripides made up the story from scant references in the mythological history.[18] In so doing Euripides revises for

17. Although the ending may be satisfying on the political level, this does not mean that all questions are resolved, particularly in terms of Apollo's role in the events and the relationship between humans and the gods.

18. The scholarly literature on *Ion* agrees that Euripides' version is unusual, but there are debates as to whether he made it all up or not; see, e.g., George Grote, *History of Greece*, 3rd ed. (London: J. Murray, 1851–56), p. 199 n. 1: "I conceive many points of tragedy to be the invention of Euripides, but to represent Ion as the son of Apollo not Xuthus seems a genuine Attic legend." D. J. Conacher, *Euripidean Drama: Myth Theme and Structure* (Toronto: University of Toronto Press, 1967) says that there is no evidence that Apollo was considered the father of Ion before Euripides. He doubts, however, that it is a Euripidean invention. He also quotes H. Gregoire from the introduction to the Budé text, who claims that both Ion and Xuthus were strangers to the Attic Ionian tradition: rather they were created for specific political purposes by the genealogizing epic of the seventh century. Xuthus was inserted into

Athens her foundation myths, and shows the Athenians the basis of the city not in its unity from a birth in Attic soil, but in the beliefs on which the city is built.[19]

The story Euripides tells in this play is subject to a variety of styles of analysis. It is a lyrical romance of enchanting poetic images; it is a source book for Freudian analysis; and it is a statement made with a view to the contemporary citizenship reforms then under debate in Athens. My particular focus in considering this play is limited to the issues cited above: autochthony, the female role in the foundation of the cities, and the place of myths at the base of cities.

2

Hermes, the servant of the gods, introduces the play with an extensive prologue. Within the prologue references to the autochthonous origins of Creusa's forebears abound. She is the child of Erechtheus (10). She places the child born from her union with Apollo in a circular cradle, "preserving the custom [*nomos*] of her ancestors and the earthborn Erichthonius" (20–21). Erichthonius the earthborn [*gēgenēs*] was entrusted by Athene to the maiden Aglauros, daughter of Kekrops, yet another earthborn character (21–24). In memory of this early source of nurture, the Erichtheidai, the children of Erichthonius, observe the custom of nursing their offspring amidst golden snakes (24–26), a custom Creusa preserves when she places a similar ornament around her son before she leaves him to die. (These ornaments and Creusa's girlhood embroidery of the two

---

the Homeric catalogue, he claims, to establish an affinity between the Ionians and the Achaeans, while the function of Ion was chiefly to associate the Ionian patronym with the state of Athens. A. S. Owen (*Euripides' Ion* [Oxford: Clarendon Press, 1939], p. xiv) remains an agnostic on when and how Ion entered Athenian legend and on the paternity of Apollo. Cf. also Nilsson, *Cults, Myths, Oracles*, pp. 61–67.

19. The comments of Nilsson, *Cults, Myths, Oracles*, p. 65, are particularly appropriate here: "Greek society and the Greek State were founded on the family, on groups of men who were supposed to have a common descent, and this idea was deeply ingrained in the Greek mind, self-evident to it, and pervaded their whole life. . . . The idea that a people, a tribe, a subdivision of the State were descended from a common ancestor was paramount, and if there was no old tradition of a common ancestor, or even if he could not possibly have existed, e.g., when new artificial subdivisions were created by an administrative reform, he was simply invented. We call such fictitious ancestors [such as Ion was] eponyms because they give their names to the people or tribe etc., in fact the relation is the inverse, the name of the eponym is abstracted from that of the people."

dragons who guarded the earthborn Erichthonius will serve as the recognition tokens at the end of the play [1427–29].) Ion is transferred to Delphi, the locus of the omphalos, the navel of the world, in his circular cradle by Hermes, after Apollo bids his brother: "Go to the autochthonous house of the famed Athenians" (29–30) and take the child to Delphi.

Two of the central themes of the play dominate in the prologue: autochthony and birth. Hermes begins with reference to his own birth as the grandchild of Atlas, the son of Maia and Zeus. In the prologue the births described are all explicitly heterosexual, and yet autochthony, as noted above, is a means of avoiding heterosexual birth and thereby the female. The tension is captured well in the first choral ode. The chorus of women attendants on Creusa call on the virgin daughter of Zeus, Athene, to implore Apollo to give their mistress an heir to "the ancient race of Erechtheus." Athene is appealed to in the very first lines of the ode as one without the aid of Eileithyia, never having invoked for herself (or her mother?) the pains of childbirth (452–53). Athene is described as being born with the obstetric aid of the Titan Prometheus (455–56). No feminine birth this, with a male as the midwife and a male as the single progenitor. The second part of the ode returns us to human births and reminds the audience how children give overwhelming happiness to mortals; the children here are sons and the mortals are fathers. Half is omitted, for the story of *Ion* focuses primarily on the mother-son relationship between Creusa and Ion. It is this tie that is at the emotional and political heart of the play, for should Ion *not* be the son of Creusa, the ties of the Athenian rulers to their autochthonous origins would be lost. Thus, the ode, in contrast to the action of the play, emphasizes the masculine side of birth, while the action of the play refocuses our attention on the female and heterosexual reproduction among mortals.

The story of Creusa's rape is repeated several times in the play. Hermes in his prologue offers the first version. He tells of Apollo's passion for Creusa, how Phoebus yoked (*ezeuxen*) her with violence (*bia*) in *gamois* (10–11), a phrase often used to describe an irregular union,[20] and how in secret she bore the child of that union and abandoned him in the same cave where she had been violated by the gods (17). Creusa first tells of her rape elliptically; it is the tale

---

20. Owen, *Euripides' Ion*, p. 68.

of a friend, not her own tale that she recites to the sympathetic, but incredulous, temple boy she meets outside the oracle. "A friend of mine says she was sexually united with Phoebus" (338). To Ion, who has asserted that the god would be ashamed by the injustices (*adikia*) of men (341), Creusa affirms simply that this friend has suffered many griefs. The pain described here by Creusa comes not so much from the violence of the act itself as from the loss of her child and her ignorance of the fate of the child. Is he alive or dead, torn by the ruthless claws and beaks of wild animals and birds? Is she a mother of a living child or not? Need she raise a tomb for the child who has died? Creusa's "friend" suffers from her ignorance, but there is a hope on Creusa's part that the god Apollo will reveal the truth at his oracle. Ion, Apollo's servant here, must restrain her from asking embarrassing questions of the god that would test the honesty of the oracle.

However, Creusa's recital of her friend's woes strikes a responsive chord in Ion. He, too, intensely feels his ignorance of who his mother is and his parentless status—particularly, we should note, his motherless status. We meet Ion first talking gently to his broom and performing the task assigned to him from childhood (102): sweeping clean the temple of Apollo. The temple in its nurturing role replaces the mother and the father. He himself is *amētōr apatōr* (109). He does not know who the woman who bore him is (313) and laments that he has "never known the breast" (319).[21] Creusa's response is to pity him: "O suffering one, I being sick have found one also sick" (320). The son needs the mother as much as the mother needs the son. In an irony only the audience can understand, Ion laments the fate of Creusa's "friend": "The same chance brings suffering to me" (359).

In the middle of the play, after she learns that Xuthus has found a son, Creusa reveals to the chorus in a song of lament what befell her, and not her friend, by the lust of Apollo. At this point she denounces men and gods; they are betrayers of the marriage bed (879–80). She then recalls Apollo leading her to the infamous cave, his violent hands grasping her wrists (892), as he, heedless of her cries for her mother, acted without shame "for the sake of

21. Cf. also line 1373 where Ion again laments that he never enjoyed the breast. It is clear that the priestess at the temple of Apollo must have suckled him, but it is also clear that he does not consider this in any way comparable to being suckled by his own mother.

Aphrodite" (896). To the sympathetic old tutor this time, she recalls the spot: "There the dreadful *agōn* [conflict][22] we fought" (939). Again there is repetition; there was not only pain from the conflict, but also from the loss of the child born from the violent rape. The story of the play is the resolution of the latter pain, for by the end, after the near tragedies of matricide, temple burning, the murder of one's child, and sacrilege against a suppliant, mother and son are united and the sense of loss both experienced is overcome. However, in the joy sensed in this final unity, the pain of the rape, so prominent before, is ignored. Creusa at the end now claims:

> I revere Apollo whom I did not revere before;
> No longer is he unconcerned about the child he now returns to me
> These gates are fair to look on for me, as is the seat of the oracle,
> Now that the anger is a thing of the past.

> (1609–12)

At the end of the play when the two protagonists have acknowledged their ties, Creusa repeats her story. This time she recalls simply that Apollo enjoyed her bed (1484). The violence of the act is forgotten in the delight of finding her son.

Myths of autochthony perform a similar function. They are unifying myths that cover up the violence at the foundation of the city. By stressing the city's unity they hide its initial disunity, its initial anguish. Apollo does not appear at the end of the play lest his presence call forth old recriminations (1557). Scholars have wondered at Apollo's apparent cowardice and either try to explain it away or see it as an indication of the play's negative portrait of the Olympians.[23] But Apollo's absence here is important for understanding what must be forgotten as cities and races are founded. The original grief must be ignored in the satisfaction of unity and creation. The city needs autochthony myths to prevent the visions of old pains from undermining the current satisfaction and stability that is about to be imposed. The mother must forget the labor pains in order to enjoy and suckle the child. The city must forget the internal conflicts that gave it birth.[24]

---

22. The word *agōn* can also mean sexual intercourse.

23. For the former view, see Anne Pippin Burnett, "Human Resistance and Divine Persuasion in Euripides' Ion," *Classical Philology* 57, no. 2 (April 1962):89–103. For the latter view, see Thomas G. Rosenmeyer, *The Masks of Tragedy: Essays on Six Greek Dramas* (Austin: University of Texas Press, 1963), pp. 113–22.

24. Cedric H. Whitman, *Euripides and the Full Circle of Myth* (Cambridge, Mass.: Harvard University Press, 1974) emphasizes in his analysis of the play the constant interplay or counterpoint between good and evil, gentleness and violence, taking as

Euripides also suggests, through the development of certain characters throughout the play, the social consequences of autochthonous foundations for the city—most specifically the exclusiveness of an autochthonous city, the almost fanatical attempt to remain pure and enjoy a freedom from the dependence on others. There is, throughout, a concern, indeed a preoccupation, with the noble birth necessary to be part of the unity that is the city.[25] The joy of Ion's discovery of his putative father in Xuthus is muted by Ion's concern with the status of his mother and the hostile reception that awaits an apparent interloper among the Athenians. He warns his "father": "They say the renowned Athenians are born from the earth, not brought in from outside. There I shall come with two marks against me: born of a foreign father and myself a bastard" (589–92). Though Ion accepts Xuthus's command that he come to Athens, he nevertheless wishes that it may turn out that his mother was not some Delphian maid, as he first suspects, but "a woman from Athens, so that there will be to me from my mother freedom to speak [*parrhēsia*]" (671–72). The pure city (*katharan polin;* 673) of Athens does not accept strangers easily. The chorus of Athenian women who have seen this reunion of "father" and "son" confirm the validity of Ion's fears: "Never let the child come into my city; abandoning his gentle youth, let him die . . . the present rulers sprung from King Erechtheus are enough" (719–24). The Athenians in this play pay constant homage to such visions of purity, a purity associated with nobility of birth. The interloper, the foreigner, threatens that purity, debases that nobility and must be accepted only under duress—as was Xuthus, the adventurer whose military prowess bought an Athenian princess as his wife, a prize in war (as she refers to herself [297]). Creusa speaks of her husband as "not of the city, but someone brought in from another land" (*ex allēs chthonos;* 290). There is an apologetic tone: she had to marry him because Athens's military weakness made the city dependent on the strength of foreign princes. It is the fear of yet another interloper into the pure city, into the pure line of the Erechtheids that incites Creusa, abetted by the prejudiced old pedagogue (cf. 735–37), to plot the murder of Ion. The foreigner, be he king or serving boy, is not welcome in the city.

---

an example the purity of the temple, which is preserved only by the threatened killing of the birds who befoul the sacred premises. "Purity . . . involves bloodshed," suggests Whitman on p. 75 with reference to lines 161–69.

25. On this topic, see esp. Walsh, "Rhetoric of Birthright and Race."

The mentality behind this preoccupation with birthline and the purity of the race is clearly one of opposition, an opposition specifically between "we" and "they"; the other is foreign and the other is dangerous. Xuthus is other because he is from a foreign land; the son he is to bring home from Delphi is also other, because he does not have ties to the royal bloodline of Athens. The other, though, can also be, and often is, the female. Exclusiveness preserves prerogatives for some. In clarifying to whom those prerogatives belong, the other is made inferior and discriminated against. Ion worries about the citizen rights he as other will lack when he is in Athens. The foreigner and the female are treated equally in this regard. Euripides' play exposes to the Athenians their exclusiveness, of which their autochthonous myth is one potent expression.

When Ion first meets the woman whom he knows only as the queen of the Athenians, he inquires in great detail about the autochthonous origins of the city of Athens. "By the gods, tell me truthfully about the myths spoken by mortals," Ion asks. Creusa offers to answer his questions. "Did the earth bring forth the father of your father?" "Erichthonius, yes . . . " "And Athene raised him from the earth?" "Into her maiden hands, but she did not bear him" (265–70). The questioning continues through the violent deaths of the daughters of Kekrops and that of Erechtheus, slain by their own father, according to Creusa, *pro gaias*, for the sake of the land that is their country, from which Erechtheus's father was born. Creusa alone survived, "an infant, just born, in the bent arms of her mother" (280). A yawning chasm in the earth (*chthonos*) hid Erechtheus, slain by the trident of Poseidon (281–82). Ion recites the myth about the earth swallowing Erechtheus. Creusa elaborates that it was the sea that struck him down. According to her version, the earth only gives birth, not death. The chasm, though, where Erechtheus was hidden is the same spot where Creusa was raped and where Ion was abandoned in his circular cradle. Throughout this passage on autochthony, the image of father recurs. Forms of *patēr* appear seven times in the twenty-five lines devoted to this story. *Mētēr* appears once, the reference made by Creusa to her own mother (280).

The parallels between the stories of Erichthonius and Ion are obvious. Ion in his circular cradle is given to another to be tended to. Ion becomes the new Erichthonius, the new founder of the race, but, significantly, despite the snakes adorning *his* casket, he has *not* emerged from the earth. The race of Ionians spread across Greece now can trace their origins back to one of woman born.[26] And indeed it is she who is crucial with regard to Ion's ties to the Athenians, for his supposed father is a foreign adventurer, whose descent from Zeus does nothing to elevate his status among the Athenians. Creusa, the descendant of Erichthonius, a woman of noble birth, is herself denied citizen rights and forced to marry this man from a distant land. Yet she, whom the Greeks see as "other," is the one who bears in her womb the eponymous hero of the Ionians. The denial of heterosexual reproduction inherent in the myth of autochthony is rejected. Not only is the woman brought back into the foundation myth, but she is also placed squarely at its center in this play that primarily extols the unity of the mother and the child.

In his prologue Hermes recalls how Creusa placed Ion's cradle in Apollo's cave and Hermes' own role in transferring it to Delphi, where the priestess of Apollo found it. At first the priestess removed the cradle from the temple, assuming that it signified the shame of some nymph, but then she took pity on the child in it. She nurtures the child to manhood. The priestess in this role appears as the only one in the play who is able to love something (one) other than what is her own. The intricacies of the whole plot and Apollo's botched plan depend on Xuthus's expected refusal to love what is not his own. He must be tricked into believing that Ion is his own son in order to accept him into his house, into his line of successors. Creusa is no less parochial in this regard than Xuthus. The thought that she might have to nurture in her home an alien child, the son of another mother, that her husband could find a child while she herself remains barren, leads—with some help from the pedagogue—to those thoughts and plots of murder. It is the priestess, the attendant on the god, what is common to all men, who stands alone in her love of what is alien to her. The city cannot show the indiscriminate love that the priestess does. The city is bounded by the demands to love what is its own. To love another makes the city vulnerable. The priestess can accept what is alien,

26. Burnett, "Human Resistance and Divine Persuasion," also sees Ion as the new Erichthonius, but suggests that Apollo as father replaces Athene as "mother." Although Burnett emphasizes the glorious divinity of Apollo, I find the negative portrait of Apollo presented by Rosenmeyer in *Masks of Tragedy* far more convincing. By keeping Apollo out of the action of the play, Euripides emphasizes the maternity of Creusa far more effectively than the paternity of Apollo.

for her role transcends the particular and moves her to the universal. Creusa and Xuthus are at the foundation of the city; in their actions and affections they attend to the particular needs of men. For them, a direct sense of what is their own is crucial. This is why the city needs myths of autochthony that make the land its own. Apollo, however, does not acknowledge this desire for one's own *on the part of the mother;* he sees only the father and assumes that his only task is to convince Xuthus that Ion is his son. Creusa, according to Apollo's plan, will learn to accept this apparent interloper as her own, i.e., he expects her to be able to do what the city itself cannot—accept a foreigner freely into its midst. His plan is to keep her ignorant of Ion's true birth (69–73), but it is precisely her refusal to accept what is not her own that leads to the heart of the action of the play.

Euripides does not offer favorable views of the exclusiveness characteristic of the Athenians in the play and in the myth of autochthony itself. The major exponent of the myth is Creusa's tutor, who appears throughout as a mindless instigator of evil actions— beginning with his sacrilegious proposal to burn down Apollo's temple. With him as the exponent, the myth loses much of its seriousness; it becomes something worthy of belief only by those who are from the lower strata of society and tied to antiquated traditions. George Walsh aptly relates these themes of exclusiveness, autochthony, and purity to contemporary political Athenian rhetoric about the citizenship laws. His insights are important, but we must also recognize the Athenian claims both within the play and outside as based on the political necessity of exclusiveness, which structures an apparent unity. This exclusiveness denied a place for foreigners in the citizen rolls of the city, but such exclusiveness is based on false myths. The dynamic interaction in the play between Xuthus and Creusa suggests the dangers of exclusiveness and the necessity for mutuality.[27]

Both Creusa and Xuthus come to Delphi seeking a child. At first they seek a child who is theirs, one to continue the line of inheritance of the Erichtheidae. They each leave accepting a child who does not belong to the other. Creusa finds fault with an Apollo who

27. Though Euripides uses this play at times to mock the exclusiveness and arrogance of the Athenians, we must also recognize the value such a sense of cohesion can have for a political community. On this point, see J. Peter Euben, "Political Equality and the Greek Polis," in *Liberalism and the Modern Polity,* edited by Michael J. Gargas McGarth (New York and Basel: Marcel Dekker, 1978), pp. 207–28.

might have taken her fictitious friend's child and raised him himself. "He did not act justly enjoying alone what was common [*koina*]" (358). And yet both Creusa and Xuthus are willing to enjoy individually what is a common endeavor. Euripides' play suggests the importance of recognizing the mutuality of male and female in the birthing patterns of humans of the city. Autochthony excludes the female: Apollo's scheme had tried to exclude the female as well by fundamentally ignoring Creusa. But the scheme does not work, for Apollo does not account for the female's rightful role in the process of procreation. Creusa rebels and refuses to accept an auxiliary role, to be the mere nurturer rather than an active participant in the creation of the next generation and the race that is to give rise to so many of the Greek cities. She thus plots the murder of the interloper who would deny her a place in the creation of children. To do this, though, she must ironically return to the autochthony myth at the base of the play, for the instrument to be used in Ion's murder comes from Erichthonius, whom, as the pedagogue now recalls, "first of your race earth brought forth" (1000; cf. 1053). Creusa's father inherited from Erichthonius two drops of the Gorgon's blood; one drop heals, the other poisons.[28] It is the poisonous drop that is to be used now to protect the woman from again being excluded from the beginnings of cities. And it is Creusa's attempted murder of her child that leads finally, through a series of events, to the revelation of her role in the birth of Ion. Without her plot, without her refusal to be simply a passive receptacle excluded from the "common pleasure," without her rejection of the stranger from her household, Apollo's plan would have worked. Against the god's plan Euripides asserts the importance of mutuality—and indeed of the female.

Like Apollo, Xuthus appears willing to disregard the role of the female in the process of procreation. He is searching for his son. He has found one. Who the mother is is an irrelevant question to him. The whole scene in which this attitude on the part of Xuthus is presented is comic, with Xuthus appearing very much the dunce throughout. He has been told by Apollo, and he believes him, that the first person he meets on going out of the temple will be his son. Xuthus rushes out and throws himself upon the bewildered Ion. Appropriately Ion says: "Are you thinking well? Or have you been

28. Whitman, *Euripides and the Full Circle*, p. 98, notes that only in this version is the Gorgon referred to as being autochthonous.

driven mad by some god?" (520). Ion can see the approaches of
Xuthus only as lascivious disrespect for the god's servant, while a
fawning Xuthus tries to make him understand and accept his new
father. But once Xuthus can finally explain, Ion asks first whether
he is Xuthus's son by present of the god or by birth. Xuthus, ignorant of the truth, asserts that it is by birth, not gift, and then Ion
asks the question neither Xuthus nor Apollo are prepared for: "Of
what mother was I born to you?" (540). Xuthus did not ask, and
neither has Apollo independently supplied this information. "De-
lighting in this the discovery of a son, I did not ask" (541). Ion, the
gentle youth, pursues the question though: "Perhaps I was born
from the mother earth." The precedent of Erichthonius is vivid in
his mind, as indicated in his earlier conversation with Creusa. It is a
point that Xuthus rejects as impossible, a clear indication of his for-
eignness to Athens. Ion, more ready to accept such tales, must
thus push further. How could he be born without the benefit of a
woman? How could he be the son of the man who stands before
him without a woman being involved as well? His search for his
mother belies the self-satisfaction Xuthus shows at his discovery.

In their subsequent discussion they conclude that there must
have been some indiscretion by Xuthus before his marriage, during
a feast at Delphi: the mother must have been some Delphian maid
whom he no longer recalls, or shows any sustained interest in recalling except under pressure from Ion. Xuthus ignores the mutuality of procreation once he has discovered a son. Ion is not so
easily distracted from the question: "O beloved mother, when shall
I see your form? Now I long more than before to know whoever you
are" (563–64). While Xuthus acknowledges Ion's wish to find his
mother, and his own curiosity to know "of what woman you were
born to me" (572–74), he gladly leaves such a search to some later
time, when perhaps (*isōs*) they will find her (575). He will not be
delayed by looking for her in Delphi; instead, they are to hasten
homeward to Athens.

Xuthus's willingness to ignore the role of the human female in the
creation of his son parallels, though without the intensity, the
powerful trial scene at the end of the *Oresteia*, where the arguments
of paternity conquering maternity are given their full expression.
As Apollo says there, the woman only nurtures the seed. Her role
is like that of a flowerpot. By her distance from female activities
and embodiment of masculine virtues, Athene, the female god who
is no female, defends the principle of asexual birth, she herself

sprung from the head of Zeus. She required no female in her creation, and neither do the autochthonous heroes of Athens's origin
require one. Nor indeed does Ion in the visions of both Xuthus and
Apollo. Ion's demand for his mother, his longing to know where it
was that he was nurtured, flies in the face of this, as does the plot of
the play itself, which will establish the importance of the mother
both Apollo and Xuthus wish to deny.

This play, like several others by Euripides, suggests finally the inadequacy of male arrogance. In the other plays this inadequacy is
often related to the arrogance apparent in war, the arrogance of
power or brute strength. Here the arrogance is simply the belief in
male genesis. It is a belief characteristic not only of men, but of the
gods as well. Euripides does not delve into the biological aspects of
heterosexual reproduction in the fashion that Aeschylus allows to
his Apollo. For Euripides the psychological aspects are powerful
enough. The child demands, longs for the maternal breast; the father ignores that demand thinking any substitute for the womb or
the breast will do. Creusa's plot to kill Ion and Ion's own sensitive
fear of his effect as a foreign interloper, as her husband's child, on
Creusa (607–20) give the lie to that vision. The enchanting youth of
the play urges compassion for the woman he does not yet know as
his mother. "Before she shared in common your misfortunes," he
says to Xuthus. Now she suffers alone. How could she not hate the
youth? (607–15). The gentleness of Ion, who deeply feels a woman's
anguish, stands in marked contrast to the boorish warrior Xuthus—
sensitive neither to the female's passions nor to the city's own need
for myths about earthborn creatures.

The most powerful, though unacknowledged, attack on the superiority of the male as father comes in the form of Xuthus's ignorance of the fact that he is the dupe of both Apollo and Creusa. He
accepts without question as his son one whom he has absolutely
no recollection of fathering. In the better-known versions of the
myth, Xuthus is indeed Ion's father.[29] By making Apollo the father,
Euripides turns Xuthus into a comical figure satisfied with his ignorance. He admits that he does not know (*ouk oida*), but he believes
what he is told by the god (542). In other words, he believes the lie.
The credulity of Xuthus here stands in stark contrast to his incredulity of the Athenian foundation myths noted earlier. At the very end
of the play, Athene admonishes Creusa: "Be silent now how this

<hr>

29. Herodotus *History* 7.94 and 8.44.

child is yours in order that pleasing opinion may hold Xuthus"
(1601–2). He who cared naught about the mother of his child is indeed no father. *His* ignorance enables Ion to return to Athens.

Xuthus's ignorance here is parallel to the ignorance and suscep-
tibility to deception with which all men must function, the uncertainty of paternity, the uncertainty of who it is who fathered the
children they think to be their own. The denigration of the female
in the role of procreation is an attempt to assert the male's participation and importance in that process, but it is a participation that
must be deduced and is not immediately obvious. Paternity, as
Margaret Mead points out, is the result of inference and speculation. Maternity needs no inference; it is easily observable in the
growing belly and the actual labor of the woman. It is the definitive
and obvious statement of male dependence upon the female. It is a
dependence the males Apollo and Xuthus deny, but that Euripides
the playwright asserts. It is also a dependence the tales of autochthony try to overcome. The exclusion of the female from the founding of cities helps to deny the threatening power she holds over
males, the knowledge of who is and who is not their child. Xuthus
would not bring Ion back to Athens if he did not believe that Ion
was his son. The importance of that belief for Xuthus is asserted
throughout the play. The control Creusa has over that belief raises
her from the status of an irrelevant individual to the very source for
the founding of cities. Euripides in this play irreverently suggests a
revision of the autochthony myth, and in so doing exalts the role of
both women and motherhood. The foolishness of autochthony
("The plain does not bear offspring," as Xuthus so obviously states)
is transcended by the lyrical and sensitive relation between mother
and son, and by the more human focus on birth from the mortal
female.

What are the political implications of such a transformation? As
suggested at the beginning of this essay, autochthony myths gave a
city its sense of unity and naturalness. The artificial boundaries
and artificial connections of a political unit were made natural by
original birth from the earth. But they also gave the city its exclusiveness and its aristocracy, its rejection of what was other and
of those not descended from the original earthborn race. Thus, Ion
expresses hesitation to return to Athens as Xuthus's son. He is a
bastard, fearful of arriving as an outsider among the autochthonous Athenians. As the bastard son of a foreigner, he is other; as

such he is denied access to the rights of Athenian citizens. He will always be an outsider. In the important speech in which Ion reflects on the hostile reception he expects at Athens, Euripides seems to be chiding the Athenian audience. Their autochthony myth, so crucial for the founding of the city, becomes a limiting, stifling influence—antithetical to Athens's vision of itself as an open city. Foreign influences, indeed foreign benefits, the sons of gods, are excluded for what has now become a petty concern with citizen purity. The search for purity can be extended so far that it destroys what it seeks to protect. As Walsh points out, Ion keeps the temple pure by chasing away the birds, but it is a bird who saves his life by drinking the poisoned libation and thus warning Ion not to drink the poisoned wine.[30] The autochthony myth, rooted in a desire for purity, must be modified. As the city grows, it must acknowledge the female, and it must accept the son of a god. Refusal to accept the other creates fools like the tutor, ready to burn down Apollo's temple and encourage the murder of a husband and then of an innocent young boy. The pedagogue illustrates the dangers of the myth on which the city is built—the danger of forgetting its fragile origins and the mutuality of male and female necessary for the creation of a race of heroes.

Some have read *Ion* as a propaganda piece written for Athenians eager to defend their citizenship laws by reference to their divine origins. However, to read the play in this way is to ignore the critique implicit in it and to obscure the subtle interplay between male and female that undermines the Athenians' self-satisfaction in their masculine polity. Clearly, *Ion* presents for the Athenians their myths concerning the founding of their city and reveals how such myths are necessary for the survival of the city. And yet the play questions myths that create impassable boundaries for women and for foreigners. The city as constituted in ancient Greece must have its boundaries, its citizenship laws that establish the meaning of friend and of enemy, of same and of other. But at the same time that those laws give order and stability, they can also limit the possibilities of the city and deny the fullness of human experience. Therein lies part of the tragic content of this comedy and therein lies the political teaching of the poet.

30. Walsh, "Rhetoric of Birthright and Race," p. 306.

Chapter Eleven

Tragedy and the Education of the *Dēmos:* Aristotle's Response to Plato

Stephen G. Salkever

1.

THE CONTEXT OF THE *POETICS*

The reader of Aristotle's *Poetics* approaches that work with great expectations. It is, after all, the only sympathetic discussion of Greek tragedy written by a man who was both nearly contemporary with the great tragedians and a first-class philosophic mind. Moreover, in spite of its form, which is both rough and incomplete (our text is only the first of at least two books on the art of poetry), it has for centuries been seen by many as a manual for the proper construction of works of imaginative literature in the West. Nonetheless, a first reading cannot help but disappoint the lover of tragedy, who will find in Aristotle's account of the meaning of tragic drama a reduction of the vivacity and profundity we experience in reading or seeing the plays to a set of prosaic formulae, which must appear either crabbed or mysterious. Most modern commentary concerns itself with unraveling the meaning of these formulae, the most famous of which is Aristotle's definition of tragedy in chapter 6: "Tragedy is an imitation of an action [*praxis*] that is serious and complete, and of a definite magnitude, written in pleasing language each form of which is used separately in the parts of the tragedy. The imitation is with persons done by means of men acting, not through narration, accomplishing through pity and fear the *katharsis* of such passions" (*Poetics* 6.1449b).[1]

---

1. This is, with minor alterations, the translation of Laurence Berns ("Aristotle's *Poetics*," in *Ancients and Moderns*, ed. Joseph Cropsey [New York: Basic Books, 1964], p. 72).

What is striking about such commentary is that however the modern scholar may interpret the meaning of "serious *praxis*" and "*katharsis*," he or she will be inclined to take a condescending view of the adequacy of Aristotle's literary criticism to its subject. The explanation for this apparent inadequacy is not far to seek: in spite of the commonly held view that the *Poetics* offers a rehabilitation of the value of poetry in response to the Platonic critique, to many "it seems obvious that he [Aristotle] had very little feeling for poetry as such."[2] Plato opposed poetry in the name of philosophy, but he at least fully comprehended the power of the poetic challenge; Aristotle's restoration of poetry to philosophic respectability appears to rest upon a trivialization that distorts the meaning of the tragic enterprise.

A deeper criticism of the Aristotelian account of tragedy is also current. It attributes Aristotle's failure as a reader of tragedy not only to his insensitivity to poetic diction but more importantly to his inability to appreciate the possibility, central to tragedy, that the human world is constituted by fundamentally unresolvable conflicts.[3] If the ubiquity and necessity of such conflict does indeed characterize tragedy, and Aristotle is blind to it, we should not be surprised by the shortcomings of the account of tragic drama we find in the *Poetics*.[4]

2. G. M. A. Grube, *The Greek and Roman Critics* (Toronto: University of Toronto Press, 1968), p. 91.

3. Alasdair MacIntyre, *After Virtue* (Notre Dame, Ind.: University of Notre Dame Press, 1981), p. 153.

4. The romantic, and today nearly universal, view that tragedy is the depiction of insoluble and profound human conflicts leads some critics to the view that Goethe, and not Aristotle, is our best guide to the significance of tragic drama. See, e.g., Albin Lesky, *Greek Tragedy*, trans. H. A. Frankfort (New York: Barnes & Noble, 1965), p. 8. Many of the best classical commentators are convinced that Aristotle was simply incapable of appreciating the achievements of the best playwrights: "Tragedy in its greatest days comported things that were not dreamt of in Aristotle's philosophy" (Gerald F. Else, *Aristotle's Poetics: The Argument* [Cambridge, Mass.: Harvard University Press, 1957], p. 446). Aristotle is not without his modern defenders, who, like John Gardner (*On Moral Fiction* [New York: Basic Books, 1978]) and Norman Gulley ("Aristotle on the Purposes of Literature," in *Articles on Aristotle*, vol. 4, *Psychology and Aesthetics*, ed. J. Barnes, M. Schofield, and R. Sorabji [New York: St. Martin's Press, 1978], pp. 166–76) see in the *Poetics* the basis for the development of a view of imaginative literature that rejects the romantic identification of poetry and metaphysical insight. While I cannot provide a general defense of the Aristotelian understanding here, I do think that such a defense is possible on the basis of my reading of the *Poetics*. Such a view would have to overcome the romantic (or, better, Nietzschean) portrait of art as a surrogate for religion or philosophy and perhaps conclude with the claim that imaginative literature, in Robert Frost's words, "ends in a clarification of life—not necessarily a great clarification, such as sects and cults are founded on, but in a momentary stay against confusion" (*The Complete Poems of Robert Frost* [New York: Holt, Rinehart and Winston, 1961], p. vi).

That the meaning and the merit of the *Poetics* are much contested should come as no surprise, given the unfinished character of the work. But the problems of interpretation have a deeper and more interesting source: the uncertainty about what the *Poetics* says involves an uncertainty about the context in which to understand it. One important temptation to be avoided here is that of treating the *Poetics* as the first distinct theory of what has come to be called aesthetics. Such an approach is convenient for modern academic purposes, but it is distorting in that it presupposes that art is a permanent, distinct, and self-moving thing, and thus a proper object of theory. But for Aristotle, art in general and tragedy in particular are no more proper objects of theory than is politics; one may theorize (or generalize) about tragedy and about politics, but there can be no separate aesthetic or political theory.[5] The assumption, contra Aristotle, that such an aesthetic is possible, obscures the meaning of the work by establishing a systematic bias against recognizing any possible link between politics and tragedy, and inclines us to treat the tragic dramas as a class of objects that reveal their own purpose and meaning without reference to any political context.

In what follows, I argue that a proper understanding of the context of the *Poetics* indicates that we must try to understand that work not as an account of some isolable aesthetic phenomenon; rather, Aristotle's discussion presupposes the thought that tragedy is not only a political institution, but more particularly a democratic one. Once this is established, we shall be in a better position to discuss the meaning of some of Aristotle's controversial and obscure claims: that tragedy achieves the *katharsis* of pity and fear, that the central figures of tragedy must be people of great reputation and good fortune but relatively ordinary virtue, and that tragedy is better poetry than epic.

If I am right, two points of departure for studying the *Poetics* suggest themselves. The first is the Athenian self-understanding of the tragedies. This is a promising strategy since Athenian tragedy presupposed a unified democratic political culture that ruled out any

5. The temptation to treat the *Poetics* as Aristotle's aesthetic theory is important, because it leads scholars like Else (*Aristotle's Poetics*, p. 443) to claim that the critic must try to interpret the *Poetics* in its own terms, without reference to other Aristotelian writings. This tendency is the source, I believe, of what John Jones calls the "almost total failure of contact between Aristotle's argument and the successive traditions of exegesis" (*On Aristotle and Greek Tragedy* [Oxford, 1962; reprint, Stanford, Calif.: Stanford University Press, 1980], p. 11). My aim is to show that the *Poetics* should be read as part of Aristotle's political philosophy (or social science—*politikē*).

distinction between popular and fine art.[6] But this assumes both that there is a certifiably accurate interpretation of the meaning of tragedy for Athenians available to us independently of what we know from Aristotle and other commentators, and that Aristotle's intention is to restate and justify his culture's self-understanding of tragedy. Such an assumption ignores the various ways in which Aristotle's work is counter-cultural, critical of many of the mores of his time.[7]

A more reliable point of entry into Aristotle's discussion of tragedy is by way of a consideration of Plato's thought. In this, as in other matters, we may confidently assume that however much Aristotle's solutions differ from Plato's, his notion of what problems require solving and much of his vocabulary for solving them are drawn from Platonic sources.[8] Most accounts of the *Poetics* do in fact begin in this way, but generally only to the extent of noting the fact that Plato's comments on tragedy are entirely negative, whereas Aristotle attempts to show how tragedy might reasonably be defended. But in order to make sense of the Aristotelian defense, we need to ask why Plato so opposed tragedy. The most common answer is that the Platonic critique of tragedy is simply an application of a general Platonic opposition to poetry or art. The *Poetics*, says John Jones, "is a defense [of poetry] against attacks scattered among the writings of Plato. . . . Plato held it against poetry that its emotional appeal is a threat to the authority of reason, that it tells lies, . . . and that works of imaginative literature are remote from reality";[9] he adds that Plato "despised art for its intellectual poverty."[10] In book 10 of the *Republic*, Socrates does claim that tragedians are the greatest imitators, that imitation is a kind of play and not serious, and that imitators know nothing of what they imitate (602b). Nevertheless, "Plato himself supplies a good deal of the material for a complete aesthetic, a defense and reasonable critique of art."[11] Thus Plato's attack on the practice of Athenian tragedy does not reflect a general hostility to imaginative literature, or to play-

6. Lesky, *Greek Tragedy*, pp. 84–86.

7. He is clearly critical of the form of democracy characteristic of mid-fourth-century Athens, of the way in which his contemporaries tended to distinguish between free person and slave, and of all prevailing views concerning justice.

8. Jacob Klein, "Aristotle, An Introduction," in *Ancients and Moderns*, ed. Joseph Cropsey (New York: Basic Books, 1964), p. 50.

9. Jones, *On Aristotle and Greek Tragedy*, p. 21.

10. Ibid., p. 52.

11. Iris Murdoch, *The Fire and the Sun* (Oxford: Clarendon Press, 1977), p. 72.

fulness and imitation as such, but rests upon a specific political judgment that the *dēmos* taken as a whole—as tragedians must take them—is radically ineducable. Aristotle's disagreement with Plato on this point provides the context for his defense of tragedy.

2.

THE PLATONIC CRITICISM OF TRAGEDY

All good poetry is understood by Plato to be an imitation (*mimēsis*) of some objective reality rather than self-expression or perfectly accurate description or enactment of reality. As such, imitation is a kind of deed (*ergon*), a particular representation of something universal (since real entities are all universals, or forms), and therefore necessarily only an approximation of the truth about being (*Republic* 5.473a). This does not imply that representation as such must or can be avoided,[12] only that a clear distinction between good and bad imitation is necessary. As the Athenian Stranger says in the *Laws*, "[w]e ourselves are poets, authors as much as possible of a tragedy that is the noblest and the best; at least, our whole culture [*politeia*] was constructed as an imitation [*mimēsis*] of the most beautiful and most virtuous way of life" (*Laws* 8.817b). Poets are imitators, not simply versifiers, and though imitation must be subject to rational criticism, it is not to be rejected out of hand.

Imitations can be judged unsatisfactory on three related grounds: because the imitation is pursued as an end in itself; because the imitator cannot give an adequate account of what he or she is doing; or because that which is imitated is not in fact real. The first case of inadequate imitation refers to the poet who can become and imitate all things. Such a poet must be turned aside from the city of *Republic* 3 in favor of the one "who would imitate the diction [*lexis*] of the decent man [*ho epieikēs*]" (*Republic* 3.398a–b). Second, and more generally, imitation is unsatisfactory insofar as imitators cannot give an intelligible reason for pursuing their activity.[13] The third

---

12. The Eleatic Stranger in the *Statesman* says that the best laws "would be imitations [mimēta] of parts of the truth written by those who know these things as much as possible" (300c).

13. In the *Gorgias*, such incapacity to justify itself is one of the two criteria for separating true from sham art: "I do not designate as an art (*technē*) anything which is irrational (*alogos*); if you dispute me concerning these things, I am ready to give a *logos*" (465a). Ordinary poets are elusive creatures, and cannot be questioned about their meaning (*Protagoras* 347c), and Socrates characteristically insists that his inter-

ground for criticizing poetry explains the second: poets tend not to be able to give an account of themselves because what they are imitating is not something stable and universal but the unstable and particular desires and dreams of their audience. Tragedians are flatterers, concerned with pleasing their audiences rather than improving them.[14] This fault is not venal, but follows from the impossibility of tragedy imitating wise and quiet characters in the theater, where all sorts of noisy and foolish humans are gathered in festive assembly (*Republic* 10.604e).

Plato is not criticizing imitation or imaginative literature because it presents myths and images rather than discursive arguments. Indeed, such productions may be a necessary part of human education, or *paideia*, the improvement of people that Socrates names as the goal of all his discourses. True, Socrates says that he is not a speaker of myths.[15] Nevertheless, he does tell myths,[16] some of his own invention as well as those prepared by others.[17] Images are not only employed by poets. Socratic *paideia* itself depends upon the successful deployment of image and metaphor, perhaps even more than on what we would call discursive argument.[18] Such language

---

locutors give such an account of themselves. As Theodorus says, "It is not easy, Socrates, for anyone who sits with you not to give an account (*logos*) with respect to himself" (*Theaetetus* 169a; see also *Laches* 187e).

14. *Gorgias* 464c–d, 502b; *Laws* 3. 700d–e.

15. He says he is not a *muthologikos* in the *Phaedo* 61b. This statement is not, of course, incompatible with his telling of myths. For a different view of myth in Plato, see Robert Zaslavsky, *Platonic Myth and Platonic Writing* (Washington, D.C.: University Press of America, 1981), pp. 29–139, who argues that the myths in the dialogues are intended as wholly philosophic accounts (but genetic ones, as opposed to classificatory or descriptive).

16. He explicitly describes himself as telling myths (*muthologō*) in the *Gorgias* 493.

17. The plan for the education of the guardians in books 2 and 3 of the *Republic* is said to be a myth, or at least like one: "Come then, just as people mythologizing in a myth [*en mythō mythologountes*] and acting at leisure let us educate these men in speech [*logō*]" (*Republic* 2.376d–e).

18. Images and the imagination are placed at the lowest level of the divided line (*Republic* 6.509e), and images are placed below knowledge in the account of education given in the Seventh Letter (342b), but the divided line itself is called an image (*eikōn;* 509a) of the best or most natural education, as is the cave story (514a, 517a–b). These are not accidental slips. Socrates' response to Adeimantus's charge (*Republic* 6.487e–489b) that philosophers are useless is not a discursive argument but the image of a ship in need of a pilot (which Aristotle cites as an instance of an argument by means of an example [Rhetoric 2.1393a–b]). Socrates says there that Adeimantus's question calls for an answer "spoken through an image [*di'eikonos legomenēs*]," and indicates that he is an inveterate imagist. The same point, that images are a necessary aspect of *paideia*, is made while speaking to Glaucon at the conclusion of the cave image (*Republic* 7.533a). See also Socrates' comment to Callicles in the *Gorgias* 493d.

by itself does not pose any challenge to the authority of reason, and so cannot be said to be a ground for rejecting tragedy as such.

Nor is it damning that poets are uncertain about their approximations. When Socrates says in the *Phaedrus* that poetry requires a certain madness (*mania*) and that this madness is not necessarily shameful (245a and 244b–c; see also *Ion* 533e), he is not softening his critique of imitation in the *Republic*, but is perfectly consistent with it.[19] In the *Phaedrus*, poetic *mania* is defended by the claim that when such madness comes from the gods it is linked with the "most beautiful *technē*," that of prophecy (*mantikē*), in terms both of word origin and meaning. The result of this prophetic madness is the production of beautiful deeds or works (*kala erga*; 245b). Not all prophecy is genuine, and there are degrees of irony involved in Socrates' saying elsewhere that poets (like corybantic priests) are out of their heads (*Ion* 533e–534a), that Anytus is a prophet since he knows all about sophists without ever having dealt with one (*Meno* 92c), and that political people generally are prophets when they speak and do great things while knowing nothing of what they say (*Meno* 99b–d). But lapses of reason and certainty, and the consequent production of myths and images, are not peculiar to professional poets and democratic politicians. They are also characteristic of Socratic imitation itself (*Charmides* 169b), and so are perhaps inescapable even for the one who knows most of all. Imagistic speaking and writing is (for Socrates) not a sign of shameful and contemptible ignorance, but the only alternative to silence about the most pressing matters, matters pertaining to how we should live.[20]

Just as myths and images are as much a part of the Socratic repertoire as of that of the poets, Plato similarly presents Socrates as being playful rather than serious as he goes about the undoubtedly

19. Aristotle says in the *Rhetoric* (3.1408b) that Socrates is being ironical in his talk about poetic inspiration in the *Phaedrus*. However, Aristotle himself gives a similar definition of poetic madness (*Poetics* 17.1455a).

20. Socrates appears at times perfectly willing to speak in spite of his own uncertainty. In the *Meno*, Socrates says that he is uncertain about the claims he has made in connection with the recollection account and the demonstration with the slave, and later characterizes his discussion of the superiority of knowledge to right opinion by saying that "I speak as one not knowing but imagining [*eikazōn*]" (98b). Other Socratic images are prefaced or followed by similar admissions of Socratic uncertainty, such as the use of the sun as metaphor for the good in *Republic* 6.506d–507a. One of the key functions of the language of imagery, then, is to clarify the intimations about reality that compose a significant portion of the intelligence of the person who knows that he does not know.

serious business of trying to make the citizens better. Not only is Socrates occasionally accused of playing by his serious adversaries (as by Callicles at *Gorgias* 481b–c), but he makes a point of calling attention to his own characteristic playfulness. In the course of a passionate defense of philosophy against its enemies in *Republic* 7, Socrates stops himself for a moment, saying: "I forgot, I said, that we were playing [*epaizomen*] and spoke rather tensely." The passionate Glaucon, a serious lover of victory (548d), responds by bolstering his ally: "No, by Zeus, you didn't seem that way to me the listener." Socrates corrects him: "But to me the speaker" (536c).[21] Consistent, dogged seriousness belongs to politicians like Anytus and Callicles, or to geometers like Theodorus (*Theaetetus* 145b–c), perhaps because they think mistakenly that skill either at political persuasion or at geometry is the peak of human wisdom. In the *Laws*, the Athenian Stranger says that one must be serious about serious things (like God) and not about unserious matters (like humans), and that most people mistakenly hold that war is the supremely serious activity (*Laws* 7.803c–d). At any rate, Socrates by his playfulness appears to have more in common with sophists and poets (*Sophist* 234a–b) than with generals and politicians—in spite of the fact that he describes himself as the true politician (*Gorgias* 521d). There is no real difficulty here: the ordinary politicians and geometers are unremittingly serious about matters of less than the greatest importance, while sophists, poets, and immature philosophers (*Republic* 7.539b) are playful for the sake of play; only Socrates has the art of being properly playful with a serious end in view. But the question now is this: why can't poets and playwrights be playful in the Socratic manner?

In all of Socrates' conversations, no matter how theoretical the subject matter, the intention is always the same: persuading people to be concerned with their virtue (*Apology* 31b), to take seriously the question of the most desirable life (*Republic* 1.344d–e, 352d). This is as true of the dialogue about the meaning of knowledge (*Theaetetus* 210b–c) as of Socrates' talk with Glaucon and Adeimantus. A concern with the edification of its benefactors is as sure a test of the genuineness of a *technē* as is the demonstrability of its practices (*Gorgias* 500c). The principal obstacle to this Socratic *paideia* is not the rival teachings of sophists or poets, but the deeply

21. Socrates also recommends playfulness in the education of youthful philosophers (*Republic* 7.537a).

human inclination to believe that the most desirable life is the life of unlimited power for the sake of pursuing whatever our hearts desire. Plato regularly describes this belief as the view that the best or most admirable person has more than anyone else (*pleon echein* or *pleonexia*), more of those things that allow such persons to achieve whatever they wish. This is the view defended by Callicles, the man Socrates calls the best possible test for Socrates' own rightness (*Gorgias* 486d), and by Thrasymachus. But it also reflects the secret dream of those such as Glaucon and Adeimantus, who are too well brought up to confess it openly (*Republic* 2.367e–368c) and would be ashamed to act upon it, but who are uneasy about their habitual shame. This almost innocent and involuntary tyrannic dream, which is the great obstacle to true *paideia*, is said by the Athenian Stranger in book 3 of the *Laws* to be the one desire common to all humans (686e–687c). This is the desire "to have all things happen according to the commands of one's own soul." Such a desire is often concealed but is reflected in the view that power and strength necessarily lead to happiness and "in our tendency to eulogy upon seeing great wealth or especially honorable family ties or any such thing." This tendency to love power in spite of what the laws or respectable people might say is said by the Stranger to be the greatest ignorance, "whenever someone does not love but hates what is in his opinion noble or good, and loves and cherishes what seems to be bad and unjust" (689a). It is this ignorance or incoherence, and not some merely cognitive failure, that Socratic *paideia* seeks to remove by all the persuasive resources at his command: arguments, myths, images, charms (*Phaedo* 77e–78a), and corybantic chants (*Crito* 54d).[22]

The most precise account of this *paideia* in the dialogues is found in the Eleatic Stranger's discussion of the noble kind of sophistic art (*hē genei gennaia sophistikē*) in the *Sophist*. The "greatest ignorance" is here said to be "thinking that one knows something while not knowing it" (229c), particularly bearing in mind the statement about the greatest ignorance in the *Laws*, thinking that power is the necessary and sufficient condition of *eudaimonia*.[23] The practi-

22. On charms, see also Pedro Laín Entralgo, *The Therapy of the Word in Classical Antiquity*, ed. and trans. L. J. Rather and John M. Sharp (New Haven: Yale University Press, 1970), pp. 108–25.

23. *Republic* 1.336a. Socrates says that Polemarchus's definition of justice (helping friends and harming enemies) belongs to some rich man who has a high opinion of what he can do, thus indicating a connection between civic friendship and the tyrannical dream.

tioners of the art of *paideia* release people from this belief by showing the ignorant that their opinions contradict one another (230b),
by practicing, that is, the sort of *elenchos* or refutation that is characteristic of Socrates. Those who receive such an education are not
merely better informed, but undergo a transformation of character
such that their anger toward others becomes gentleness and a self-
directed sense of shame (230b–d; on gentleness as the outcome of
elenchos, see *Theaetetus* 210b–c and *Meno* 100b).

With an eye to Aristotle, it is important to note that the Stranger
calls this process of *paideia* through *elenchos* rather than direct admonition (and noble sophistry as a whole) by the name of the cathartic art (*kathartikē*; 231b). Since *katharsis* is the central element of
the Aristotelian definition of the proper function of tragedy, but
is a word that appears much more frequently in Plato than in
Aristotle, it is very important to notice its significance here. The
word *katharsis* and its cognates are clearly used in several senses by
Plato, some traditional and some novel.[24] Laín Entralgo distinguishes five separate meanings, of which the *katharsis* in our passage in the *Sophist* constitutes the fifth. The first four senses are:
(1) the traditional meaning of "cleansing" of a thing of all that is not
itself, in the way in which a sieve may be used to "purify" grain
(*Timaeus* 52e); (2) the traditional religious meaning of ritual purification or lustration; (3) the "purgation" from a body of impurities that cause disease, the usage characteristic of Hippocratic
medicine (*Republic* 3.406d); and (4) the peculiarly Platonic sense of
the soul being "purified" by being separated from the body after
death (*Phaedo* 114b–c). None of these senses seems quite to capture
the way the word is used to characterize *paideia* in the *Sophist*,
though all tend to identify *katharsis* with a process of restoring or
transforming a thing so that it becomes properly or naturally itself.
The cathartic *paideia* described in the *Sophist*, which I argue to be
much like Aristotle's use of *katharsis* in the *Poetics*, refers to such a
transformation, though not by any removal of impurities (either
lustral or purgative); rather, *katharsis* works here through the introduction of order into otherwise disorderly or incoherent souls
(whose opinions are like those of "wanderers" [*planōmenoi*; 230b]
and so are subject to *elenchos*), with the result that involuntary ignorance and tyrannical dreams are removed and the educated per-

24. Laín Entralgo, *Therapy of the Word*, pp. 127–38.

son becomes better. The process here is not one of removal, but of giving the soul its proper form and order.[25]

It is clear that the Socratic practice of cathartic *paideia* uses all the devices associated with poetry and tragedy—myths, lies, metaphors, divinations, and jokes, as well as more or less straightforward deductive inferences. Then why is it impossible to conceive of an art of poetry or tragedy that has been redeemed in the same way that Socrates may be said to have redeemed the sophistic, rhetorical, and political arts? The most general reason has to do with the futility of trying to provide a common or public education in virtue.[26] Socrates, as educator, can bring about a *katharsis* of individual souls, but he could not (even if his *daimonion* permitted him to try) educate an entire city all at once—he must live privately rather than as a man of the *dēmos* (*idiōteuein alla mē dēmosieuein*) or else he will be put to death in no time (*Apology* 31d–32a). This belief about the impossibility of public education does not only apply to democracies. The Athenian Stranger in the *Laws* criticizes Sparta and Crete not only because they put the least of the virtues—courage or virility (*andreia*)—first (a criticism taken up by Aristotle in the *Politics*), but also because they educate their young in a mass or herd and not singly (*Laws* 2.666d–667a).[27] But the project of public *paideia* is especially problematic in a democracy, since the multitude (*to plēthos*) can never be brought to accept the existence of an objective standard of the beautiful or noble that is different from their own desires, and so cannot be philosophic and will always blame philosophers, as will those private individuals who want to please *to plēthos* gathered together in a mass (*Republic* 6.493e–494a), individuals like ordinary sophists and especially tragic poets (*Republic* 6.492a–c).[28] Especially tragedians, since they—unlike sophists— must submit their work to the judgment of all sorts of humans (*Gorgias* 502b–e; *Laws* 2.665e) gathered in a very noisy theater (*Laws* 9.876b). It is thus no surprise that tragedy, the form of poetry that is most persuasive and delightful to the *dēmos* (*dēmoterpestaton te kai*

25. This is like the Hippocratic conception of medical treatment, in which health is understood as the proper ordering of the elements of the body. See Laín Entralgo, *Therapy of the Word*, p. 132.

26. Aristotle accepts the superiority of private *paideia*, though on the same basis as the superiority of private doctoring, *Nicomachean Ethics* 10.1180b.

27. This suggests that the remarks concerning the education of the guardians in *Republic* 2 and 3 can hardly be taken as a Platonic "theory" of education.

28. Only "the many" believe that the sophists are the corrupters of youth. In fact, it is the sophists who are corrupted by the many (*Republic* 6.492a).

psuchagōgikōtaton; Minos 321a), will support and reinforce the dream of tyranny, the belief that the best life is the most powerful life (*Republic* 8.568a–b; *Laws* 8.889e–890a), the belief that is the least common denominator of human aspirations and, as such, the only opinion that integrates and gives form to the otherwise disorderly *dēmos*. Tragedy lends a false air of seriousness (*Laws* 7.817a)[29] to the unifying opinion of democracy, but this impropriety is not caused by any bad or corrupt intention peculiar to tragic poets; rather, the political context of tragedy is such that it is utterly impossible for a tragedian to be both successful and at the same time a practitioner of genuinely cathartic *paideia*.

3.

ARISTOTLE AND THE EDUCABILITY OF THE *DĒMOS*

For Plato, all human goods derive their value from their effectiveness as stays against the confusion caused by *pleonexia*, and there may surely be insoluble conflicts among such goods—the ever-present tension between Socrates and the city, and between philosophy and *nomos* as forms of order, are the most fundamental and permanent of such conflicts. But this difficulty, serious though it is, is more a consequence of serious attempts to solve the problem of disorder than a key to the heart of the problem itself. Since order or form is both needed and not spontaneous (or generally desired), education is necessary for its establishment. Since the ignorance reflected in the shapeless tyrannic dream is both deep and not accidental, an education equal to conquering it cannot take the form of mere preaching or admonition (which is the traditional way of the fathers and the many; *Sophist* 229e–230a), but must be indirect and charming on the model provided by Socratic *elenchos*. Tragic drama as Plato knows it can never perform this function because of its dependence upon democratic public assemblies, which always reinforce the ignorance *paideia* seeks to overcome.[30]

29. See also the characterization of a particular definition of color as "tragic" in *Meno* 76e. That must also mean, I think, "falsely serious." Aristotle also uses the adjective "tragic" in something like this sense (perhaps "overly dignified") at *Rhetoric* 3.1406b.

30. The Platonic opposition to democracy no more follows from an unreasoned prejudice against the poor or the lower classes than his estimate of the need for order reflects an obsessive philosopher's preference for logical consistency. Democracy is the regime next worst to tyranny because of the disorderliness it tolerates (*Republic* 6.557a–558c).

As we shall see, Aristotle's assessment of the possibilities of democratic education, and hence of the value of tragedy, are very different from Plato's; nonetheless, his understanding of the principal obstacle to human well-being is much the same as that of his teacher. The central antithesis in Aristotle's moral vocabulary is the distinction between the *spoudaioi* and the *phauloi*, between those who are serious about living virtuously and those who are concerned with particular pleasures in a disorderly way.[31] Most people prefer the disorderly life (*zēn ataktōs*; *Politics* 6.1319b); but for Aristotle this preference does not reflect any corruption peculiar to the lower classes, but rather our common biologically human attachment to living, an attachment ordinarily much stronger than any commitment to an ordered conception of how we should live (*Politics* 3.1278b).[32] But however natural, in one sense, our inclination to *pleonexia* may be, the fact remains that we can be happy only insofar as we live according to a reasonable order of the sort that may be indicated by the *nomoi* (laws) of our city or culture.[33] The *paideia* provided by the *nomoi* will be adequate insofar as it causes us to choose not "to have more [*pleonektein*] either of money or of honor or of both" (*Politics* 2.1266b). Since such an education may run counter to our powerful attachment to our own survival, it presents an extremely difficult problem of persuasion; while it is surely difficult to determine what is just in human affairs (given conflicting human goods), "still it is easier to hit upon this than to have it accepted by those who have the power to get more [*pleonektein*]" (*Politics* 6.1318b). Still, this is what education and the laws must aim to do (*Politics* 2.1267b).

31. As Else says (*Aristotle's Poetics*, pp. 71–78), the closest English equivalent to *hoi phauloi* is not "the vicious" but the Southern American "the no-account." The *phauloi* are defined as those who aim at no definite end, but at *pleonexia* (*Nicomachean Ethics* 9.1167b). They do not take seriously the problem of living well, but are concerned only with the unlimited acquisition of particular things: money, honor, and somatic pleasures (1168b). The distinction is a traditional one, but Aristotle differs from tradition (as does Socrates in the *Republic* 1.347a–b) in associating *pleonexia* not only with the love of money and of physical pleasure but with the love of honor as well. This has, as we shall see, important consequences for Aristotle's discussion of the relative merits of oligarchy and democracy.

32. In his discussion of the economic art in book 1 of the *Politics* (1257b–1258a), Aristotle says that some people mistakenly think that the function of the art is to increase one's property without limit (*apeiron*): "The cause of this disposition is being serious [*spoudazein*] about living but not about living well. As the desire for life is unlimited, so also the desire for the things productive of life is unlimited."

33. An argument for this reading of the relation of laws to human happiness is given in Stephen G. Salkever, "Aristotle's Social Science," *Political Theory* 9 (1981): 488–92.

To this point, Plato and Aristotle are in full agreement: the greatest injustices are caused by disorderly tyrannical dreams, which are manifested primarily in the love of money and the love of honor (*Politics* 2.1271a)[34] and in the mistaken belief that an orderly life such as is lived within a genuine culture or *politeia* (i.e., one whose goal is education in virtue) is slavery rather than salvation (*Politics* 5.1310a). But whereas Plato holds that the many as such are not open to the sort of persuasion at which good laws and education aim, Aristotle takes a very different view. This difference begins to appear in the *Politics* in the discussion in book 3 of whether the best *polis* should be ruled by the few people who are best or by the multitude (*to plēthos;* 1281a).[35] It would seem obvious that the best should rule, but Aristotle initially sets out an argument that denies this. His claim is that while each individual member of the many (*hoi polloi*) may not be a serious man (*spoudaios anēr*), the many "when coming together admit of being better than those who are best, not individually, but as a whole [*hōs sumpantas*]." Since a *polis* has several functions, and must provide for the security as well as the virtue of its citizens, a city in which the many are mixed with the better may be capable of the best judgments; this is supported by the analogy that impure (*mē kathara*) food mixed with pure is more nourishing than a small amount of pure food alone. The discussion concludes (1283b) with the tentative assertion that nothing stands against the possibility that the many may sometimes be better than the few, "not as individuals, but as a whole" (or "in a crowd"; *hōs athroous*). We are left to wonder about the circumstances under which a *dēmos* is such that it may be made more *katharos*, and about the agency through which this *katharsis* occurs.

In language directly antithetical to the Platonic position taken in the *Gorgias*, Aristotle says that often a crowd (*ochlos*) judges better than an individual, since the many are often less corruptible than the few, less likely to be overcome by anger and so to err (*Politics* 3.1286a). This claim is reinforced in book 4 by the proposition that "the graspings [*pleonexiai*] of the wealthy subvert the regime [*politeia*] more than those of the *dēmos*" (1297a). The basis for Aristotle's

34. Aristotle calls these injustices voluntary, Plato involuntary, but this is a quarrel over definition: for Aristotle, *voluntary* means originating with the agent, for Plato it means with the full understanding of the agent.

35. I am taking *plēthos* and *dēmos* as equivalent terms, as does W. L. Newman (*The Politics of Aristotle*, vol. 4 [Oxford: Clarendon Press, 1902], p. 517). The same equivalence in Plato can be seen in Alcibiades' speech in the *Symposium*.

preference for democracy over oligarchy is not a romantic idealiza-
tion of the virtues of every *dēmos*, but the empirical claim that the
wealthy will tend to be motivated by the love of honor and the *dēmos*
by the love of gain (*kerdos*), and that the greatest crimes, the greatest
pleonexia, are consequences of the unlimited love of honor and pref-
erential regard (*Politics* 2.1267a). The form of *pleonexia* that infects
the *dēmos* is easier to check than that which drives the wealthy, so
that under certain circumstances a democracy can be a regime in
which a substantial degree of political virtue is realized.

These circumstances are primarily economic, having to do with
both the amount and the kind of wealth the citizens possess. Democracies can be the most measured or reasonable (*metriōtatē*) of
those regimes that do not aim explicitly at virtue, because in the
best democracies the laws are permitted to rule rather than the citizens (*Politics* 4.1289b, 1292a), thus reducing the occasions for the
vice caused by *pleonexia*. These democracies are those in which the
dominant element is composed of farmers or herdsmen of middling
wealth (1292b; *Politics* 6.1318b); such people have substance enough
to live as long as they work, but not much leisure, and so will be
inclined to rule according to laws (1292b). Thus they will be open to
the sort of reason (*logos*) that the laws approximate, given the objectivity of the *nomoi* and their braking effect on *pleonexia* (*Politics*
4.1295b).[36]

Aristotle's conception of the best agrarian democracy does not
evoke images of fully committed republican citizenship. Nor does
he hold that in the best democracy each person is simply consumed by private affairs; people of middling wealth neither flee nor
are eager for rule (*Politics* 4.1295b). The best democracies are in-
formed by a particular civic opinion, an opinion that is conservative
(rather than acquisitive or ambitious) toward familial prosperity
and strongly committed to the laws as the instruments of this con-
servation. Such an opinion can be indirectly supported by economic regulations, sumptuary laws, and the like, but it cannot be
adequately secured without a system of *paideia*, of education in virtue appropriate to the limits of the regime. The most important task
of democratic education is to secure the public against what Aristotle regards as the greatest threat to democratic opinion and vir-

36. Overly wealthy people are inclined to hubris and major crime, overly poor
people to smaller villainy (1295b), and the former inclination is much more difficult
to subdue than the latter (1267a).

tue, which is the extravagant teaching of demagogues concerning the meaning of freedom (*Politics* 5.1340b).

The substance of this teaching is that freedom consists not in ruling and being ruled in turn, but in living as one likes (*Politics* 5.1310b; 6.1317b). Its danger is that it obscures the distinction between the reasonable order supplied by the *politeia* and the unreasonable constraints of slavery, and so leads its adherents to suspect that citizenship and slavery are inseparable, thus opening the way to what Plato calls the tyrannical dream and the greatest ignorance, the view that power and mastery are the true sources of happiness. Unlike Plato, Aristotle appears to believe that a form of public *paideia* that opposes the spread of this dream is possible,[37] though generally neglected (*Politics* 5.1310a) and extremely difficult. But the discussion of *paideia* in the unfinished eighth book of the *Politics* does not address this question directly, since it is concerned primarily with the education of the young and with music education in a relatively narrow sense. It is possible to see the *Poetics* as a continuation of the discussion of political education, and the Aristotelian characterization of the function of tragedy as a prescription for the treatment of the dream of *pleonexia* that continually threatens to erode the core of otherwise healthy democracies.

4.

THE AUDIENCE FOR TRAGEDY

The *paideia* in question must be understood as pertaining not only to children,[38] but in the broader sense defined in *Politics* 2 as "customs, *philosophia*, and laws" (1263b).[39] This reference to philosophy as a central part of the project of educating against *pleonexia* and injustice cannot refer to a need to make the citizens adept at the science of understanding the eternal and immovable things, but rather to education in what might be called literary culture (*philosophia* clearly has this meaning at *Rhetoric* 2.1394a).[40] Such an edu-

37. It will be more possible in democracies than in oligarchies, insofar as love of gain is a less severe obstacle to *paideia* than love of honor.

38. Warren D. Anderson, *Ethos and Education in Greek Music* (Cambridge, Mass.: Harvard University Press, 1966), pp. 137–38.

39. A similar usage is at *Politics* 7.1337a, where he says that all *paideia* and *technē* aim at filling up nature's deficiencies.

40. Carnes Lord, "Politics and Philosophy in Aristotle's *Politics*," *Hermes* 106 (1978):354–55.

cation, like Socratic *elenchos*, operates indirectly; it neither admonishes nor implants moral rules, but prepares its auditors to use their leisure well, to act virtuously and thoughtfully rather than under the influence of *pleonexia*, even when circumstances (such as war or the fear of punishment) do not compel them to do so. It is in this sense that *philosophia* is said to be a necessary preparation for a virtuous *diagōgē*, or way of life, to allow the possibility that leisure be used decently rather than as an occasion for self-aggrandizement (*Politics* 7.1334a).[41] Tragedy and epic poetry might well be seen as the heart of such an education, which is both broadly philosophic and aimed at non-theoretical people, and the function of these arts could then be understood as similar to Socratic *elenchos* in that they aim at cultivating the desire to live according to reasonable laws based on a perception of the connection between orderliness and happiness. Can the *Poetics* be interpreted as defining the purpose of tragedy in this way?

For Aristotle, the definition of any natural entity or of any art has two elements: the work or end (*ergon* or *telos*) that distinguishes the entity or art from all others, and the means through which this *ergon* is specifically accomplished. For instance, the *telos* of a *polis* is the virtuous life of its citizens,[42] and the means it employs are the rule of laws and the process of ruling and being ruled in turn. Aristotelian definitions are intended to allow us to identify genuine cases of the thing defined, and to distinguish them from false pretenders. The definition of tragedy in chapter 6 of the *Poetics* follows this pattern: "Tragedy is an imitation of an action that is serious and complete, and of a definite magnitude, written in pleasing language . . . done by means of men acting, not through narration, accomplishing through pity and fear the *katharsis* of such passions" (1449b). Most of this definition refers to the means by which tragedies achieve their *telos*: the *mimēsis* of a *spoudaia praxis*, later expanded by specifying that the action must involve a shocking reversal of fortune that befalls a person of middling virtue and great repute as an inevitable consequence of a great mistake (*hamartia*)

---

41. For *diagōgē* as "way of life" rather than the trivial "pastime," see Newman, *Politics of Aristotle*, vol. 3, pp. 449 and 488, and Anderson, *Ethos and Education*, p. 270.

42. I am simplifying Aristotle's account here; in order to achieve its definitive end, a genuine *polis* must also achieve the preliminary ends of citizen survival and civic integration. These preliminary ends are also means to the definitive end, but may at times conflict with it. See Salkever, "Aristotle's Social Science," pp. 492–94.

committed and later comprehended by the protagonist (13.1453a); embellished language, immediately defined as the alternating employment of meter, musical mode (*harmonia*), and melody; the use of dramatic roles rather than narration, later refined by saying that the plot (*mythos*) of the drama itself is more important than the character, thought, diction, or looks of the characters; and the arousal of pity and fear, later expanded by saying that it is through the imitation of pitiable and fearful incidents that tragedy produces the pleasure that is proper to it.

The *Poetics* as a whole has much to say about the means by which tragedy does its work, but almost nothing about the end these means accomplish.[43] To be sure, the plot (*mythos*) is said to be the first element and "like [*hoion*] the soul of the tragedy" and the production of a plot rather than a certain character is said to be the goal for tragic *mimēsis* (6.1450a). But since tragedy is an art rather than a natural kind, it cannot contain its own *telos*; the plot no more embodies the end of tragedy than medicine embodies health or the political art virtue. In the same chapter, the work of the plot, and hence of tragedy, is said to occur because it persuades (*psychagōgei*; 1450a), but we are told nothing more about the character of this persuasion or about who is to be persuaded (25.1461b). Similarly, Aristotle says that the goal of tragedy is producing the sort of pleasure that arises from pity and fear (14.1453b); but since for Aristotle human pleasures must always be understood relative to the kind of person experiencing them, since pleasures vary with ways of life (*Nicomachean Ethics* 10.1176a), the definition of tragic pleasure provided by the *Poetics* is necessarily incomplete.

Tragedy must be persuasive relative to some opinion, and pleasant relative to some way of life. The difficulty of grasping the work of tragedy is only compounded by Aristotle's reference to *katharsis* as the specific accomplishment of tragedy, since this word has, as we noted in discussing Plato, several different meanings. Whichever of those meanings is correct here, *katharsis* shares with persuasion and pleasure the character of being definite only in relation to some goal that purging, purifying, or whatever, achieves. Thus in saying that tragedy must be pleasurable, persuasive, and cathartic, Aristotle tells us that the tragic art is successful only if it manages

---

43. This is characteristically Aristotelian: the *Politics* and *Ethics* say very little about the meaning of living well, and the *Metaphysics* is hardly voluble on the primary instance of being.

to move its audience from some point to some other; the nature of this motion, and the nature of the audience to be moved, requires further consideration.

In the long history of the interpretation of Aristotelian *katharsis*, three major views are prominent.[44] The earliest holds that *katharsis* refers to a form of religious expiation (the sense in which the term is used in *Poetics* 17.1455b).[45] Since the middle of the nineteenth century, a majority of commentators have held that it refers instead to the homeopathic treatment of emotional disorders in the manner of Hippocratic medicine (the way the word is used in *Politics* 7.1341a–1342a).[46] More recently, several writers have urged that the term has neither a medical nor a ritual connotation, but refers instead to a kind of clarification or enlightenment.[47] Though interpretations vary, the commentators agree, generally implicitly, that the interpretive strategy for understanding tragic *katharsis* must be indirect; since Aristotle himself says so little about the meaning of this key term, the best interpretation will result from the best characterization of the nature of the audience tragedy specifically addresses.

This seems quite sound, since every *technē*, including the tragic, aims at some good or at some need or deficiency it intends to fill (*Politics* 7.1337a). Moreover, all discourses must be shaped not only by the character of their subject matter (*Nicomachean Ethics* 2.1103b–1104a), but also by the type of evidence those who are to be moved or persuaded are in the habit of accepting: "Some people do not accept statements unless they are expressed mathematically; others, unless they are expressed by way of examples; and there are some who demand that a poet be quoted as a witness" (*Metaphysics* 2.995a, trans. Apostle). The nature of tragic discourse can thus be inferred from two aspects of the nature of its audience: what the audience needs, and what kind of persuasion the audience is prepared to accept.

Readers of the *Poetics* are thus correct in trying to define the

---

44. For reviews of the history of the interpretation of *katharsis* in the *Poetics*, see D. W. Lucas, *Aristotle: Poetics* (Oxford: Clarendon Press, 1968), pp. 273–90, and Laín Entralgo, *Therapy of the Word*, pp. 186–201.

45. For a variant, see Else, *Aristotle's Poetics*, pp. 374–75 and 437–38.

46. See Jacob Bernays, "Aristotle on the Effect of Tragedy" (Breslau, 1857), trans. Jonathan and Jennifer Barnes, in *Articles on Aristotle*, vol. 4, *Psychology and Aesthetics*, ed. J. Barnes, M. Schofield, and R. Sorabji (New York: St. Martin's Press, 1978), pp. 160–62, and Lucas, *Aristotle: Poetics*, pp. 282–86.

47. Laín Entralgo, *Therapy of the Word*; Laurence Berns, "Aristotle's Poetics"; and Leon Golden, "The Clarification Theory of *Katharsis*," *Hermes* 104 (1976):437–52.

function of tragedy relative to the needs and limits of its audience, but the characterization of this audience is usually insufficiently precise insofar as it assumes the adequacy of three categories for classifying audiences: the audience must be either emotionally disturbed (and hence in need of purgation), or normal and pious (and hence in need of purification), or normal non-philosophers (and hence in need of clarification or enlightenment). But these alternatives fail to do justice to the complexity and subtlety of Aristotle's social psychology and so result in unnecessarily vague inferences concerning the purpose of tragedy.[48] Though the question of the specific audience for tragedy is not directly considered in the *Poetics*, we can learn a great deal about that audience, and hence about the purpose of tragedy, from Aristotle's discussion of the characteristics of different audiences in the *Rhetoric*. An examination of this discussion will, I believe, suggest that the appropriate audience for tragedy, the audience open to and in need of tragic *katharsis*, closely resembles the citizenry of the better sort of democracy outlined in the *Politics*.

Aristotle does not explicitly name tragedy as a branch of rhetoric, but it seems safe to assume that it is: many of his examples of rhetorical devices are taken from tragedies, and the *ergon* of rhetoric is said to concern "those things concerning which we deliberate" (*Rhetoric* 1.1357a), that is, things that can be other than they are, preeminently human actions (*Nicomachean Ethics* 3.1112a–b), the things imitated or represented by tragedy. Moreover, rhetoric, like tragedy, aims at persuasion not through arguments but by the use of examples *paradeigmata* (*Rhetoric* 1.1356a–b). Thus the subject matter of tragedy is much the same as that of, say, Aristotle's political philosophy or social science—each seeks to be persuasive concerning the question of good and bad actions. But the two modes of discourse differ in their style of argument and so are appropriate to different audiences. On the whole, persuasion by example is appropriate "in the presence of such listeners as are incapable of taking in many things in one view [*ou dunatai dia pollōn synoran*] or of following long or remote chains of argument [*logizesthai porrothen*]" (*Rhetoric* 1.1357a). Assuming the rhetorical character of tragedy, then, we can say that the tragic audience will be no more

48. It is as if we were to draw inferences about the nature of Socratic *elenchos* on the basis of whether Glaucon, Meno, Charmides et al. are troubled or sound. The problem with these categories is not that they lead to false judgments, but to overbroad ones.

philosophic than it is emotionally unstable. This is not at all to say, as we shall see, that the members of such an audience are incapable of serious deliberation about political matters, or of learning with pleasure from rhetorical imitations (*Rhetoric* 1.1370a–b).

While the art of rhetoric aims at persuasion concerning matters of action in general (*Rhetoric* 1.1355b), the art of tragedy is specifically concerned with those actions that arouse fear and pity. These emotions are discussed at length in *Rhetoric* 2, where fear is defined as "the painful or troubled feeling arising from the imagination of an imminent evil which causes destruction or pain" (1382a). Not all prospective setbacks evoke fear; for instance, no one fears "becoming unjust or slow-witted," but only those things likely to cause great pain in the immediate future. The same things that excite fear when they are about to happen to us evoke pity when we see them about to happen to others (1386a), especially if these others are sufficiently like those near and dear to us: "pity is a kind of pain upon seeing the deadly or painful evil happening to one who does not deserve it, such as one might expect to come upon himself or one of his own [*ē tōn hautou tina*]" (1385b). Fear and pity are thus not separate or separable emotions, since both arise from the solicitude we feel for ourselves and those closest to us; Aristotle in no way suggests that pity is a transforming sublimation of fear.[49]

Normally, fear comes as a kind of shock; only those who are weak, like the very old, perpetually think they are about to suffer from all sorts of evils. But fear is not, unlike terror or sudden anger, the sort of shock that generates an irrational response; rather, the experience of fear is a motive to deliberation: "fear makes men deliberate [*ho gar phobos bouleutikous poiei*]" (1383a), presumably because a sense of danger, as long as it is not so strong as to arouse unbearable terror, will cause us to think and to consult one another about the best ways of warding off the evils that threaten us.[50] The experience of fear may thus at times be a very salutary thing for the

49. Jones makes the point clearly as follows: "One should hyphenate Aristotelian pity-and-fear because it is a mistake to think of pity in isolation and interpret it, as some have done, in a spirit of Christian altruism (*Aristotle and Greek Tragedy*, p. 39 n.)." Cf. Berns, "Aristotle's *Poetics*," pp. 75–77.

50. In this important respect Aristotle's account of fear as a rationalizing emotion is, perhaps surprisingly, not at all unlike that of Thomas Hobbes. This was well known by Leo Strauss (*The Political Philosophy of Hobbes*, trans. Elsa M. Sinclair [Oxford: Clarendon Press, 1936], p. 35): "The central chapters of Hobbes' anthropology . . . betray in style and contents that their author was a zealous reader, not to say a disciple of the *Rhetoric*."

potentially rational animal, and when it is, the best way for a speaker to arouse an audience to fear is by reminding them that "others greater [*meizous*] than they have suffered . . . at the hands of those from whom they did not expect it, and in ways and at times when they did not think they would suffer" (1383a). This passage suggests the political importance of fear and states the proper technique for arousing that emotion in a way that approximates the account of tragic peripeteia or reversal (chs. 10, 11) and of the character proper to the tragic protagonist (ch. 13) set forth in the *Poetics*. We may thus tentatively surmise that the function or goal of tragedy is to arouse the sort of fear that makes political deliberation possible.

Fear and the pity that depends upon it inspire deliberation, and are in this way distinct from emotions like anger (*orgē* or *thymos*), "the painful desire for revenge for a real or apparent slight to oneself or one's own when the slight is undeserved" (*Rhetoric* 2.1378a; see also 1368b–1369b). The very proud, the very angry, and the very manly (like Achilles; 1378b–1379a) cannot feel fear or pity because they are incapable of anxiety about evils to come; people can feel pity "who are not in a manly passion [*hoi mēte en andrias pathei ontes*], such as anger or confidence (for these are unreasoning [*alogista*] about the things which will be), nor those of a hubristic disposition (for such are also unreasoning about future suffering)" (1385b). Those who are capable of fearing and pitying are said to be those who are more experienced, more timid, more sensible, and weaker than the powerful and heroic. Such people are said to be "correct reasoners" (*eulogistoi*) about the possibility of suffering, as are "those who have children, and parents, and wives; for these are part of them, and are such as to suffer the evils of which we have spoken" (1385b). Fear, pity, and the consequent inclination to deliberation do not therefore belong to all humans—certainly not to the noble and spirited citizen soldiers—but only to those whose self-understanding and social situation are in a middle position (*hoi metaxu*) between heroic self-sufficiency and wretched desolation.

A very sharp picture emerges in the *Rhetoric* of the sort of person who is open to fear and pity, and so inclined to respond to threats with cautious deliberation rather than resignation or revenge. His view is that those who are very young, or very wealthy, or of very noble birth, or very powerful, will be inclined to be lovers of honor and victory (rather than of wealth), manly, hubristic, and incapable

of fear (1389a).[51] In sum, an excess of good fortune tends to produce a fearlessly arrogant and thoughtless character (1391b), while
it is implied that too little good luck results in weakness and shame-
less timidity in action and thought.[52] The capacities for fear, pity,
and deliberation thus go together[53] and are especially to be found
among those of mediocre fortune, so long as such people are not so
cynical as to think that there are no decent humans (*epieikeis*), and
hence no undeserved evils (1385b).

Fear and pity are humanizing emotions insofar as they support
the deliberative life, the sort of life that constitutes human virtue
within the realm of human actions: they are to practical wisdom
what wonder is to theoretical speculation. Tragedy stimulates these
emotions in people capable of experiencing them, people who are
in a sort of mediocre position with respect to wealth and intelligence, precisely the sort of people who are said in *Politics* 4 to find
it least difficult to follow reason (*logos*) in practical matters (1295b),
the group that composes the major part of the middle class or agrarian democracy. Such people are neither solitaries nor perpetually
busy in the assembly and marketplace, and it is among them, on
those intermittent occasions when they leave their homes and families to meet in assembly, that the tragic emotions can take hold; but
to what end? To answer this question is to understand the function
of tragic *katharsis* and *paideia* within the context of a democratic polity, whose citizens require neither a purgative cure for emotional
disorders nor ritual purification but protection against the nearly
universal human inclination to act unjustly whenever we have the
power to do so (*Rhetoric* 2.1382b; *Politics* 6.1318b; *Politics* 7.1324b),
and the specifically democratic inclination to equate freedom and
power.

5.
TRAGIC KATHARSIS AND DEMOCRATIC EDUCATION

To achieve its goal properly, tragedy must arouse the emotions of
pity and fear by the imitation of a serious action (like the self-

51. And so incapable of pity, except for the young; but even their pity is not from
fear but rather from *philanthrōpia*, which seems to signify a naive generosity about
human merit that makes *any* suffering seem undeserved (1389b).
52. Such characteristics are explicitly attributed to the old (1389b–1390a).
53. Aristotle does oppose fear to reasonableness in the *Nicomachean Ethics*
(10.1179b–1180a), but the context there is different, and concerns the need, when
educating the young, to transform childish fear into mature shame.

discovery of Oedipus). Aristotle is especially precise in listing the features an appropriately tragic action must include. First, the action must involve a shocking and terrible misfortune (*Poetics* 9.1452a) that happens or is about to happen to some apparently fortunate person (13.1455a). Aristotle's point here is that the most noticeable trait of the well-drawn tragic figure must not be his or her virtue,[54] although a thoroughly vicious man (*sphodra ponēros*) is an even less likely tragic sufferer. Rather, the main character of a tragedy must be someone of relatively average virtue, and so like us, but of strikingly high social reputation and good fortune (1453a), such as Oedipus or Thyestes. The successful tragedian will persuade an audience that the mighty may, contrary to our expectations, suffer great evils, and so confound, momentarily at least, the opinion that power and wealth are sufficient for happiness. It is in this sense that the tragic events occur contrary to opinion (*para tēn doxan*; 9.1452a).

Tragic events are set in motion by a serious mistake (*hamartia*) made by the central character; misfortune must result neither from accident nor through divine agency or fate (1452a), but as a result of an error of the protagonist's resulting in some disastrous action. For Aristotle the lesson of genuine tragedy is not the Christian moral that the mighty are brought low as a result of their hubris or through some deep-seated "tragic flaw."[55] We may, however, see the occurrence of the tragic mistake as loosening the hold of the hubristic opinion that the mighty are immune to the consequences of serious error by virtue of their power.

Finally, the misfortune whose imitation effects tragic *katharsis* must be of a particular kind: the disaster or threatened disaster that is the occasion for the drama must be neither personal nor political, but a shocking blow directed against the order of the household or

54. The sufferer of tragic misfortune must not simply be a decent person (*epieikēs*) because, Aristotle says, such suffering is neither fearful nor pitiable but disgusting (*miaron*). See Lucas, *Aristotle: Poetics*, pp. 140–41.

55. Nearly all modern commentators agree in treating *hamartia* as a mistake based on ignorance, rather than as a deep "tragic flaw" foreshadowing original sin (cf. Berns, "Aristotle's *Poetics*," pp. 76–77). Lucas's judgment seems incontrovertible: "the essence of *hamartia* is ignorance combined with the absence of wicked intent" (*Aristotle: Poetics*, p. 302; similarly, see Else, *Aristotle's Poetics*, pp. 376–86, and Jones, *Aristotle and Greek Tragedy*, p. 15). This reading is demanded by Aristotle's use of the word elsewhere (e.g., *Nicomachean Ethics* 3.1110b), especially given the fact that the tragic errors discussed in the *Poetics* all involve a mistaken judgment about the identity of particular persons, as of Oedipus concerning his father and Iphigeneia her brother. Tragic *hamartia* is thus not a fundamental flaw, but "a mistake as to certain details" (Else, *Aristotle's Poetics*, p. 383).

family. In chapter 14, Aristotle asks, "What sorts of incidents appear terrible or pitiable [oiktra]?"[56] From the definition of pity
given in the *Rhetoric* (1385b), i.e., *pain arising from the spectacle of* undeserved suffering, we might expect the answer to be that calamities wrought by an unjust upon a just person are the truly pitiable
events. But this is not what he says here; instead, the answer given
is that a destructive act (a *pathos*, as defined in 11.1452b) is pitiable
only if it occurs among *philoi*, rather than among enemies or persons indifferent to one another. The tragic thrill or *frisson* (*phrittein*;
1453b)[57] that captures the spectator or reader of a tragedy must be
brought on by an unexpected break in a relationship of *philia*, a relationship defined here in a precise and uncommonly narrow way
by Aristotle's examples: events are pitiable when "calamities occur
among *philiai*, such as when brother kills brother, or son father, or
mother son, or son mother." The *philia* intended here is not the
broad "friendship" that is the ordinary meaning of the word, but is
clearly and uniquely a family or blood relationship.[58] It is for this
reason, Aristotle goes on to say, that tragedies concern only a few
families or households (*genē* or *oikiai*; 1454a). He makes the same
point in chapter 13 (1453a), giving as example six families that experienced disaster—all in the form of a slaying of kin as the result
of a *hamartia*.[59] This choice of a few families as the means of arousing tragic pity was not, we are told, the result of art, but of chance
(*ouk apo technēs all' apo tychēs*; 14.1454a). Tragedians discovered that
it was the stories of these families—stories of the fatal disruption of
the *philia* of the household—that were most likely to produce the
sensation of pity, of serious and unmerited suffering, in the minds
of their audience.

This use of *philia* in the narrow sense of blood relation is unusual
and worth noting. The term occurs frequently in the *Politics*, where
it is used to describe the emotional ties among citizens that are necessary for the survival of the *polis*; political *philia* is thus said to be
"the greatest of goods for cities" (*Politics* 2.1262b). There we are
told that there are two causes of *philia*: the sense that another person is in fact one's own (*to idion*),[60] and the shared sense that some-

---

56. Lucas (*Aristotle: Poetics*, p. 151) says that *oiktra* here is synonymous with
eleeina, especially given the pairing of *deina* and *eleeina* in 1456b.

57. See Lucas, *Aristotle: Poetics*, pp. 149–50.

58. Else, *Aristotle's Poetics*, p. 415; Lucas, *Aristotle: Poetics*, p. 151.

59. Else, *Aristotle's Poetics*, pp. 391–98.

60. A sense similar to the concern for self extended to one's family described in
Rhetoric 2.1385b.

thing is truly lovable; the first form of *philia* being familial and the second political. The two are separate but related as means to end: intermarriage is a necessary condition for political *philia* (3.1280b). In the extensive discussion of *philia* in the *Nicomachean Ethics*, the most powerful form of *philia* is said to be familial, not based upon any agreement about justice or virtue but arising simply from the affection we feel for our own (8.1161b–1162a). Familial (*syggenikē*) *philia* is thus the most powerful human friendship, but it is perhaps the least definitive or perfect (*teleia*) friendship, being less distinctly human than either political friendship or the highest form, that which is based on neither blood nor political ties, but occurs "among good people and those who are similar in virtue" (1156b).[61]

This brief consideration of the varieties of Aristotelian *philia* tells us something important about the audience for tragedy specified by the *Poetics*. Such an audience will respond with fear and pity to deeds that threaten to violate a certain order of *philia*. This order, however, is not that of the *polis*, or of any other community based on an agreement about justice or virtue, but the hereditary or biological community of the family or household. As tragedians have discovered by experience, the events that appear (*Poetics* 1453b14) terrible or pitiable *to this audience* are those clearly destructive of familial *philia*. We may thus infer that such an audience is primarily composed neither of independent self-aggrandizers or seekers after wisdom, nor of committed citizens, but of people like the moderate democrats described in the *Politics*, those to whom the most important goods are those connected with their homes and families.

By recalling what has been said about the principal elements of a good tragedy—the status of the major characters, the *hamartia* that causes the tragic calamity, and the aspects of life this calamity disrupts—we are now in a position to draw some conclusions concerning the way in which such a tragedy may function to protect its audience against the inclination to act unjustly whenever the opportunity arises. What such an audience learns from viewing or

61. This distinction between power and perfection is characteristic of the Aristotelian perception of the human condition, and reflects the fact that our strongest desires are for living together, rather than for the good that defines us as a species, living well. See Stephen G. Salkever, "Beyond Interpretation: Human Agency and the Slovenly Wilderness," in *Social Science as Moral Inquiry*, ed. N. Haan et al. (New York: Columbia University Press, 1983), pp. 213–14. For a discussion of the distinction between political and familial *philia* in the *Politics*, and of Aristotle's view that the former is dependent upon the latter, see Arlene W. Saxonhouse, "Family, Polity & Unity: Aristotle on Socrates' Community of Wives," *Polity* 15 (1982):214–17.

reading a tragedy is threefold: first, that serious mistakes are possible, and one must therefore act with caution; second, that wealth, social prestige, and the power to do whatever we want do not necessarily bring happiness, and one must therefore resist the tendency to identify freedom and happiness with power; third, that the familial order is as fragile as it is precious, and so requires the support of institutions such as the laws if it is to be maintained. But to refer to the tragic effect as a form of learning is perhaps to attribute to Aristotle a more didactic notion of the tragic function than is in fact the case; surely he nowhere says or implies that the tragedian supplies the audience with a stock of moral rules or maxims, ready for application. Instead, tragedy for him involves the arousal of pity and fear and the subsequent direction of those emotions toward a certain class of objects—a focusing of concern rather than direct teaching or admonition. The transformation the audience undergoes resembles the effect of Socratic *elenchos*, which encourages inquiry and gentleness indirectly by removing the ignorance that arises from *pleonexia* and turning one's anger toward oneself. If we use the key Aristotelian terms *form* and *matter* metaphorically, as Aristotle himself often does,[62] we can say that the function of tragedy is the unobtrusive imposition of a certain form upon a certain kind of matter (the democratic audience) by encouraging the acceptance of a certain opinion about what is truly fearful; not the weakness of the powerless, but the mistakes of the especially powerful.

Another Aristotelian way to describe this focusing or informing would be to say that the work of tragic *katharsis* is neither that of purgation nor of purification, nor yet of direct teaching or enlightenment, but is part of the process of transforming a potentially good democracy (with proper land distribution, economic regulations, and so on) into one that is actually such, in the sense in which soul is said to be the first actuality (*energeia* or *entelecheia*) in relation to the potentiality inherent in a particular kind of body or matter (*De anima* 2.412a–b). The suggestion here is not that tragedy has the power to move its audience immediately and decisively to a better course of action, but that it can make its audience more inclined to act well, or at least not to act badly. The *katharsis* of the

---

62. For example, in a *polis* the population is matter and the *politeia* form; the members of a chorus are matter and tragedy or comedy the form; the notes in a musical composition are the matter, the musical mode the form (*Politics* 3.1276a–b).

demotic audience understood in this way would be like that experienced by the individual who benefits from the cathartic *paideia* embodied in Socratic *elenchos*. That which lacks *katharsis* is here understood not as something requiring purge or lustration, but rather that which is primarily potential and in need of being shaped.[63] As we have seen, for Aristotle a *paideia* relative to the goals of the regime (*politeia*) is the best way of disposing any group of citizens to participate in the way of life or order that characterizes that regime; tragedy is the most effective *paideia* appropriate to the best democracy.

One major objection to this conception of tragedy may be that it wholly lacks the nobility the word tragedy suggests to us. But for Aristotle the work of tragedy, like the way of life of the best democracy, is neither heroic[64] nor contemptible (as Plato might have thought), and his praise of the tragic art is itself carefully modulated. This can be seen from the argument for the superiority of tragedy to epic poetry that concludes the *Poetics*, an argument that may be understood as a response to an antidemocratic preference for epic such as that expressed by the Athenian Stranger in the *Laws* (2.658d). He begins his defense by accepting the premises of tragedy's detractors, that the better *technē* is that which is pleasing to the better audience, and that at the present time (the fourth century), epic appeals more to an audience of *epieikeis*, while tragedy, replete with posturing actors and whirling *aulētai*,[65] is more pleasing to the *phauloi* (26.1461b–1462a). But this should not be taken as a criticism of tragedy as such, any more than the contemporary situation of extreme democracy in Athens can be taken as proof of

63. Additional support for the plausibility of this reading is provided by the fact that Aristotle does use the adjective *katharos* in the sense of having form or actuality in his discussion of sexual reproduction in the *Generation of Animals*. The central theme of this discussion is that the female contributes the matter for new life, via menstrual fluid, while the male contributes the form or principle of motion (*Generation of Animals* 1.730a); the female and male contributions are to one another as the potentiality and actuality of new life. In the course of that discussion, Aristotle characterizes menstrual fluid as follows: "the menstrual fluid is semen, not *katharon*, but requiring being worked upon [*deomenon ergasias*]" (728a). *Katharsis* thus appears as a process of increasing definiteness: becoming more actually what a thing potentially is.

64. On the complete absence of both the word and the concept of the tragic hero from the *Poetics*, see Jones, *Aristotle and Greek Tragedy*, pp. 11–20. As Jones notes (p. 20 n.), the central characters of a well-made tragedy are of interest *not* as individuals, but as members of certain families (*Poetics* 14.1454a).

65. *Aulētai* were performers upon the double-reed *aulos*, an orgiastic instrument, which is almost universally, but utterly wrongly, translated as "flute." See Anderson, *Ethos and Education*, p. 8.

the deficiency of democracy as such. The contemporary decay of both tragedy and politics are noted in the *Rhetoric:* "Those who are skilled at vocal tricks nearly always carry off the prizes at contests, since at present actors have more power than poets, and also in political contests, on account of the badness [*mochthēria*] of the regimes [*tōn politeiōn*]" (3.1403b). To defend tragedy, then, it is necessary to distinguish the art from its current practice, just as is the case with Aristotle's defense of democracy and of the political art in general. Aristotle must have been aware that he was, as Else says, "championing the cause of an art that was practically dead,"[66] at least for the time being.

But an accurate judgment of tragedy must consider the power of its plot (*muthos*) to move an audience, since this is, metaphorically, the soul or essence of tragedy (*Poetics* 6.1450a), and not the scenic and musical accoutrements that have corrupted it, and which are equally capable of corrupting the performance of epic poetry. And if the *muthos* alone is considered, then Aristotle says tragedy must be considered superior to epic in achieving the end (*telos*) or performing the function (*ergon*) that the two share, that of producing the pleasure that attends the arousal and *katharsis* of pity and fear (*Poetics* 26.1462b). It is superior in achieving this goal simply because it is more compact, unified, and vivid in the presentation of its *muthos*, in its characteristic way of representing *praxis* (1462a–b).[67] But this empirical claim, that short and vivid imitations are more gripping than longer and less colorful ones, will be true, it seems fair to say, only given an audience of a particular sort: one susceptible of being roused to fear and pity, and one not likely to be moved or pleased by long and elaborate arguments (*Rhetoric* 1.1357a). Once again, it is apparent that Aristotle's preference for tragedy does not represent a universal aesthetic judgment in abstraction from social context, but indicates his judgment that

66. *Aristotle's Poetics,* p. 636. Else goes on to say that, in the fourth century, "'tragedy' had given way to 'theater.' The best analogue would be the 'writer' in Hollywood, in his position vis-à-vis actors, directors, and production magnates." For Aristotle the decline may be said to have begun with Euripides, whom he nonetheless defends and calls "the most tragic of poets" (*Poetics* 13.1453a) for his capacity to elicit pity and fear. Jones nicely characterizes Aristotle's feelings about Euripides, saying that his attitude "is like that paradoxical sense of advance into decline which an education in eighteenth-century music leads many of us to experience towards Beethoven" (*Aristotle and Greek Tragedy,* p. 242).

67. The length of the tragic *muthos* is limited by the requirement that it be "easy to remember" (*eumnēmoneuton*) (*Politics* 7.1451a). The size of a *polis* must be similarly limited relative to its function. See *Politics* 7.1326a–b.

the tragic art is crucial to the successful actualization of a good democracy.

There is, then, nothing grandly elevated about the pleasure of tragedy, as Aristotle understands it. The value of a pleasure is relative to the value of the way of life it accompanies, and it is quite clear from the *Poetics* that nothing in the reading or viewing of tragedy can match the "extraordinary pleasures" those who are "philosophers by nature" can obtain from the careful observation of plants and animals (*Parts of Animals* 1.645a), to say nothing of the remote ecstasies of first philosophy. But it would be equally mistaken to view the tragic effect as trivial or despicable simply because it does not ascend to the heights of human possibility;[68] I think Aristotle would say that such an attitude is characteristic of the optimism and inexperience of youth (or of Socrates made young and fair). The problem or disability that tragedy addresses, the misperception of freedom and happiness that can and does undermine the possibility of a decently democratic way of life, is one of the most pressing and difficult tasks imaginable (now as then), and one tragic poetry is uniquely capable of ameliorating. The tragic *katharsis* is indeed a clarification, not concerning the highest things, but concerning matters that affect all of us in ordinary political life.

68. It is perhaps because of such a mistake that we may be unwilling to consider Aristotle's account as a plausible rendering of the meaning of tragic art.

Contributors

Michael Davis teaches philosophy at Sarah Lawrence College and has written articles and reviews on Plato, Aristotle, and Shakespeare. He has been especially concerned with moral and political philosophy and with their metaphysical implications. He is the author of *Ancient Tragedy and Modern Science* (1986).

J. Peter Euben is Professor of Politics and the History of Consciousness at the University of California, Santa Cruz. He has published a number of essays on classical and contemporary political theory and essays on education and the professions.

Warren and Ann Lane received their doctorates in the History of Consciousness at the University of California, Santa Cruz, where they now teach.

Anthony J. Podlecki is Professor of Classics at the University of British Columbia, Vancouver. He is the author of articles on Greek history and literature, translator of Aeschylus's *The Persians* (1970), and author of *The Political Background of Aeschylean Tragedy* (1966), *The Life of Themistocles* (1975), and *The Early Greek Poets and Their Times* (1984). A translation of and commentary on Aeschylus's *The Eumenides* is forthcoming.

Stephen G. Salkever teaches Political Science at Bryn Mawr College. He has published articles on Greek, eighteenth century, and contemporary political philosophy.

Arlene W. Saxonhouse is Professor of Political Science at the University of Michigan, Ann Arbor. Her main interests are classical and early modern political thought, and her recent publications include *Women in the History of Political Thought: Ancient Greece to Machiavelli* (1985) and "From Tragedy to Hierarchy and Back Again: Women in Greek Political Thought," *American Political Science Review* 80 (1986).

Joel Schwartz is Associate Professor of Government at the College of William and Mary. He teaches courses on the history of political theory and the philosophy of the social sciences and was the 1985 recipient of the

Thomas Jefferson Teaching Award. He is the author of "Participation and Multisubjective Understanding: An Interpretivist Approach to the Study of Political Participation," *Journal of Politics* (1984), and "Liberty, Democracy, and the Origins of American Bureaucracy," *Harvard Law Review* (1984).

Charles Segal is Benedict Professor of Classics and Professor of Comparative Literature at Brown University, Providence. His recent publications include *Tragedy and Civilization: An Interpretation of Sophocles* (1981), *Poetry and Myth in Ancient Pastoral: Essays on Theocritus and Virgil* (1981), and *Dionysiac Poetics and Euripides' Bacchae* (1982). Forthcoming publications include *La Musique du Sphinx: Mythe, langage et structure dans la tragédie grecque, Pindar's Mythmaking: The Fourth Pythian Ode, Language and Desire in Seneca's Phaedra,* and *Interpreting Greek Tragedy: Myth, Poetry, Text.*

Laura M. Slatkin teaches in the Department of Classics at Columbia University. Her primary interest is archaic Greek poetry.

Froma I. Zeitlin is Professor of Classics at Princeton University. She has written on ancient prose fiction and Greek drama, and on topics relating to myth and ritual. She works extensively with Greek notions of gender and sexuality and is the author of *Under the Sign of the Shield: Semiotics and Aeschylus' Seven Against Thebes* (1982).

General Index

action: in Greek tragedy, 184; and Oedipus, 215
actress, political: Antigone as, 163, 165
Adkins, A. W. H., 44, 217
Aegisthus, 93, 94
Aeschylus, 67, 78; democratization of mythical period, 77–78; discontinuities in *Oresteia*, 236; and human thought, 27; and *Republic* of Plato, 11; and Sophocles' *Antigone*, 136; and story of Oedipus, 189; and technique of tragedy, 71
Agamemnon, 91, 93
Ajax, 146, 148, 155; and foresight, 147–48; of Homer, 155; suicide of, 153–54
analogical thought: and A. Gramsci, 4; and A. MacIntyre, 18; and political theory, 3–5, 6
analytic philosophy. *See* philosophy
Anderson, W. D., 289, 290, 301
Antigone, 125, 137, 178–79; as exemplary human being, 164; as Homeric hero, 174; politics of, 216; and Thebes, 123, 137; as a woman, 180
Apollo: as cause of action, 196–99; and Oedipus, 200
Archilocus, 192
Arendt, H., 33, 236; and Aeschylus, 38; and drama, 1
Argos, 85
Aristophanes, 245, 246
Aristotle, 100, 185–88, 191, 202, 206–8; account of tragedy, 275; and myths of tragedy, 190; and rule of many, 287; social psychology of, 293; and tragic pleasure, 291
arrogance, male: in Euripides, 271
Arrowsmith, W., 23, 222–25, 241, 245–46, 250
Arthur, M. B., 114
asexual birth, 270
Athens: army of, 87; and empire, 82; and Oedipus, 139; and Persia, 79
Atossa, 81
Atreus, house of, 118
Austin, C., 116
authority, 97, 189

autochthony, 113, 114, 121, 258, 265; Athenian myth of, 254–55; and authority, 256; and civic unity, 255, 272; and Democratic Athens, 257; and exclusion of women, 259, 269; and foundation of city, 273; in Plato, 252, 258; and politics, 254; and problems of foreigners, 267; and violence, 256

Bacchylides, 201
Bacon, H. H., 53, 121, 129, 217, 221
Balogh, E., 213
Barthes, R., 44–46, 74
Benardete, S. G., 83, 126, 142
Bercovitch, S., 210
Bernays, J., 292
Bernstein, R., 16, 19, 41
Beye, C. R., 23, 223, 243
Bowra, C. M., 139, 169, 189, 210
Braudel, F., 19
Braun, R., 177
Browning, R., 45
Burian, P., 134, 141, 211
Burkert, W., 70, 241
Burnett, A. P., 223, 231, 245, 264, 267

Cambridge School: and study of Greek tragedy, 43
Cameron, A., 187
character, tragedy of: in Sophocles, 192
citizen: as hero, 230
city, problem of: in *Ajax*, 159
civilization, 55
classical: normative meaning of, 2–6
Conacher, D. J., 224, 238, 260
Cook, A., 224, 229
Cooper, L., 188
Cornford, F. M., 2, 43, 110, 195
corruption: of Athens, 222, 246; of city in *Antigone*, 175, 180; disclosed by Euripides, 249; of language, 225; in *Orestes*, 227, 248; structural or systemic, 224; Thucydides and Euripides compared, 225; of tragedy (*see also* political corruption)
Creon, 124–25; conflict with Antigone, 180; decree of, 169–75; leadership of, 98; speech of, 170; as stage tyrant, 94

307

Index of Greek Terms

Designer: Adriane Bosworth
Compositor: G&S Typesetters, Inc.
Text: 10/13 Palatino
Display: Palatino
Printer: Braun-Brumfield, Inc.
Binder: Braun-Brumfield, Inc.